AMERICAN SOCIALIST TRIPTYCH

CLASS : CULTURE

SERIES EDITORS
Amy Schrager Lang, Syracuse University, and Bill V. Mullen, Purdue University

TITLES IN THE SERIES:

Amy Schrager Lang, *The Syntax of Class: Writing Inequality in Nineteenth-Century America*

Eric Schocket, *Vanishing Moments: Class and American Culture*

Angelo Herndon, *Let Me Live*

Walter Mosley, *Workin' on the Chain Gang: Shaking Off the Dead Hand of History*

James C. Davis, *Commerce in Color: Race, Consumer Culture, and American Literature, 1893–1933*

John Marsh, Editor, *You Work Tomorrow: An Anthology of American Labor Poetry, 1929–41*

Marcial González, *Chicano Novels and the Politics of Form: Race, Class, and Reification*

Fran Leeper Buss, Editor, *Moisture of the Earth: Mary Robinson, Civil Rights and Textile Union Activist*

Clarence Lang, *Grassroots at the Gateway: Class Politics and Black Freedom Struggle in St. Louis, 1936–75*

Pamela Fox, *Natural Acts: Gender, Race, and Rusticity in Country Music*

Carole Srole, *Transcribing Class and Gender: Masculinity and Femininity in Nineteenth-Century Courts and Offices*

Lorraine M. López, Editor, *An Angle of Vision: Women Writers on Their Poor and Working-Class Roots*

Matthew H. Bernstein, Editor, *Michael Moore: Filmmaker, Newsmaker, Cultural Icon*

John Marsh, *Hog Butchers, Beggars, and Busboys: Poverty, Labor, and the Making of Modern American Poetry*

Mark W. Van Wienen, *American Socialist Triptych: The Literary-Political Work of Charlotte Perkins Gilman, Upton Sinclair, and W. E. B. Du Bois*

Liam Kennedy and Stephen Shapiro, Editors, The Wire: *Race, Class, and Genre*

Andreá N. Williams, *Dividing Lines: Class Anxiety and Postbellum Black Fiction*

AMERICAN SOCIALIST TRIPTYCH

The Literary-Political Work of Charlotte Perkins Gilman, Upton Sinclair, and W. E. B. Du Bois

Mark W. Van Wienen

THE UNIVERSITY OF MICHIGAN PRESS

Ann Arbor

FOR NATHANIEL, MIRANDA, AND BENJAMIN

First paperback conversion 2014

Published in the United States of America by
The University of Michigan Press
Manufactured in the United States of America
♾ Printed on acid-free paper

2017 2016 2015 2014 5 4 3 2

A CIP catalog record for this book is available from the British Library.

Library of Congress Cataloging-in-Publication Data

Van Wienen, Mark W.
American socialist triptych : the literary-political work of Charlotte Perkins Gilman, Upton Sinclair, and W.E.B. Du Bois / Mark W. Van Wienen.
p. cm. — (Class : culture)
Includes bibliographical references and index.
ISBN 978-0-472-11805-2 (acid-free paper) — ISBN 978-0-472-02808-5 (e-book)
1. Gilman, Charlotte Perkins, 1860–1935—Political and social views. 2. Sinclair, Upton, 1878–1968—Political and social views. 3. Du Bois, W. E. B. (William Edward Burghardt), 1868–1963—Political and social views. 4. Socialism and literature—United States—History—20th century. 5. Socialism and literature—United States—History—19th century. 6. Socialism—United States—History—20th century. 7. Socialism—United States—History—19th century. I. Title.
PS1744.G57Z88 2012
810.9'3581—dc23

2011023785

978-0-472-03566-3 (pbk. : acid-free paper)

ACKNOWLEDGMENTS

For a study that explores the interconnectedness of individuals in human societies, and which seeks to offer a fuller account of this interconnectedness, it is altogether fitting to begin with thanks for the many people and institutions that have helped to make this book possible. Thanks are due first to my mentor, Cary Nelson, who has been unfailingly supportive from my time in graduate school and ever since.

My colleagues in the Department of English at Northern Illinois University have also been magnificent. Special thanks to colleagues there who have read portions of my manuscript during various stages of its creation: Keith Gandal (now at the City University of New York), James Giles, Mark Kipperman, and Diana Swanson.

I have also been blessed with several smart and diligent research assistants. Julie K. Kraft helped with initial research of the W. E. B. Du Bois materials when she was an undergraduate student and I an assistant professor at Augustana College, Sioux Falls, South Dakota. At Northern Illinois University, graduate students Sang-Wook Kim, Meagan Peabody, and Brett Stumphy assisted with research on Upton Sinclair's EPIC campaign and with the voluminous papers related to the Scottsboro trials.

The institutions where I have worked while this book has been in the making have also been uncommonly generous in their financial support. My research in the summer of 1999 was supported by an Augustana Research and Artistry Fellowship, while at Northern Illinois University a portion of the work for this book was funded by a spring 2008 sabbatical leave and a 2010 Summer Research and Artistry Award. Moreover, a portion of the production cost of this book has been supplied by a subvention provided jointly by the Department of English, College of Liberal Arts and Sciences, and Graduate School at Northern Illinois University. Special kudos to Phil Eubanks, Christopher McCord, and James Erman for their assistance in making the subvention happen.

At another critical juncture in 2003, this book was supported by a yearlong fellowship from the National Endowment for the Humanities. That grant was transformative not only for this book project but for my academic career. I am also deeply appreciative of a grant from the Lilly Library, Indiana University, Bloomington, supporting research in its collections through an Everett Helm Visiting Fellowship.

And then there are the special collections libraries that have preserved materials important to the history of American socialism. Without these collections and the people who have helped me in accessing them, this book could not have existed. I thank the following libraries, their administrators and staffs: Bancroft Library, University of California, Berkeley; Beinecke Library, Yale University; and Lilly Library, Indiana University, Bloomington. Thanks, too, to the catalogers and microfilmers at the Schlesinger Library on the History of Women in America, Radcliffe College, Cambridge, Massachusetts, and at the university library at the University of Massachusetts, Amherst, who have made the papers of Charlotte Perkins Gilman and W. E. B. Du Bois, respectively, readily available via microfilm. Not least, I thank the libraries and librarians at Augustana College, Sioux Falls, and Northern Illinois University, especially their indefatigable interlibrary loan personnel.

I gratefully acknowledge the permission of *American Quarterly* and *African American Review* to republish materials that originally appeared in those journals. For their assistance in shepherding the manuscript through the submission, editing, and publication process, I heartily thank acquisitions editor LeAnn Fields, her editorial assistant, Scott Ham, and project manager Marcia LaBrenz. Thanks also for the constructive feedback of the three anonymous readers commissioned by the University of Michigan Press and for the careful copyediting of Richard Isomaki.

For a study about social interconnections and interdependence, it is slightly ironic that certain personal acknowledgments take the form, almost, of an apology for times when the author was far away on the porch or basement study, lost to family and friends because he was so intensely invested in the lives of "Charlotte," "Upton," and "W. E. B." I stand largely unabashed in my thanks on this point only because my family members were so generous in their support of this project. Thanks to my parents Margaret and Bill Van Wienen, my parents-in-law Eveleen and Walt Windholz, my sister, Marcia Van't Hof, my brother-in-law, Mark Van't Hof, and their son Braden. Since Mark's untimely death in February of 2008, I have come to see him as Virgil to my Dante, a comparison altogether unfitting on my side, for I do not pretend to have written a *Divine Comedy* (though it does have three parts), but mostly right on his, so impeccable was his writing and deeply compassionate and generous his character.

I thank my wife, Anne Windholz, who more than anyone else has shared all the ups and downs of this project from beginning to end: read chapters, advised, served as sounding board, and never wavered in her love and support. A final debt of thanks is to our children. They have inspired me by their budding aspiration to make the world more just and humane. To Nathaniel, Miranda, and Benjamin I dedicate this book.

CONTENTS

AUTHOR'S NOTE

During the publication process, sections of manuscript were deleted to reduce the book's length. Fuller discussions of some topics can be found at the *American Socialist Triptych* website, www.press.umich.edu/p/american-socialist-triptych.

—Mark Van Wienen

ABBREVIATIONS

In the notes I have abbreviated three of the archival collections cited frequently, as follows:

CPG Archive	Charlotte Perkins Gilman Archive, Schlesinger Library on the History of Women in America, microfilm edition
Du Bois Papers	Papers of W. E. B. Du Bois, microfilm edition, University of Massachusetts, Amherst
Sinclair MSS	Sinclair Manuscripts, Manuscripts Department, Lilly Library, Indiana University, Bloomington, Indiana

INTRODUCTION

TOWARD A LITERARY HISTORY OF (SOCIAL) DEMOCRACY IN AMERICA

This book focuses upon three prominent American socialists who also happen to be essential figures in the study of modern American literature. To be sure, Charlotte Perkins Gilman, Upton Sinclair, and W. E. B. Du Bois aspired to careers in writing and intellectual work prior to their becoming socialists. Du Bois in fact wrote the work that made his name as an intellectual, *The Souls of Black Folk,* prior to expressing any overt interest in socialism, and he is nowadays regarded primarily as an advocate of African American civil rights. Gilman's socialism is also not widely recognized; today she is seen almost exclusively as an early feminist. Sinclair alone of my three featured writers is well known as a socialist—and that has not necessarily been an asset to his literary reputation. Yet for Du Bois and Gilman as well as Sinclair, a conscious commitment to socialism became central to the writers' intellectual, political, and literary identities early in their careers, and this commitment remained strong throughout the rest of their lives. My aims in this study are to examine how and why they made this commitment, to explore what their shared—and divergent—viewpoints say about socialism in the late nineteenth and early twentieth centuries, and to consider the relevance of their socialist literary work to the history of their times—and ours.

They are a somewhat miscellaneous trio: almost the only thing uniting them was a shared belief that the common wealth of the United States should be controlled democratically and shared equitably by all citizens, and that this could be achieved through the collective organization of society's less privileged members. But it is precisely their diversity that testifies to the versatility of socialist ideals and practices in the United States in the late nineteenth and early twentieth centuries and to the wide influence of socialism in American culture of that era. Each, in fact, is representative of a distinct direction taken by socialism in the United States. Gilman reflects socialist elements in the protest politics of the 1890s—in the Edward Bellamy Nationalism, Populism, and Fabianism in which she was active at the very start of her literary career—even as she was becoming the foremost advocate of feminism in American socialism and of socialism in American feminism. Sinclair signifies not only the more assertively proletarian, Marxist brand of socialism that emerged at the turn of the century with the founding of the Socialist Party of America, reflected in his famous muckraking novel, *The Jungle;* his career overall also shows the progressive infiltration of socialist ideas into the mainstream of American politics, exemplified especially in his nearly successful 1934 run for the California governorship, which helped to strengthen the case for Roosevelt's New Deal. Du Bois joined the Socialist Party only briefly in the second decade of the twentieth century, the Communist Party only in the early 1960s during the final three years of his life, but from soon after the turn of the century onward, socialism infused Du Bois's writing and activism, providing a discourse by which he sought to cultivate political solidarity among blacks and to hold whites accountable on matters of racial justice. His work reflects the symbiotic relation between the socialist movement and black intellectuals and the tension between them as well.

On the one hand, *American Socialist Triptych* offers an in-depth study of each of these three major authors, challenging interpretations of them that have tended to downplay or sidestep the socialism of Gilman and of Du Bois, while seeking to renew interest in Sinclair's socialism as a topic of critical discourse. On the other hand, this book uses Gilman, Sinclair, and Du Bois as representative of the socialist movements of which they were a part. Viewed collectively, they provide a means of gauging the potentials, shortcomings, and accomplishments of American socialism over five decades, between 1890 and 1940. If, as many historians and critics have suggested, the 1930s and the Great Depression were the key moments when American political-economy turned leftward, resulting in the establishment of important elements of the welfare state that have persisted to this day, the groundwork for that turn was laid in the previous decades, during which, for the first time in American history, democratic government became an instrument rivaling the power of private business enterprise, and in which socialists of various kinds played no small role.

American Socialist Triptych also has something to say about American literary history, as literary history. In tracing the narrative of Gilman's, Sinclair's, and Du Bois's socialism, I often draw upon nonfiction prose, letters, diaries, speeches, and public documents as well as fiction, which does no more or less than follow the lead of the writers themselves, who in their political advocacy employed about equally both conventional genres of creative writing and other genres. Gilman, Sinclair, and Du Bois were hardly on the cutting edge of modernist experiments in narrative form. Yet their adaptations of realist fiction to their political aims, particularly their innovative combinations of realistic with utopian modes, meant that the kinds of writing employed by Hamlin Garland and William Dean Howells in support of Populism and Nationalism continued to do important cultural work in the second and third decades of the twentieth century in support of socialism, hence bridging the methods of realism with those employed in documentary and proletarian fiction of the 1930s. In the hands of Gilman, Sinclair, and Du Bois, not only did literary fiction record the social and political currents of modern American history; it also helped to write that history. These authors demonstrate continuity across the supposed break between premodern and modern literary periods, even as they illustrate a set of writing practices integrating political and literary aims at a time when many modernists were seeking separation between these aims.

By telling the interconnected stories of Gilman, Sinclair, and Du Bois as socialists, I seek in this book to enter into several current conversations taking place in literary history, literary criticism and theory, and social theory. For each of these fields, I believe something may be gained by an examination of Gilman, Sinclair, Du Bois, and their socialist comrades—not least because a fuller recollection and understanding of the really existing socialist movement in the United States ought to be relevant to scholars and citizens interested in cultivating a more equal, just, and sustainable social order today.

Most proximately, there is the work done on U.S. radical writers of the twentieth century. Especially of late, scholars in this field have gravitated to the connections between American writers and the political party that was most implacable in its hostility toward American capitalism, the Communist Party. The first generation of literary historical scholars adopting these emphases, headed by Daniel Aaron, James Gilbert, and Walter Rideout, traced the roots of 1930s literary Communism back to the second decade of the century, finding parallels between the beginnings of American modernism and of American literary radicalism.[1] More recently, the critical tendency has moved away from an examination of the evolution of American Communism, toward a narrower focus upon the one period when the Communist Party built something approaching a popular following, the Depression decade of the 1930s. That decade provides the historical rubric for a score of monographs and essay collections published over the past twenty-five years, including work by Paula Rabinowitz, Barbara Foley, Bill Mullen, James Smethurst, and Robert Shulman.[2] Even when the radical literary project continues to be more broadly conceived historically, the Communist Party typically remains the fulcrum. A focus on Communism remains manifest, for example, in works as culturally and historically diverse as William Maxwell's *New Negro, Old Left: African-American Writing and Communism Between the Wars* (1999), Alan M. Wald's *Exiles from a Future Time: The Forging of the Mid-Twentieth-Century Literary Left* (2002), and Barbara Foley's *Spectres of 1919: Class and Nation in the Making of the New Negro* (2003).[3]

Thanks to these and other scholars, we know a considerable amount about American Communist writers and about left literary activity in the 1930s. But far less is known about the involvement of American writers in other kinds of American socialism and during periods other than the 1930s. If from one standpoint the fact that so many literary and cultural critics have fastened upon American Communism and the Great Depression appears to represent a consensus about their importance, from another standpoint these emphases represent serious scholarly and political risks. If a central—very likely *the* central—aim of left scholarship is to retain a working historical and political knowledge of American socialist traditions, then the focus of this scholarship upon Communism and the Great Depression risks critical myopia. In *Revolutionary Memory: Recovering the Poetry of the American Left,* Cary Nelson offers a warning about the state of our knowledge of radical traditions in poetry: "We are not, in short, even ready to produce a complete bibliography of American poetry of the Left, let alone a reasonably comprehensive account. . . . By far the largest gaps in our knowledge, however, are not from the Red decade of the 1930s, . . . for which good accounts can be given, but rather from the half-century that leads up to the 1930s."[4] Nelson's comments might be extended to refer to deficiencies in our knowledge not only of radical poetry but of left literature and culture generally. I would add that the critical emphasis on the 1930s that Nelson cites, though it *need* not lead to an exclusive focus on the Communists, has in practice been tantamount to this.[5]

To a significant extent, my study of Charlotte Perkins Gilman, Upton Sinclair, and W. E. B. Du Bois is complementary to the large body of criticism on Communist-affiliated writers in the 1930s. Their work formed a precedent for the later Communist activity; Sinclair and Du Bois, especially, were on parallel tracks with the Communists during much of the 1920s and 1930s. Perhaps most importantly, I concur with the majority of the scholars in the field in finding that the Great Depression provided the key opening for structural changes in the political economy of the United States—the profound crisis of capitalism that socialists had long been predicting, although not the final crisis that the most dogmatic Marxists had pronounced as inevitable. I allow, too, that the positions advanced by Communist Party members (sometimes at the urging of the Comintern authorities, sometimes in spite of them) were often highly progressive, especially on questions of gender and racial equality. The deep appeal of the Communist Party to African American intellectuals was the practical consequence of these positions.

This is not to say, however, that a recovery of the socialism of Gilman, Sinclair, and Du Bois is merely a matter of filling in a few details in an intellectual and political map we already know from inquiries into the Communists and the 1930s. The socialist philosophies and social democratic strategies of Gilman, Sinclair, and Du Bois, grounded in the pre–World War I analyses of the Second or Socialist Internationale, were distinctively different from those of the Third Internationale, or Comintern, inaugurated with the success of the Bolshevik revolution. Most fundamentally, the latter held that the only way to effect genuine social equality was by the revolutionary overthrow of the Western liberal democracies as well as the surviving monarchies—all seen as fatally intertwined with capitalism—and this position demanded acceptance of political violence as necessary and efficacious in the establishment of a workers' government. The Second Internationale, in contrast, held it possible that social equality could be achieved by gradual, parliamentary, and peaceful means. Such a position did not rule out the possibility of violent confrontation or the necessity of political compulsion, and indeed the relation between these, on one hand, and political liberty and harmony, on the other, is a central tension in the work of all three of my featured writers. Still, the philosophical and political difference between the internationales is as substantial as it is practically unexamined in literary critical studies of socialism in the United States.

American Socialist Triptych must, therefore, enter into some contention with the preponderance of scholarship upon the "Red decade" and literary Communism. Besides the question of extralegal political violence, which is either openly accepted or (more often) pointedly sidestepped in discussions of Communist writers, another key issue is that the supposed ideological advantages of Communism were manifested in practice (at best) with great inconsistency. Witness the widespread phenomenon of disillusionment among

African American writers, most prominently Richard Wright and Ralph Ellison, after a few years of passionate involvement in the party.[6] In light of the demise within the past twenty years of the really existing socialist states promulgated under the Comintern, we must also call into question what had been the strongest argument in favor of the Communist tradition: its practical efficacy. And as the outrages of Stalinism and of Mao's Cultural Revolution have been revealed, we must ask, too, about the supposed ideological sophistication and progressivity of the whole movement that identified socialism with revolutionary Marxism and then with Communism. What, exactly, is the ethical appeal and political value of ideological positions that could be implemented in the United States only in partial and extremely localized fashion, and where they were implemented more fully, in the U.S.S.R. and China—we should not mince words here—resulted in some of the most homocidal and autocratic political regimes in human history?

I cannot, for example, endorse the critical procedure advanced by Kate Baldwin, who in her study of African American writers and Cold War–era Communism argues that W. E. B. Du Bois's idealizations of Stalinism may be warranted as a critical counterweight to the racism, economic exploitation, and intolerance of American society in the 1950s. Baldwin faces a delicate balancing act in reading Du Bois's late work, as she tries "to tread the fine line between over-identifying Du Bois with the ruin of the Soviet empire—and hence assigning to his idealism a necessarily 'tragic' fate—and underidentifying or not fully appreciating the ways in which Du Bois allied himself with the Soviet Union through a consciousness of outsider status and thus a counter to what he insisted were the monolithic goals of a post–World War II Americanization."[7] I share Baldwin's goal of keeping alive social democratic ideals and of opposing U.S. imperialism. But neither Baldwin's account of "overidentifying" nor her conception of "underidentifying" seems aware of the risk of forging ties with an authoritarian and homicidal dictatorship just because such ties will show unequivocally one's contempt for American capitalism. Ultimately, the dilemma of untangling Du Bois's socialism from Stalinism is an unnecessary one, interesting and (even) feasible as it may be as an intellectual exercise, for Du Bois's socialism long predated his apologetics for Stalinism. Du Bois's dialogue with socialism was no less rich prior to the very existence of the Third Internationale, and in its pre-Stalinist manifestations it had immeasurably more to offer as a viable model for our present thinking about social democracy.

The same thing may be said in more general terms: American socialism, like international socialism, had a much longer and more viable history than the one associated with the Communist Party and focused upon the Red decade of the 1930s. As a corrective and an alternative to this typical focus, my attention in *American Socialist Triptych* will be centered upon the activity of American radicals and progressives in the period between 1890 and 1920, in which Gilman, Sinclair, and Du Bois are representative figures and were sometimes influential players. As my concluding analysis of Sinclair's "End Poverty In California" campaign will show, even in the 1930s the Communist Party was far from offering the one genuinely progressive alternative to the status quo. Moreover, the degree of leftist success in the 1930s was not an aberration, but depended upon the radical activism of other groups predating by decades the Communist Party and the Bolshevik revolution. Within this framework, it is the relative political quiescence of the 1920s that becomes something of an aberration: Not the defining moment in American letters that it appears to be with emphasis on the usual canonical authors—T. S. Eliot, Fitzgerald, Hemingway, Faulkner—but rather a pause between much more extended periods of radical and progressive activity before as well as after the decade of the "lost generation." Socialist ideas and ideals suffered during the world war and in American reaction to the Bolshevik revolution, but they were kept alive by radicals and progressives who had cut their teeth before the war as well as new arrivals on the left—and thereby kept culturally and politically viable when needed to face down the crisis of worldwide depression. Ultimately, then, New Deal successes in introducing social democratic and socialistic practices are indebted far less to political pressure exerted by the Communists than to a foundation of socialist ideas, and to a large cohort of political progressives shaped by those ideas, that originated a generation or half a generation earlier.

As with literary histories focused upon leftist writers, so with the wider range of literary and cultural critics and theorists who assert an interest in socially transformative progressive politics: the contemporary conversation may be enriched by opening a dialogue with Gilman, Sinclair, and Du Bois, and some of what the nineteenth- and early twentieth-century socialists have to say may be critical of the conversation's current direction. It is in fact remarkable how often the leading critics and theorists of literary studies over the past thirty or so years employ a single word that has long-standing ties to the leftist political tradition: *radical, radicalism, radicalize.* That word in its several variants operates as a kind of linguistic talisman, coming up repeatedly at climactic points in critics' arguments. Here is Jacques Derrida in *Of Grammatology,* hailing Nietzsche for "Radicalizing the concepts of *interpretation, perspective, evaluation, difference,* and all the 'empiricist' or non-philosophical motifs that have constantly tormented philosophy throughout the history of the West."[8] New Historicist Stephen Greenblatt rejects "the *O altitudo!* of radical indeterminacy," but argues for an interpretation of *King Lear* of which he claims, "The possibility of such a radical undermining of the orthodox position exists, and not merely in the cool light of our own historical distance."[9] Elaine Showalter declared in 1985 that the fullest expression of feminist criticism "demanded not just the recognition of women's writing but a radical rethinking of the conceptual grounds of literary study," a movement accelerated by "radical critical thought from other countries."[10] A little later, Judith Butler's *Gender Trouble* declares: "One ought to consider the futility of a political program which seeks radically to transform the social situation of women without first determining whether the category of woman is socially constructed in such a way that to be a woman is, by definition, to be in an oppressed situation."[11] Not to be outdone in invocations of "radicalism," Fredric Jameson recently speaks not only of modernist writers as employing "radical artistic practices" and registering "radical change . . . in the social world outside" but also of a "radicalism" that goes right into the depths of human subjectivity, to "betray a radical depersonalization of the bourgeois subject" and a profound desire "for some new existence outside the self, in a world radically transformed and worthy of ecstasy."[12]

The references to "radically transformed," "radicalizing premises," "radical critical thought," and so on, are of obvious interest to this study seeking to describe the perspectives of American writers who aligned themselves with allegedly "radical" political groups and philosophies. But just what do these citations of *radicalism* signify in the work of theorists and critics of the last thirty years, all of them in the vanguard of our profession at the time the works cited above were published? All, to one extent or another, appeal to the word's Latin root, *radix,* which of course means nothing other than "root" itself. As for what the theorists are purporting to identify as the root of all significance, there are two principal tendencies, often used in combination. The first is the prevalence of the linguistic turn, greatly catalyzed by Derrida and poststructuralism generally, signaled in Showalter's hailing of "radical critical thought from other countries," and exemplified in Butler's interrogation of the social construction of "the category of woman." The second, also demonstrated by Butler and carried to its logical extreme by Slavoj Žižek, is the interiorization of radicalism and politics, wherein what would appear to be an arena of social change through traditional, identifiably political apparatuses becomes instead a struggle within the psyche of every individual, beginning with the critic him- or herself. Given Fredric Jameson's reputation as a diehard Marxist critic, it is particularly remarkable that his book *Singular Modernity*, quoted above, embodies both the linguistic turn and the tendency toward interiorization. While continuing to insist upon his Marxist credentials, Jameson feels compelled to point out that "the base/superstructure distinction . . . [is] only mentioned once by Marx, in a not very central place" and to declare the widespread "displacement onto language and terminology of political struggle today."[13] Nowadays for Jameson, the "radical artistic practices" of modernism are not to be identified with radical social change itself (a slippage all too common in other critics); they are instead held to be cultural indices of "radical change" in society and harbingers of the "radical depersonalization of the bourgeois subject."[14]

Other critics and theorists have joined Jameson in suggesting their "radical" interpretations also have implications in the area of progressive politics—and politics as usually considered, having to do with how societies organize themselves, how they manifest relations of power, and how they produce and distribute material and other goods. Not only feminist, gender, and neo-Marxist critics lay claim to progressive political visions; so have deconstructionists and New Historicists, at least after their initial "O altitudo" phases.[15] But what, exactly, is the kind of politics wrought by the linguistic and psychological emphases of recent literary criticism and theory?

The common denominators among these theorists and critics are an opposition to institutions as inherently coercive, and a corresponding championing of the freedom of human subjects from constraint. The sharp impact of Michel Foucault's thought and diminishing influence of Karl Marx's is key to understanding the difference, beginning with the fact that the Marxist-socialist emphasis upon material relations of production is displaced in Foucault by a focus upon discursive power-relations. The centrality of discursivity in Foucault, of course, reinforces perfectly the linguistic interest of English professors and their colleagues in cognate disciplines, whereas the shift from economic exploitation to "micro-physics of power," cultivated through a variety of disciplinary and institutional practices,[16] increases dramatically the forms of social relations that might be compassed within the struggle for justice. Marxism focuses upon the emancipation of a particular class with the clearest social grievance, the proletariat, from a particular form of economic exploitation, capitalism, with the end result of class equality. For Marx and virtually all socialists both preceding and succeeding him, equality is the foundation for true liberation. Foucault's project, in contrast, emphasizes that *all* members of society are constrained by social discipline, with the differences between social roles (proletarian vs. bourgeois, female vs. male) being less significant than the overall effects of social control. Although it is difficult to locate in Foucault a fully fledged emancipatory vision (only power), interpreters of Foucault have extrapolated such a vision in which social power might be challenged at more or less any point, with more or less equal effectiveness. Such an assertion of the equal political significance of most every cultural phenomenon has been a bonanza for literary scholars, who have proceeded to elaborate how social reality can be challenged and changed through a virtually limitless variety of forms of literary resistance and stylistic subversion. Meanwhile, lacking any means to distinguish between the subjects of social control (as all are equally controlled), practitioners of Foucauldian power-analysis render the egalitarian aim of Marxism and socialism virtually meaningless; in its place, because all subjects alike are subject to disciplinary practices, is the struggle to "free" them and particularly (adopting the model provided by psychoanalysis) to liberate the play of desire.

This notion, that political power might be subverted and transformed by whatever literary or cultural textualities happen to come to hand, is challenged directly by Gilman, Sinclair, and Du Bois. Canonical as their writing has become in recent decades, all three were passionately insistent upon the socially instrumental and political function of their own work, which to a large extent they generalized to all literary work. They believed that certain kinds of writing might foster social change, and it was critical for them to seek these out, for they also held, conversely, that many kinds of writing accomplished little at all in the way of social transformation; most writing did no more than reinforce existing social norms. Using the example of the Dutch painters, Gilman suggested in 1904 that the usual role of art was to accentuate the existing ideology, to make "Holland Hollander," although she also allowed that literature, especially fiction, might foster the imagining of new social realities: "that power of seeing over and under and around and through, of foreseeing, of constructing hypotheses, by which science and invention profit as much as art."[17] More bluntly, Upton Sinclair declared in 1925: *"All art is propaganda. It is universally and inescapably propaganda; sometimes unconsciously, but often deliberately, propaganda."*[18] W. E. B. Du Bois spoke in virtually the same terms, playing the curmudgeon just a year later at the height of the "New Negro" Renaissance: "All art is propaganda and ever must be, despite the wailing of the purists. I stand in utter shamelessness and say that whatever art I have for writing has been used always for propaganda for gaining the right of black folk to love and enjoy. I do not care a damn for any art that is not used for propaganda."[19] The instrumentalism of their writing asserts, moreover, the importance of a social and material world beyond textuality: a world important enough to sacrifice, quite willingly, the pleasures of the text and the stylistic performance, however adroit and culturally resistant such a performance might be. In short, these writers state the case for conceptions of politics and society reoriented to class struggle, in which the contest for material resources is fundamental, and social structures are typically assembled by and for the benefit of men ahead of women, whites over people of color, and owners above workers.

To find a body of recent critical work sympathetic with the frankly materialist and instrumentalist emphases of Gilman, Sinclair, and Du Bois, we must examine the work of a distinct minority among literary and cultural critics—often also critics of minority literature and culture—or move altogether outside the orbit of literary studies into social and political theory. Perhaps the most in sync with the triptych writers, and perhaps the most implacable critic of the linguistic and psychological turns of recent "radical" theory, is the Marxist-feminist literary theorist Teresa Ebert. Ebert writes scathingly that most postmodernist and poststructuralist theories, by focusing upon linguistic and ideological struggles, have accomplished little more revolutionary than validating their own status as "privileged mental workers." "Post-al" theories, as Ebert calls them, practically erase basic distinctions between material needs and immaterial desires, such that "Lack and need become superfluous concepts and, as such, have to be erased: this is a world (class) for which the problem is no longer the problem of poverty (need) but of liberty (desire)."[20] Ebert's perspective is instructive, and not least by the fact that her bluntly materialist position is very much a minority voice even among contemporary critics who profess some allegiance to Marxism.

Black studies has also provided a significant forum for scholars in disciplines other than English to dialogue critically with literary scholars who have defined radical political change in primarily discursive, psychological, or stylistic terms. Kenneth Warren's critique of "The End(s) of African-American Studies" analyzes the work of Robin Kelley and other literary scholars wherein "politics tends to get reduced to a matter of meaningful aesthetic expression and the correct exegesis of that expression rather than concerted action directed toward definable goals."[21] In *W.E.B. Du Bois and American Political Thought*, Adolph Reed dresses down the cultural politics of Houston Baker and Henry Louis Gates Jr. in order to dispute the priority in literary studies of politics of indirection, subversion, and cultural diffusion, as opposed to more conventional understandings of politics as advocacy, hegemonic struggle, and collective organization. By showing that more recent traditions of black social justice activism are descended genealogically from Du Bois's work, Reed even offers implicit evidence showing the long-term relevancy of the socialist tradition in which Gilman and Sinclair as well as Du Bois participated.

Coming from several disciplinary spaces, sometimes responding to disciplinary discourses touting quantitative measurement of economic value, one recent trend in progressive social thought essentially seeks to split the difference between the materialism of Ebert and the psychological and linguistic emphases of the "radical" postmodernists. Chantal Mouffe's *On the Political* speaks of "liberty and equality for all" as the foundational aims around which political and ethical consensus might be gained—a reasonable and seemingly even obvious practical suggestion until one considers the ways that the two terms have been played against one another in the history of U.S. politics as well as in the theoretical debates described above.[22] Along much the same lines, Lisa Duggan's *The Twilight of Equality?* concludes with a counterbalancing emphasis upon "Love *and* Money," with a dual focus on "pleasure *and* collective caretaking, love *and* the egalitarian circulation of money." Ultimately, Duggan envisions the necessity of fundamental challenge to prevailing cultural *and* economic categories, "radical transformation of cultural categories" and "a socialist transformation of the institutions of political economy."[23] Mouffe and Duggan attempt to balance bottom-line definitions of economic inequality and classically Marxist conceptions of class politics with multiple definitions of the social good and the proliferation of recent justice struggles. Here they are joined by a handful of literary scholars such as Eric Lott, who in *The Disappearing Liberal Intellectual* issues a warning to liberals with a "general preference for agitating around class and economic inequality to the exclusion of other exploitations," suggesting as alternatives "the history of African-American liberation movements, radical women's uprisings, and other insurrectionary energies."[24]

This is a critical balance I must seek in my own study. Implicit in the very choice of representative figures in my triptych is the aim of including "African-American liberation movements" and "radical women's uprisings" on equal terms with more mainstream, more visible versions of American socialism. Moreover, in spite of their passion for literary instrumentality, the writing of Gilman, Sinclair, and Du Bois, like all literature whether of the most prosaic or experimental sort, operates inescapably on the level of cultural or ideological work. On other points, too, there are strong commonalities between Gilman, Sinclair, and Du Bois and the current group of social democratic theorists. In distinction from the Communists of their day and dogmatic Marxists such as Teresa Ebert in ours (as avid a supporter of militant revolutionism as any past devotee of the Comintern), they either emphasize or imply the importance of using the existing political and legal structures for bringing about economic transformation, however radical. Mouffe explicitly repudiates the necessity—or even the possibility—"of an act of radical refoundation that would institute a new social order from scratch." She insists, instead, that "a number of very important socio-economic and political transformations, with radical implications, are possible within the context of liberal democratic institutions."[25]

At the same time, Gilman, Sinclair, and Du Bois also offer a potentially salutary challenge for today's theorists who go to such extraordinary lengths to insist upon the equivalence of all justice struggles. The problematic, if productive, paradigm was articulated as early as Laclau and Mouffe's *Hegemony and Socialist Strategy,* which in 1985 asserted not only that there are multiple forms of social oppression under modern capitalism (a mainstay of Marxist analysis concerning gender oppression, suppressed nationalities, and so forth) but also that those forms are relatively distinct and autonomous from one another and that, therefore, the justice claims and freedom struggles of each oppressed group must remain relatively separate and independent. Yet Laclau and Mouffe further (and reasonably) insisted that the only way for oppressed, outsider groups to be empowered was through a dynamic coalition politics: "In our view," they argued, "the building of a new hegemony implies the creation of a 'chain of equivalence' among the diversity of democratic struggles, old and new, in order to form a 'collective will,' a 'we' of the radical democratic forces."[26] As with the literary critics surveyed earlier, it is possible to see here the influence of Foucauldian anxieties about social control and the dream of social freedom complicating the Marxian narrative—and not necessarily positively. Although these critics seem less vulnerable to Ebert's charge of replacing need with desire, it is not clear that the formulations balancing the Foucauldian drive for liberation with the Marxist goal of equality—Mouffe's "liberty and equality for all," Duggan's "Love *and* Money"—actually result in a practicable and compelling socialist strategy.

Even as Gilman and Du Bois insisted upon the importance of women and racial minorities within social democratic coalitions, they joined Sinclair and other socialists in emphasizing economic determination and insisting upon economic equality as the basis for all other forms of social freedom. At those moments when today's social democrats stress the autonomy of the new political struggles as a way to demonstrate the inadequacy of economic analysis, they tend to reify economics into a limited conception of "class." On some occasions, as when Mouffe speaks of "all the democratic struggles which have emerged in a variety of social relations and which, we argued, could not be apprehended through the category of 'class,'" and when Lott warns against liberals' "general preference for agitating around class and economic inequality to the exclusion of other exploitations," they appear to reduce the flexible category of economic relations to a static, narrow social category.[27] Such a reification makes class just one among several subject identities, and of course to prioritize class interests above the interests of exploited minorities, women, or GLBT people would be to violate the core principle of equality. But economic analysis (whether in the Marxist or in other socialist traditions) cannot be equated to partisanship for a particular, clearly defined set of individuals. If, to be sure, Sinclair sometimes conceives of the proletariat in terms of the white, male, European stereotype, Gilman and Du Bois show us that prioritizing the mode of production and the problem of economic exploitation, as Marxism and socialism do, can and should mean attending first and foremost to the needs of women, blacks, and other disadvantaged groups that are more economically exploited than the white, male proletariat (or even largely excluded from economic life). Indeed, economic analysis can actually function as a mediating frame of analysis that allows for a more fundamental articulation of common interests between various exploited groups than simply an assertion of the necessity of a series of ad hoc political alliances against a common but ill-defined foe, variously identified as social repression, disciplinary power, or political oppression. Such an analysis of economic relations may also make possible a relative prioritization of immediate political goals: not an absolute privileging of economic over social issues, but a conditional emphasis upon material needs.

From the example of the triptych writers, we can see, too, that the different relationships of various disadvantaged groups to the means of social production may result not only in different relative priorities, but in rather different kinds of political action than if—as prompted by the formula of equivalency—they were pursuing their own goals mainly according to their own lights. The tension lies in whether "love" and "money" can, after all, be pursued by everyone simultaneously, or whether some group's pursuit of its desires might, in fact, interfere with not only the desires of another group or individuals but even their basic material needs. In response to the effort to balance goals of "love" and "money," liberty and equality, for all individuals simultaneously, the triptych writers often offered a differential understanding of the relationships of various individuals and groups to social power—and hence an understanding that different groups will need to behave differently for there to be a coordinated and coherent, counterhegemonic socialist strategy. To take just one preliminary example: Charlotte Perkins Gilman saw that the difference between middle-class and working-class women was qualitative as well as quantitative, for the former could enjoy significant wealth even as they altogether lacked status as socially productive individuals, whereas the latter had some status as productive individuals (and were exploited by it) even as they had very little wealth. Consequently, the remedies for their situations were starkly different: middle-class women had to become traitors to their class, giving up their privileges as bourgeois consumers even as they sought recognition as producers by moving into the workforce; working-class women already had recognition as producers but needed to gain in their privileges as consumers, needing to obtain control over the full product of their labor.

All of this is not to suggest that Gilman, Sinclair, and Du Bois were paragons of egalitarian ethics and social democratic political judgment. Gilman, Sinclair, Du Bois, and their cohort of activists offer instead a series of case studies exemplifying both the possibilities of egalitarian activism within the United States and the challenges of such activism. Ultimately, the most fundamental difference between this study and recent theorizations of "liberty and equality," "love and money," is not about aims, or even social democratic strategy, but about their emphasis on general theory and a focus upon recent events and my focus on a historical methodology and a longer view. I seek in *American Socialist Triptych* to describe not so much how social democracy *might* be—the ideal conditions that might yet yield social democracy, "a 'chain of equivalence' among the diversity of democratic struggles," to quote Laclau and Mouffe—but rather how historical events actually *did* conspire to realize a degree of social democracy in the United States. It tells this narrative both by entering into dialogue with historians and biographers and by using primary texts extensively, not only literary texts but also unpublished manuscripts, diaries, and personal correspondence. In adopting these historiographic methods rather than the higher theory of Ebert, Laclau and Mouffe, Foucault, or Derrida, *American Socialist Triptych* is oriented toward the specificity of what has actually happened with, and to, socialism in the United States. This is not to discount the importance of the ideal; indeed, among the phenomena that have "actually happened" in the United States is the projection of a variety of socialist futures. The interaction between pragmatic and idealistic versions of socialism—often called "scientific" and "utopian" socialism—is central to the story I have to tell, beginning directly in the next chapter and more or less throughout. Yet the narrative will consider with at least equal attention those aspects of historical contingency—the resistance of institutions and practices to change, and the necessity of using institutions in order to effect change—that complicate the pure and direct pursuit of egalitarian ideals and also those historical aspects—moments of serendipity—that create opportunities in spite of the theoretical shortcomings of the activists involved.

I should like finally to offer a few words on the book's strategy and organization by way of the overarching metaphor I have adopted for this work: the triptych. In its original medieval usage, a *triptych* is a three-panel, dually hinged and usually movable, allegorical mural created for medieval Christian churches and chapels. The three parts of the mural were employed variously: they might represent a snapshot of a single scene with three focal points; they might describe a single narrative arc with beginning, middle, and end and typically moving from left to right; or they might present three separate, though interrelated saints' lives or biblical narratives.[28] In all its variations, the heart of the triptych is the composite and dialogic effects gained by viewing the three panels together. So, too, with my triptych of American socialist writers. To begin with, there is a logical and chronological progression from Gilman and the pre-1900 socialists on the one side, to Sinclair and the Socialist Party in the middle, and on to Du Bois and Black Nationalism on the other. But in terms of socialist ideology, the progression is by no means absolute. As the triptych is meant to be viewed as a whole, with the ever-present possibility of comparisons back and forth between the panels, so too this socialist triptych demands reading the earlier story of Gilman in constant dialogue with the later two, virtually synchronous stories of Du Bois and Sinclair, for in her work we find a socialist-feminist interrogation of the latent patriarchy of the other two. It demands also that the work of W. E. B. Du Bois be brought into critical relation with the main line of the socialist tradition defined by the careers of Gilman and Sinclair, neither of whom ever entirely grasped the importance of antiracism to socialist strategy.

Here it is useful to recall the medieval penchant for the grotesque often reflected in the triptych, whereby the very holiness of the represented characters or narratives might be brought into question by the manner of their presentation (the Last Judgment, for instance, seems particularly arbitrary in its division of the damned and the saved, whose naked forms are indistinguishable from one another except for their radically differing eternal destinations).[29] The diversity of the triptych as a genre, often focusing upon events in the life of Jesus but also taking as subjects the Virgin Mary, the Last

Judgment, Adam and Eve, various saints, and even the visages of patrons, also suggests that no single triptych pretends to tell the whole narrative that the church seeks to convey to spiritual seekers and believers. The central narrative thread may be held in common—whether social equality in this world or salvation in the next—but the ways of elaborating upon the story are multiple. So, too, I do not profess that Gilman, Sinclair, and Du Bois were in all ways exemplary of the best in American socialist traditions—only that their work is often prophetic and consistently instructive. I also do not assert that work done by other scholars upon other socialist traditions ought to be disregarded. I merely offer that, in addition to the chapel of progressivism and the shrine to Communism, we might consider the authenticity of another American social democratic narrative, this socialist triptych of Gilman, Sinclair, and Du Bois.

Besides the triptych of representative socialist writers, fundamental to this project at its conception, another tripartite scheme has emerged through the process of research, writing, and rewriting, reflected in the three-part organization of the chapters into groups. The scheme emerges from the tension between Gilman's, Sinclair's, and Du Bois's work as political activists and their profession as writers. The political and literary functions were practically coterminous for these writers. Yet unquestionably, there were choices these writers could and did make about how precisely to manifest their political commitments in their writing, and they certainly made choices at various times about how closely they aligned themselves, and involved themselves, with specific political groups and campaigns. Moreover, even as the literary politics of Gilman, Sinclair, and Du Bois must be understood within the context of the groups and movements of their times, their political literature must be understood within the framework of literary tradition, genre, and reception. Consequently, this book will sometimes focus more upon how the triptych writers used their literature toward immediate political ends, and sometimes more upon how politics is reflected in, and acts upon, literary form.

Part I will consider especially the interconnections between the political and the literary at those moments in the authors' careers when they initially identified themselves with socialism, a procedure that will also serve to introduce American socialism in the decades of the 1890s and the following two decades. In Part II, which has a slightly later focus concentrated on the second and third decades of the twentieth century, the argument is closely tied to the development of a literary critical genre that was the favored mode of all three of my featured socialist writers, a genre that I shall call realist-utopian fiction in deference to the two widely acknowledged literary genres that it merges. These genres, I shall argue, have been interdependent upon each other from the outset and have developed in relationship with the progressive-socialist movements of their era. In addition to this argument's implications for the standard literary histories of the late nineteenth and early twentieth centuries, an exploration of the literary production of Gilman, Sinclair, and Du Bois allows an examination of the several different relationships of the literary profession and of intellectual work generally with political activism. Even as their careers reflect a constant desire and the possibility of literary production doing immediate political work, those careers also show the productivity and the necessity of longer-term cultural work. At various points in the second and third decades of the twentieth century, the triptych authors paid relatively greater attention to their own literary endeavors and pulled back from direct political activism. But for them, certainly—and perhaps for other American writers—the shift in focus did not reflect a diminishment of political interest so much as a redirection of socialist strategy from immediate political action to less direct cultural work. The two chapters comprising Part III examine the interaction of the longer-term work with political action, showing how, at the key historical moment of the Great Depression, the cultural work combined with a renewal of direct action to bring about political and institutional change.

Although this progression reflects the compromises and the long-term commitment necessary to bring about just a degree of socialist change in the United States, it also inspires some degree of hope for a more egalitarian future by social democratic change. If the history of U.S. socialism in the later years of the nineteenth century and opening years of the twentieth century remains immanent in many of our contemporary institutions, practices, and ideological formations—and, after all, elements of the welfare state, key provisions of Social Security established in the 1930s, do remain with us—then that history may tell us of both the potentials for progressive transformation and the pitfalls of attempting such a transformation in the opening years of the twenty-first century. Although there is considerable difference between the way literary critics have come to imagine social liberation in the twenty-first century and the way these socialist literary figures imagined it in their times, and while there is appreciable though more subtle difference between the formulations of the new social democrats and these old ones schooled in the Second Internationale, the notion of a common American history of "radicalism" suggests also that the various concepts that today's academics offer under those terms have, at their root, a common aim of genuine social equality in material as well as psychological dimensions. This book is written with such a possibility in mind, coupled with an awareness that, for all our interest in justice and equality, contemporary scholars of American culture and literature are lacking in resources for learning the history of nonviolent, democratic, and radical politics within their fields. It is my hope that *American Socialist Triptych* will be such a resource.

PART ONE

SOCIAL DEMOCRACY IN AMERICA

CHAPTER ONE

LOOKING BACKWARD, WORKING FORWARD: FIN DE SIÈCLE SOCIALISM ACCORDING TO CHARLOTTE PERKINS GILMAN

In approaching the history of socialism in the United States, we immediately face the problem that historians have widely assumed socialism has never amounted to much here—even, among some specialists in the field, that in this country there has been no socialist movement worthy of the name. Werner Sombart's *Why Is There No Socialism in the United States?* (1906) was notably premature in its negative judgment upon the movement, drawing conclusions well before the high points of Socialist and Communist Party activity. His gloomy analysis has nevertheless set the standard for later commentators. Two of his points of criticism—that greater social mobility (or the appearance thereof) has prevented working-class solidarity in the United States, and that the U.S. two-party system has thwarted the influence of radical parties of all kinds—certainly must be reckoned with by any study of American socialism, including this one. Initially, though, it is the basic assumption, "no socialism in the United States," that demands our attention. Among the many critics that have shared the Sombartian premise, it is the wide—and contradictory—variety of explanations of the assumption that stands out. On the one hand, as characterized in Daniel Bell's seminal *Marxian Socialism in the United States,* American socialism has been too rigidly theoretical and utopian ever to gain traction in the quotidian, workaday world, "trapped by the unhappy problem of living '*in* but not *of* the world,' so it could only act, and then inadequately, as the moral, but not political, man in immoral society."[1] On the other hand, as caustically dismissed in Brian Lloyd's *Left Out: Pragmatism, Exceptionalism, and the Poverty of American Marxism, 1890–1922,* socialism in the United States has been theoretically slack, altogether too pragmatic and accommodating toward American conditions to effect any real change in them, "attempt[ing] the impossible—defeating the enemy while waving the enemy's flag."[2] Obviously, these points of view are incompatible. But then what are we to make of the assumption of socialism's failure, shared by both? Should we conclude that American socialism was sometimes overly pragmatic, sometimes overly utopian, but nearly always the wrong one at the wrong time? Or if, as often happens in such debates, there is an element of truth on both sides, then is it possible that American socialists have sometimes gotten the balance right, a conclusion that must force us to rethink the assumption with which Sombart started us more than a century ago?

Here it may be objected—by exponents of socialism and its opponents alike—that socialism is not by any means about the right balance between extremes. One of the most famous formulations in the socialist tradition, after all, is Marx and Engels's unequivocal assertion that "only by the forcible overthrow of all existing social conditions"[3] could the proper foundation for socialism's ultimate goal, the classless society, be laid. Yet in the same document containing this assertion, the epoch-making *Communist Manifesto,* Marx and Engels sought precisely to stake out the middle ground between their socialist predecessors and the defenders of existing conditions. The writings of the early socialists Robert Owen and Charles Fourier, English and French promoters of communal schemes by which people of all classes were to meet on equal terms, might be "full of the most valuable materials for the enlightenment of the working class,"[4] but in Marx and Engels's estimation, the communitarian socialists had been sorely lacking in their understanding of the fundamental facts of class division and struggle in modern society and, therefore, had done little more than seek to impose their own "fantastic" conjured-up ideas upon material reality. Theirs were forms of socialism utterly divorced from the real. The bourgeoisie, for all their faults, could be credited with a more realistic appraisal of the relations between classes under capitalism. At the founding moment of Marxism as an internationally recognized movement among the available forms of socialism, Marx and Engels claimed for themselves not the most extreme position, not the most fundamental radicalism, but the middle ground recognizing the down-and-dirty reality of the class struggle—even as did the bourgeois—and yet claiming also the higher ethical ground of human equality—together with all other socialists, of however pragmatic or utopian a hue. Presently, in Engels's 1881 treatise *Socialism: Utopian and Scientific,* the practical and righteous mean would have a name, "scientific," but even before its coinage, Marxists, non-Marxist socialists, and nonsocialist progressives have fought for a claim upon that mean. What theory and practice, socialists have wondered and argued over, would have enough leverage upon existing society to make a new, socially egalitarian order practicable, yet would at the same time remain distinct enough to establish the conditions for genuine egalitarianism, not the same old capitalist inequality in a new guise?

In the context of this search and this argument, the larger number of American socialists asserted the possibility that the United States could become a classless society by a gradual, democratic, and nonviolent path. Some, indeed, insisted that genuine socialism could be successfully introduced *only* by such a path. Unorthodox as this may seem from a latter-day perspective colored by the socialist-capitalist antinomies of the Comintern and the Cold War, in the latter years of the nineteenth century American socialists of this type were not bucking but participating in an international trend. To understand where they were coming from, we need to know something of the genealogy of socialism in the nineteenth century, in which Marxism offered just one of several theoretical lenses, and in which socialists had to come to terms with other anticapitalist but not necessarily socialist movements—including anarchism on the international scene, Populism within the United States. These socialist and socialistic movements simply did not register with a commentator such as Sombart, who had a very specific, Marxist and trade unionist notion of what socialism looked like. But these various movements set the stage both for the subsequent development of American socialism and for the infusion of certain social democratic practices in American culture more generally. Ultimately, the later development of a socialism more oriented to Marxist notions of class struggle—closer to what we think of as socialism in the twentieth and twenty-first centuries—tended to suppress forms of socialism that were more willing to assimilate other forms of radical critique and could be more readily assimilated into the wider culture. The initial steps of both processes—the assimilation and the suppression—become visible through the early career of Charlotte Perkins Gilman, who was an activist in both the Edward Bellamy Nationalist movement and the Populist movement, and who developed a synthesis of feminism and socialism that emerged in conversation with multiple socialist sources—a synthesis that has all too often been disregarded by later socialists and their historians alike.

REALLY EXISTING SOCIALISM IN THE UNITED STATES, CIRCA 1890

"French and English, with the American enthusiasm of Bellamy."

The socialism Gilman encountered when in 1890 she became active in the movement can be defined quite narrowly and with considerable precision and, at the same time, connected with a variety of groups and perspectives that are not so easy to describe by a simple rubric. In her autobiography, *The Living of Charlotte Perkins Gilman,* she explained that "My Socialism was of the early humanitarian kind, based on the first exponents, French and English, with the American enthusiasm of Bellamy."[5] Such a genealogy is precise about the beginning of the socialist movement that Gilman embraced early in her career as an intellectual. Along with thousands of other American progressives, she counted herself an adherent of Edward Bellamy Nationalism by 1890, a political phenomenon whose existence can be dated definitely to the weeks immediately following the 1888 publication of Bellamy's utopian novel, *Looking Backward: 2000–1887.* For his part, responding to questions about why the movement was called "Nationalism" instead of "socialism"—a distinction that has prompted at least one critic of the movement to claim it *wasn't* socialist[6]—Bellamy explained in an 1894 *New Nation* editorial that the latter term was simply not exact enough. Bellamy notes that socialism is "a generic and not a specific term," that a socialist might be defined broadly as any person "who accepts and works for the definite principle of organizing trade and industry collectively, by having land and industrial capital owned by the community (in some form), and operated co-operatively for the equitable (not necessarily the equal), good of all." Nationalism, Bellamy suggests, "contain[s] all the meaning of socialism" thus defined, but it also specifies the form of collective ownership as the Nation while insisting that the common wealth be shared not just equitably but *equally* among individuals.[7] Such a definition establishes a definite ideological content for the socialism with which Gilman affiliated as well as a clear point of historical origin.

The other elements of Gilman's definition of her socialism tend, however, to complicate as well as to enrich the picture, particularly because Gilman and her comrades in the 1890s were far from being the first U.S. citizens to be interested in socialism's "first exponents, French and English." Gilman was alluding to the early nineteenth-century movements founded by the Englishman Robert Owen and the Frenchman Charles Fourier—the very socialists disparaged by Marx and Engels in the *Communist Manifesto.* Owen was a Welsh textile manufacturer and philanthropist, famous for his model textile factory and company town, who by 1824 had became determined to redress the working conditions not merely of his own employees but of all workers. His plan was to plant small cooperative communities throughout

England and the United States, which might serve as winning models for the eventual transformation of society as a whole. Charles Fourier, a traveling-salesman-turned-philosopher who developed his system of collectivist, egalitarian "phalanxes" approximately ten years later, was also a communitarian, seeking to effect a wider transformation of society through the inspiration of communities that grew their own food and supplied most of their other material wants by traditional handicrafts. There was reason for Marx and Engels to concede that Owen and Fourier provided "most valuable materials for the enlightenment of the working class," for the intellectual architecture of their movements was genuinely inspiring: Owen, Fourier, and their followers denounced the antisocial effects of private property and economic competition, insisted upon the equality of women with men, and declared that human beings might achieve their full potentiality if placed in nurturing and cooperative social environments.[8]

Owen looked specifically to the United States as the most fertile ground for his prototype agricultural and industrial communities.[9] The United States had, after all, been a site of various communal experiments in cooperative and egalitarian economics since the beginnings of European settlement. The most famous of the first permanent European colonists, the Pilgrims, were communards motivated by religion—common ownership of property being one of the articles of the Mayflower Compact. While the Plymouth governor, William Bradford, began to allow some forms of private property within three years, confessing that human depravity prevented the realization of the communal ideal anywhere short of heaven, American religious communities with happier views of human nature continued to see communal property as practicable on earth, and included the Shakers, the Amana colonists, and the Hutterites.[10] So it was that Owen came to the United States in the late 1820s armed with a degree of hope that he might find individuals willing to join egalitarian communities following his highly idealistic, though secular, philosophy. He personally supervised the formation of ten settlements, and nine more hailing Owen as their inspiration were formed in the 1830s and 1840s.

Fourierite communities in the United States followed closely on the heels of the Owenite experiments. Although their namesake never set foot in the United States, the Fourier phalanxes were actually more numerous and longer lived. Fourierism benefited from having articulate and influential American advocates: chiefly, Arthur Brisbane, whose books such as *The Social Destiny of Man, or Association and Reorganization of Industry* (1840) and *A Concise Exposition of the Doctrine of Association, or Plan for the Reorganization of Society* (1843) combined translations of Fourier's writings with Brisbane's own commentaries; and *New York Tribune* editor Horace Greeley, who permitted Brisbane to write a regular front-page column on Fourierism from March 1842 to September 1843. The publicity generated by Brisbane and Greeley led, in turn, to a boom in commune building—thirty-seven Fourierite settlements in thirteen states, almost all established during the 1840s.[11]

The knock against communitarian socialism was its supposed impracticality. Marx and Engels's criticism, that Owen and Fourier operated on the level of beautiful ideals divorced from material realities, was echoed in other quarters. Nathaniel Hawthorne, who lived in the Brook Farm cooperative community supported by Ralph Waldo Emerson and other Transcendentalists, made the community a matter for satiric and tragic fiction in *The Blithedale Romance.*[12] His most explicit commentary upon Brook Farm, in the novel's final chapter, suggested that communes would never succeed because enterprising individuals would prefer the competitive world of the capitalist marketplace, whereas the loafers who hoped to gain from cooperation would never be able to make such a community self-sustaining: "Where once we toiled with our hopeful hearts, the town-paupers, aged, nerveless, and disconsolate, creep sluggishly afield. Alas, what faith is requisite to bear up against such results of generous effort!"[13] Hawthorne's objections somewhat bizarrely mix the two, diametrically opposed kinds of latter-day criticisms of American socialism, for just before his narrator, Coverdale, voices the impracticality of the communal arrangement, he also faults Blithedale for being insufficiently idealistic, "lapsing into Fourierism, and dying, as it well deserved, for this infidelity to its own higher spirit."[14] Socialism in America, it seems, can be neither practical enough nor idealistic enough. Yet again, for whatever reason the judgment of history appears to back up Hawthorne's adverse judgment as well as Marx's and Engels's. The Brook Farm community had been defunct for several years by the time *The Blithedale Romance* was published, and though it lasted but six years, it was one of the longer lived socialist communes. Most of the Owenite communities disbanded after a year or two, with only the longest lived reaching the six-year mark, a distinction shared by the Coal Creek Community of Indiana and Fruit Hills in Ohio. The Fourierite communes did only somewhat better: a majority lasted for two years or less, while just six out of thirty-seven lasted six years or longer.[15]

Through the middle and later decades of the nineteenth century, the main line of socialist development in the United States did not reject the philosophy of the Owenite and Fourierite experiments so much as it sought to place socialism upon a more practical basis. The communes had foundered, analysts felt, because they had been forced into competition with capitalism on a completely unequal footing—small islands of subsistence economics engulfed by a system with vastly greater resources, backed up by the allure of greater material consumption and an altogether hostile individualistic ideology. To have a fighting chance, socialism needed to be introduced on a much greater scale, meaning that not merely small groups of individuals needed to be persuaded of the value of socialism but a massive number, likely even a controlling majority of the citizenry. It was the perceived necessity of this greater scale that led to Bellamy's insistence that socialism be instituted nationally, but on this point Bellamy was neither alone nor the first among American advocates of social equality.

The historical landscape of the later nineteenth century was dotted with movements that sought large-scale alternatives to capitalism as practiced in the United States. Part of the complexity of comprehending socialism in the period lies in sorting out just how to classify these alternatives: some did not advocate common ownership of property and thus would permit capitalism in some form to be maintained, while others did not seek strict social equality but rather equal opportunity or (as with current advocates of liberation) radical freedom. But if these do not count as socialism—according to either the narrower definition preferred by Bellamy or the broader one—then they might count as *socialistic,* in the sense that they contributed to a critique of capitalism and offered collectivist or at least less individualistic remedies. A case in point is the Single Tax, minutely explained in Henry George's 1879 treatise, *Progress and Poverty.* George's reform scheme was a straightforwardly confiscatory national tax upon land speculation, which, by rendering the ownership of untilled land unprofitable, sought to enable practically any American citizens who so desired to own their own small farms. Without demanding the abolition of private property, George's proposal sought to use government intervention on a single point to redirect individualist and entrepreneurial energies in ways that would result in a more equitable society—hence adopting the key socialist goal but an incompletely socialist means. Another awkward ideological mixture can be seen in the development of the Knights of Labor, whose leaders adopted the Owenite socialist philosophy of cooperation between labor and management, even as they organized America's first great industrial union, welcoming into one organization unskilled as well as skilled workers, blacks as well as whites, women as well as men. Because of their tremendous size—by the mid-1880s, over 700,000 members[16]—and limited opportunities for an Owenite education of the rank and file, the Knights were practically fated to enter instead into direct conflict with the captains of industry.

The evolution from communal socialism to the modern mass movement was not left entirely in the hands of ad hoc reformers and pragmatists, however. In attempting to persuade Americans of the feasibility as well as the desirability of socialism, American socialist theorists also sought to get a boost by demonstrating, as Marx and Engels had sought to do, that historical forces were driving toward precisely the egalitarian and generous society that comprised the socialist socio-ethical ideal. This was exactly the contention of Laurence Gronlund's 1884 book, *The Cooperative Commonwealth,* which in fact drew heavily upon Marx and Engels's ideas and even turns of phrase. Just as Marx saw the Paris Commune of 1871 as the beginning of revolutionary action in Europe, which would undoubtedly spread and deepen through the inexorable process of capitalist accumulation and labor exploitation, Gronlund predicted that the tumultuous American railroad strikes of 1877 were just the beginning of an inevitable cycle leading to revolution in the United States, as time and again capitalist overproduction would lead to economic crisis, economic crisis to labor unrest, and unrest to increasingly brutal suppression, until "in the fulness of time we shall have a labor revolt that will not be put down."[17] Echoing one of the more famous images of the *Communist Manifesto*—"What the bourgeoisie, therefore, produces, above all, is its own grave-diggers"—Gronlund announced, "This 'Individualism,' which has created and nourished Capital and is making it bigger and bigger, is at the same time digging the grave of Capital."[18]

Yet precisely at the moment of declaring the historical, dialectical materialist triumph of socialism across the board, at the very point where Gronlund's argument and his rhetoric aligns most closely with the *Manifesto,* Gronlund's argument turns in a quite different direction. Once historical and material forces have established the direction of social change, Gronlund imagines a tipping point at which the majority of citizens will acknowledge the inevitability of that change, approve of its results, and so give it their democratic assent: "As soon as the people learn not to be scared by the word 'Socialism'; as soon as they learn the true nature of the State and see whither they are drifting, the Cooperative Commonwealth will be the only *expedient* system."[19]

Edward Bellamy went still further in predicting the inevitability of socialism in America, finding the catalyst for revolution not in labor activism, as did Gronlund, but in the dreaded adversary of labor: monopoly capitalism. When the protagonist of *Looking Backward,* Julian West, falls into a state of suspended animation in 1887 and awakens in 2000 to find his native Boston much improved by one hundred years of life under a socialist commonwealth, nothing astonishes him more than the news that the great transformation from monopoly capitalism to state socialism took place with absolutely no violence or bloodshed. No doubt having in mind the violent insurrections of 1877 or, perhaps, the Haymarket riot, Julian West must be assured several times by Dr. Leete, his host on the cusp of the twenty-first century, that the emergence of socialism was greeted by the vast majority of citizens as reasonable and desirable. Indeed, the monopolies that many had felt "threatened society with a form of tyranny more abhorrent than it had ever endured" are presented by Leete as actually paving the way for the final monopoly, the Nation. Dr. Leete informs Julian that "early in the last century," the twentieth century, that is,

> the evolution was completed by the final consolidation of the entire capital of the nation. The industry and commerce of the country, ceasing to be conducted by a set of irresponsible corporations and syndicates of private persons at their caprice and for their profit, were entrusted to a single syndicate representing the people, to be conducted in the common interest and for the common profit. The nation, that is to say, organized as the one great business corporation in which all other corporations were absorbed; it became the one capitalist in place of all other capitalists, the sole employer, the final monopoly in which all previous and lesser monopolies were swallowed up, a monopoly in the profits and economies of which all citizens shared.[20]

Once they recognized the groundwork for the great monopoly being laid by the progressively larger industrial syndicates, even the laborers found they could bide their time, wait for the inevitable coming of the one collective that must necessarily be controlled by the central national government "representing the people." And once practically all citizens recognized the productive efficiency realized through economies of scale and the elimination of redundant competitive industries, the demand for social ownership of the means of production became nearly universal: "Public opinion had become fully ripe for it, and the whole mass of the people was behind it. There was no more possibility of opposing it by force than by argument."[21]

Such a conception of a gentle and orderly path into the cooperative commonwealth was not, of course, a matter of consensus among socialists—neither in the United States nor elsewhere. Marx railed against Henry George's Single Tax: "Theoretically the man is utterly backward! He understands nothing about the nature of *surplus value*."[22] In 1880, Engels felt compelled to return to the critique of Fourier, Owen, and other early communitarians and socialist philosophers, organizing the debate between the non-Marxists and Marxists by terms that have since become widespread as terms of dismissal and approbation. *Socialism, Utopian and Scientific* sought to reject non-Marxian socialism as impossibly out of touch with reality, Marxian socialism as in the know about the objective conditions of society and history. Although a supporter of Bellamy Nationalism at the very beginning of his socialist career, Daniel De Leon soon became America's most ardent and vocal exponent of rigorous Marxist revolutionism and dialectical materialism. For De Leon as with Marx and Engels, history was driven essentially by class struggle; those socialists who wished for an easy road to revolution were indistinguishable from social reformers. Building upon the binary opposition articulated by Engels, De Leon asserted in an 1896 speech that genuine socialism "takes Science by the hand, asks her to lead, and goes withersoever she points." Such scientific socialists "move as intelligent men; we do not mutiny because, instead of wings, we have arms, and cannot fly as we would wish," and they do not insist upon nice moral distinctions in seeking "Revolution—peaceful or bloody, and the peacefulness or the bloodiness of it cuts no figure whatever in the essence of the question."[23]

Among the protest groups that De Leon scorned were the Populists, whom he classed (along with the Knights of Labor and Henry George) as "movements that bred hopes in the hearts of the people" but were doomed to fail because they operated upon "denials of scientific facts." Yet even as the People's Party had by then passed its apogee as an independent movement—De Leon jeered that "it went up like a rocket, and is now fast coming down a stick"[24]—the evidence provided by American history and by the socialist movement in America to that date did not back up the "science" of militant Marxism nearly as unequivocally as De Leon would have had his hearers believe. The impermanency of the cooperative communes had demanded reconsideration of their small-bore, experimental approach. Yet arguably, Marxist revolutionists were basing their suppositions upon still more slender historical reeds than were the socialists who envisioned a gradual transformation effecting a cooperative commonwealth. Marx believed he had gained enough empirical evidence from the Paris Commune of 1871 to draw specific conclusions in his pamphlet *The Civil War in France* about the historically ordained form to be taken by the dictatorship of the proletariat. But the Commune had been possible in the first place only on account of the French military debacle of the previous fall in the Franco-Prussian war; it had been imperiled from the start, and was brutally crushed by regrouped elements of the French army after just seventy-three days. Even the least successful of the secular communes, whose philosophies served to inspire later American socialists of a gradualist and cooperative bent, lasted longer than this, and the longer-lived Fourierite groups sustained themselves for a decade or more: Utopia in Trialville, Ohio, lasted for eleven years; the Alphadelphia Phalanx in Michigan and the North American Phalanx in New Jersey both for thirteen; and the Hopedale Community in Massachusetts for twenty-five. Provocatively, the last American Fourierite phalanx was founded in the same year that the French army was routed at Sedan, setting the stage for the Commune. The Kansas Cooperative Farm did not grab headlines; it struck fear into the hearts of few; it did not inspire any imaginative literature so far as I know, and it remained functioning until 1884.[25]

As in Paris in 1871, those occasions when violent labor disturbances took place in the United States hardly produced much evidence that here lay the path to an egalitarian socialist society, although one could certainly make the case that these were events driven by powerful historical determinants. The Great Upheaval of 1877 was in many respects America's version of the Paris Commune. In that year spontaneous strikes among railroad workers in Pennsylvania and West Virginia led to widespread destruction of railroad property, armed confrontations in which some militiamen decided to support the workers, and protest meetings in some towns in which the workers, deliberately invoking the spirit of the Commune, declared the establishment of labor governments.[26] The revolutionary rhetoric of the strikers seemed, however, only to embolden their antagonists, for federal troops swiftly, brutally, and completely crushed the strikes, and majority popular opinion turned sharply against the workers and their grievances. Something similar happened to the Knights of Labor, whose rank and file, despite the nonconfrontational stance of their leaders, went out on strike repeatedly in the mid-1880s, almost as soon as they reached a critical mass in membership. Initial successes led to spring 1886 strikes against James Gould–owned railroads in the Southwest. Then sabotage and other acts of violence by some Knights-affiliated strikers provided warrant for law enforcement officials and company militias to strike back with violence of their own, and within weeks the Knights were forced to accept wage cuts and other concessions (and union membership fell almost as swiftly as it had previously risen, to around 100,000 by 1890).[27] The year 1886, moreover, brought the Haymarket disaster, which showed that the link between radical labor leaders and violence need only be plausibly *imagined* in order to justify the widest-ranging persecution. No one claimed that the seven anarchist leaders who were convicted of murder charges had actually thrown the bomb that killed eight police at Haymarket Square, Chicago, yet Haymarket cemented in the popular imagination the image of the bomb-throwing anarchist that in the United States has served to define—and to discredit—anarchist socialism to this very day.

In Europe during the same period, socialist reaction to the Commune and the demise of the First Internationale were establishing the groundwork for a new, less confrontational approach. Although the intellectual supremacy of Marx's thought was so well established by the 1870s that every European socialist party claimed Marxism as its official ideology, European socialists were offering widely varying applications of that ideology to the practical difficulties they faced after the defeat of the Paris Commune. The preferred socialist strategy was parliamentary and gradualist, effectively implemented by the 1875 merger of the two major German socialist organizations to form the Social Democratic Party, and codified by the 1889 formation of the Second International. During the First Internationale, it was the minority position, maintained by Marx's arch-foe Ferdinand Lassalle, that revolutionary change might be possible by nonviolent and legal methods. In the Second Internationale it became the official majority line of the international movement, preached by prominent Marxists August Bebel, Eduard Bernstein, and Karl Kautsky. During the Second Internationale, Engels himself even occasionally countenanced the possibility of socialist revolution through parliamentary means, especially in countries with democratically elected governments such as the United States.[28]

In the United States, meanwhile, as if to fulfill all that Gronlund had prophesied as possible under American political and social conditions, the utopian literary projection and rhetorical persuasion of Edward Bellamy's *Looking Backward,* published just two years after Gronlund's *Cooperative Commonwealth,* served to fuel a nationwide movement. Bellamy's *Looking Backward* had a tremendous popular readership, with somewhere between 160,000 and 300,000 copies of the book printed in the first two years, between 500,000 and one million within the first decade.[29] Nationalist clubs devoted to studying its blueprint for the future sprang up almost immediately, too, numbering 158 clubs in twenty-seven states by the end of 1890, when Charlotte Perkins Gilman first affiliated herself with one of them.[30] Gronlund was enthralled by *Looking Backward,* to the extent that he instructed his booksellers to push sales of Bellamy's book instead of his own, and he threw his energy into supporting the Nationalist movement. Largely on the strength of his observation of the Bellamy Nationalist phenomenon, Gronlund came to assert all the more unequivocally that socialism could be achieved without violence, through the institutions already existing in the United States. By the time he issued a new, revised version of *The Cooperative Commonwealth* in 1890, he eliminated his prediction that socialists could await the revolution with folded arms. Replacing this (formerly) scientific-socialist deduction were Gronlund's (newly) scientific-socialist prognostications about the pivotal role to be played by popular control of the state, which he saw Nationalism as helping to effect.[31]

In many ways Nationalism was the lineal descendant of Owenism and Fourierism—as Gilman would later suggest—for the movement insisted upon the principles of strict equality and the obligation of all to labor as well as upon the possibility of a natural, harmonious progression from capitalist competition into socialist cooperation. Along with Gronlund and other Marxists, Nationalism had also come to terms with industrial and technological modernity, embracing modern industrial production as the means to provide material abundance for all. Bellamy and other Nationalists further asserted, however, the need for a mass politics as the means to achieve a national transformation in political economy. Recognizing their own limitations—a movement reaching into many but not all states, and appealing more to intellectuals and bourgeois progressives than to a cross-section of the population—Nationalists sought to connect with a wider political movement. Consequently, Nationalist representatives attended the founding convention of the People's Party in 1892 and chose to support Populist efforts to supplant the established national parties.

Even as they were precise about the necessary scope of socialist organization and held high standards for the egalitarian criteria by which socialist success would be judged, Nationalists were flexible about the forms of progressive activism that might count as favorable to their cause. If, after all, monopoly capitalism could be turned to the ultimate advantage of the cooperative commonwealth, what movement aiming at social betterment could not be assimilated? It was not especially difficult, therefore, for Bellamy and other Nationalists to affiliate themselves with the Populist movement and the People's Party in the 1890s. Whereas De Leon scorned the Populists, Bellamy touted them. In an 1893 editorial, "This Revolution is Beginning Like all the Great Ones," Bellamy speculated that "petty" Populist measures such as free silver coinage would in due course proceed to "the plain issue between the public conduct of all industry for the equal common benefit, and the present irresponsible system of private capitalistic rule for private ends." Indeed, when Bellamy compared the People's Party with the Marxist but gradualist social democratic parties of Europe, he found the political demands and strategy of the American People's Party to be more aggressive. Referring to the moderate political strategy approved at the 1893 international socialist congress held in Zurich, Bellamy chided the "conservatism" of the German social democrats, "which looks like failing devotion to the ultimate socialist ideal" and "pretty mild sort of talk compared with the utterance of our people's party conventions." Bellamy's criticisms echo Marx's own of the reformist direction taken by the German Social Democrats as early as the 1870s, as Bellamy asks puckishly, "Shall we have to export socialism?"[32] Writing in much the same vein a few years later, Gilman's assessment of the international socialist movement is both broadly inclusive of groups being systematically excluded from the ranks of the Socialist Internationale and pointedly partisan toward the People's Party: "The social movement of to-day is felt in each civilized country, but varies in form according to the local conditions. In Russia we have nihilism; in Italy and Spain, anarchism, communism and Socialism. In Germany Socialism, strict and strong. In England a more ethical and educational form of Socialism. In America what we call Populism is our indigenous movement in the same direction."[33]

While the philosophy of Nationalism is relatively easy to define, as the Nationalist organization always remained closely associated with the originating vision of Bellamy in *Looking Backward,* the task of defining Populism is fairly daunting, for the 1890s movement derived from many quite different sources and flourished in several regions of the country—the Southeast, Southwest, and upper Midwest—each of which gave the movement its own distinct constituency and different, even sometimes contradictory, aims. One of the leading historians of the movement, Lawrence Goodwyn, steadfastly resists classifying nineteenth-century Populist ideology under the categories of either capitalism or socialism: "Populists were not capitalist reformers, as we understand that phrase in modern political language; neither were they socialists. Though their mass movement literally grew out of their belief in the power of man as a cooperative being, they also accepted man as a competitive being."[34] Manifestly in the South, less so in the Midwest and Southwest, Populism was a movement of white farmers who felt threatened from below by black labor as well as from above by white-owned banks, railroads, and granaries. The history of Populism is, therefore, checkered by racism varying in kind and degree from region to region.[35]

Populists were united, however, by a consistent and far-reaching contempt for capitalism as practiced in nineteenth-century America. Even if, as Goodwyn suggests, the Populists were by no means united upon any particular, systemic alternative to capitalism, and if their attitude might be seen as preindustrialist nostalgia—very much the same spirit that had animated the communitarian socialist groups—those practical measures and reforms they advanced certainly meet the standard of being socialistic. The key demands uniting the People's Party nationally were for a government with much broader powers in the economic sphere. In all three major planks of the platform ratified in Omaha in 1892, the People's Party advocated either outright nationalized ownership or federal administration oriented more to public good than, as at present, to private gain. "Money," railroads and telegraphs, and "Land," Gene Clanton explains, "Having been usurped by corporations and privileged individuals . . . had to be reclaimed and superintended by means of public agencies, owned and administered by the community at large."[36] Using the *Communist Manifesto* as a yardstick, we may note that Marx and Engels's proposals there include nationalized banking, public ownership of transportation and communication, and land reform promoting smaller-scale farming and a more even distribution of population between country and city. While the reforms of the People's Party definitely fell short of the abolition of capitalism, they represented practical measures that could be, and in some cases actually were, implemented. The subtreasury plan of southwestern Populists created a cooperative market among farmers for crops, land, and equipment standing as a buffer to the "free," capitalist market. It was one of the boldest and most creative challenges to market capitalism ever attempted in the United States.[37]

As De Leon's metaphor of the rocket suggests, the People's Party was remarkably and swiftly successful. In its regions of strongest support and during the economic crises of the early 1890s, the People's Party surpassed the popularity of the two established parties. An organization called the Farmers Alliance and Industrial Union, the immediate predecessor of the national People's Party formed by midwestern and southern farmers and remnants of the Knights of Labor, had already fielded candidates in the election of 1890, eleven of whom won seats in the U.S. Congress.[38] In 1892, with the further support of the Nationalists and other reform groups, this political organization under the new banner of the People's Party won two governorships. Its presidential candidate, General James Weaver, won five states as well as over 8 percent of the total national vote. Although by the time of the midterm elections of 1894 the People's Party retained only seven seats in the U.S. House of Representatives, it held six seats in the Senate and elected hundreds to state office and controlled or won influence in state legislatures throughout the Midwest and South.[39]

The subsequent career of Populism—which De Leon characterized as a "stick" returning to earth—I will be taking up in the third and final section of this chapter. At this point, suffice it to say that De Leon's dismissive attitude may be seen as strongly colored by defensiveness over the limited electoral success of his favored, more doctrinaire Marxist party, the Socialist Labor Party. When in 1892 General Weaver received over one million votes for U.S. president, the candidate of the Socialist Labor Party garnered 21,000.[40] De Leon's argument was that historical forces were on the side of his version of scientific socialism, but the empirical evidence of the past several decades suggested, rather, that history was on the side of those socialists who found parliamentary, conciliatory, and gradual means as the more promising path into the classless society.

Bellamy, Gilman, and other Nationalists who threw their support to the Populists did not imagine that the movement represented a fully realized socialism—nor even that its ideals amounted to a fully formed socialist vision. In a sense, however, they actually cleaved more closely than the more doctrinaire Marxists did to the basic Marxist principle that socialism might be realized only within the framework of actually existing, material social relations. Bellamy and his followers extended this principle to the realm of political ways and means—effectively in accord with the Second Internationale—by asserting that socialism could be substantially advanced through progressive, merely socialistic popular movements and the existing political and legal apparatuses. The American Revolution appeared, in fact, to afford socialists a useful precedent and native national rhetoric for the popular control of industry. Bellamy hastens to draw the parallel early in *Looking Backward*, as Dr. Leete ties the common sense of economic revolution to the political revolution of 1776, as by the end of the nineteenth century "the people of the United States concluded to assume the conduct of their own business, just as one hundred-odd years before they assumed the conduct of their own government, organizing now for industrial purposes on precisely the same grounds that they had then organized for political purposes."[41] In her first extant public speech—given in 1890 before one of the Nationalist Clubs dedicated to the propagation of Bellamy's ideas—Charlotte Perkins Gilman spoke on "Human Nature" both to dispute that capitalism offered a clear extension of human nature and to assert that the natural development of American culture pointed to socialism. Gilman urged her audience to imagine themselves extending an antiauthoritarian trend initiated in the Protestant Reformation:

> [We] sat under religious tyranny [for a] long while—didn't know we could help it! But as soon as a few men were big and brave enough to *take*

> their right to religious freedom, why they did it, at awful cost—but to the world's great gain. We come from those men!
>
> We sat under royal tyranny for a long while—didn't know we could help it. But as soon as a few men were big and brave enough to *take* their right to political freedom, why they did it—at awful cost again, but helping the whole world. We come from those men!
>
> And still we sit under the tyranny of money, and most of us don't know yet that we can help it. But as soon as we grow big and brave enough to *take* [our] right to economic freedom—why we can do it, and help the world as it was never helped before.
>
> *We are those men!*[42]

From the vantage point of the early 1890s, Gilman and her comrades saw a substantial American tradition of socialism that did, indeed, stress the possibility of common ground between most members of most social classes and insisted upon the possibility of nonviolent social change. And that tradition would include not merely Bellamy's "American enthusiasm" and the American exponents of Owenism and Fourierism, but the cooperative visions of the Knights of Labor, Laurence Gronlund's adaptations of Marxism, Henry George's socialistic Single Tax, and even the egalitarian ideals of the nation's founders and its first European settlers. Looking backward from 1890, Gilman and her socialist comrades found an independent, varied, and genuinely radical legacy upon which to build. Looking at the present, they saw in the emerging Populist movement a number of signs of popular resistance to capitalism, democratic control of industry and finance, and reform schemes tending toward social cooperation over competition. Looking forward, they sought to do the cultural and political work that might bring "the whole mass of the people" to throw their support to the cooperative commonwealth. In Gilman's words, Americans needed to do no more or less than be "big and brave enough" to assume their natural "right to economic freedom."

POPULISTS AND WOMEN AS AGENTS OF REVOLUTION

> "Woman, the house-servant, belongs to the lowest grade of unorganized labor."

On a later day, when revolutionary Marxist-Leninism was to gain ascendancy in international socialism, Gilman would largely buy into the sharp dichotomy drawn by De Leon in the 1890s. She, of course, would gravitate to the pole of the binary opposite of De Leon's, when in her 1935 autobiography she not only asserted the kinship of her socialism with the Bellamy movement and the "humanitarian" French and English types but also insisted that "the narrow and rigid 'economic determinism' of Marx, with its 'class consciousness' and 'class struggle' I never accepted, nor the political methods pursued by Marxists."[43] There were of course substantial differences between Gilman's and De Leon's brands of socialism—between socialism that envisages legal and nonviolent methods as efficacious to the accomplishment of its ends, and socialism that foresees extralegal and violent methods as necessary. But I would also have us consider that these distinctions were never quite so sharp as De Leon saw them to be in the 1890s or Gilman believed they were in the 1930s. This is evident from a close examination of Gilman's writings of the 1890s: both those commenting directly upon the Nationalist and Populist movements and those in which Gilman expounded the theoretical relationship of women and socialism, especially in conversation with the feminist tenets of Nationalism. In other words, the socialism in which Gilman participated and to which she contributed was not only gradualist but revolutionary, and not a merely superficial challenge to the existing social order but a rigorous and radical one.

When Charlotte Perkins Gilman attended the 1896 International Labor and Socialist Congress, convening in London, her reports upon the congress stressed the parallels between protest movements in the various European countries and the United States. Her report on the congress, quoted above, stressed the commonalities not merely between social democracy, communism, and Populism but between nihilism, anarchism, and English Fabianism. It was with Fabianism that Gilman evidently felt the strongest connection among the various forms of socialism that she came into contact with at the congress: her report was the first of many articles Gilman would publish in the *American Fabian*, the organ of the U.S. offshoot of the English Fabian Society. Still, it is the blurring of distinctions that is most striking in Gilman's 1896 accounts of international socialism. Gilman's diary from the days of the 1896 congress, for example, differentiates only slightly between her warm regard for the Fabians and her esteem for the Marxians in attendance: "Meet the Fabians, long honored. Bebel, Singer, Liebnecht, Lafargue, Eleanor Marck Aveling, etc.—lots of great names there."[44] Besides *seeing* August Bebel at the congress, the day before it opened she spoke on the same platform with him at a Hyde Park peace demonstration.[45] Indeed, it seems that Gilman was then more open-minded in her socialism than were the mainline

Marxists. Later on the very day that the congress refused to recognize the anarchists' credentials, carrying on the precedent set by Marx and Engels during the First Internationale, Gilman reports going to hear the anarchists at their parallel meeting: "Go in evening to Anarchist meeting in St. Martin's Hall. Krapotkine [*sic*]—Elisee Reclus—Louise Michel—*very* interesting."[46]

Not only in 1896, when Gilman's contacts with socialists were as numerous and varied as they would be at any time in her career, but also in 1890, when she made her first connection to a socialist group by becoming involved in the Pasadena, California, Nationalist Club, Gilman's writings testify that she and her Nationalist colleagues envisaged their movement as something rather different from a matter of gentle humanitarian reform. Certainly, Gilman's first speech before the Pasadena club, "On Human Nature," provides an indication of the difference between the ethos of the non-Marxian Nationalist movement and the Marxist Socialist Labor Party that De Leon would soon be associated with. The horticultural imagery that infuses the speech, for example, substantiates Mark Pittenger's argument that reform socialists drew upon the Lamarckian evolutionary views stressing *adaptation,* whereas revolutionary socialists emphasized *struggle.*[47] Yet the speech's rhetoric consistently undermines the apparent contrast between the terms. Although certainly Gilman's embrace of Lamarckianism shows the preference of Gilman and her colleagues for social development through cooperation rather than antagonism, it also reveals a desire for change to be swift and thorough, more than orderly and conservative:

> Here we all are today, suffering from this and suffering from that and suffering from the other, and calling it "the common lot of humanity"! Lot indeed!
>
> Are we trees? Are we houses? Are we stuck in the ground and fenced in that we call life a "*lot*"? It would seem so.
>
> But it is *not* so. We can move and leave that lot. And what is more we can dig and ditch and plow and plant until that lot is a garden of Eden—if we choose.
>
> And we do choose. We heartily object to our lot as we find it; and we propose to so alter that lot that the former owners would not recognize it.[48]

Gilman's garden metaphor appears not so much to undermine the need for dramatic social change as to make such a change more palatable to her audience. Moreover, that change is actually premised on the idea of class division and conflict, of owners who set the terms of current suffering, and of occupants who, seizing control of their "lot," will transform it according to their own pattern.

In this case, it appears that the difference between Marxian and non-Marxian socialism lies not in an absence of "class consciousness" and "class struggle" in Nationalism but in a different conception of these terms. Marx and Engels asserted that the critical fault line between the classes lay between the bourgeois and the proletariat—under contemporary conditions, a division so closely in halves that a protracted class struggle would clearly be demanded for the proletariat to win power. Bellamy, Gilman, the Nationalists generally, and the Populists whom they supported placed the principal division between the large capitalists (plus their dependents and their immediate subordinates) and virtually everyone else—meaning that a tremendous majority had an interest in the establishment of socialism, and merely had to be shown this fact and then persuaded to act upon it politically. The philosophy here articulated by Gilman has been called "producerism," which, Michael Kazin explains, defines "productive labor" as including not only "the urban proletariat" but also independent "craftsmen . . . small merchants and manufacturers, and farmers of all regions and incomes," in contrast to the classic Marxist tradition specifying that productive work is done only by manual, industrial laborers.[49] Gilman's conception of the kinds of workers who belonged to the productive majority was always extensive. In 1893, for instance, she asserts that "the people, the poor people and the middling people, are so large a majority that they have only to decide on their course and take it."[50] As applied by Gilman and others in the Nationalist and Populist movements, working-class and middle-class people shared a common economic cause and therefore shared a foundation for common class consciousness. Without denying that working-class people suffered the most vicious abuses of capitalism—indeed, even while acknowledging and denouncing these abuses—they asserted that the vast majority of Americans were worse off under capitalism than they would be under collectivism. They were, therefore, natural allies rather than fundamental, historically determined foes, as postulated in the bourgeois-proletarian split of classic Marxism.

For a time in the early 1890s, the rising influence of the People's Party seemed to show that democratic control over industry could be established peacefully, by established legal and political means. In "What the People's Party Means," a speech delivered before a People's Party meeting in 1893 near the high tide of Populist influence, Gilman saw the ultimate success of the producing majority of workers as assured. To "some [who] talk of necessary bloodshed—say that this great change can never be effected without loss of life," Gilman had this to say:

> They forget, these alarmists, the enormous—the ridiculous disproportion between The People and—and what? What possible opponents shall we have to slay?
>
> The capitalists? Are we to have a war between the capitalists and the laborers? For shame! The uncounted thousands—yes millions of working men; full armed with productive skill—wealth-makers—world-builders—shall these make war upon the inconsiderable handful of rich men, helpless non-producers that they are, mere dependents upon our favor—make war upon them as a thousand to one?
>
> Impossible.[51]

While the unfolding Populist revolt meant a vindication of gradualist tactics in the theoretical debate with militant socialists, it promised to bring practical results and real consequences in the struggle with the captains of industry. Like other pronouncements by Populist activists (as well as her earliest Nationalist statements), Gilman's rhetoric also challenges the notion that Populist change would lack a revolutionary transfer in power. She treats with definite relish threats of dispossession and the prospect of police authority responsive to the will of the people: "Society does not make war upon a handful of thieves. It arrests them, restrains them, sets them to work. Capital punishment—or may I say capitalist punishment—is unnecessary."[52]

Here and elsewhere during the ascendancy of the People's Party, Gilman's enthusiasm for the party could lead her to inflate its actual power. Yet even in her most impassioned partisan orations, Gilman also analyzed the social contingencies standing in the way of revolution as well as the opportunities making it possible. In short, rather than assuming that the forces of history would effect revolutionary change without any particular effort or conscious direction, she asserted the need for critique of the movement, redirection, and exhortation. To begin with, Gilman argues that more fundamental than voting rights, and indeed hampering anything like a constructive usage of those rights, is the very economic inequality that the People's Party would seek to address. In "What the People's Party Means," therefore, Gilman questions the orderly progress from political independence to economic independence, mapped out in *Looking Backward* as a straightforward progression, "the people of the United States conclud[ing] to assume the conduct of their own business, just as one hundred-odd years before they had assumed the conduct of their own government."[53] The problem is that the political independence of 1776 is largely illusory as long as voters remain unfree as economic agents:

> We have our religious life.
> We have our political life.
> We have our industrial life.
>
> In the first two we have made ourselves free, but because we are slaves in the last we are helpless in all.[54]

Without industrial freedom, Gilman continues, men "vot[e] this way or that as their masters direct, voting in idiotic triumph for the very measures that hold them down—mere cats paws for the artful ape behind."[55] For all Gilman's gloating over the productive strength of the People and the parasitic weakness of the capitalists, what she calls the "poor rich" appear to get the last laugh, as she recognizes how both false consciousness and economic inequalities between the classes prevent an effective political coalition.

It is noteworthy, however, that "What the People's Party Means," Gilman's fullest statement of support for the People's Party, does not end with her analysis of how economic inequality complicates coalitions across class lines; that is where she begins. Thus, her effusions about the overwhelming majority of "wealth-makers—world-builders" are framed by the challenge of getting that majority to vote as one, and they constitute an effort to get them, beginning with her immediate audience, to do just that. Much critical analysis of class relations gravitates toward an individual's or group's being—what he, she, or they are. Gilman's own representation of the difficulties of forming an interclass Populist coalition makes clear reference to the relevance of such analysis. But this speech and other Gilman texts are ultimately less focused upon being bourgeois, proletariat, or some other class position, than upon an ethical practice concerned with doing something through these class positions and something about their fundamental inequality. Whereas critics of Nationalism, most notably Arthur Lipow in *Authoritarian Socialism in America: Edward Bellamy and the Nationalist Movement,* suggest that its activism was all about shoring up and celebrating the class position of the bourgeoisie, Gilman's work emphasizes an interrogation of that class position: an effort to show the bourgeois that their real, long-term interests lay not with the capitalist monopolists but with the common workers. Her work also offers a sustained critique of the ways that, at present, bourgeois advantages did in fact work to drive a wedge between their fellow members of the producer class.

During her brief tenure at *The Impress,* the organ of the Pacific Coast Woman's Press Association that she edited in 1893–94, Gilman wrote scathingly of the collaboration of middle-class consumers, both men and women, in maintaining the capitalist status quo. Although the periodical was short lived, it gave Gilman the opportunity to editorialize on the Homestead strike of 1892, the Pullman strike of 1893, and also on a smaller strike of female garment workers in New York City. Regarding the garment workers strike, Gilman quoted at length from the *New York Tribune,* which stated the workers had earned only "from $3 to $5 a week, working from 7 in the morning until 6 in the evening" and that, while on strike, they "have been driven to lives of shame to keep from starving." To this sensational account Gilman added, scathingly:

> Whose is the shame? Does it not redden your cheeks, you women of respectability and refinement, who are always eager for bargains, and you men who buy "cheap" shirts, without a thought of the wages paid to the makers of them? And you merchants, who think you are doing a clever thing when you can increase your profits some five or ten percent, regardless if the increase is squeezed out of the life and soul of the sewing woman,—is not her blood on your hands? But who of us is not partaker in this guilt? Who of us can plead not guilty to the charge: "These are the images ye have made of me!" And what are you going to do about it? Read the line again—*have been driven to lives of shame to keep from starving.*[56]

The appeal to middle-class propriety is plain enough, as it evokes melodramatically the "lives of shame" that the young, female garment workers have been driven into. Yet the argument also takes a turn that leads squarely to confrontation of her audience's and even Gilman's own bourgeois tendencies. Here she sees plainly the consequences of middle-class consumer behavior within the capitalist system, as well as the discrepancies, both potential and actual, between working-class and middle-class interests.

Even as elsewhere in *The Impress* Gilman applauds collectivist reforms wherever they emerge—a theme borrowed directly from Bellamy's *New Nation,* the organ of the Nationalist movement—she preaches all the more vigorously the need for middle-class people to embrace changes in their social and economic systems that do not make exploitation of the working classes necessary, or even possible. In calling for radical economic changes that would transform the social and moral landscape of the nation, changes that would dramatically alter middle-class as well as working-class life, Gilman sees the alteration in middle-class life as betterment. But she also recognizes that the alteration may mean sacrifices in lifestyle and relative economic advantage; for some in the middle classes, ethical betterment may have to compensate for economic loss. The possibility that Gilman here opens is that people of middle-class standing, if rightly guided and goaded by ethical imperatives, may well make political and social choices that sacrifice their own immediate economic benefit for the greater material and moral good of their society.[57] That middle-class people, women as well as men, have not yet risen to the challenge speaks not just to the fractures in the Populist coalition, but places the far greater share of responsibility upon the middle-class women and men who are supposed to act as allies of blue-collar workers in the grand producing-class coalition.

Gilman's analysis of middle-class women was not confined, however, to their belonging to the middle class on terms similar with their male relations. In the 1890s she also initiated the lines of feminist critique for which she is today known, an enterprise shared by socialists both among the Nationalists and in the international movement. Gilman argued that women of whatever class, like proletarians, were exploited under capitalism; they, like the workers, stood to gain much from revolutionary change, and, hence, they too were specially positioned to lead that change. Here, as on the question of class struggle, the differences between Gilman and the Marxists, though real enough, were not absolute, and where differences do exist, it is not always evident that the Marxists were the keener analysts.

Populism, Gilman saw, would stand to benefit women tangibly, though it did not address their concerns directly. That the middle classes as well as proletarians were vulnerable under capitalism was a point of interest to middle-class women as well as middle-class men, proletarian women as well as proletarian men. That the votes being asked for by the People's Party belonged to husbands, sons, fathers, and coworkers meant a different relationship between women and the party, but it did not change women's potential interest in the success of the party or the potential importance of their mobilization as part of a People's revolt.

But Nationalism pledged more. Even in *Looking Backward*, which pays only minimal critical attention to women's roles, women were to have an equal share of the nation's wealth and, hence, economic independence from men. The underemphasis upon gender equality in Bellamy's groundbreaking novel, which has provided a clear opening for critics to jeer at its portrayal of women as consummate shoppers and objects of romantic interest, was largely rectified in the much fuller analysis of women's equality in the final major work of his career, *Equality* (1897), published just shortly before Bellamy succumbed to tuberculosis. Long before this, however, an observant follower of the movement such as Gilman could hardly miss the feminism integral to the Nationalist movement. The economic dependency of women and its resulting harm—the fundamental starting points for *Women and Economics*—are mapped out by Edward Bellamy in the *New Nation* of 1891, when Gilman had been active in the movement for over a year and was likely to have read the Nationalist organ.[58] In one of his "Talks on Nationalism," for instance, Bellamy's persona Mr. Smith meets a "Women's Rights Advocate." While agreeing with her on the importance of women's suffrage and other reforms, Mr. Smith asserts, "I am interested in it merely as an entering wedge for obtaining the economical equality of women with men which nationalism proposes. I tell you frankly that I should be opposed to woman suffrage if I did not look forward to nationalism, because to give the suffrage to a class likely to remain dependent upon the favor of another class would be to make a mock of it."[59] The "W.R.A." readily agrees—"Oh, no, Mr. Smith, you can't tell us women anything we do not already realize as to the humiliation of pecuniary dependence, either as daughters or wives"—lending weight to Mr. Smith's conclusion that under Nationalism women will "through life, be not only economically equal with every man, but absolutely independent of any man."[60]

Bellamy's skepticism about the importance of voting rights for women finds its echo in a curious statement in Gilman's autobiography—that she saw suffrage as "reasonable and necessary" but "by no means as important as some of its protagonists held"—as well as in Gilman's admission in an 1890s letter to Houghton, her cousin and husband-to-be, that she could not "fire up" on "Woman Suffrage pure and simple."[61] More specifically, Gilman's series of "Classes in Socialism," written for the *American Fabian* soon after returning from the International Labor and Socialist Congress, are uncannily like Bellamy's "Talks" of 1891. In Gilman's discussions, like Bellamy's, the expert manages the questioners so adroitly that only the most recalcitrant are not persuaded of the merits of collectivism. In the first of the lessons, while satirizing the Politician, Millionaire, Manufacturer, and Average Man who have learned from their professions "How to take care of myself, of course!" Gilman highlights the difference in women's socioeconomic position by the

Average Woman's lesson: "How to get somebody to take care of me, of course!"[62] While suggesting through her Average Woman the ludicrousness of women's dependency, Gilman in this article only implies the remedy. But as far back as 1891 Gilman had given the answer, much the same as Bellamy's during the same period: "The Way Up"—the title of an 1891 lecture by Gilman—lies in "pecuniary freedom."[63]

Indeed, on questions of gender, it is difficult to see exactly where to draw the lines of influence within the Nationalist movement. Certainly Gilman was initially attracted to the Nationalist movement in part because of its stance on gender equality. But several of *Equality*'s fuller elaborations upon gender matters suggest Gilman's potential influence upon her Nationalist mentor. Take, for example, the matter of women's clothing. As part of the elaborate conceit by which *Equality* was supposed to update *Looking Backward* without actually revising the original utopian vision, Bellamy explained that Edith Leete and her mother had worn long dresses merely as costumes so as to keep from offending the Victorian sensibilities of Julian West. Almost immediately when Edith reveals this secret to Julian (by then her betrothed), she changes her outfit, donning a typical twentieth-century garment, tailored but comfortably fitted and essentially the same for women and men, "since their bodily conformation is on the same general lines." The new clothes are nevertheless stimulating to Julian's romantic interest, as when they go for a walk together "the buoyant grace of her carriage and the elastic vigor of her step as she strode now by my side was a revelation of the possibilities of an athletic companionship which was not a little intoxicating."[64] For readers acquainted with *Herland,* it is almost impossible not to hear an echo of Julian's observation on Edith's "athletic companionship" in the initial encounter of the male adventurers Van, Jeff, and Terry with the lithe, gymnastic women who will later become their companions.[65] More likely, though, is that it is Bellamy who echoes Gilman, rather than vice versa, for already in 1891—and on many other occasions prior to 1897—she had announced: "It is just as right for a woman to be beautiful as it is for a man to be beautiful; but except for neck and arms there is no comparison in beauty between an agile muscular graceful young man and the tassel-shaped mass of cloth that is all we have of woman in her usual costume."[66]

Whether in matters of clothing, physical development, or psychological health, Gilman sees women's lack of development as stemming from the one crippling cause: lack of economic independence. For Gilman, the remedy of economic independence was to be achieved not simply by being granted an equal share of the purchasing power of the nation. In contrast to the impression given by *Looking Backward* that, in the future socialist society, material abundance would be available to all people and especially women with minimal work, Gilman stresses repeatedly that society will become wealthier and happier when the social and economic equality of women enables—and demands—that women do more work, better work, and a greater variety of work. "Until every one of us women has some part in the work that is for mankind," Gilman declares in the 1892 talk "How Our Work Affects Us," "we cannot be *great.*" Although some women have begun to move outside the traditional roles of mother and domestic, Gilman opines that they have not yet "applied their energies to any other service that the world has claims upon her as a producer, a distributer, a manager, some human functionary." Were women to take up these roles, Gilman asserts, both women and men would find themselves the better for it: "Holding steadily in view the formative effect of work upon character—remembering that the same natural laws which make man make us,—seeing plainly that any or all of these are not enough to make the race grow as it should—it becomes apparent that each one of us needs work in the world which will not only please some one else, not only earn our bread, but which will react upon us to our constant betterment."[67]

Not infrequently, common points of reference between Gilman and Bellamy on women's issues extend to Marxian socialists and anarchists as well. The equation of marriage with prostitution, for instance, was asserted across a broad spectrum of socialist theoretical work. Indeed, it is a theme so well known in Marx and Engels and in the writings of anarchists such as Emma Goldman and Voltairine de Cleyre that the remarkable point is, no doubt, its appearance in the (relatively) conservative writers Bellamy and Gilman.[68] Perhaps most intriguingly, in "Socialism as the Cure for The Social Evil" Gilman explains the hostile attitude taken by respectable married women toward prostitutes not as a matter of morality but of economic competition within the marketplace: "Countless thousands of poor women whose necessity forces them to underbid their virtuous competitors . . . offer the same wares at far less price!" Shifting her metaphor slightly (and consistently with the Marxist concept of labor power as commodity), Gilman asserts, "The virtuous women form a rigid union, and the vicious women fill the rank of unorganized cheap labor."[69] Much the same set of relations between economics and sexuality is narrated by Dr. Leete in "What the Revolution Did for Women," chapter 20 of *Equality,* which asserts that the "essence" of marriage "in the eyes of the law and of society was its character as a contract, a strictly economic *quid-pro-quo* transaction."[70] This economic transaction was at bottom the same outside of marriage as within it.

As with American socialists' attitudes toward revolution and class struggle, so too with their feminism: the differences between Marxian and non-Marxian socialism were by no means absolute. And whereas Gilman's and Bellamy's analysis of gender is particularly close, reflecting an evolving dialogue in which Gilman's work consistently reflects its Nationalist roots and, at the same time, may push Bellamy to expand and refine his feminism, there are other places where Gilman's work actually shows greater kinship with gender analyses in the Marxist tradition.

These feminist-socialist currents and cross-currents can all be found in *Women and Economics*, the summation and fullest extension of Gilman's socialist analysis of gender. Notwithstanding the fact that Gilman later claimed that no bibliography had been compiled for the 1898 book because "the books I had read bearing on the subject . . . were only two! One was Geddes's and Thompson's *Evolution of Sex*, the other only an article, Lester F. Ward's, in that 1888 *Forum*,"[71] the connections between Gilman's thought and Bellamy Nationalism emerge almost immediately. In the book's opening chapter, Gilman asserts that the root of women's inequality is their economic dependence upon men, hence rearticulating an argument she, Bellamy, and other Nationalists had been making for over a decade: "Their labor is the property of another: they work under another will; and what they receive depends not on their labor, but on the power and will of another."[72] Although *Women and Economics* never uses the words *socialist* or *socialism* (nor Nationalism, Fabianism, or Populism, either), the first chapter of *Women and Economics* also lays bare some of the connections between Gilman and other socialist traditions. Whereas the focus in *Looking Backward* falls upon women's equality with men in terms of purchasing and consuming power—as women have an equal share in the common wealth of the nation—Gilman's emphasis in the opening of *Women and Economics* falls upon gender equality in production.[73] Thus, in the opening chapter of *Women and Economics* Gilman remarks of human beings, signified by the conventionally generic "man": "Climate affects him, weather affects him, enemies affect him; but most of all he is affected, like every other living creature, by what he does for his living. Under all the influence of his later and wider life, all the reactive effect of social institutions, the individual is still inexorably modified by his means of livelihood: 'the hand of the dyer is subdued to what he works in.'"[74] Applied specifically to women, the connection between identity and labor means that most women of whatever class are valued primarily according to their sexual functions; but to be human, as Gilman tells her readers women assuredly are, demands a wider field of possibilities in the relations of production: "The desire to produce—the distinctive human quality—is no longer satisfied in a status that only allows for reproduction."[75]

Not only does Gilman's analysis of women's economics follow up on this premise about the importance of *production* to women's identity and independence, but her argument moves toward an explicit statement of the relationship between proletarianized work, the central concern of Marxist and most other socialist analyses, and women's work. To begin, Gilman argues that women's household labor as well as reproductive labor is exploited by men. The domestic labor that women do, in spite of not being directly accounted for in the capitalist market, does in fact produce what Marxists call "surplus value": "The labor of women in the house," Gilman notes, "enables men to produce more wealth than they otherwise could; and in this way women are economic factors in society."[76] But that economic value is transferred entirely and immediately to the husband's property: whereas the paid laborer at least has the compensation of the wage as the price of exploitation, the married housekeeper has her work appropriated directly, as a slave's labor is seized under chattel slavery. The comparisons Gilman draws to describe women's predicament are, therefore, between women and horses, and women and "valets," a point she puts with disarming understatement: "If the valet is the property of the man, is obliged to perform [useful] service, and is not paid for it, he is not economically independent."[77] Continuing this line of reasoning, Gilman argues that women have effectively been cut off from the modern labor movement: instead of sharing in the productive advantages of specialization and cooperation, women's domestic work is pathetically unskilled, inefficient, and isolated. Therefore, within every marriage—especially middle- and upper-class marriages—there is effectively a class divide between bourgeois and proletarian. According to Gilman, the chasm supersedes all ideals of romantic love, domestic partnership, and shared social status: "The woman in marrying becomes the house-servant, or at least the housekeeper, of the man. . . . Married lovers do not work together. . . . They are economically on entirely different social planes, and these constitute a bar to any higher, truer union than such as we see about us." Later Gilman remarks, "Woman, the house-servant, belongs to the lowest grade of unorganized labor."[78]

Here Gilman's distinctiveness lies in the particular emphasis she provides to this comparison. She bids fellow socialists not to overlook the parallels between proletarians and women, and to give expression to the theoretical observation by making the liberation of women coequal with the liberation of workers. But the parallels themselves appear in socialist theory of many varieties. In Bellamy's *Equality*—at the printer during exactly the same months as was *Women and Economics*[79]—Dr. Leete explains to Julian West: "Now, the key to the fetters the women wore was the same that locked the shackles of the workers. It was the economic key, the control of the means of subsistence. Men, as a sex, held that power over women, and the rich as a class held it over the working masses." This common problem demands, obviously to Dr. Leete and to his creator, Bellamy, a common solution: "economic equalization, which in the sexual as in the industrial relation would at once insure the substitution of co-operation for coercion."[80]

Both *Equality* and *Women and Economics* were, moreover, preceded by other socialist texts in the Marxist tradition that noted the very same homologies between women and male workers. One of the most important, Friedrich Engels's *Origin of the Family, Private Property, and the State: In the Light of the Researches of Lewis H. Morgan,* was a treatise written after Marx's death using notes compiled by him. It was published in English in 1891; the fact that Morgan was an American social anthropologist makes it all the more likely that it would have attracted Gilman's interest.[81] Like *Women and Economics, Origin of the Family* goes beyond the assertion that women earn their keep by sexual labor to consider the value of the unpaid labor women do in their households, arguing that otherwise "bourgeois" women are proletarianized by their work at what we now call "homemaking." This is true as a matter of historical process, Engels argues, for with the "patriarchal family" and especially its successor "the monogamian individual family," "The administration of the household . . . became a *private service.* The wife became the first domestic servant, pushed out of participation in social production." It is also true, Engels maintains, in the current bourgeois family: "Today, in the great majority of cases the man has to be the earner, the breadwinner of the family, at least among the propertied classes, and this gives him a dominating position which requires no special legal privileges. In the family, he is the bourgeois; the wife represents the proletariat."[82]

Gilman's *Women and Economics* cannot even lay claim to being the first book by a socialist to focus primarily upon women's exploitation—fellow socialist-feminist Jane Addams singled it out not as the first book in the field *about* women, but the first one *by* a woman[83]—for August Bebel's *Woman and Socialism* was available in English already in 1885. Bebel had theorized that the women's movement, even when fixated on legal and political rights, might well exert progressive, collectivist leverage paralleling that of the radical labor movement. Even though suffragists may express hostility toward economic change, Bebel asserts that "all the same, the hostile sisters have, to a far greater extent than the male population—split up as the latter is in the class struggle—a number of points of contact [with the radical labor movement] on which they can, although marching separately, strike jointly."[84] Bebel goes so far as to emphasize that the apparently narrow class interests of women are bound to coincide with those of the radical labor movement because ultimately both redound to the good of all society: The feminist activist, Bebel says, "who aims at the solution of the Woman Question to its full extent, is necessarily bound to go hand in hand with those who have inscribed upon their banner the solution of the Social Question as a question of the whole human race. These are the Socialists, that is, the Social Democracy."[85] And still further, Bebel asserts that the full emancipation of women is a matter not merely of good socialist practice—an "agitational" issue—but of "necessity" an issue of socialist "principle": "*There can be no emancipation of humanity without the social independence and equality of the sexes.*"[86]

The key theoretical difference separating various socialists was not whether women as a class were exploited, nor even whether the situation of women was analogous to that of the proletariat, but rather the degree to which women could be looked to as agents of revolution. Certainly women are a class of individuals exploited under capitalism. Are they also a self-conscious, collective mass capable of revolutionary leadership? For Engels, they clearly are not. Only working-class women, he reasons, have had their labor transferred into measurable capital; only they have been concentrated into a mass through industrialization, and therefore only they are capable of revolutionary action—fighting alongside proletarian men.[87]

For Bebel, in contrast, feminist women are capable of revolutionary leadership, even if they "march separately," provided only that they agitate for "the solution of the Woman Question to its full extent." Bebel does not even consider it necessary for women to be aware of their connections to the proletarian movement; they might even be "hostile sisters" toward their brothers in the labor movement. Edward Bellamy's projections about the role of the women's movement in social revolution trace much the same double movement for emancipation. Although he looks for the eventual coordination of women's and workers' campaigns, he too does not see overt alliances or deep self-consciousness as being necessary at first. "Unable to see beyond the end of their noses," Dr. Leete reports, women were inclined to hold individual men liable for the subordination and abuse of individual women, and thus the popularity of the temperance movement. Or they were ambitious only of "securing the right to vote, together with various changes in the laws about property-holding by women, the custody of children in divorces, and such details." Once begun, however, this movement "by no means revolutionary" led eventually to a frontal attack against the fundamental economic system, for as the omniscient Dr. Leete explains, "It was the system which permitted human beings to come into relations of superiority and inferiority to one another which was the cause of the whole evil."[88]

For Gilman—who had spent much of the 1890s mobilizing middle-class people, and especially middle-class women, for the Nationalist and Populist movements—the revolutionary potential of women seemed obvious. The conclusion of *Women and Economics* even appears to reverse the usual Marxist priority of the working-class movement over the women's movement, as she writes, "Where our progress hitherto has been warped and hindered by the retarding influence of surviving rudimentary forces, it will flow on smoothly and rapidly when both men and women stand equal in economic relation."[89] But when in her study Gilman draws connections between her immediate subject and the labor struggle for equality, she adopts formulations that—like Bellamy's—concur in their essential points with Bebel's analysis. Gilman joins Bebel and Bellamy in noting the initial narrowness, the partisan interest, of the (ultimately) revolutionary movements for women's and workers' liberation:

> Both make a class issue of what is in truth a social issue, a question involving every human interest. But the women naturally feel most the growing healthful pain of their position. They personally revolt, and think it is they who are most to be benefitted. Similarly, since the "laboring classes" feel most the growing healthful pain of their position, they as naturally revolt under the same conviction. Sociologically, these conditions, which some find so painful and alarming, mean but one thing,—the increase of social consciousness.[90]

Although in *Women and Economics* Gilman's attention is mostly focused upon the social consequences of women's economic disenfranchisement and the wide benefits of gender equality, she accords the working-class movement a coequal status to the women's movement, as she speaks of "the twin struggle that convulses the world to-day,—in sex and economics,—the 'woman's movement' and the 'labor movement.'"

One of Gilman's innovations in *Women and Economics* is the degree to which she sees proletarian-capitalist and male-female relations as interrelated and even overlapping. Following immediately upon her remarks about the labor movement, Gilman articulates how gender relations and gendered behaviors impact economic life throughout society: "in the economic world, excessive masculinity, in its fierce competition and primitive individualism; and excessive femininity, in its inordinate consumption and hindering conservatism." But Gilman seeks to establish not only the importance of women's equality to class equality—clearly the critical and controversial point from the standpoint of socialist debates—but also the importance of class equality to women's equality—which becomes the critical point in feminist debates, and especially so given the degree to which Gilman is today seen as a feminist first and a socialist hardly at all. Both points are clearly in view when Gilman deliberately parallels the women's movement—as we have seen, a "concerted movement . . . seeking a common good"—to the labor movement: "So with the labor movement. It is not alone that the individual laborer is a better educated, more highly developed man than the stolid peasant of earlier days, but also that with this keener personal consciousness has come the wider social consciousness, without which no class can better its conditions."[91] The definite implication is that this "wider social consciousness" must include a consciousness of women's equality (and indeed of human equality in general), and that a lack of such consciousness will prevent the male-dominated labor movement from bettering "its conditions."

What this close comparison between Bebel, Bellamy, and Gilman shows is the pervasiveness of women's rights as a theme—even a central theme—in the socialist theory of the 1890s. The revolutionary potential of feminism cuts across the divide that later appears so sharp between Marxist and non-Marxist socialism. Even the differences between Gilman and Engels are not as tremendous as they would first appear. In spite of her very different conclusion regarding the revolutionary potential of women, Gilman's reasoning is so close to Engels's as to amount to, not a separate socialist intellectual tradition, but an explicit refutation within a common tradition. For, remarkably, the common experience mobilizing women into a social and political force is *not* their common dependency upon men but rather their shared experience of entering the workforce in ever greater numbers. "For a while the introduction of machinery which took away from the home so many industries deprived woman of any importance as an economic factor," Gilman observes, "but presently she arose, and followed her lost wheel and loom to their new place, the mill. To-day there is hardly an industry in the land in which some women are not found."[92] At the same time—in effect contesting Engels's focus on proletarian women—she notes that the "increasing army of women wage-earners, who are changing the face of the world by their steady advance toward economic independence" includes middle-class women seeking professional work, "young girls [desiring] to have a career of their own," as well as working-class women.[93]

In Gilman's most incisive account of the relationship between women of various classes, women's solidarity is based on two interrelated, essentially Marxian concepts: a shared self-consciousness as productive laborers, and a shared consciousness of economic exploitation. "The progress of social organization," she explains, "has produced a corresponding degree of individualization, which has reached at last even to women,—even to the lowest grade of unskilled labor." But Gilman finds in women a self-consciousness about their class that Engels explicitly denies. She continues, "The woman's movement rests not alone on her larger personality, with its tingling sense of revolt against injustice, but on the wide, deep sympathy of women for one another. It is a concerted movement, based on the recognition of a common evil and seeking a common good."[94] In theory, all women should be socialists.

Much of Gilman's subsequent career as an intellectual would be dedicated to trying to make them so—and to explaining why so many were not. Hence, in following Gilman's work into the first decades of the twentieth century, I will be focusing primarily upon the relation of socialism to the women's movement and the women's movement to socialism. Meanwhile, however, there is something to be said and concluded about the fate of the Nationalist and Populist movements with which Gilman was so active in the 1890s.

THE POPULIST LEGACY

> "Radical, socialistic Democracy."

Just as De Leon said, in 1896 the People's Party was in steep decline. Even while Gilman was making her acquaintance with the full range of socialist groups and representative leaders at the International Labor and Socialist Congress, the group that she had hailed as the American manifestation of the movement was being co-opted by a Nebraska Democrat, William Jennings Bryan, making the first of what would be three unsuccessful runs for the presidency. Nationalism was on the wane as well; within two years its inspiration and leader would be dead. Upon her return to the United States Charlotte Perkins Gilman associated with the very small offshoot of the English Fabian Society, and she would never again affiliate herself so closely with a major political group as she had with the Nationalists and Populists. What, though, was the legacy of Nationalist and Populist ideas and ideals when the groups espousing them faded, with even avid supporters such as Gilman falling away?

At least according to the predominant interpretation of the People's Party and the Populist movement, there was good reason for disillusionment. It seems that the coalition of labor and farmers, working-class and middle-class Americans, was all too easily torn apart when the mainstream parties took notice of a few of their grievances. After the elections of 1892 and 1894, the Populist success had reached the point where the party's policies and rhetoric—and their voters—began to attract serious attention from the two parties of longer standing, and especially the party generally in the minority since the Civil War, the Democrats. It was the hope of capturing Populist votes that led Bryan, then a young, charismatic congressman, to take the free coinage of silver—part of the People's Party platform—and make it the centerpiece of his 1896 run for the presidency. Considered the Waterloo of the People's Party by its major historian, Lawrence Goodwyn, the Bryan campaign sought and gained the Populist presidential nomination as well as the Democratic nomination by little more than the "free silver" platform plank and a good deal of antiestablishment rhetoric. Goodwyn argues that the election of 1896 meant not only the sacrifice of Populist autonomy; it also meant the national repudiation of Populist values. When Bryan lost to William McKinley, ideals of economic justice for small landholders and workers were decisively beaten back by the power of corporate capitalism and party-machine politics.[95]

Yet this negative assessment of the Bryan movement seems unduly attached to the demise of Populism as a separate movement and overly skeptical about the genuineness of the Democratic Party's assimilation of its ideals. After all, the People's Party was itself compromised by its amalgamation of reactionary and progressive ideas, its mix of egalitarianism and race prejudice, capitalist accommodations and socialistic proposals. Why not consider not only how Bryanism co-opted the membership and party structure of the People's Party but also how Populism infiltrated the ideology of the Democratic Party? Unlike the labor uprisings of the 1870s and 1880s, which were crushed by the combined power of government and business and (at best) worked toward the amelioration of the labor-capital conflict only indirectly and eventually, the Populist uprising of the 1890s succeeded directly and definitely in changing the course of one of the major American parties.

One measure of this change in course is the degree to which Populist rhetoric became incorporated into the Democratic Party platform, the degree to which this rhetoric persisted, and the extent to which rhetoric eventually translated into policy. In his examination of party platforms and election rhetoric of the major parties' leading candidates, John Gerring has argued that the leadership of Bryan and his influence upon the Democratic Party, especially as exerted in his three runs for the presidency, redirected the party—"*Populist* in tone and in policy"—in fundamentally new ways. Dating a "Populist" era in the Democratic Party from 1896 to 1948, Gerring sees Bryan as "the rightful father of the Progressive–New Deal Democratic party, bringing to it a regulatory style and redistributive purpose found hitherto only outside the mainstream of American party politics."[96] My own analysis of Democratic Party platforms concurs with Gerring's, while I note also the ways that many elements of the national Democratic prospectus that Gerring calls Populist were also socialistic. The 1892 Democratic platform, upon which Grover Cleveland was elected to his second term, had obsessed over the issue of Republican-instituted tariffs on international trade—the abolishment of which Democrats posed as friendly to working people as a means to reducing the cost of living, but which in fact almost certainly was no better than a wash because the reduction of market costs also would have a depressive effect upon wages. The 1896 Democratic platform on which Bryan ran was dramatically reoriented. The minting of silver coinage, with the aim of loosening the money supply, was not the most fundamental of the Populist reforms, but it would bring a definite benefit to the heavily mortgaged small farmers of the Midwest and South, and thus a shift in the direction of redistributing economic power from the greater moneybags to the lesser. Just as significantly, for the first time a major American party took an explicit stand for active government mediation in the conflict between labor unions and businesses: "We are in favor of the arbitration of differences between employers engaged in interstate commerce and their employees, and recommend such legislation as is necessary to carry out this principle," the platform declared.[97] To put the matter in the terms offered by Gilman's idealization and critique of the Populist movement, we might say that the Populist tilt of the Democratic Party from 1896 onward led "The People" to see not only their "political life" but also their "industrial life" as identified, increasingly, with the life of "working men."

With Bryan continuing as a national leader of the Democratic Party for the next two decades, its presidential candidate again in both 1900 and 1908, the party's platform continued to move in directions originally mapped out by the Populist Party and its labor allies. Already in 1896, the Democratic Party had positioned itself as hostile toward corporate trusts and monopolies. The platform of 1900 amounted to a declaration of war. "We pledge the

Democratic party to an unceasing warfare in nation, State and city against private monopoly in every form," the platform thundered, while later it expanded on the theme: "Any attempt by corporations to interfere with the public affairs of the people or to control the sovereignty which creates them, should be forbidden under such penalties as will make such attempts impossible."[98] The 1900 platform also, significantly, declared war on war, defining the unequivocally imperial outgrowths of the Spanish-American War, the colonization of Puerto Rico and the conquest of the Philippines, as the preeminent issues of the election, announcing that "no nation can long endure half republic and half empire" and warning "the American people that imperialism abroad will lead quickly and inevitably to despotism at home."[99]

By 1900, the Populist Party was but a shell of its insurgent self, just four years before. Yet after the turn of the century, the impact of Populism continued to ripple through national politics. With the sudden emergence of Theodore Roosevelt, it came to affect the Republican Party as well as the Democratic Party. Nominated as vice president in 1900, Roosevelt had made his name by opposing the old-style politics of the Democratic machine in his home state of New York; in effect, his political positions in favor of municipal reform and strong centralized government aligned him less with the economic and social conservatives that had dominated the Republican Party since the end of Reconstruction, and more with the muckrakers and reformers whose ideology formed the urban counterpart of the antiestablishment, populist movement within the Democratic Party, oriented to rural protest. Even as the assassination of William McKinley by Leon Czolgosz meant the political death knell for anarchism, it elevated Theodore Roosevelt to the presidency, thus suddenly bringing TR's brand of progressivism—for a time—to the forefront of Republican Party politics. Czolgosz's action set back the radical liberty he had hoped to advance and advanced the state power he had hoped to thwart. But because the anarchists were opposed not only to capitalism but also to the kind of state direction that nineteenth-century socialists had come to see as necessary to surmount the limits of communitarianism, the McKinley assassination not only precipitated the rise of Theodore Roosevelt but also facilitated socialist aims: the greater involvement of the state in the many realms into which Theodore Roosevelt's administrations ventured, including federal policing of industrial monopolies, the public management of wilderness lands, and the national regulation of food and drug manufacturing. Hence, although Czolgosz's action had not done much for anarchist aims, it had resulted in a measure of progressive change. The assassination could therefore be used both to demonstrate the efficacy of violent direct action and to disprove it, helping to ensure that the debate over political uses of violence would be kept alive within American socialist circles in coming decades.

Beginning in the next chapter, we will need to explore in more detail the complex, paradoxical relationships between the most radical and despised individuals within the socialist movement, the most progressive of Republican presidents (who would not be the last Roosevelt credited with saving capitalism from itself), and the next generation of moderate American socialists who came of age after 1900, oriented more to issues of urban industrial labor than to those of agrarian protest. Meanwhile, summing up the longer-term impact of Nationalism and Populism upon American politics, we may note that the efforts of Roosevelt and successive "trust busters" actually interrupted the cartelization of American industry that Bellamy had anticipated as the graceful segue from capitalism to state-directed socialism. Yet the less absolute demands and programs of the Populists, which the Nationalists had accepted as entering wedges for socialism, did in fact redirect the national politics of both parties—and especially of the Democratic Party—in durable ways. Although the Democratic Party effectively conceded the progressive mantle to Roosevelt when their 1904 presidential nomination went to New York supreme court justice Alton Parker, the party's platform remained marked by elements of populism introduced by the Bryan movement. The 1904 platform, for example, asserted the principle that corporations ought not receive more than their "just share of the joint product of capital and labor" and declared, in an unmistakable broadside against the ideological defenders of capitalism, that "the rights of labor are certainly no less 'vested,' no less 'sacred' and no less 'inalienable' than the rights of capital."[100]

The return of Bryan to the top of the Democratic ticket in 1908 ushered in the most militantly Populist, prolabor, and anticapitalist platform yet. With the Republican Party pulling back from Rooseveltian Progressivism, the Democratic Party under Bryan effectively claimed the Progressive mantle and then some. The first substantive paragraph of the document hailed the "various investigations [that] have traced graft and political corruption to the representatives of the predatory wealth, and laid bare the unscrupulous methods by which they have debauched elections and preyed upon a defenseless public through the subservient officials whom they have raised to place and power."[101] The platform asserted the right not only of the Interstate Commerce Commission to regulate commerce across state lines but also of the states to regulate commerce within their borders; it called for the end to judicial injunctions in capital-labor disputes, long and infamously used to criminalize strikes; it also demanded recognition of labor unions; and it advocated laws making employers liable for injury and death of their employees on the job. The document moved toward its close with a flourish of Populist rhetoric: "The Democratic party listens to the voice of the whole people and gauges progress by the prosperity and advancement of the average man; the Republican party is subservient to the comparatively few who are the beneficiaries of governmental favoritism." The final statement of the 1908 platform declared a remarkable political-economic principle in favor of "such an administration of the government as will insure, as far as human wisdom can, that each citizen shall draw from society a reward commensurate with his contribution to the welfare of society."[102] Such a declaration falls short of the economic equality sought by socialism, but it links, for the first time in a U.S. major-party platform, two of the cornerstones of socialist philosophy: the responsibility of government to superintend American industry, and the obligation of all citizens to contribute to the common welfare.

Of course the Bryan platforms were those of the *losing* party every time out. As such, they represent the Populist-influenced ideology of the party never quite able to gain majority endorsement, whether in the 1890s or the following decade. But in their incorporation into the official platform of one of the major national parties, socialistic ideals articulated in the Populist and socialist movements of the 1890s were indeed working their way—by subterranean means though in perceptible degrees—into the mainstream of American politics.

The writing of W. E. B. Du Bois supplies one final piece of evidence not only that socialism and socialistic policies *could* be linked to the major political parties, especially the Democratic Party, but also that they *were* linked by observers of the time. At the time Bryan was making his third run for the presidency, Du Bois had already gained critical acclaim for his landmark study of black culture, economics, and political life, *The Souls of Black Folk;* there he had presented himself as both the successor and the alternative to Booker T. Washington. It is perhaps not surprising that Du Bois would consider support for the Democrats over the Republicans, for his rival, Washington, had recently been feted by President Roosevelt at the White House, and yet the party of Lincoln had done little for African Americans since the end of Reconstruction besides a meager dole of patronage positions in government. Du Bois had recently initiated the Niagara movement, an all-too-short-lived effort to draw African American leaders into an organization rivaling Washington's Tuskegee juggernaut. Still, the reasons given by Du Bois for his endorsement of Bryan in the *Horizon*, the Niagara-movement journal that he edited, were little short of remarkable. Du Bois argued that under Bryan's guidance the Democrats had become anti-imperialists, opponents of corporate wealth that held in its "crushing grasp" "no group of Americans . . . more than Negroes," and even implacable foes of the southern Bourbons by virtue of their "radical socialistic Democracy."[103] Du Bois had become familiar with the German labor movement and social democracy since the 1890s, when he had conducted graduate study at the University of Berlin; he had begun exploring the possibilities of socialism as a way for black Americans to achieve that equality in all phases of life he had called for in *The Souls of Black Folk.* Yet he had not fully embraced the socialist label, and his identifying and praising the "radical" and "socialistic" tendencies of the Democratic Party—for an audience he was attempting to weld into a cohesive group, no less—suggests just how noncontroversial and indeed attractive those tendencies were. Moreover, as a relatively neutral observer of both socialism and the Democratic Party, Du Bois appears to be reflecting not a partisan argument about Bryan but a commonplace observation of his platform and proposals.

The suggestion is that in American political life in this period, it was logically possible, and perhaps even politically advantageous, to be a member of one of the major parties *and* be "socialistic," if not actually socialist. To be a socialist was *not* to be foolishly utopian. Capitalism was not the only possible, really available political economy in the United States, and militant insurrection utterly overturning "all existing conditions" did not need to be the only path to the classless society or the cooperative commonwealth. This was the testimony of most American socialists of the 1890s even as it was Du Bois's observation in 1908, and just as it was the conviction of the European socialists who in the same era operated under the aegis of the Second Internationale.

Du Bois, along with Gilman, Sinclair, and other socialists, was not unrealistic about the obstacles along the reformist and nonviolent path. In one of his *Horizon* editorials, Du Bois characterized the "radical socialistic Democracy" of Bryan as a party within a party, engaged in an "impossible alliance . . . with an aristocratic caste party" of southern Democrats.[104] Yet Du Bois obviously did not see this alliance as so fully "impossible" as to negate the progressive pull of Bryan, not so hopeless as to compel Du Bois and other African Americans to look elsewhere for political allies. This in fact was the pattern that marked Du Bois's career as a socialist, soon to commence. Du Bois, along with Sinclair and Gilman, sought to pull American politics and economics into increasingly radical and socialistic directions even while asserting, as they did so, that U.S. politics and economics were flexible enough to accommodate these directions. Du Bois believed he recognized, and Gilman, Edward Bellamy, and other Nationalists definitely sought to advance, just this kind of socialist trajectory within American Populism. That Gilman, Sinclair, and Du Bois all followed a similar strategy throughout their careers both shows their abiding faith in the possibility of socialism in America and suggests their observation of a really emerging "radical socialistic Democracy" there.

CHAPTER TWO

THE MULTIPLICITY OF AMERICAN SOCIALISM: UPTON SINCLAIR AND THE "PARTY OF AGITATION," 1901–1914

For all of the hopeful indications of the rising tide of progressivism, the American socialist movement ended the nineteenth century and began the twentieth at a critical juncture. The popular organizations that had espoused socialist and socialistic measures in the 1890s, especially the Nationalists and the Populists, had either lost their momentum or been coopted by the mainstream parties. The more militant parties, De Leon's Socialist Labor Party for example, had never gained anything like a national following. Into the breach stepped the Socialist Party, formed in 1901 when the splinters of several disintegrating, smaller Marxian parties determined to present a united front, adopted the parliamentary style of the Second Internationale, and found a charismatic, coalition-building leader in Eugene Debs.

In very many ways, Debs and the Socialist Party of America (SPA) picked up where the gradualist, non-Marxian socialists of the previous decade had left off. The path followed by Daniel De Leon, whereby early acquaintance and involvement in Nationalism was succeeded within a few years by a swing far into doctrinaire revolutionary Marxism, was not the norm among U.S. socialists. More typical was the progression of Debs. While in jail following the federal suppression of the Pullman strike of 1894, which he led as president of the American Railway Union, Debs professed that his turn into socialism was aided by Bellamy and Gronlund as well as the German Marxist Karl Kautsky.[1] He considered himself a Populist after his imprisonment as well as before, and throughout his years as leader of the Socialist Party and perennial presidential contender, Debs exhibited tendencies toward popular inclusiveness and political expediency as well as antipathy toward capitalism, characteristics of the gradualist, predominantly non-Marxist socialism of the 1890s.

The legacy of 1890s socialism is clear as well in the early work of Upton Sinclair. Strongly reminiscent of Gilman's Populist peroration against violence is Upton Sinclair's 1904 piece published in the *Appeal to Reason* and addressed to Chicago stockyard workers: "You Have Lost the Strike! Now What Are You Going to Do About It?" Although a twenty-six-year-old socialist neophyte who had never himself worked at the stockyards or even yet visited them, Sinclair already knew by the light of socialist principles just how the workers would need to proceed and what they must avoid:

> *You think, perhaps, that I mean mobs and insurrections, dynamite and gatling guns. I do not.*
>
> *I speak to Americans.*
>
> *I speak to men whose ancestors did the fighting; whose fathers left them freedom as their birthright who handed down to them a weapon by which they might forever guard it for their own.*
>
> *That weapon is the ballot.*
>
> *THE BALLOT!*[2]

Even as Sinclair synthesizes socialist militancy with Americanism, he makes clear, as Gilman had, that the violent methods of direct-actionists were not needed under American conditions.

Like Gilman and many other socialists coming of age around the turn of the century, Sinclair had also read and synthesized his Edward Bellamy. In the long dialogue on socialist theory that comprises most of the penultimate scene of *The Jungle,* the fictional dialectician Nicholas Schliemann seems to have drawn practically half of the details of the coming socialist society from *Looking Backward.* One of the key features of Bellamy's commonwealth, the sharp split between the regimentation of industrial life and the freedom of social life, can be found in one of Schliemann's most memorable and conceptually fundamental aphorisms: "Communism in material production, anarchism in intellectual."[3] Also like Bellamy, Schliemann envisages the possibility of much shorter terms of work for laborers, and much more productive industrial production, by eliminating the inefficiencies of overproduction in a competitive environment; and like Bellamy, he sees the "ultra-modern profession of advertising" as representing all that is wrong with industrial competition, wasting energy to persuade consumers to buy items they do not need, or otherwise to justify the existence of "ten thousand varieties of a thing for purposes of ostentation and snobbishness, where one variety would do for use."[4] Schliemann and Bellamy are further agreed on the basic principles for using production cost rather than market value in determining the prices of most goods and services.[5]

It would be a mistake, though, to flatten out entirely the difference between the socialist movement that caught Sinclair's imagination in 1904 and the Nationalist movement that inspired Gilman's devotion in 1890. The generational shift in personnel was accompanied by a broadening of the socialist movement's scope. The movement expanded leftward, so that groups such as the newly founded Industrial Workers of the World would be more difficult for Sinclair to dismiss than, say, the Socialist Labor Party had been for Gilman. (Indeed, once Sinclair spent more time in the movement, it would be more difficult for him even to reject "mobs and insurrections, dynamite and gatling guns" as he had initially.) The movement also expanded further into the mainstream, so that Socialist Party regulars began to focus upon the respectability of the party, and members of the major parties began to endorse political and social remedies that had previously been backed only by socialists and "muckrakers." Although Gilman, as already noted, showed a surprising openness to a variety of militant (though not violent) philosophies, the diversity of American socialism between the turn of the century and the beginning of World War I was such that Sinclair, in trying to assimilate its breadth and intricacies, was led to attempt an almost Whitmanian synthesis of contraries, extending even to the anarchist "propaganda of the deed." That he emerged with a functional socialist praxis at all—and with some definite results to show for his effort—is a testament to the dialectical work of socialism within U.S. culture as well as to Sinclair's own personal intellectual accomplishment.

BRAIN WORK AND THE REVOLUTION

> "Meantime, in the realm of thought, his life was a perpetual adventure."

For some critics of Sinclair, an account of the author's views on socialism is closely connected with the profession of authorship itself, particularly as conditioned by the higher social status of writers as compared to working-class people whom socialist writers purport to represent. In the 1930s, the distinguished critic and then-Communist fellow traveler Granville Hicks averred that Sinclair's novels are often told "from the point of view of the middle-class convert to radicalism" and concludes that "he has never eradicated the effects of his bourgeois upbringing. Though his aim had been socialistic, his psychology has remained that of the liberal."[6] In what has remained for over thirty years the definitive description of Sinclair's creation of *The Jungle,* Michael Folsom also points to a bourgeois psychology. The novel's infamous ending seems to Folsom to reveal that Sinclair was interested most of all in his own fate as a professional writer: "Sinclair, who had spent a whole book immersed in the lives of laboring people, was ultimately most interested in the intelligentsia and its problems. A Socialist was, for him, someone who could make or write an argument."[7] Recent Sinclair biographer Kevin Mattson goes so far as to characterize the entire American Socialist Party as aligned with Sinclair's literary caste. "The Socialist Party that Sinclair would join was composed largely of lawyers, journalists, and teachers," Mattson reports, making it a relatively genteel and timid organization, "derided" by "some who were more revolutionary" as "slowcialism."[8]

Similar conclusions have been reached regarding the social status of authors and the particular brand of socialism espoused by Gilman and Du Bois, as well, and therefore it seems fitting to treat the issues together—and before proceeding very much further in my larger argument. Gilman's genteel roots and bourgeois upbringing are treated as an impediment, for example, by biographer Mary Hill. While Hill acknowledges the hardship Gilman faced during her childhood years, when her mother, abandoned by her husband, maintained her family by shuttling them between the households of a long succession of relatives—"forced to move," the young Charlotte Perkins wrote, "nineteen times in eighteen years, fourteen of them from one city to another"—Hill steadfastly denies that these experiences in any way qualified Gilman for identification with the working class: "Though Charlotte had seen hard times, she was not working class."[9] Class status and political quiescence are, for Hill, indissolubly linked: "Like many people of her class and heritage, Charlotte had learned from thinkers more than activists, men who emphasized religion, science, and keen educational training as reformers' tools, not farm and labor meetings, strikes, or galvanizing fights."[10] Such a characterization of Gilman's politics has been extended to the socialist and socialistic groups with which Gilman affiliated. "In the spate of utopian novels inspired by *Looking Backward,*" Mark Pittenger notes, the "brain workers" who were to forge the new, egalitarian society and then administer it "were very often either scientists or engineers, and almost never proletarians."[11]

The character of W. E. B. Du Bois's socialism has been imputed less from Du Bois's genteel but economically uncertain upbringing in a single-parent household than from the class status of his decidedly well-heeled associates on the board of the NAACP, some of whom were socialists and are widely credited with influencing Du Bois's brief stint with the party in 1911–12. Adolph Reed's *W.E.B. Du Bois and American Political Thought* follows Manning Marable in suggesting that Du Bois's socialism was adopted from his peers on the NAACP board and that it was of a "conservative variety." Wilson Jeremiah Moses's *The Golden Age of Black Nationalism* likewise specifies Du Bois's early editorship of *The Crisis* as "fall[ing] into the period when Du Bois toyed with the idea of non-revolutionary white-collar socialism" and cites his kinship with liberals, progressives, and moderate socialists including Jane Addams, Mary White Ovington, William English Walling, and Charles Edward Russell.[12] Whatever may be said for or against the political and intellectual acumen of Du Bois, Sinclair, Gilman, and other socialist intellectuals, criticism of them can boil down to just this: they were of middle-class origin; their politics, therefore, cannot make any genuine claim to represent the working class.

Viewed as formal arguments, such a dismissal amounts to little more than an ad hominem derogation. If genuine socialist theory and praxis are necessarily dependent on a proletarian occupation or family of the theorist-practitioner, we would have to dismiss outright scores of socialist intellectuals including leading American socialists left, right, and center: Daniel De Leon, Victor Berger, Morris Hillquit (not to mention Karl Marx and Friedrich Engels).[13] If, however, such applications of identity politics are overly simplistic, it is reasonable to observe that a person's standpoint, although it does not simply *determine* how that person thinks and acts, does *affect* how he or she thinks and acts—and particularly, speaks and acts in political terms.[14] And so we should ask: To which class or classes *did* Sinclair, Gilman, and Du Bois belong? What bearing did their class position have upon their politics? And what do their cases tell us more generally about the supposedly bourgeois origins and self-serving intentions of the socialist groups in which they participated?

For all three writers, though in slightly different ways, answers to the question of class status prove to be far less straightforward than the simple label of "bourgeois" or "middle class" would designate. As Sinclair recounts in his autobiography, during his childhood years there was enough contact with better-heeled relations that Sinclair could occasionally sleep under "silken coverlets in a fashionable home" and his family could seek and gain some respite during economic emergencies. In weeks when his improvident and alcoholic father was unable to pay the rent, Sinclair records that "my mother paid a visit to her father, the railroad official."[15] Refuge with relatives did little to alleviate the specific sufferings of downward mobility, however. Sinclair's largely autobiographical *Love's Pilgrimage* recounts that "Thyrsis," the male protagonist, and his parents "always paid what they owed; but they were not always able to pay it when they owed it, and they suffered all the agonies and humiliations of those who did not pay all. . . . There was endless wrangling and strife and worry over money; and every year the task was harder, the standards lower, the case more hopeless."[16]

Sinclair's teenage years were a period of relative upward mobility. He largely supported himself—and at times his mother—first by writing children's stories and jokes for periodicals and later by penning serialized military adventure stories.[17] He did this even while attending high school, two years of college at the City College of New York, and then more college and graduate school at Columbia University.[18] But education brought Sinclair a keener appreciation for classic literature, which contributed to his ambition to produce "a serious novel," so that the achievement of a higher level of education led him—paradoxically—back to the brink of poverty. Sinclair recalls: "When, at the age of twenty-one, I became obsessed with the desire to write a serious novel, I came to loathe this hackwork, and from that time after I was never able to do it with success, even though, driven by desperate need, I several times made the effort."[19] Complicating Sinclair's writing ambition further was his marriage to Meta Fuller in 1901 and the birth of their son, David, in 1902. This complication, too, was generated by various ideological prescriptions: chiefly, the bourgeois expectation that the nuclear family should be supported by the man of the household. Although Sinclair might have fallen back on the support of Meta's fairly prosperous family, Upton, Meta, and David instead lived in the most bohemian of economic circumstances, living as squatters in rural areas, sleeping and working in tents or shacks. While Upton was writing *The Jungle*, for instance, the Sinclairs lived in conditions of physical privation severe enough to qualify as an experiential correlative for the desperation of the packing-town immigrants, as he suggested in his autobiography: "Did I wish to know how the poor suffered in wintertime in Chicago? I had only to recall the previous winter in the cabin, when we had only cotton blankets, and had put rugs on top of us, and cowered shivering in our separate beds."[20]

The parallel suggested by Sinclair is an approximate one, for whereas the Rudkus family has their hardship dictated by a series of heavily determined circumstances (their capability only for unskilled manual labor, their ignorance of American customs and laws, and above all the meagerness of the total resources of their extended family), the Upton Sinclair family at least appears to have had some choices open to them. The separation between working-class and bourgeois was by no means absolute, however. Sinclair's authorial profession exposed Sinclair and his family to the vicissitudes of the capitalist marketplace in particularly naked fashion. At the very outset of Sinclair's career, the kind of literary work that held the clearest promise for making a living was the most proletarianized. The anonymous jokes and the military stories written under pseudonyms meant an almost complete appropriation of his intellectual labor, and to earn little more than twenty dollars a month he had to produce as many as thirty thousand words a week.[21] Sinclair knew from his early experience as a hack writer what it must be like to be a Jurgis Rudkus, at first capable of any kind of Herculean task, but within a year or two beaten physically and mentally and unable to keep pace. When, subsequently, Sinclair aspired to produce literature of a higher caliber—when he sought to move from the equivalent of the literary proletariat to the more bourgeois reaches of the profession—he traded the hope of social gain and an ideological wage for almost absolute financial uncertainty. If, in some measure, the uncertainty and privations were chosen, they were choices scripted within a set of ideological and social expectations that maintained the boundaries of class divisions under capitalism. The arbitrariness of the choice and the boundaries might make the bourgeois subject all the more inclined to follow the expectations fastidiously, but that arbitrariness also affords a certain knowledge and an impetus to rebel—to call out the merely meretricious distinctions by which social and economic inequality is organized. In short, the instability of the writer's petit bourgeois class standing might make the writer particularly jealous of minor privileges, or it might constitute the essential basis for alliance with the working classes. Here, then, was another, specifically political dimension of choice available to some among the bourgeois.

We may offer a very similar portrait of Charlotte Perkins Gilman's class standing and its social and political implications, with the principal variations having to do with the ways gender difference shaped Gilman's professional experience and political attitudes. Whereas Sinclair's father was improvident, Gilman's father altogether abandoned his family. Her mother was able to provide for herself and her children primarily by casting the family upon the charity of variously hospitable relatives, an arrangement that led to Charlotte Perkins's nineteen relocations before reaching adulthood. During the ten years of her marriage to Walter Stetson, Charlotte experienced somewhat greater domestic stability, but at the price of nearly absolute female dependency upon the male breadwinner and, after the birth of her daughter

Katharine, the enforced period of retirement from mental work prescribed by her physicians, which resulted in the near total breakdown described in "The Yellow Wall-Paper."

In the formative period of Gilman's development as an author and political thinker, between her 1889 separation from Walter and her 1900 marriage to her second husband, George Houghton Gilman, Charlotte Perkins Gilman never earned a middle-class wage and, in spite of some unmistakable bourgeois pretensions, never lived in a securely bourgeois household. A passage from one of her class talks written late in 1892, "Our Domestic Duties," represents a problematic class bias in her writing, when she speaks with condescension of manual laborers: "Putting east and west together the 'maid of all work' does not get more than 4.50 a week. That makes $8.00 a week [when room and board are added]. If you want to stretch that and call it 9—even if it were ten—ten dollars for 7 days work is but a dollar and a half a day. And that is what we pay to the common laborer, the hod carrier, the digger and lifter and breaker of stones."[22] But the passage also reveals a working-class wage scale that Gilman herself was seldom able to match. At the end of a good month over a year later, January 1893, Gilman by the evidence of her diary was earning no more than they: "Have done about fifteen pieces of salable work this month—three lectures, three poems, nine articles of one sort or another. Received $40.00 therefor so far. Fair work for an overworked invalid."[23] Such examples of Gilman's meager earnings can be multiplied many times over from the evidence of her *Diaries.* Month after month her income failed to meet her expenses, and she and her household survived by cash gifts from friends and family, a long succession of loans, and a string of vacated leases and disgruntled landlords. The situation only improved marginally when, after her divorce from Walter was finalized in 1894, she sent her daughter east to live with him and his new wife, and she took to the national lecture circuit. "I was many times entirely out of money," and "My margin was always narrow," she recalls.[24]

Gilman's class position, like Sinclair's, emerges as far more complex than just "bourgeois" or "proletarian." For much of their early lives, they inhabited the ambiguous space between class designations, embodying that conundrum of class definition aptly described by Raymond Williams, in which they perceived their social position as middle class, "conscious of relative social position and thus of social distinction," while at the same time they experienced an economic situation no more elevated than an unskilled, manual laborer, as both "sell and are dependent on their labour."[25] Rather than critiquing the idea of "class consciousness" from an assured middle-class standing, Gilman, in the 1890s at least, is critiquing it from the standpoint of someone *between* classes—whose rejection of middle- and working-class definitions is based precisely on her experience of straddling them.[26] Moreover, Gilman's and Sinclair's financial hardship during their childhood and a decade or more of their adult lives raises questions about the middle-class standing of other leaders in the socialist movement, the "brain workers" who Pittenger supposes form a separate class with interests distinct from wage laborers. What we commonly imagine as the greater security of white-collar labor—the salaried job with benefits—was simply not the experience of Gilman, Sinclair, or their peers. If, for the sake of argument, we accept the premise that Gilman's and Sinclair's class standing *was* in fact middle class, this raises questions about what precisely we should mean by the term as applied to people living one hundred years ago. It is virtually a truism of American labor history that workers, especially skilled ones, were relatively conservative because they could hope to earn virtually the same income as their petit bourgeois counterparts.[27] The corollary, however, is seldom considered: that these "bourgeois" with little economic clout and less security might make common cause with workers of similar means, and that the lives of neither group were comfortable enough for them not to want better than that permitted under market capitalism.

W. E. B. Du Bois makes the third triptych writer who grew up in a household in which the mother was the breadwinner and the father either improvident or altogether absent. Willie's mother, Mary, from the downwardly mobile but respectable Burghardt clan of Great Barrington, Massachusetts, gambled on marriage with the well-mannered, Haitian-born, and light-complexioned Alfred Du Bois. Within two years of "Willie" Du Bois's birth, she had lost the wager; Alfred moved on and out of Great Barrington, and neither mother nor son saw him again. As with the childhood situations of Sinclair and Gilman, the father's dereliction was countered by some basic sustenance provided by Mary's extended family, which was supplemented by her taking on domestic work. When Mary was partially crippled by a stroke, other townspeople in Great Barrington pitched in as well, and the network of social support worked just well enough that in adulthood Du Bois could recall "no poverty" in his childhood, though he recognized as well that "our family was certainly poor."[28] Du Bois's intellectual aptitude and scholarly achievement provided a way out of poverty and into contact with a world of privilege, but as a young adult he was always dependent upon wherever the current scholarship or present job opportunity led him. Although he was the first African American to win the Ph.D. from Harvard University, he was denied the still higher honor of being the first to earn the Ph.D. from the University of Berlin because renewal of his U.S. scholarship was capriciously denied just one semester short of the completion of his program.[29]

As for the influence of the socialists on the board of the NAACP, it should be mentioned at the outset that the wealth of the board members did not stipulate any particular place on the party's ideological spectrum: John Haynes Holmes, a sometime guest editor on *The Crisis,* was a Social Gospeler; William English Walling, sponsor of the motion to give Du Bois responsibilities as the association's director of research, was a radical, a sympathetic witness to the failed 1905 revolution in Russia; Charles Edward Russell was on the conservative wing of the socialist movement; Mary White Ovington, probably Du Bois's closest confidante on the board, was in the social democratic mainstream.[30] The question of Du Bois's class status around the time he became a socialist has as much to do with Du Bois's professional roles—as editor of *The Crisis* and director of NAACP research—in relationship to the board as a whole. As the one African American on the NAACP's founding board and the second-best-known person of color in the United States—behind only Booker T. Washington—editor Du Bois was the single indispensable individual at the association's founding.[31] But even while Du Bois's prestige in the black community ought to have made him first among equals on the NAACP board, his prerogatives as *Crisis* editor were hedged by the official oversight that the board exercised over the journal and the fact that Du Bois, unlike every other member of the board, was not independently wealthy. Oswald Garrison Villard, one of the most powerful board members and one of those most hostile to socialism, was also the landlord of *The Crisis,* whose offices were provided rent-free in the same Manhattan building that housed the Villard-owned *Nation* and *New York Evening Post.*[32]

Like Sinclair, and unlike most blue-collar and many white-collar workers, Du Bois had the privilege of a certain choice in his profession at the time of his first affiliation with the Socialist Party. Truly, in 1910 he stood at the brink of a decision that would define the trajectory of most of the rest of his professional life: he could continue his career of teaching and research at Atlanta University, or he could decide, as he did, to come to New York and become editor of *The Crisis.* What in his situation Du Bois could *not* choose, however, was to cut his ties with white, capitalist philanthropy, for Atlanta University and his Carnegie-endowed studies in Negro life were just as dependent upon it as were the NAACP and *The Crisis.* When the Slater Fund had refused to renew his scholarship for the critical final semester at the University of Berlin, Du Bois had seen how uncertain the support of such philanthropy could be. Repeatedly in the coming years Du Bois would clash with the NAACP board over association policy, including the basic question of whether *The Crisis* would function as an independent journal at Du Bois's discretion or as an organ of the association with editorial control directly vested in the board. From the outset, he knew that he served at the pleasure of his colleagues on the NAACP's directors; editor Du Bois always remained in essence an employee of the association.

That certain of Du Bois's philosophies and tastes had elitist implications is hardly surprising, given the kinds of personal and ideological pressures that were brought to bear through his world-class education and well-heeled company on the NAACP board. Yet the hybrid mix of Du Bois's background and experience—birth and childhood just above the poverty line, diligent and politic effort to make his way in the world, contact with the rich and powerful in adulthood—afforded him an uncommon range of choice in how he employed his own intellectual gifts and attainments. Contact with the lowly and the high-born gave him, much as with Gilman and Sinclair, the experiential capacity for understanding the situation of the poor and working class as well as a position of cultural and intellectual leverage that could be employed to change that situation. Even as Du Bois celebrated black America's Talented Tenth, he preached the necessity for that tenth to bring up with them, as they rose, the other nine-tenths of black America. Whereas, in helping to found the NAACP, Du Bois presumably supported the association's avowed goal of racial integration—by one interpretation, the means by which the most socially and economically advanced blacks might join their proper class without the stigma of race—the *Crisis* editor rapidly came to champion a quite different ideal, racial solidarity, which continually worked to break down class differences within black communities.

For all three triptych writers, the operative issue was not what their social class *was*, but what they *did* with and through their class position. The general answer as to what they *did* with their class position is fairly straightforward, if incomplete: they became socialists. Although to be a socialist around the turn of the century might mean a number of different things—a point that I will take up in the next section, with a closer consideration of what it meant for Upton Sinclair at the time he joined the party—it can also be said that to join the socialist movement, to recruit others to join that movement, and to advocate socialist solutions to social problems did mean, even for the most conservative of socialists, a greater equality in the distribution of the common wealth, resulting immediately in the diminution of class distinction and tending ultimately to the elimination of class difference altogether.

The critical issue is not the class status of intellectuals or of socialist intellectuals, but the question of how to make intellectuals socialist—or, for that matter, how to make any and all citizens socialist. Sinclair's work particularly highlights this issue. He was not as concerned with what kind of socialists "brain workers" would be, as he was concerned with how to do the brain work necessary for all workers, whether of head or hand, to become socialists. In the baldest terms, we may say that the transformation of a proletarian—or for that matter, a pastor, millionaire, or writer—into a socialist requires intellectual work. On this issue, Sinclair's position squares with the clear evidence of socialist party-building in the United States as elsewhere: namely, that even as not all, or even a majority of, exploited workers like Jurgis Rudkus became socialists, not all bourgeois intellectuals or, for that matter, wealthy industrialists rejected the moral summons of socialism. Regardless of occupation or class, nobody became a socialist by the mere pressure of economic and social determinants. The groundwork for socialism might well have been laid by such factors. Nonetheless, to recognize their social and economic circumstances as exploitation and to recognize their power to change those circumstances, individual workers and citizens had to become *educated.*

The point is repeatedly evident, for instance, in the process by which Jurgis becomes a socialist in Sinclair's *The Jungle.* The polemical and didactic passages toward the ending of the novel, which seem to lend substance to Folsom's and other critics' claims that Sinclair's socialism is for intellectuals only, are in fact the very passages that illustrate the means by which a regular proletarian, Jurgis, gains an intellectual mastery of his social circumstances and of their remedy through socialist transformation. They are also the means by which Sinclair, however cumbersomely, ensured that the novel would introduce its readership of various classes to the core principles of socialism. Immediately after the speech in which Jurgis is first acquainted with socialism, he is handed over to one of the party's organizers, a Polish tailor named Comrade Ostrinski who can explain socialism to Jurgis in his own language. Thereafter, while in the current order of things he remains a menial laborer, his mind grows: "he was just a hotel-porter, and expected to remain one while he lived," but "in the realm of thought, his life was a perpetual adventure. There was so much to know—so many wonders to be discovered!"[33]

The Jungle does not in any way suggest that Jurgis, the former stockyard worker and current hotel service worker, occupies the same role within the socialist movement as the party intellectuals and itinerant party organizers. The novel pointedly shows, however, that their roles are not mutually exclusive. In the closing scene of *The Jungle,* in which the election results of 1904 are reported before a Socialist meeting in Chicago, the roles of intellectual and rank-and-file are portrayed as complementary to one another. The oratory of the speaker helps his hearers to envision the actions of individual voters as a coherent mass movement: "as he swung his long arms and beat up the crowd, to Jurgis he seemed the very spirit of the revolution."[34] But it is the casting of Socialist votes by the rank-and-file that constitutes the fundamental political act, and each voter must in turn take up the task of party building and political education: "It rests with you to take your resolution—now, in the flush of victory, to find these men who have voted for us, and bring them to our meetings, and organize them and bind them to us!"[35] Hence intellectual development along the lines of class analysis is fundamental to the socialist identity of a proletarian such as Jurgis Rudkus, just as it is necessary for intellectuals like Sinclair, Gilman, and Du Bois to become socialists.

For Gilman and Du Bois, it must be said, there could not be quite the same steady flow in the circuit between intellectual leadership and mass action, moving from political education to revolutionary voting behavior and onward to further education and the creation of a widening circle of socialists voting and organizing according to their convictions. In short, Gilman and Du Bois belonged to groups whose suffrage was altogether forbidden or severely restricted and whose citizenship rights were limited in other ways as well. For them and other knowledge workers disenfranchised by gender, race, or other factors, the bond between the knowledge worker and others from their group could only be strengthened. For Sinclair and other white male socialists in the United States, the very smoothness of the circuit between leadership and mass action could leave them indifferent to the rights of less visible and less powerful women and minorities. The potential for gaps within radical political groups, then, is not only a matter of brain workers being separated by experience and perspective from rank-and-file manual laborers but also of an entire, potentially vanguard class—say, white proletarians—finding that their experience and perspective may separate them from others still less socially privileged. All of this complicates, rather than resolves, the difficulty socialists including Gilman, Sinclair, and Du Bois faced in welding together disparate groups of American citizens and half-citizens, proletarian, bourgeois, and even propertied classes into a working social democratic coalition. But these difficulties also challenge any assumption that the brain worker is unfitted for participation in the class struggle, if only because they underscore the necessity of the best kind of intellectual work, regardless of the current occupation of the intellectual worker, to formulate their solution.

THE DIVERSITY OF AMERICAN SOCIALISM, CIRCA 1906

"Communism in material production, anarchism in intellectual."

As it happened, there was no shortage of ideas among American socialists. The election of 1904 described in the closing pages of *The Jungle* marked the beginning of what has been called the "golden age" of the socialist movement in America, a period lasting until the beginning of the Great War in which the party made steady gains in the popular vote, placed a representative in the U.S. Congress, elected mayors in Milwaukee, Schenectady, and over fifty other municipalities, and gained majorities on the councils of many of these cities.[36] It was also a period of remarkable diversity in the socialist movement. One commentator notes that "the Party was far from homogeneous or orthodox in the present sense of that word, although before 1920 such differences were generally accepted as normal and desirable aspects of the process of developing a viable mass party."[37] And this is considering only the Socialist Party proper. The American socialist movement also included, further to the left, a persistent cadre of anarchists and a steadily growing anarcho-syndicalist union, the Industrial Workers of the World. On the right, there were significant numbers of adherents to the Social Gospel, and socialist ideas were manifest, perhaps unsystematically but nonetheless tangibly, among the Progressives of both major parties. Most of these varieties of socialist activity are evident in Upton Sinclair's writing and activism beginning with *The Jungle* and continuing through his campaign on behalf of the victims of the Ludlow Massacre. Broad as his sympathies and intellectual curiosity were, Sinclair developed in his work a compelling case that the various forms of socialism did, in fact, work effectively together—even when the various factions might sincerely distrust each other.

Something of the diversity of the socialist movement is apparent among Sinclair's initial mentors in the movement. As with Du Bois's early socialist mentors, it would at first seem that the considerable power of these individuals would produce some homogeneity in their socialist perspectives. But there is virtually no consistency at all in their socialist views and affiliations. Leonard Abbott, described in *Love's Pilgrimage* as the first person to give "Thyrsis" socialist literature to read, was an editor at the *Literary Digest*, director of the Free Speech League, and principal of New York's Ferrer School (named after the martyred Spanish anarchist Francisco Ferrer). George Herron, also mentioned prominently in *Love's Pilgrimage,* was well known in the Social Gospel movement—and somewhat notorious—at the time Sinclair met him. His extramarital relationship with the wealthy socialite Carrie Rand had led to a highly public divorce, his resignation from church ministry, and marriage to Rand, who subsequently used her inheritance to endow the Rand School for Social Research. J. A. Wayland, the initial publisher of *The Jungle,* earned a fortune from land speculation in the West, was the founding editor of *The Coming Nation* (1893–95) as well as its immediate successor, the *Appeal,* and thus provides a tangible link between Nationalism and Populism and the era of the Socialist Party.[38] Gaylord Wilshire was a real estate magnate from Southern California whose self-named magazine (*Wilshire's*) was a frequent publisher of Sinclair's earliest socialist articles. Presented as "a drawing-room edition of Mephistopheles" in *Love's Pilgrimage,* Wilshire was an advocate of syndicalism and, for that advocacy, was forced to move his magazine first to Canada and then to England in order to evade government censorship of his publications.[39]

The diversity of American socialism is practically flaunted in the closing pages of *The Jungle,* the infamously didactic monologues and dialogues upon socialist theory and praxis. Once apologizing for the rambling and expository style of these chapters, Sinclair confessed, "I ran wild at the end, attempting to solve all the problems of America; I put in the Moyer-Haywood case, everything I knew and thought my readers ought to know."[40] This very effort at comprehensiveness and didacticism, however, is a boon to our effort to describe American socialism near the beginning of its ascent into political prominence. To begin with, socialist variety is on display in Sinclair's cast of characters, both fictional and nonfictional. Comrade Ostrinski, Jurgis's tutor, presents the party-building and electoral strategies that were the main line pursued by the Socialist Party of America throughout its major period, 1901–20. As we have seen, the electoral strategy is subsequently dramatized in the closing, election-day scene as well. But Sinclair's interest in socialist leaders and philosophies ranges far and wide, as indicated by his brief character sketches of real-life socialists whom he generally does not name but describes with enough detail for readers to identify. There is Eugene Debs, of course, who is identified as one of the "two standard-bearers of the party" whom Jurgis hears during the 1904 election season, and described as "a man of electric presence, tall and gaunt, with a face worn thin by struggle and suffering."[41] Besides pointed allusions to the radical publishers Wayland and Wilshire, noted above, characters that suggest the leftward extension of the socialist movement include Jack London, described as someone "who had tramped the country and been sent to jail, had lived in the Whitechapel slums, and been to the Klondike in search of gold," and Daniel De Leon, readily recognizable to socialist readers in the figure of the "Little Giant" who Sinclair says had "written a veritable encyclopedia upon the subject [of capitalism], a book that was nearly as big as himself."[42] To broaden the socialist spectrum still further, Sinclair elsewhere includes reference to "Mrs. Gilman"—Charlotte Perkins Gilman, of course—as the author of books on women's economics and domestic cooperatives.[43]

The Jungle portrays the polyglot nature of the socialist movement most fully, perhaps, through the fictional comrades Schliemann and Lucas, the contrasting characters who generate the long dialogue in the novel's penultimate scene. Several critics have attempted to establish definitively Sinclair's factional preference within the socialist movement by discerning which of these characters the narrative seems to favor. The effort appears to be more daunting than it might first seem, however, because for every critic (Michael Folsom, Isabel Díaz) who is certain that Sinclair prefers Lucas, there is another critic (Scott Derrick, June Jacobs) who presents irrefutable evidence that Schliemann is the favorite.[44] The upshot of this critical stalemate, I would maintain, is that Sinclair's narrator succeeds in being largely sympathetic to *both* of these socialists, no small feat given how different their philosophies are. Whereas Schliemann is positively contemptuous of Christianity, describing it as "the Arch-fiend's deadliest weapon," which "oppressed [the wage slave's] mind, and poisoned the stream of progress at its source," Lucas the Social Gospeler sees the Christian Bible as "one long cry of the human spirit for deliverance from the sway of oppression" and Jesus as "the world's first revolutionist, the true founder of the Socialist movement"; Lucas also stresses the pragmatic advantage of being able to appeal to the social conscience of the many people who call themselves Christian. Schliemann accepts the notion of Jesus as "revolutionist" only insofar as it permits him to put in a good word for revolutionary violence, as he characterizes Jesus as "a practical man"—someone who "would take pretty little imitation-lemons, such as are now being shipped into Russia, handy for carrying in the pockets, and strong enough to blow a whole temple out of sight.'"[45] While Lucas provides the argument for moral suasion and the capture of existing institutions, Schliemann provides one for direct action and—at least under certain circumstances—violence against those institutions.

Notably, *neither* of these major spokesmen for socialism is typical of the Socialist Party line. Both are introduced as "Socialists." But as a Christian minister advocating the Social Gospel, Lucas would not be typical of the party with its resolutely secular ideology. And Schliemann *should* not, in point of fact, be a member of the party, although it is conceivable that he might be "one of the minds of the movement" without being a card-carrying party member.[46] Schliemann openly declares himself to be a "philosophic anarchist," a point of view evident also from his convictions that "socialism was simply a necessary step toward a far-distant goal, a step to be tolerated with impatience," that "the end of human existence was the free development of every personality, unrestricted by laws save those of its own being," and that presently, with the abolishment of the profit system and of state authority, "Society would break up into independent, self-governing communities of mutually congenial persons."[47] For holding such views openly—as well as sympathizing with the Russian direct-actionists—Schliemann ought to have been among the anarchists barred from the party from its inception.

Moreover, in offering Schliemann as the representative of anarchism, Sinclair puts a far more congenial face on anarchism than might have been expected—indeed, a far more positive face than Sinclair appears to have originally intended in his design for the novel. Recall that Sinclair's 1904 *Appeal to Reason* article, "You Have Lost the Strike! Now What Are You Going to Do About It?" had drawn a bright line between the methods of democratic socialism and those of the anarchists and other violent revolutionaries. Much the same attitude was reflected in Sinclair's précis of the novel providing advance advertising for its serial publication in *Appeal to Reason:* "Then the hero goes out and hears about anarchism. Anarchists and the social crime and terror that make them have not yet been put into fiction. The hero is making bombs—and then he learns about Socialism."[48] The ending that Sinclair actually wrote shifts his representation of the typical anarchist from something close to the popular stereotype, a bomb-hurling madman, to a portrait of a far-seeing and erudite social philosopher. Moreover, Schliemann's quip about Christ the practical revolutionist makes Schliemann a supporter of revolutionary violence not merely in the abstract but in relation to a historical event: the Bolshevik Party's failed coup against the czar in 1905. Not only does the novel's dominant theorist endorse revolutionary violence *before* the fact, when knowing support means collaboration, but the novel's narrative point of view also condones the violence and its foreknowledge *after* the fact, when Sinclair might have wished to distance this character (and himself) from the revolution, given both its violence and its failure.

That Sinclair was aware of tensions within the party stemming from its diversity is clear enough from the minimal common ground that the novel describes as binding the socialist movement together. There appear to be just three planks that might be agreed upon as a shared socialist platform. The first is the principle of "no compromise" articulated by Comrade Ostrinski and reinforced by the election-day speaker, which seems to allow for a variety of means to socialist ends (including especially parliamentarianism) so long as all socialist parties remain united in their opposition to capitalism. The second and third are the "two carefully worded propositions" upon which the sparring debaters Lucas and Schliemann can agree. One is a statement of the socialist goal broad enough to include state socialism as well Schliemann's favored communes: "common ownership and democratic management of the means of producing the necessities of life." Another articulates with slightly more detail the means to this end, "the class-conscious political organization of the wage-earners."[49] It is an articulation that shows some influence of Marxism upon Sinclair and the post-1900 socialist movement, although by using the term "wage-earners" instead of the "proletariat" Sinclair offers a formulation broad enough to accommodate the full range of pre-1900 producerist thinkers and to include, with minimal friction, brain-laboring, piecework writers such as himself and Gilman, and even the salaried but very much supervised editor Du Bois.

For the most part, though, *The Jungle* envisages the tensions as productive. Implicitly as well as explicitly, *The Jungle* is all about inclusiveness, about entertaining all kinds of socialist philosophy and praxis and about contemplating the possibility that most of them would, in the end, be compatible with the aim of progress toward social democracy. Not only does Schliemann remain cordial toward Lucas in their spirited debate, but the very representation of Schliemann embraces contraries that Sinclair appears to have believed were in no way incompatible. Although Schliemann is a character at least as radical as De Leon, we have already noted some of the ways in which his utopian vision is heavily cribbed from that of Edward Bellamy, supposed to be among the most conservative of American socialists. Such a synthesis might seem implausible. The fact that Schliemann is definitely identified as a capital-*S* Socialist, when in fact the party refused to recognize anarchists, may well suggest something is amiss with his characterization. Yet even as Sinclair was writing *The Jungle,* another set of incidents was beginning to unfold that exhibited for Sinclair the productive interactions possible along the radical-to-progressive spectrum.

The Haywood-Moyer case was a narrative he had hoped to include in the novel as one of the many things he had "thought my readers ought to know." In December 1905, during a strike of the Western Federation of Miners, the union leaders Charles Moyer, William Haywood, and George Pettibone were abducted by agents of the governors of Colorado and Idaho, carried away to Idaho on a special train that abrogated extradition procedures, and made to stand trial for conspiracy to commit murder. The murder victim, the former governor of Idaho, had been killed by a bomb while Moyer, Haywood, and Pettibone were in Colorado, but such facts were apparently not supposed to stand in the way of retribution against radical labor leaders. In response, the labor and socialist movements swiftly mobilized. Eugene Debs proclaimed in the *Appeal to Reason:* "If they attempt to murder Moyer, Haywood and their brothers, a million revolutionists, at least, will meet them with guns."[50]

Appeal editor Fred Warren devised a publicity stunt that demonstrated the partial nature of American justice as applied to the radical labor movement. Warren wondered, editorially, what would happen if some other prominent but respectable public figure were wanted for murder, had fled to another state, and was kidnaped so that he could stand trial. What if that person were a state governor? Warren had in mind the former governor of Kentucky, William Taylor, who had murdered his Democratic gubernatorial opponent and taken refuge in Indiana, where a fellow Republican governor refused to extradite him. Accordingly, the *Appeal* announced a $1,000 bounty to kidnap Taylor and return him to Kentucky to face murder charges. It was purely a publicity maneuver, Warren explained; the state of Kentucky had already announced a bounty ten times greater, and the governor of Indiana had made plain all along that he would continue to harbor his fellow Republican. Indeed, the present governor of Kentucky (again a Republican) proceeded to pardon Taylor of a crime for which he had been indicted but never tried. Later, in 1909, government prosecutors bolstered Fred Warren's case about the prejudices of the capitalist judiciary, as the then-pardoned former governor Taylor testified against Warren in a libel suit that resulted in Warren's conviction, a sentence of six months, and a fine of $1,500.

As framed by the contemporary historian of the *Appeal,* the lesson of the fight to save Haywood, Moyer, and Pettibone and subsequently, too, of the fight to free Warren, was all about the class war: "The revolutionary little sheet and its fighting editor emerged with colors flying, while the routed forces of Capital fled in confusion and dismay."[51] Yet even as the cases against Haywood, Pettibone, and Moyer, and against Warren showed clearly the lengths to which capital would go to protect its interests, the "capitalist" courts did ultimately acquit Haywood, Moyer, and Pettibone of all charges, as the juries did not fail to overlook the defendants' iron-clad alibis. Sinclair also could not miss the fact that Warren's campaign, ultimately highly successful as an anticapitalist protest, had been carried on not in the streets but in the public (and more or less free) press. Sinclair's own public activities in the case had included organizing an eminently respectable protest meeting at Carnegie Hall to demand that President Taft pardon Fred Warren, to be led by a blue-chip list of socialists and progressives: Charlotte Perkins Gilman; Lincoln Steffens, muckraking journalist and author of *The Shame of the City;* Edwin Markham, the protest poet of "The Man with the Hoe"; civil rights lawyer Samuel Untermyer; and Clarence Darrow, the renowned criminal defense lawyer then representing Warren on appeal.[52]

A relatively swift outcome of the Warren case likewise served to reinforce the value of working within as well as confronting the existing system. Prior to Sinclair's scheduled meeting at Carnegie Hall—and long before armed revolutionaries had arrived in Washington—Fred Warren received a presidential pardon. On February 4, 1911, journalist Frederick Upham Adams confided to Sinclair the details of the behind-the-scenes denouement. The pardon had been won by a series of conventional political maneuvers: the intervention of Warren's congressional representative; the influence of "the new Solicitor General, a personal friend of mine and of our line of social economics"; and Adams's own presentation of the facts of the Warren case in an article delivered to President Taft. In his letter to Sinclair, Adams saw reason to hope that both socialists and "mere" authors might exert influence at the highest levels of government: "So far as I am aware this is the first instance in which a mere author has forced an overthrow of a verdict affirmed by a Court of Appeals, and it is the first instance, to my knowledge, in which an executive of any nation has exercised clemency on behalf of a Socialist."[53]

At the same time, Sinclair reckoned that the left-wing threat was almost as important as the right-wing rapprochement. Debs's threat, and militant workers to back it up, made Adams's behind-the-scenes dealing possible. Hence, during the golden age of the Socialist Party, Sinclair interested himself less in sectarian party-building activities than with exploratory dialogue with syndicalism and that still more radical version of "direct action" defended by his fictional character Schliemann—anarchism. Both *The Jungle* and Sinclair's immediately subsequent nonfiction work, *The Industrial Republic* (1908), cited the Russian anarchist Petr Kropotkin, whose *Fields, Factories, and Workshops* was taken as the leading authority on the productivity of modern agricultural methods.[54] During a stay in England in 1912, Sinclair opened a correspondence with Kropotkin. Soon he arranged a meeting with Kropotkin as well, who was living in exile in England at the time. Years later, Sinclair continued to describe Kropotkin as one of the leading men of international socialism: *"I went to see him in Brighton England; he kissed me on both cheeks and I can still feel his bushy whiskers. One of the noblest of men!"*[55]

Sinclair was then on his way home from receiving a no-fault divorce in the Netherlands, his marriage to Meta Fuller having disintegrated (a topic to be covered in detail next chapter). He—along with the woman who would soon become his second wife, Mary Craig Kimbrough—stayed in England for several weeks with his early socialist mentor Gaylord Wilshire and his wife, Mary. But it was not love alone that was in the English air in 1912. While in England, Sinclair also collaborated politically and professionally with Gaylord, who had landed there along with his syndicalist magazine in flight from censorship threats first in the United States and then in Canada. At the time Wilshire was also filling in as editor at an English magazine, *The Syndicalist*, whose erstwhile editor had been imprisoned for his actions during the British rail transportation strike of 1911–12. Sinclair helped with the editing of both magazines, taking positions straddling the division between the IWW and the Socialist Party.[56] In a debate between himself and Wilshire published in the October 1913 *Wilshire's*, "A Butterfly Net for a Rhinoceros Hunt," Sinclair sought alternately to placate and to provoke: "I grant you that the workers will never win by politics alone. The masters would take away the vote just as quickly as they would the right to strike. But why not fight *with both sword AND shield*? . . . I want to get you to discuss this question . . . that of *both* political and industrial action, carried on, each in its proper time, and each supplementing the other—each *protecting* the other."[57] Whereas Sinclair defends the value of political action and hence of the Socialist Party, he concedes a number of points made by Wilshire, who maintained that the economic power wielded by the workers, because relatively independent of anything the capitalists might decree, was less vulnerable than their voting rights.

On her own 1896 visit to England, Charlotte Perkins Gilman had found herself similarly impressed by the anarchists whose credentials had been denied by the international socialist congress. On her return to the United States, she had touted anarchism as the Russian equivalent of U.S. Populism. Gilman, though, had focused her energies on building up the U.S. version of the Fabian Society. Back home in the United States in 1913, Sinclair threw himself into further direct collaboration with syndicalists and anarchists. He was a participant in the Paterson textile strike and workers' pageant of that year, as he organized a picket of Fifth Avenue shops by silkworkers in the days leading up to the pageant at Madison Square Garden.[58] Rose Pastor

Stokes, an IWW leader and one of the principal organizers of the pageant, responded enthusiastically to Sinclair's plans for the picket: "A group of women pickets in front of Fifth Avenue shops, bearing really striking legends, to thrust in the faces of the indifferent ladies who *wear* the silks they make, would create something of a stir—and more—in the press. Of course some of the women would get arrested, but it would have to be the silk workers themselves who are to carry these banners—and they are used to arrest."[59] Although the pageant itself was one of the great publicity successes in the history of political theater and political art, in practical terms the Paterson labor action ended in failure; the strike was broken and the IWW's effectiveness brought into question.[60] Sinclair's assessment of the failure of the Paterson strike, included in his debate with Wilshire, criticized the SPA as well as the IWW. Sinclair credited rank-and-file members of the New York party with cooperating with the Paterson IWW during the strike, and he criticized the IWW for undermining the party's efforts to fight the New York and New Jersey authorities politically. But his argument also conceded the syndicalists' major premise: "The politicians in the Socialist Party [must] come to understand that the working classes care nothing about old age pensions (or, at any rate, ought not to), but that the purpose of a Revolutionary party is to back up the Revolutionary unions while they reorganise the industries."[61]

Whether in the negative example of the Paterson strike or the positive experiences of the Haywood, Pettibone, and Moyer and Fred Warren exonerations, Sinclair found affirmation for the broadest synthesis of social democratic activism, from the merely liberal-progressive to the most radical-left. Such coalition politics had been suggested in *The Jungle.* It was still more fully and broadly articulated in *The Industrial Republic: A Study of the America of Ten Years Hence.* In a futuristic fictional scenario that served as the frame for an essentially nonfiction analysis, Sinclair hypothesized that socialism might be instituted in the United States as early as the election of 1912. Contrary to the cry of the election-day speaker at the conclusion of *The Jungle* who trusts only the party of the workers to carry out the socialist transformation, *The Industrial Republic* suggests the role of the Socialist Party need not be anything more than a catalyst, a kind of bogey threatening chaos if social revolutionary changes are not instituted: "The Socialist party is a party of agitation rather than administration; but it is of vital importance that it should everywhere exist, as a party of the last resort, a club held over Society. Everywhere the cry will be: Do this, and do that, or the Socialists will carry the country."[62] The particular set of politicians and the party carrying out the social democratic transformation was of relatively little consequence,

Sinclair reasoned. Even a sensation-seeking populist such as William Randolph Hearst, Sinclair hypothesizes, might serve the purpose, as he might aver "with his ten thousand and tenth declaration that he is not a Socialist" yet nevertheless do the work of socialism: "upon a platform of Americanism . . . equal rights for all" effecting "federal ownership of all criminal monopolies."[63] At the same time, Sinclair imagines a critical role not only for mainstream populists and for the Socialists but also for labor unrest and violence of various kinds:

> There will be two or three million—perhaps five or ten million—men out of work. . . . They may have forced Congress to provide them some temporary employment—which will, of course, be the first taste of blood to the tiger. They will certainly have been waging strikes of a violence never before known—they will have been shot down in great numbers, and they may have done a great deal of burning and dynamiting. That some particularly conspicuous individual like Mr. Rockefeller or Mr. Baer may be assassinated, seems more than likely; that a "Coxey's Army" of much larger size will have marched on Washington, seems quite certain.[64]

Thus we see the root of Sinclair's support for the syndicalists and sympathy for the anarchists as well as his appreciation for the insider politics of Frederick Upham Adams.

Affirmation for such a wide left-wing collaboration came from the broadest of historical currents as well as the closest personal experience. If on some points—as in the setback at Paterson—Sinclair was offering utopian projections contrary to the reality of intraparty conflict, he was also reflecting upon genuine and broad-based socialist successes—including one national movement for safe food production in which Sinclair had, of course, been directly involved. For much of his career, Sinclair's line on *The Jungle* was that it had fallen short of his mark: "I aimed at the public's heart, and by accident I hit it in the stomach."[65] Such an estimation is consistent with the conclusion at the closing of the novel itself, that a mere "municipal-ownership Democracy" was insufficient to resolve the deep-seated class inequalities exposed by the novel. It is also consistent with his declaration in the aftermath of the Paterson strike, that the "working classes care nothing about old age pensions (or, at any rate, ought not to)." Yet this kind of posturing, the drawing of sharp ideological lines and ramping up of demands, may be seen as participating precisely in the pattern of Socialist agitation for revolutionary change that—by its very extremity and insistence—might make necessary and even palatable more moderate reforms moving U.S. political economy that much closer to social democracy.

This is what *The Jungle* did when it hit Americans in the stomach. The novel did not stipulate the terms of the Pure Food and Drug Act; it was far from the first expression of concern and outrage against the processing of foodstuffs in the United States. By 1905 two other well-known socialists, Algernon M. Simons and Charles Edward Russell, had written articles on the meatpacking industry, and comprehensive food safety regulations had been drafted into legislation under the tutelage of government researcher Harvey W. Wiley. Robert Crunden reports that 190 bills seeking regulation over food and drug production had been introduced between 1879 and 1906, but only eight minor laws had actually been enacted.[66] What *The Jungle* produced was not new information or new proposals, therefore, but a groundswell of popular outrage linked with the threat of radical political alternatives. The outrage—and the threat—caught the attention of legislators and President Theodore Roosevelt to a degree sufficient to result in the passage of the Pure Food and Drug Act by the end of June 1906, less than five months after the appearance of Sinclair's novel in book form.

Whereas Sinclair's quip about America's stomach suggests how far America needed to go to achieve socialism, the fact that federal officials had already crafted legislation that would create the first effective public oversight over the production of food underscores the degree to which social democratic reform was something that could—and did—take place through the process of ordinary democracy and the action of salaried bureaucrats and major-party politicians. Insofar as President Roosevelt was responsive to public pressure and willing to enter into dialogue with a known Socialist (the letters back and forth between the president and Sinclair are featured in Sinclair's *My Lifetime in Letters*), it seems that the scenario Sinclair laid out immediately thereafter in *The Industrial Republic* was not so terribly far-fetched. Old party ideologies meant little when the Socialist Party was gaining ground at the polls, when a series of journalistic exposés (some by socialists, some by liberals) showed the degree of corruption and mendacity in politics and business, and when, consequently, Progressivism was a banner flown by one or the other of the major political parties, and sometimes by both.

The elitism of the Progressive Era has been described by a number of commentators; its reliance upon half measures and palliatives has been decried by successors of Sinclair who express their contempt for such reforms as "municipal-ownership Democracy" and "old age pensions."[67] Yet the reforms generated during the Progressive Era moved consistently toward a more active federal government role in the supervision and regulation of industry; they moved steadily in the direction of making the government an agent representing the general public, including consumers, workers, and children. From a Socialist perspective, the public was receiving half a loaf, and a worm-eaten and stale half loaf, at that. But it was a half loaf, nonetheless, and the Progressive Era laws, policies, and agencies provided the foundation for further, more ambitious and social democratic reforms to come. Under Theodore Roosevelt, the formerly ineffectual Sherman Anti-Trust Act was actually enforced in celebrated cases against J. P. Morgan and John D. Rockefeller. The Interstate Commerce Commission, also created in the nineteenth century but never effective, was for the first time armed with sufficient regulatory authority and staffed with enough officials to carry out a number of its tasks. With the expert advice and advocacy of government researcher Wiley and the support of Roosevelt, the furor over *The Jungle* led to federal oversight not merely of the meatpacking industry but of all foods and drugs transported across state lines.[68]

Meanwhile, following Roosevelt's shellacking of the "safe and sane" Democratic candidate of 1904, Alton Parker, the Democratic Party became increasingly united behind William Jennings Bryan's reformism.[69] In the election of 1912 the Progressive label was aggressively claimed by Woodrow Wilson (as well as by Roosevelt, running as the presidential candidate of the new, short-lived Progressive Party). Wilson's record as a reformer was at least as important historically as Roosevelt's. In an initial burst of legislation orchestrated by Wilson, the Democrat-led Congress created the Federal Reserve and the Federal Trade Commission, both agencies that gave the federal government an important toehold in the regulation of the nation's business, and they passed new antitrust legislation, the Clayton Act, which included a provision that prevented antitrust legislation from being wielded against unions (one of the few ways that the old Sherman Act *had* been consistently applied and upheld). A second round of legislation, similarly ambitious and progressive, resulted in a national law prohibiting child labor, an eight-hour workday on the railroads, a system of disability compensation for federal workers, a national credit program for farmers, and a steeply progressive federal income tax.[70]

Throw in the creation of the National Parks Service under Roosevelt, a harbinger of the federal government's subsequent role in environmental policy, and the passage of the constitutional amendment mandating direct election of senators, ratified during Wilson's first administration and a direct response to the domination of business interests in the Senate, and we may find plenty of cause for concluding that the Progressive Era was, in fact, progressive, and in ways that bore fingerprints of many socialist ideals and proposals. It might have seemed far-fetched for Sinclair to imagine in 1908 that a mainstream politician might carry out a socialist program. Who could think of the socialist movement representing so potent a force when its presidential candidate, Eugene Debs, could carry no more than 3 percent of the vote? Who could believe that the breadth of socialist ideas might reach so far into the popular political culture of the United States? Yet Roosevelt himself suggested that his progressivism was a response to radicalism, a stance that echoed Sinclair's proclaimed tactic: "Do this, and do that, or the Socialists will carry the country." In Roosevelt's words: "I am a radical who most earnestly desires the radical program to be carried out by conservatives. I wish to see industrial and social reforms of a far-reaching nature accomplished in this country, . . . but I want to see that movement take place under sober and responsible men, not under demagogues."[71] Roosevelt was not a radical in any of the senses that would satisfy either the socialists of his day or the various radicals of ours, but the provenance of "radical" as he uses it certainly has everything to do with "far-reaching" changes necessary for social democracy, even as they fall short of its full realization.

THE LUDLOW MASSACRE AND THE FALL OF THE SECOND INTERNATIONALE

> "I assure you that to shut your ears to these voices is not courage—it is obstinacy, it is suicidal stupidity. If you persist in doing it, you bring down the storm upon your own head, you have only yourself to blame for what may happen to you."

Through Sinclair's busy first decade as a Socialist, the author-activist had seen the benefits of a broad and diverse socialist movement, one in which even those elements that had been expelled from the party or never been admitted to it had an important role to play. At the close of that decade, on the eve of the Great War that swiftly ended the Second Internationale, Sinclair was to launch one more major foray into labor activism and socialist politics. In the process, he was compelled to confront the potentially fatal limitations of the anarchist-socialist-progressive coalition politics that he had come to tout. The particular cause was that of the victims of the "Ludlow Massacre," striking coal miners and their families who had been attacked, and some killed, by agents of the Standard Oil Company and the state of Colorado on

April 21, 1914. Sinclair learned the particulars of the miners' plight when a delegation of union leaders and Ludlow miners' wives addressed a New York City gathering on April 27, 1914. Sinclair learned that wages in the coal industry were high only on paper, for there were numerous ways that the companies made work in the mines unprofitable and perilous. Workers were not guaranteed any fixed number of working hours, and they were paid only by the weight of coal actually extracted, so time spent in shoring up unstable passages was effectively unpaid work. Consequently, coal miners in Colorado were four to eight times more likely to die at their trade than miners in the coal fields of Illinois, Iowa, or Missouri. Payment was often in scrip, spendable only at the company store, and the mining towns as well as the mines themselves were company property, so all rents were collected by the company and access to the towns closely controlled by the company.[72]

In spite of the desperation of those conditions, the United Mine Workers (UMW), the primary labor union active in the coal fields, sought merely recognition as the collective bargaining agent of the miners when it led a strike in 1913–14.[73] But the intransigence of the mine owners, spearheaded by the Standard Oil–affiliated Colorado Fuel and Iron Company, led to an escalating spiral of violence. By mid-April the strikers and their families, evicted from the mining companies' towns, were living in tent cities erected near the routes to the mines, where they hoped to head off scabs the company was likely to try to bring in. At one of the largest, housing some 1,200 people near Ludlow, Colorado, troops of the Colorado state militia (payrolled by the coal companies) moved in, razed the tent city, opened fire, and killed twenty-three workers and family members, including two women and eleven children who were asphyxiated in a cellar dug beneath a tent platform.[74] After this catastrophe, miners struck back by burning mine properties and for a time seizing control of the town of Trinidad. Quiet was restored only when President Wilson mobilized the National Guard.[75] In 1915, the official government investigator of the strike asserted that the Ludlow "rebellion constituted perhaps one of the nearest approaches to civil war and revolution ever known in this country in connection with an industrial conflict."[76]

Sinclair's response to the Ludlow Massacre brought together much of what he had learned and found effective by way of socialist agitation over the previous decade. Recalling his tactic during the Paterson strike of bringing the protest right to the doorstep of power and privilege, Sinclair arranged a public protest at the Broadway Avenue headquarters of the Standard Oil Corporation. The action also drew upon other models for radical action:

Fred Warren's adroit use of publicity in the mainstream media and the IWW's free speech fights, in which Wobblies spoke on public streets in defiance of local ordinances, were arrested en masse, and soon overwhelmed jail capacity. On April 29, 1914, Sinclair and four other protestors notified the police of their intentions, were arrested for disorderly conduct, and—refusing to pay the fine—spent three well-publicized days in prison. Meanwhile, growing numbers of other picketers continued to appear before the doors of the Standard Oil Company, and city authorities were compelled to leave them alone for fear of flooding the city's jails. By the time Sinclair and the other protestors were released, thousands of spectators had witnessed the picket and newspapers had broadcast word of the Ludlow Massacre throughout the country.[77]

Sinclair reached out for allies across the radical-to-progressive spectrum and found them in many quarters. While he was in prison, his new wife, the Mississippi-born patrician Mary Craig, led the picketers on Broadway. Sinclair's mentor Leonard Abbott assumed overall direction of the protest, sending picketers, including many anarchists, to the Rockefellers' New York City residence as well as to the Standard Oil headquarters.[78] Another prominent anarchist joining the protest was Alexander Berkman, recently released from prison after serving his time for attempting to murder Henry Clay Frick during the Homestead Strike. Others on the picket line were sympathetic liberals, mostly literary types who two decades later would be called fellow travelers: the journalist Lincoln Steffens, poets George Sterling and Clement Wood, novelist Alexander Irvine, and suffragist Elizabeth Freeman.[79] Also there were members of the Church of the Social Revolution, a radical Social Gospel fellowship headed by Bouck White, whose members went to the Rockefellers' usual place of worship in New York City and disrupted services on May 10, whereupon they were hauled out by police and arrested.[80]

Sinclair also found an assortment of allies in Colorado, when over the coming weeks he went there to see the labor conditions for himself, to conduct research for a possible book, and, as he recalls in his *Autobiography*, "to make publicity there, and to write it."[81] One ally, children's court judge Ben Lindsey, dropped his regular court business in order to accompany a delegation of the wives of Ludlow strikers for an audience with President Wilson.[82] Another was Democratic state senator Helen Ring Robinson, who gave Sinclair inside information on a series of legislative maneuvers at the closing of the state assembly's spring session. Specifically, she revealed that the Republican-dominated legislature had rushed through without debate a measure ghostwritten by the coal industry that pledged the state government to "render all assistance . . . in the enforcement of law and the maintenance of order." Meanwhile, Republican governor Elias Ammons was reassuring President Woodrow Wilson that the state legislature was providing "mediation" between labor and management.[83]

Sinclair's principal publicity stratagem was to advertise this discrepancy between the state government's professed interest in the common good and its actual collusion with the fuel companies. Competing newspapers provided Sinclair with friends as well as foes to his cause. When Sinclair sought to publicize the governor's false assurances to the president, the Associated Press stonewalled him. The *Denver News*, however, helped to expose both the governor and the rival Associated Press newspapers by sending its Washington, DC, correspondent to question White House officials. The AP's report held that Wilson had "expressed satisfaction with the situation after he had received Governor Ammons' reply"; the correspondent affiliated with the *News* found that no one at the White House had expressed any such approval of the governor's handling of Ludlow affair.[84] Other journalists provided national alternatives to the line distributed by the Associated Press. George Creel, then a muckraking Denver newsman (later during World War I, the director of the Committee for Public Information), published an article in *Everybody's* magazine strongly supportive of the Colorado strikers and highly critical of the coal operators. John Reed, a few years before he became famous as a correspondent of the Russian Revolution, published an article in the *Metropolitan* magazine favorable to the Colorado strikers alongside another by a second correspondent praising Mother Jones, in Colorado to support them.[85] Notably, too, the Wilson administration was hardly in collusion with the Colorado state government when it denied being satisfied with the state's "mediation" effort.

On the train home back east on May 26, 1914, Sinclair attempted to reach out still further for friends or—failing that—at least to make additional publicity. Improbably, he composed a personal letter to John D. Rockefeller, Jr., at the time the chief executive in charge of day-to-day operations at the Standard Oil Company. Sinclair knew a considerable number of millionaire socialists; why not multimillionaire or billionaire socialists? It was not the first time he had written a personal letter to a second-generation robber baron. In 1913 Sinclair had addressed an open "Christmas Letter" to Vincent Astor, the heir and executive-in-waiting of another of America's wealthiest families, and Astor had offered a rejoinder in his own letter to the press.

The letter to Rockefeller is, in any case, remarkable for its attempt to synthesize moderate and radical positions. Sinclair informed Rockefeller that a month previously, just when the Ludlow Massacre had been reported and initial decisions about the protests had been debated, one of his friends, "a well known novelist," had drafted an open letter to be cosigned by Sinclair and many other notable public figures. The letter had charged Rockefeller with murder, and was so "direct and unqualified . . . that it would probably lead to someone's attempting to kill you—and then there would be a reaction, and the cause of the miners would be set back." Sinclair said that he had persuaded the novelist, along with others, to suspend publication for a time, to see if the administration of Standard Oil might meanwhile relent in the hard line taken against its striking workers. Sinclair thus positions himself as the voice of moderation: he counsels against violence, and restrains those whose actions might, even as a matter of unintended consequence, precipitate it. Simultaneously, however, he lends his voice to condemnation of the Standard Oil Company and of Rockefeller personally. In the same paragraph in which he raises quite directly the prospect of the anarchist propaganda of the deed, he indicates the moral warrant for that "propaganda," pointedly telling Rockefeller that he regards him as a murderer of the Ludlow miners and reminding the magnate that the legally sanctioned penalty for a murderer is death. Ultimately, Rockefeller himself will be responsible for whatever ill might befall him, as Sinclair concludes (with some hyperbole about the press's unanimity): "All the organs of public opinion are full of evidence against you, of condemnation of your attitude; and I assure you that to shut your ears to these voices is not courage—it is obstinacy, it is suicidal stupidity. If you persist in doing it, you bring down the storm upon your own head, you have only yourself to blame for what may happen to you."[86] Sinclair thus offers a defense for the anarchists even as he protests that he does not himself subscribe to their philosophy.

Unlike Vincent Astor and Theodore Roosevelt before him, John D. Jr. never dignified Sinclair with so much as a line of response. And this time capitalists were not the only ones who did not share in Sinclair's outrage. Conspicuously absent from the picket lines were members of the mainline Socialist Party. The day after his release from prison, Sinclair had dispatched telegrams to Socialist Party offices throughout the country inviting them to extend the protest throughout the United States. Its argument was of a piece with the view that socialists should act in concert with the radical workers' movement to protect their efforts to appropriate the means of production. Meanwhile, he addressed his plea to the New York party in a letter: "There are branch offices of Standard Oil in every town. Cannot you or the National Executive Committee recommend that mourning pickets appear before these offices?"[87] Rejections from party locals, especially in New York City, were swift, curt, and in some cases public. Julius Gerber, secretary of the New York County local, dismissed Sinclair's actions as "self-advertising noise"—and in the *New York Times,* no less.[88] Subsequently New York (and national) party leader Morris Hillquit wrote to explain that he had never felt Sinclair's " 'silent mourning' was a manifestation of Socialist activity," and that "rightly or wrongly, I consider all such movements as distinctly harmful to the cause of Socialism, principally because the unthinking public is but too prone to hold the Socialist Party responsible for them."[89]

Moving toward ever greater respectability, proving perfectly capable of administration and government service (rather in contrast to Sinclair's declaration in *The Industrial Republic* that the Socialists were a party of agitation), Socialists such as Gerber and Hillquit had come to think of the socialist movement as the property of the Socialist Party alone—and *their* understanding of the party, at that. It was on this basis that they sought to exert party discipline upon the wayward Sinclair. Ironically, at the same time that the public was showing some signs of accepting the party, these party officials maintained a robust skepticism about the intelligence of average American citizens, the "unthinking public." Sinclair's assumptions were fundamentally different on both counts. The socialist movement was certainly not owned by any one group, but was the sum of many different groups seeking a common goal, even if by different and apparently contradictory means. Sinclair further assumed that the public, the great majority of Americans, *could* think critically about their political and social life. It was unquestionably the purpose of the picket he had organized to *get* them to think, just as it had been the purpose of the Ludlow workers delegation to get *him* to.

When the anarchists shifted the protests to Tarrytown, New York, near the Rockefeller estate, it showed their inclination to see the conflict in personal terms where Sinclair had seen it in institutional ones. When Sinclair, returning from Colorado, chose to support them, he indicated his continuing willingness to collaborate with them even when their philosophies clashed. When some of the citizens of Tarrytown responded with tentative support for both the anarchists and Sinclair, the wisdom of trusting the public was in some measure borne out. To begin with, the anarchists' appeal to personal accountability appears to have hit the mark with a number of progressives in the Tarrytown community, although not without some caveats and complications. A local landowner, Annie Gould, provided her private property for a meeting in support of the anarchists' rights to free speech, though she did so, contradictorily, on the conditions that no anarchists be put on the program.

Predictably, when the meeting was held on June 14, it was disrupted by anarchist hecklers.[90] Moreover, suspicions that they were being double-crossed seemed to gain credibility after the meeting, for the advice from village officials offered there—that protestors could be free of harassment from the local police by standing on a narrow band of land owned by the City of New York—entirely backfired when the Tarrytown police proved to be no respecters of municipal boundaries. They attacked anarchist protestors, including Alexander Berkman, pursued them with billy clubs flying, and thrust them aboard the return train to the city.[91] And yet these legal outrages swayed Gould and other Tarrytown residents toward still greater sympathy for the anarchists. A *Tarrytown Daily News* editorial upon the June 22 melee found that the reaction of the police "reflected no credit on the village."[92] The perspective of Annie Gould was being reshaped by the irony that those who purported to represent law and order had been neither lawful nor orderly. "I am dreadfully disappointed and ashamed of the conduct of the Tarrytown toughs last night," she wrote to Sinclair. "Nothing could be more anarchistic than their treatment of people whom they reviled as anarchists." She concluded that in Tarrytown "there is an element, vulgar and brutal that is more dangerous than the much abused I.W.W." [93]

All this changed on the Fourth of July 1914, when back in New York City three anarchists were blown to pieces while trying to assemble a bomb. The explosion was so powerful that it destroyed the top three stories of a seven-story tenement building and killed a woman in an adjoining apartment. The bomb, Alexander Berkman later explained, was being produced with the intention of assassinating whichever of the Rockefeller magnates the anarchist militants could first get to.[94] One of the anarchists killed in the blast, a young French-Canadian named Arthur Caron, was well known by both Upton and Craig; he had been a regular on the picket line. A notebook containing Craig's name was found in one of Caron's pockets, leading police to call upon her first to identify his body.[95] Craig could not bring herself to go and neither could Sinclair.[96] In the aftermath of the tragedy, Sinclair wanted to come to speak to the citizens of Tarrytown in person—to speak in defense of Caron and of himself as well, for he had offered a personal testimonial to Caron's character between the events of June 22 and those of July 4. Annie Gould asked him to stay away. "The bomb explosion does take it out of our hands," she reflected; "The tragedy of it seems to impose a great silence."[97] Until that tragedy, Gould and others had been willing to be critical of their neighbor, the world's most powerful scion of capitalism, and had been receptive to the ideals of social democracy, if not anarchism. Sinclair had been an effective advocate for socialism. So had the anarchists as long as they remained courageous advocates of free speech and helpless victims of state violence. But no longer.

Sinclair would persist in defending violent direct action as a reasonable response, if not the response he himself advocated, to capitalist violence. In an open letter he wrote in response to Gould's refusal to help him stage another public meeting, Sinclair explained his equivocal position. While avoiding a direct defense of Caron's conspiratorial bomb-building, Sinclair turned his attention to the $30,000 annual bequest of the Rockefeller family financing the Tarrytown municipality, and to the pending trials of ten anarchists charged with disorderly conduct at the June 22 demonstration (not the police and their deputies, of course):

> I can only say that violence breeds violence, and did so long before I was born into the world to tell you about it. I point you to the example of all history; I point you to Russia to-day. You are letting yourself be turned into a little Russia to-day, under the irresistible influence of a $30,000, a month payroll. I can only declare to you my solemn conviction that you will not solve the weighty problems you have before you by your present program of sending ten entirely innocent people to jail for a period long or short.[98]

Yet in several ways involving both professional and personal decisions, Upton and Mary Craig began to distance themselves from the kind of political struggle in which they had engaged as a response to Ludlow. Expenses associated with the Standard Oil protests had largely drained the Sinclairs' bank account. The anthology *The Cry for Justice* was conceived, in part, as a moneymaking proposition to shore up their finances. Sinclair received a $1,000 advance for the book from its publisher, and work on his anthology of social protest literature kept him occupied throughout much of the rest of 1914, to the exclusion both of other political activities and work on his novel that was to recount the events of the Colorado strike and Ludlow Massacre.[99] The anthology included anarchist works along with many more mainstream figures (Thomas Jefferson, Abraham Lincoln), yet this continued intellectual interest in the anarchists no longer translated into standing shoulder to shoulder with them on picket lines. Geographically, too, the Sinclairs were placing distance between themselves and their activities of April, May, and June 1914. Most of the work on *The Cry for Justice* was done at a house at Croton-on-Hudson lent the Sinclairs by Frederick C. Howe, U.S. commissioner of immigration.[100] With work on the anthology mostly complete in the late spring of 1915, the couple removed to the summer home of Craig's family, the Kimbroughs, in Gulfport, Mississippi. In the fall they were on the move again. The initial draft of *King Coal* was begun in Gulfport and completed in Southern California, which was to become Upton and Craig's permanent residence for the rest of their life together, over forty years.[101] Upton Sinclair's activity within socialist politics and protest, which had been almost continuous between the publication of *The Jungle* and the Fourth of July catastrophe, became channeled more through his writing. As for Craig, Fourth of July 1914 may have been even more fundamentally a watershed moment, for her husband's close scrape with anarchist violence served to justify tendencies that emerged later toward conservatism, secrecy, protectiveness, and paranoia.

The wider consequences of violent action in response to Ludlow were also almost entirely to the detriment of labor. Although the Rockefellers had only been menaced, never actually harmed physically, the horribly botched assassination plot rippled far beyond the lives of the three anarchists and the innocent bystander that had been lost. The hope of a positive publicity campaign in sympathy with the Ludlow miners—the kind of national outcry that Sinclair and his comrades recognized as having been the key to *The Jungle's* political success—was utterly lost. Following government investigations that had begun in the spring, Woodrow Wilson in September made a proposal for settling the strike: striking miners were to be rehired, state laws were to be reinforced, and a grievance procedure instituted, although the union was not to be recognized and picketing was prohibited. The UMW immediately accepted. The Standard Oil subsidiary in the coal fields, the Colorado Fuel and Iron Company, led the other coal operators in flatly rejecting the proposal, pledging instead to establish their own, internal board of arbitration "for the peaceful adjustment of any differences that may arise."[102] This "permanent and impartial body" rapidly evolved into a full-fledged company union. In December, with replacement workers and defectors from the union operating the mines at nearly full capacity, the UMW draining its coffers, and the election in November bringing into state office the "law and order" candidates backed by the coal companies, the miners voted to end their strike. By the fall of 1915, the workers voted to approve the company union first proposed a year earlier, a body that government investigator George P. West recognized would "deceive the public and lull criticism, while permitting the Company to maintain its absolute power."[103]

Ironies abounded in the timing of the July Fourth incident. In the very month in which Arthur Caron was killed making a bomb meant for a family that had directly benefitted from the suffering and the deaths of their employees—and Caron roundly condemned for his anarchist philosophy and plot—a war was breaking out in which millions of young men would be killed senselessly, and *those* killings lauded as a righteous patriotic duty. In the tiff between Sinclair and the pols of the Socialist Party over picketing the Standard Oil Company, the mainline socialist leaders had worried that Sinclair's protest over the Ludlow Massacre might not be a properly respectable form of socialist activism. Then in August 1914, likewise in accord with their respectability as responsible mainstream parties, all of the major Socialist parties of Europe voted in favor of war credits in their national parliaments, thus acting in support of a war that sent millions of proletarians to their deaths and led to the dissolution of the Second Internationale. The very forces of respectability and parliamentarianism that had made for the Internationale's success undermined it in a fortnight. Violence on the most massive scale was permissible as long as it was in defense of the ancien régimes and the capitalist and imperialist status quo. But violence against the state—and even nonviolence when the state prescribed violence in its defense—those were treasonous and outrageous.

Many socialists resolved these contradictions by accepting their logic: if violence were justified in defense of an obviously faulty social order, how much more would it be justified in the promotion of equality and freedom? The nations of Europe had sowed war, with the respectable pols of the Social Democracy pitching in, and together they reaped the whirlwind of the Third Internationale. Other socialists including Sinclair, Gilman, and Du Bois found they had to live with the apparent double standard, whereby capitalists and imperialists could maim, oppress, and kill with relative impunity while socialists who so much as contemplated violence were branded enemies of society. To persuade their fellow citizens that social democracy would make their lives better, not worse or just the same, socialists would need to hold themselves and their movement up to higher ethical standards in their political tactics as well as in their ultimate aims. Sinclair came to this position gradually and somewhat reluctantly. He had collaborated with the anarchists, defended Arthur Caron gamely even when he had been revealed to be a co-conspirator in a bomb plot. Yet he recognized that the errant bomb blast had not only been self-destructive for Caron but also destructive of any further progress in the case against Standard Oil and the Rockefellers. He would defend anarchists and syndicalists again. In the 1920s, he helped to found the Southern California branch of the American Civil Liberties Union largely in defense of the free-speech rights of the Industrial Workers of the World. He also became one of the leading public voices defending the rights of Nicola Sacco and Bartolomeo Vanzetti. In doing so, however, he would distinguish sharply between the violent praxis they sometimes espoused and the benevolent socialist philosophy they preached. He honored their willingness to suffer and even to die for their cause and condemned the courts and politicians who persecuted them, but he also criticized them for their advocacy of violence in return for violence. In subsequent discussions, including many arguments with Communists over the question of violence, Sinclair cited his experience with Caron and the Tarrytown anarchists. On the right wing of the socialist movement, Sinclair saw the Progressive present and dreamed the possibility of a social democratic future. On the far left, he saw the face of Arthur Caron and turned away in grief and remorse. That way, he finally resolved, lay madness.

CHAPTER THREE

THE FEMINISM OF AMERICAN SOCIALISM: GILMAN AND COMPANY AT WORK, IN LOVE, AND ON TRIAL

The career of Charlotte Perkins Gilman and her brand of socialist feminism provide further evidence for the continuity of American socialism before and after the turn of the century. Although Gilman, like other pre-1900 socialists, tended to eschew the socialist label and regard Marxism with some anxiety, the perspective upon women's equality that she learned in the Nationalist movement and elaborated upon in her own intellectual work was, in fact, shared by Marxists before the turn of the century and proved deeply influential upon American socialists after it. The Nationalists made gender equality a central tenet of their philosophy, as had the Knights of Labor and the Fourierites before them. The Fabian Society, in whose American branch Gilman was active, took the economic situation of women as both paid and unpaid laborers to be a core area of research and activism.[1] At its founding in 1901 the Socialist Party of America ratified a platform that included "equal civil and political rights for men and women" among its "immediate demands," and women exercised a visible role in the organizational life of the movement through independent socialist clubs.[2] In a concession primarily to southern delegates, the People's Party did not include a women's rights plank in its platform.[3] Many individuals in the Populist movement were strongly committed to women's equality, however. The ardent Populist and realist author Hamlin Garland, for example, focused his attention upon the subject in his best novel, *Rose of Dutcher's Coolly*.

There was something of a generational change in the direction of feminism within the socialist movement, but the change transcended the Marxist and non-Marxist divide. Garland was part of the younger generation of socialists who came of age in the 1890s and the following decade, in which Gilman was in the avant-garde and Upton Sinclair in the immediately following wave, who sought not only to agitate for gender equality but to implement that equality in their private relationships. This was in keeping with Gilman's feminism as it developed in the 1890s, for Gilman's complicated understanding of the relationship between bourgeois ideologies of gender and the durability of capitalism predicated that socialists must both attack gender inequality in the public sphere and seek to transform their own private relationships. This further refinement, a matter of praxis as well as theory, also showed just how far the socialists had to go. On the theory of gender equality, Gilman and some of her comrades articulated a dialogic understanding of the relationship between the political and the personal long before these became the catchwords of a later generation of progressive feminists. In application, however, socialists often did little better than their nonsocialist peers—as we will see in the latter half of this chapter by an examination of the personal relationships of Garland, Sinclair, Du Bois, and Gilman herself.

THE IDEOLOGY OF BOURGEOIS MARRIAGE

> "That relic of the patriarchal age,—the family as an economic unit."

At bottom, Gilman's exploration of gender ideologies may be seen as a response to this fundamental question: if the benefits of women's economic and social equality were so transparently clear, as they were to Gilman, Bellamy, and other socialists, then why were *all* women not actively involved in the movement for equality? Why were a considerable number of women mobilized, instead, in an antisuffrage campaign? Why were so many women in the suffrage movement content to agitate merely for a narrow definition of political equality? Gilman had arrived at a similar impasse at the height of her Populist enthusiasm, when exulting in the democratic philosophy of the People's Party she had also wondered whether a democratic majority could actually be persuaded to vote the party ticket.

In *Women and Economics,* Gilman's reassurance that women's industrial development was laying the groundwork for social, legal, and political equality is balanced by deep concern about the ideological webs that continued to entrap women. While "What the People's Party Means" asserts that conservative ideologies are mostly foisted upon workers by political parties external to them, *Women and Economics* explores the ways that repressive domestic ideologies are fostered by women themselves. Whereas Edward Bellamy and August Bebel, like Gilman, are able to articulate the necessity of women's equality, and whereas they too, like Gilman, assert the complementarity of the women's movement to the labor movement, they are not as alive as Gilman is to the ways that the bourgeois home both subordinates women and encourages them to *will* that subordination. Hence, Gilman sees the dismantling of marriage and the home as conventionally understood and experienced not merely as a natural consequence of economic equality, but as a critical catalyst of that equality.

Here Gilman's closest kinship is not with Bellamy or Bebel but with Engels in *Origin of the Family, Private Property, and the State* (a book available in English by 1891). Engels argues that bourgeois marriage, wherein the wife is dependent upon the husband ("the breadwinner"), remains paradigmatic for all classes. For Engels, the pervasiveness of this bourgeois paradigm of marriage serves as a principal constituent in the stability of capitalism: "Modern society is a mass composed solely of individual families as its molecules." He concludes, therefore, that women can be liberated and the social order made fully egalitarian only when "the quality possessed by the individual family of being the economic unit of society [is] abolished."[4] Gilman concurs that modern industry and its system of wage labor constitute more progressive social formations than the institution of bourgeois marriage and the sexual-economic bargain (at least to the extent that wage labor and marriage can be seen as semiautonomous formations). Marriage as presently constituted, Gilman argues, joins "a permanently individual process with a progressively collective one."[5] Gilman's further explication of this arrangement amounts to an extended gloss on Engels's somewhat cryptic suggestion about the harm done by "the individual family" as "economic unit." She shows how the economic arrangements of the family breed ideologies and behavior injurious for both women's and all society's development:

> [This combination] has affected the economic relation of society by bringing into it a tendency to individualism with sex-advantage, best exhibited in the frequent practice of sacrificing public good to personal gain, that the individual may thereby "support his family." We are so used to considering it the first duty of a man to support his family that it takes a very glaring instance of bribery and corruption in their interests to shake our conviction; but, as a sociological law, every phase of the prostitution of public service to private gain, from the degradation of the artist

to the exploitation of the helpless unskilled laborer, marks a diseased social action.[6]

Women and Economics provides one argument and example after another to demonstrate women's various roles in the reproduction of capitalism. It is problematic enough that women's activity as "non-productive consumers" creates demand for capitalist manufactures. More fundamentally, women's economic function shapes the urge to capital accumulation that is the very basis of capitalism, "the habit and desire of taking, as divorced from its natural precursor and concomitant of making." Women's unpaid work as child-rearers becomes central in this cultural work, Gilman asserts: "We have made for ourselves this endless array of 'horse-leech's daughters, crying, Give! give!' . . . What wonder that their sons go into business 'for what there is in it'! What wonder that the world is full of the desire to get as much as possible and to give as little as possible!"[7] Gilman ultimately finds, in essence echoing Engels's conclusion, that the only way for social progress to occur is to abolish "that relic of the patriarchal age,—the family as an economic unit."[8] It seems, in fact, that the chief differences separating Gilman and Engels—the distinctive nature of women's class oppression and women's potential for revolutionary leadership—actually make dismantling the present sexual economics of marriage all the more essential from Gilman's perspective. Gilman's critique of feminine ideology makes clear that the women's movement must address not only legal and political equality for women but also women's complicity in social and economic competition and inequality.

Bellamy and Howells and other older colleagues in the Nationalist and Populist movements were disinclined to follow Gilman in her analysis of the particulars of patriarchal ideology. In Bellamy's *Equality*, the retrospective stance of the narrative diminishes the possibilities for exploring the process of challenging patriarchy; only the accomplished and general fact of gender equality and its ongoing benefits to the social good are delineated. But the younger generation of men and women active in Nationalism and Populism was another case. Indeed, although we do not find the same range of sweeping social analysis offered by Gilman and Engels in the younger intellectual-activists such as Upton Sinclair and W. E. B. Du Bois, we find vigorous efforts to apply the principles of equality, independence, and even sexual freedom to the institution of marriage in general—and their own marriage relationships in particular.

Again, much of the critical ground on these themes appears to have been covered by Gilman first, although the fact that Gilman's early statements on marriage and sexuality appear in unpublished speeches suggests that no direct influence is indicated but rather a general diffusion throughout the American socialist movement of critical analysis of bourgeois marriage and the family. Gilman's critique begins with the upbringing of girls along rigidly applied gender lines. She writes in "Our Excessive Femininity," a talk from 1891, that "from her cradle to her grave" social conditioning acts upon every woman toward the ends of enhancing sexual attractiveness and thereby ultimately winning a husband. Gilman elaborates:

> The superior daintiness and ornamentation of her attire, and the special care required to keep it decently, call on her for self consciousness, and strongly develop the conviction that it is for her *looks* she is valued.
>
> She must not romp and climb as boys do, she must "act pretty." And is praised and petted for the sweet wheedling ways which, alas, will prove strong aids to her later life.[9]

Although Gilman discusses sexuality with Victorian indirection, her early talks also underscore the need for sex education for young women *prior to* marriage. Thinking not in terms of sexual enjoyment but sexual reproduction, to be sure, Gilman offers a prescription for young women that would insist upon their equal standing with their future husbands in matters sexual as well as economic, political, and so on. She asks sarcastically, "Did you ever hear of such a thing as a young woman carefully trained to understand her special powers and duties as a wife—the dangers that await her—how to guard and govern herself and be the wise helpmate of the man she joins her life to? You are horrified at the thought. What! Have a girl understand marriage before she is married! Revolting! Impossible!"[10]

Later in her career, Gilman would spell out one particular "danger" more explicitly, as her 1911 novel *The Crux* presented a young heroine who is placed at grave risk—both to herself and her offspring—because she is ignorant of the signs of syphilis in her dashing but dissolute suitor. Already early in her association with Nationalism, however, Gilman was outlining plans not just for sex education but for greater openness and flexibility in the marriage contract. In an 1892 lecture entitled "A Married Child," she denounced the "horror" and "absurdity" of marriage being a "contract" that is "binding, and, speaking generally, irrevocable."[11] In this instance, Gilman stressed the need for women to be well-developed human individuals before marrying instead of advocating a loosening of the marriage contract. Even as she was writing, however, she was in the process of acting out the latter implication of her denunciation of the marriage contract. In 1894, after five years of separation from her first husband, Walter Stetson, she was granted a divorce. Thereafter she took to the lecture circuit, traveling almost constantly for the next five years as she sought both to make a living by intellectual work and to seek the widest exposure for that work. In its economic, social, and sexual dimensions, Gilman was seeking to live out the socialist-feminist concepts she was to limn in *Women and Economics*.

Subscribing to these concepts—and presently, too, attempting to live them out—was the fellow Populist Hamlin Garland. His literary work and politics provide an intriguing case study of the extent to which feminist attacks against bourgeois ideology and feminist efforts to transform the particulars of gender relationships were integral to the rising generation of socialists—including men as well as women who declared themselves committed to feminism. Garland's collection of stories detailing the hardships of midwestern rural people, *Main-Traveled Roads*, had appeared to favorable reviews in 1891. Hoping in part to trade upon his newly won prestige as an author and, in any case, hoping to assist the People's Party in its inaugural round of elections, Garland had rushed three novels into print in 1892—all with explicit Populist political themes. Soon thereafter, more than one literary critic has opined, Garland's involvement in politics sharply declined. Although, as Joseph McCullough observes, "Most of Garland's activities and fiction of 1891–92 resulted from his participation in the Populist revolt," he also asserts that after 1892 Garland almost entirely removed himself from direct involvement in the movement.[12] None of the critics seem to consider the possibility that Garland's Populist and socialistic views are expressed after 1892 through his representation of women's social-economic predicament and his advocacy of a solution.

A comparison of Garland and Gilman on these points lends considerable support for this overlooked hypothesis. We know from Gilman's *Diaries* that Garland and Gilman met in 1892, when both were involved in Populism; then as well as later, in 1898, they shared the same speakers' platform.[13] Whether or not Gilman was directly influential upon Garland's views on gender, the two shared essentially the same convictions on the subject. *Rose of Dutcher's Coolly*, which appeared in 1895 and is considered by most critics Garland's best full-length novel, follows almost exactly the paradigm for women's social and economic independence that Gilman spelled out in her speeches of the early 1890s.

Parallels to Gilman's discourse on the economics of marriage abound in

Garland's novel. The novel's college-educated heroine, Rose, speaks of a profession as a matter of course—and as a means to break free from patriarchy: "I feel dependent upon my father and I ought not to be; I'm out of school; I'm twenty-three years of age, and I want to do something. I must do something—and I do n't want to marry as a—as a—because I am a failure." Interpreting her faltering speech for her, her friend Isabel says directly: "You mean you do n't want to come to any man dependent." After which Rose confesses: "I must be intended for something else than a housewife, because I never do a bit of cooking or sewing without groaning."[14] At the novel's romantic ending, the essential economic point is maintained: Rose chooses to marry only when her partner has acknowledged her professional promise as a poet to be at least as great as his own as an aspiring novelist. She thus comes into the marriage confident both that her husband will consider her an equal and that she will have an economically viable career. The narrator, at least, is confident both of the happy partnership and the successful career: "It was well, it was inevitable, and it was glorious to set her face toward wifehood and fame with such a man as companion, friend and lover."[15]

Rose's engagement to Warren Mason, highly charged with romantic energy at the end, is at first entered into in the least conventional and most pragmatic manner. The terms offered by Mason in his letter to Rose address the inflated sanctimoniousness and the rigid permanency that Gilman objected to in the conventional marriage contract, even if Gilman herself might have blushed to flirt so closely with an open marriage: "I exact nothing from you. I do not require you to cook for me, nor keep house for me. You are mistress of yourself; to come and go as you please, without question and without accounting to me. You are at liberty to cease your association with me at any time, and consider yourself perfectly free to leave me whenever any other man comes with power to make you happier than I."[16] Equally critical from the point of view of the sexual-economic bargain described and critiqued so scathingly by Gilman is the fact that Mason's proposal does not claim the husband's traditional (and legal) right to sexual relations and children: "You can bear me children or not, just as you please," he proposes.[17] This is practically an open marriage in sexual terms; it is also a marriage that does the utmost, within existing constraints, to establish the wife as equal to and independent from the man.

It goes without saying that such constraints would provide considerable obstacles outside the world of fiction. But in this way, the novel does no more or less than complement Garland's earlier Populist fiction: *A Spoil of Office* names the wide-scale Populist and socialistic reforms that would create the social and economic context for gender equality. Meanwhile, however, a marriage such as the one Garland imagines for Rose and Mason will serve to chip away at the sexual-economic relation and its pernicious ideologies—cultural work that must be accomplished both to complete and to catalyze the egalitarian social transformation. On these points, of course, Gilman serves as the implicit interpreter of Garland's pattern, rather than its being spelled out explicitly. But Garland's critique of obligatory domesticity and the sexual-economic bargain, together with his insistence upon women's socially useful and remunerative work as its antidote, demonstrate plainly his participation in a socialist-feminist discourse shared with Gilman and others in the American socialist movement.

With the fame Gilman won by *Women and Economics* and the rapid publication of three books between 1900 and 1904, Gilman's influence becomes much less a point of conjecture and more a matter of fact. Regardless of Gilman's attitudes about the direction taken by post-1900 American socialism, other socialists looked to *Women and Economics* and her other writings on the subject of women's equality as fundamental building blocks of socialist theory and praxis—and not least her prolific and eager new socialist comrade, Upton Sinclair.

Gilman is featured in the compendium of socialist thought and politics at the conclusion of *The Jungle,* where Sinclair glosses both Gilman's theory of the class system of domestic economy, "the domestic drudge being either the wife or a wage-slave," and one of Gilman's key transitional remedies: cooperative housekeeping, assisted by technological innovations such as the vacuum and the automated dishwasher.[18] In his next new book, *The Industrial Republic,* Sinclair went so far as to defer entirely to Gilman's analysis of ten years previous: "Suffice it to say that the Socialist battle is the battle of woman, even more than it is the battle of the workingman. I cannot do better than to refer the reader to another book in which the whole question of the effects which age-long conditions of economic inferiority has [*sic*] wrought in the minds and bodies of women is discussed in scientific and yet fascinating form—Mrs. Gilman's 'Woman [*sic*] and Economics.'"[19] Meanwhile, Sinclair used the immediate proceeds from sales of *The Jungle* to implement Gilman's proposals for cooperative housekeeping and professional child care, buying the buildings of a former boys' school in Englewood, New Jersey, for the purpose of housing his family and an assemblage of artists, writers, and other professionals within commuting distance of Manhattan. While "Helicon Hall"—the name had been inherited from the boarding school—lasted for less than six months, a casualty of fire and underinsurance, the venture had drawn twenty-four inhabitants at its opening and housed eighty at the time of the disastrous fire in March 1907.[20]

And even the Helicon Hall experiment only begins to indicate Gilman's impact upon Sinclair. Early in his marriage with Meta Fuller, Sinclair urged his new wife to read "The Yellow Wall-Paper" and *Women and Economics,* intent (in his ham-handed way) that they should live according to the precepts of gender equality, that his wife should seek the means by which to establish that economic independence held by Gilman to be so critical to women's equality, and that his wife should be on guard to protect herself from patriarchal oppression—most immediately, to protect herself from *him.* For her part, Meta Fuller Sinclair quickly became an enthusiastic devotee of Gilman.[21] Through the years immediately leading up to *The Jungle* and the years immediately following, the core challenge in Sinclair's day-to-day literary, professional, and personal life unquestionably centered upon gender inequality. That is, in his relationship with his wife Meta Fuller Sinclair, Upton Sinclair both suffered and benefited from male-centered and patriarchal social organization, and he also sought earnestly if not always effectively to agitate for a world in which men and women would be independent economically, equal socially, and free sexually. The corresponding struggle led—among other results—to the emotionally intense and highly autobiographical novel *Love's Pilgrimage.*

Sinclair's dedication of the novel expresses plainly the book's central concern with gender inequality: "To those who throughout the world are fighting for the emancipation of woman I dedicate this woman's book."[22] Notably, the dedication is not directed to women in general but to activists who are seeking gender equality, and it plainly assumes that men as well as women might seek women's emancipation. At the same time, the novel does not presume that politically progressive men and women have the same perspective on gender equality, for the narrative is focalized through a male perspective and does not presume to tell the story of gendered experience from a woman's perspective. The novel does not merely march its readers through an exposition of the gender inequality fundamental to contemporary marriage. It also dramatizes through "Thyrsis," the male protagonist, the complex psychology of patriarchy within men, which lays many snares and reserves many compensations even (or especially) for a husband trying diligently to treat his wife as an equal. The drama is all the more compelling, the difficulty of actually achieving equality in relationships demonstrated all the more strongly, given that the intensely autobiographical nature of the novel means that the boundaries between the protagonist's and the author's egoistic self-justifications are seldom clearly drawn. It is as if Walter Stetson were to rewrite "The Yellow Wall-Paper" from the perspective of John, the doting and patronizing physician-husband.

The book is extraordinary for its frankness. A startling childbirth scene refers repeatedly to the "agony" of "Corydon" (Sinclair's pseudonym for Meta), usually with the responses of Thyrsis counterpointing blunt physical description. As the child's head appears, Sinclair remarks: "The doctor's hands were red with blood now, like a butcher's." His narrator does not pull back from mixing clinical detail and sensationalism even when the child emerges from the womb—"A thing hideous—impish—demoniac! A thing purple and dripping with blood—ghastly—unthinkable—monstrous—a spectre of nightmare dreams!"—but goes right through to the delivery of the placenta: "[The doctor] was talking to the young nurse, giving her instruction, in a strange, monotonous tone. 'The placenta,' he was saying, 'often has to be removed; we do it by twisting it round and round—very gently, of course. Then it comes—so!' There came a rush of blood, and Thyrsis turned away his head."[23] Scenes such as this led to objections from Hamlin Garland and Charlotte Perkins Gilman, both of whom Sinclair had sent a draft of the complete manuscript for their commentary. Although the inventor of "veritism" had to confess that "it reads as if it were all fact—a real human document," he hesitates to endorse fully Sinclair's "extreme and self-revealing candor." Gilman was more blunt: "I object not only to what seems to me an unnecessary explicitness of detail; but, most extremely, to the publication of such intimate matters regarding your wife."[24]

From a socialist point of view, the striking fact of the childbirth scene and its aftermath is the way that it summons the male witness of female agony to a renewed commitment to socialist agitation. Thyrsis's impassioned response recalls the conversion experiences described in *The Jungle* and in another early Sinclair novel, *Samuel the Seeker* (1910), and gains special emphasis coming as it does at the very end of the first of the novel's two parts:

> Some day the world would hear about it—some day the world would think about it! . . . They did not realize it now—else how could it be that women, who bore the race with so much pain and sorrow, should be drudges and slaves, or the ornaments and playthings of men? Else how could it be that life, which cost such a fearful price, should be so cheap upon the earth? For every man that lived and walked alive, some woman had had to bear this agony; and yet men were pent up in mines and sweatshops, they were ground up in accidents in factories and mills—nay,

worse than that, were dressed up in gaudy uniforms, and armed with rifles and machine-guns, and marched out to slaughter each other by tens and hundreds of thousands![25]

Sincere and stirring as this is, Thyrsis's (and by extension, Sinclair's) response is problematic if one's socialism calls for gender equality as well as the abolition of labor exploitation. By using the woman's child-bearing scene as the call to arms, Sinclair places femininity at the center of the socialist project, to be sure, but does so in much the same way that cults of the Virgin Mary place the Holy Mother at the center of Christianity, by idealizing the object of devotion beyond human identity and agency, and accentuating instead the agency of the masculine devotee.

Whether or not the narrator—or the author—of *Love's Pilgrimage* is fully alive to such ironies is an open question. The subsequent narrative in Part II of the novel certainly piles them on, in any case. Corydon reads Gilman's *Women and Economics* first and is responsible for Thyrsis's becoming acquainted with it (a point of apparent contrast with Sinclair's biography, as Sinclair reports that it was *he* who introduced Meta to Gilman's writings). But it is Thyrsis who particularly seizes upon the book as contributing to his wider socialist education, leading to his reading of Lester Ward (Gilman's inspiration), August Bebel, and Havelock Ellis and to a generalization about the path to social progress that is essentially Gilman's: "So Thyrsis perceived the two great causes in which the progress of humanity was bound up—the emancipation of labor and the emancipation of women; to educate and agitate and organize for which became the one service that was worth while in life." And even as Thyrsis is becoming converted to socialist agitation and organization under this twin banner—the same two-track scheme described by Gilman and Bebel—he applies the analysis of *Women and Economics* invidiously to Corydon herself, for he also realizes from Gilman "that women had not always been clinging vines and frail flowers and other uncomfortable things; and the hope that they might some day be interested in other matters than fashion and sentiment and the pursuit of the male, was not a vain fantasy and a utopian dream, but was rooted in the vital facts of life."[26]

To make progress on the track of gender equality and thus, as the narrator of *Love's Pilgrimage* says, to unleash the "mighty force that in the end would revolutionize all human ideas and institutions,"[27] the protagonists and their real-life counterparts are tasked with finding some solutions for the variety of everyday conundrums posed in the novel. To begin with, the interdependency of economic inequality and bourgeois ideology would seem to create a classic vicious circle: How is Corydon supposed to escape the domestic ideologies of dependency if she has no remunerable productive skills? But then again, how is she to develop such skills as long as she is conditioned to be psychologically and materially dependent? Just as problematic are the corresponding dilemmas confronting Thyrsis. For instance, how is *he* to escape the patriarchal ideology of head-of-household and provider when he is, apparently, the only one in the marriage partnership able to produce remunerative work? There is no public support for impecunious young artists (as there would be, briefly, in the 1930s). There is no public system of day care that would enable both young people to find paying work. Instead, there is what Thyrsis calls "the economic screw": "It pressed upon him, and through him it crushed her. All things that he sought to be and could not be, all things that he would not be and was; all that was hard and unloving in him—his irritability and impatience, his narrowness and bitterness—in all this he showed her that cruel force that was destroying them both."[28] A rationalization for unsympathetic and harsh behavior this may be, but it is also an account borne out by the particulars of their experience.

These issues lead to some intensely practical questions: To what extent can asymmetrical relationships (including traditional ones in which the male is the principal breadwinner, the female the principal child-care provider and domestic) be tolerated, or must be endured, even as socialists work for the creation of a just and equal society? And what first steps might be taken so as to make partnerships more free and equal, and to dissolve them more readily when one or both partners find themselves intolerably unfree and unequal in their relationships? For a starting point, Sinclair looks to the solution suggested by Gilman and elaborated in the unconventional marriage vows offered by Hamlin Garland in *The Rose of Dutcher's Coolly.* Even before Thyrsis and Corydon exchange vows, in fact, they agree that their partnership is to last only so long as it is mutually beneficial; the ad hoc vow is invented by Corydon, who makes her pledge first: "I take thee, Thyrsis, to be the companion of love, and I will stay so long as thy soul is better with me than without. But if ever this should cease to be, I will leave thee; for if my soul is weaker than thine, I have no right to be thy mate."[29]

As the couple drifts apart emotionally and Corydon finds herself drawn into flirtations with other men, first a Socialist artist from the town, then a young clergyman who visits her regularly when she undergoes surgery and hospitalization, Corydon and Thyrsis apparently have an opportunity to act on the escape clause in their vows. When Corydon confesses her romantic attachment to the clergyman, Mr. Harding, Thyrsis writes Harding to inform him of the unconventional nature of their marriage vows. Seeking to encourage Harding and Corydon's union, Thyrsis proceeds to discourse upon the foolish socioeconomic underpinnings of the institution of marriage, culminating in a peroration upon the wage system as pertaining to gender roles.[30] Adapting an analysis offered by Gilman as well as Engels and Emma Goldman, Thyrsis concludes that there is no essential difference between marriage and prostitution. Alas, though, Thyrsis is betrayed by a combination of his own social ineptitude and the conventionality of Corydon and Harding. The minister is altogether spooked; he suddenly gives up his congregation and goes abroad. Moreover, when Thyrsis reveals that he is not so attached to Corydon as to wish to continue their miserable coexistence, Corydon is far less happy about the prospect of loving Mr. Harding than she is distressed at Thyrsis's "poor sort of compliment he had paid her."[31] Finally, it is not at all clear—here as elsewhere—that Thyrsis's personal aspirations and expectations are as socially progressive as he believes them to be. Even if the marriage tie had been severed, the result would be merely an individual achievement. It has no particularly collectivist end unless one believes, as Thyrsis perhaps does (and Sinclair likely did), that the movement for social progress will be advanced if he is free to do his work unfettered by a challenging marriage. As for Corydon, the best that she can hope for is that her new partner will be more gainfully employed than her old one.

If this is a more realistic ending than would be provided if Corydon and the pastor were to run away together, there are also elements of high idealism in the endurance of the feminist-socialist marriage of Thyrsis and Corydon. In a dialogue between the two characters that comprises a two-page envoi, they agree all the more strongly that they are incompatible as a couple, looking forward to the day when they can write another volume in the story, "Love's Deliverance," in which Thyrsis will go "out into the wilderness and [find] himself" and "new love [will come] to Corydon." But they acknowledge that it will be a "long story" awaiting a wider social revolution: "When the Revolution is here—when there are no longer priests nor judges nor class-taboos—then out of the hunger of our own hearts we shall have to shape our sex-ideals, and organize our new aristocracies." In effect, they suspend the personal satisfactions of Thyrsis "finding himself" and Corydon finding "new love" while they work together to bring about that revolution—meanwhile, testifying in the very daily, material being of their relationship the imperfections of the prerevolutionary institution. It appears even that Thyrsis will refrain from calling their relationship a "love" relation, when the novel ends upon his solemn and—from Corydon's point of view, at least—

painful declaration: "Let us redeem our great words from base uses. Let that no longer call itself Love, which knows that it is not free!"[32] It would seem that such relationships must continue to exist for (at least) as long as there is no socialist transformation of society. But it would also seem that self-conscious living in (or even just endurance of) a vexed relationship such as Thyrsis and Corydon's will spur the revolutionary social impulse.

AN INCOMPLETE REVOLUTION

> "The present mincing horror at free womanhood must pass . . . not by guarding the weak in weakness do we gain strength, but by making weakness free and strong."

For Upton and Meta Sinclair, the heroic struggle to bring a new society into being through the shell of their troubled marriage was not long lived. Even as reviews of *Love's Pilgrimage* were appearing in 1911, newspapers in New York City and across the country were reporting upon the stranger-than-fiction disintegration of the Upton and Meta Sinclair marriage. The catalyst was an affair between Meta and Harry Kemp—figured in *Love's Pilgrimage* as the radical artist whose flirtation first awakens Corydon to the possibility of sharing her love between two men. Kemp had been mentored by Sinclair, who saw in the younger, struggling poet a version of himself some years previous. Sinclair interceded with the wealthy soap-manufacturer and social progressive Samuel Fels to support Kemp with a $250 stipend, and Sinclair invited Kemp to visit him and Meta at the bucolic, Single Tax colony of Arden, New Jersey, where they were then living.[33] Sinclair had also tutored the twenty-eight-year-old Kemp upon matters of love, sex, and marriage, writing to him with advice about marital commitments that is closely parallel to the vows taken by Thyrsis and Corydon, and for that matter by Rose and Mason: "You must have it clear between you that if the time should develop you upon different lines, so that either finds that the other is hindering his or her highest intellectual and spiritual achievements, there will be an agreement to part, with the best wishes and the noblest unselfishness."[34] With the history of his own marriage clearly in view, Sinclair warned that the aspiring male writer must insist upon the economic independence of his wife, who "must be a woman of sufficient intelligence and spirit to scorn to have you attempt to support her in idleness upon the proceeds of your genius."[35] Having implied a degree of dissatisfaction with Meta, who had no visible means of support other than her relation with Upton, and having explained that Meta and he had essentially an open marriage, Sinclair would seem to be inviting some occasion for the "noblest unselfishness" he offers. Not long after Kemp arrived in July 1911, he and Meta began an affair.

Sinclair himself witnessed one rendezvous in the cabin of Scott Nearing, another of the residents of Arden that summer.[36] In spite of his declared principles, Sinclair's first reaction was to explode with jealous anger. On August 23, 1911, Sinclair instructed his lawyer to file for divorce in New York City on grounds of adultery; Harry Kemp was named as Meta's lover. The next day the newspapers were filled with salacious details of the case; they kept at it for weeks as the principals held various press conferences and the case made its way through the court system.[37] It may be true, as William Brevda argues, that "there probably would never have been the sensational Sinclair-Kemp divorce scandal which followed if Upton Sinclair had remained true to the principles of the radical love theorists and his own principles in his novels *Love's Pilgrimage* and *Love's Progress* and recorded in his 'love program for a poet' that he had written for Kemp."[38] Yet ultimately, the chief difficulty for the parties to the divorce trial was that, after initial acrimony, they became altogether too amicable too quickly. Less than a week after Sinclair filed for divorce, he appeared alongside Meta and Kemp at a news conference in which each took turns advocating his or her advanced ideals of love and partnership. Meta spoke of searching for her "soul-mate"; both she and Kemp advocated trial marriages; Sinclair took up a version of communal child care that he had learned from Charlotte Perkins Gilman, speaking in favor of the "endowment of motherhood by the State."[39] The problem was that New York law not only stipulated adultery as the sole grounds for divorce but also forbade collusion between the plaintiff and defendant. A certain level of hostility was legally mandated for Upton and Meta to be successful in achieving the freedom both, by now, ardently wished. In the end, the divorce suit failed entirely in the New York courts. A favorable decision of the trial judge was overturned in the end precisely because Sinclair's relationship with Meta and Kemp had been too accommodating at the beginning, as Sinclair was ruled to have been complicit in promoting the affair between Meta and Kemp.[40]

As far as Sinclair's articulation of socialism and feminism goes, the key issue is not the degree of Sinclair's hypocrisy, highlighted in Brevda's detailed account. That there will be some gap between the ideal and actuality is, after all, assumed. The question is, rather, whether and how Sinclair continued to work to close that gap between his egalitarian gender ideals and patriarchal assumptions and practice. Closely linked to this is the question of how Sinclair reacted to the adverse criticism in the press—no small matter for a writer who craved popular appeal and who understood its importance in order to effect social change. How did the very public disintegration of his first marriage affect his fusion of socialism and feminism?

The record is, at best, mixed. The novels that immediately followed *Love's Pilgrimage* also focused on issues that Sinclair saw as being of special concern to women. Writing just after Gilman had published her novel upon the dangers of venereal disease, *The Crux* (1911), Sinclair brought out a triad of novels that focused upon that same subject: *Sylvia* (1913), *Damaged Goods* (1913), and *Sylvia's Marriage* (1914). Subsequent fiction by Sinclair actually featured a number of characters much more independent, forceful, and feminist than Corydon. A miner's daughter is the most dynamic character in his next novel, *King Coal* (1917), based upon Sinclair's field research subsequent to the Ludlow disaster. His major novels of the 1920s, *Oil!* (1927) and *Boston* (1928), likewise include strong women characters playing central roles. Yet in these subsequent novels Sinclair's radicalism treats the issue of women's equality as secondary, never as the central or even coequal concern it had been in *Love's Pilgrimage* and the immediately following novels. A commitment to women's equality as essential to socialist conceptions of equality remained constant. At the same time, it appears that the creative tension of being in a challenging marriage—the kind of partnership described at the conclusion of *Love's Pilgrimage,* in which the socially progressive man is pushed by an assertive woman demanding *her* rights—was precisely what was missing subsequently in Sinclair's career. Sinclair's relationships with women, particularly with his second wife, reverted to more traditional patterns, and this reversion, it seems, was matched by a corresponding retreat on women's equality.

Initially, the differences between Meta and Mary Craig Kimbrough might not have been apparent. Upton and Meta had met Mary Craig at a visit to the sanitariums of Battle Creek in the summer of 1909.[41] Aspiring to be a professional writer, Craig had moved north from her home on the Mississippi Gulf coast and was staying at the Arden colony in the summer of 1911. At first she was more Meta's confidante than Upton's. At one point after the adultery scandal broke, the trio of Meta, Craig, and Kemp were reported to have gone to the Jersey shore, where they went sunbathing *au naturel* and read aloud from Havelock Ellis's *Sex in Relation to Society.*[42] But when in the spring of 1912 Sinclair traveled to the Netherlands to obtain a divorce under the more lenient Dutch laws, Mary Craig Kimbrough followed him across the Atlantic, meeting him in England at the Wilshires'.[43] The partnership formed in England proved a lasting one. Craig and Upton were married in spring 1913 back in the United States, and they remained together until her death in 1961.[44]

The longevity of the Upton-Craig partnership shows quite plainly those elements of Sinclair's marital ideal that he considered most essential—and they were not those that resulted in full equality and independence for the new Mrs. Sinclair. Mary Craig Kimbrough did not come to Sinclair with the economic independence he had recommended to Kemp as the ideal for the literary man's wife. Soon after her relationship with Sinclair began, she abandoned her literary career.[45] Economically speaking, she was the frugal domestic manager that so much chagrined Charlotte Perkins Gilman. Her husband wrote books denouncing capitalist speculators; while capitalism lasted, however, Craig took advantage by speculating in land in the Los Angeles area where she and Upton made their home, even buying up land on the cheap during the Depression.[46] Most of all, Craig was eager to assist Sinclair in his work as the great writer and activist they both believed him to be. One of Sinclair's two recent, major biographers reports that Craig "devoted herself to advancing his career" to the immediate detriment of her own professional aspiration.[47] The other biographer notes that Craig was interested, early in their marriage, in becoming active in the women's dress-reform movement but soon concluded, "I knew I couldn't afford any kind of crusade; Upton had a monopoly on this in our family."[48] Briefly tempted to join an important feminist cause that Charlotte Perkins Gilman strongly espoused, Craig decided to subordinate her political commitments to her husband's. In his marriage to Craig, we might conclude that Upton Sinclair continued to appreciate and experience the benefits of bourgeois marriage and "the family as an economic unit"—what his socialist colleague and mentor Gilman had called dismissively "that relic of the patriarchal age."

Sinclair was not alone among socialist-feminists in this experience. Although few socialists had their marriage blow up quite so dramatically as Sinclair's first partnership had, other socialists who married had to confront much the same clash of egalitarian ideals and unwieldy personal circumstances, and many found themselves making similar compromises in resolving the conflict.

Hamlin Garland, for instance, pursued a woman that would seem to fulfill his vision of the ideal partner sketched in *The Rose of Dutcher's Coolly:* talented, independent, potentially a professional able to make her own reputation and earn her own living. In 1898, when he met Zulime Taft, Garland was thirty-eight and wary of the entanglements of marriage. Recently returned from four years of art study in Paris, Taft was the younger sister of the well-known sculptor Lorado Taft and herself skilled both as a painter and sculptor.[49] Already at the stage of courtship, however, it seems clear that Hamlin Garland visualized his intended in straightforwardly bourgeois terms. Garland reported to his younger brother: "She is a great girl. I have discovered that she plays the piano very well and reads music with care. She is a superb housekeeper and *likes* it. She paints landscapes with a modern touch and may be able to illustrate my work."[50] By 1905, after six years of marriage, two children, and the responsibilities of playing hostess for a popular literary figure, Zulime had given up all ambition of making her mark as an artist. As Garland biographer Jean Holloway remarks, "The bold feminism of Garland's blueprint for matrimony had been quietly discarded in the day-to-day responsibilities of marriage," the wife's artistic and professional ambitions being compensated by "the obvious contentment which reigned in the Garland home."[51] Of course, the husband is compensated by the domestic contentment *and* the satisfaction of professional ambitions. The same, asymetrical bargain came to be accepted by the Garlands' children, both daughters. Upon her marriage to a professional singer, one of the daughters quoted her mother on the question of unbalancing career and marriage, thus: "I'd rather be a first-class wife than a fourth-class artist."[52]

W. E. B. Du Bois's relations with his wife and other romantic partners represent a still more disturbing story of contradiction between feminist philosophical commitment and patriarchal behavior. In his essay collection *Darkwater* (1920), Du Bois describes the enfranchisement of women and of blacks as having coequal importance, an argument that echoes Gilman's and Sinclair's calls for parallel labor and women's rights movements. Du Bois argues that to exclude women from democratic participation means to construct a government "deliberately" ignorant of the needs of a majority of its citizens: "Women do need the ballot. They need it to right the balance of a world sadly awry because of its brutal neglect of the rights of women and children. With the best will and knowledge, no man can know women's wants as well as women themselves. To disfranchise women is deliberately to turn from knowledge and grope in ignorance."[53] In a chapter titled "The Damnation of Women," Du Bois cites "Charlotte Gilman" for her analysis of "cheap women," women who outnumber men in a particular city or region and therefore desperately underbid each other in the sexual-economic market (whether through prostitution or its legalized equivalent, marriage).[54] It is clear elsewhere in "Damnation" that Du Bois integrated the argument of Gilman's *Women and Economics* fully into his own feminist views, for the "Damnation" of the title identifies not only prostitution but also the social conventions that bar most women from doing socially remunerative work besides having children: "Only at the sacrifice of intelligence and the chance to do their best work can the majority of modern women bear children. This is the damnation of women." Du Bois takes up the feminist call for leniency toward extramarital sex as well: "The world wants healthy babies and intelligent workers. Today we refuse to allow the combination and force thousands of intelligent workers to go childless at a horrible expenditure of moral force, or we damn them if they break our idiotic conventions."[55]

The formal, Latinate dedication of *Darkwater* is to Du Bois's wife: "Ad Ninam / May 12, 1896." The date specified was their wedding day. In contrast to Sinclair's and Garland's marriages, however, Du Bois's marriage to Nina never pretended to be anything but a Victorian, separate-spheres relation. She had been his student at Wilberforce University, Ohio, but seems to have attracted Du Bois not for any notable intellectual gifts but because she was beautiful and well mannered, and because he had decided he should marry before he turned thirty.[56] Her primary maternal and domestic roles are apparent from the fact that *The Souls of Black Folk* mentions her only as the mother of Du Bois's recently deceased baby boy, mourned so deeply in "Of the Passing of the First-Born." The one sentence devoted to her in the opening, autobiographical essay of *Darkwater* runs as follows: "In 1896, I married—a slip of a girl, beautifully dark-eyed and thorough and good as a German housewife."[57]

But affectionate and dutiful as W. E. B. Du Bois generally was toward Nina Du Bois, he was also well versed in the Victorian double standard. "On the Damnation of Women" was strong in defense of the virtues of black women. When speaking of women in general Du Bois focuses upon the need for independence, as does Gilman and Sinclair. When speaking of black women, his emphasis shifts to the power of mothers and of maiden modesty:

> No other women on earth could have emerged from the hell of force and temptation which once engulfed and still surrounds black women in America with half the modesty and womanliness that they retain. I have always felt like bowing myself before them in all abasement, searching to bring some tribute to these long-suffering victims, these burdened sisters of mine, whom the world, the wise, white world loves to affront and wantonly to insult. I have known the women of many lands and nations,—I have known and seen and lived beside them, but none have I known more sweetly feminine, more unswervingly loyal, more desperately

> earnest, and more instinctively pure in body and in soul than the daughters of my black mothers.[58]

Read biographically, as indeed the first-person singular pronouns invite, there are hints both of the experienced man of the world, an appreciation of women of many types "I have known," and of deep guilt, the urge to "abasement" before black women who are so "loyal," "earnest," "pure," and "victimized." By the time *Darkwater* was published, Du Bois had had at least two long-running extramarital affairs, one with his literary protegé on the *Crisis* staff, Jessie Fauset; a third such affair was rumored already during Du Bois's time as a professor at Atlanta University after the turn of the century, and there were many other casual sexual relationships.[59] Levering Lewis reasonably suggests that Du Bois's strong, publicly stated feminism actually enhanced his appeal to talented and progressive women: "Many liberated women were strongly predisposed to admire a liberated man whose writings espoused not only equal political rights for women but equal pay for equal work in all the professions, as well as the radical right to control their own bodies."[60] But Lewis also notes that Du Bois habitually used his position as *Crisis* editor to leverage physical and sexual intimacy with female members of the office staff as well as women like Fauset with literary aspirations, for whom Du Bois was a key professional gatekeeper.[61] For these women as well as his economically dependent wife and daughter, the sexual escapades of the (publicly) feminist Du Bois are especially problematic because most of his lovers were *not* free and equal partners.

The asymmetry of gender relations in this period is apparent, too, in the marital experience of Charlotte Perkins Gilman. Gilman's marriage presents much the same story as the Sinclair and Garland marriages but from the point of view of the gifted female striving for independence. Gilman's first marriage, to the aspiring artist Walter Stetson, might be seen as exemplifying the ideal of the literary-artistic partnership subsequently articulated in Garland's *Rose of Dutcher's Coolly* and in Garland's own courtship of Zulime Taft. Although premised upon the professional freedom and independence of both partners (if not quite their economic independence), Charlotte's marriage to Walter foundered upon the maternal and domestic responsibilities that Charlotte (at first) willingly accepted even while trying to find a career outside the home. Like Upton Sinclair and Hamlin Garland, Walter might have been intrigued by a partner with artistic inclinations but also looked to Charlotte to play all the conventional bourgeois roles, roles that

Charlotte came to find burdensome. Indeed, they nearly drove her insane, as famously fictionalized in "The Yellow Wall-Paper."

It may be said that Charlotte and Walter's marriage was doomed for essentially the same reason that Meta and Upton's marriage was: in each case, neither partner was willing to have his or her career or well-being compromised by the professional and personal aspirations of the other. There were other parallels as well. Child care was certainly a central issue for both Sinclair and for Gilman. Sinclair won custody of his only son upon his divorce, but then almost immediately sought various child care and boarding-school arrangements that placed his day-to-day supervision in the hands of professionals. Gilman took care of her only daughter during the five years when she was separated from Walter, 1889–94, then resolved the perennial problems of living and working as a single mother by giving up custody of Katharine and sending her back east.

Like the breakup of the Upton-Meta union, the separation and divorce of Charlotte and Walter was covered as a salacious and outrageous scandal by the press. As California divorce laws appeared at first to provide Gilman with insufficient grounds for divorce, in 1892 Walter initiated the proceedings in Rhode Island. In essence, the complaint was that Charlotte's career as an intellectual and political activist had prevented her from fulfilling her wifely responsibilities. Among the grievances listed in his divorce filing, Walter complained that Charlotte had begun working out at the gym and had "developed into a very muscular woman," that she had given up wearing corsets and "waist belts," and that she had become a "crank . . . . loud in her clamor for dress reform and physical reform." Literary endeavors occupied all her days, Walter explained, and Charlotte was consumed with all manner of radical enthusiasms, chiefly but not limited to Nationalism:

> "At that time she was loaded down with the works of Bellamy.
>
> "She took up in course, however, the different reforms, and she said she expected to lend her aid to all the reform movements that were to be started in the future.
>
> "On various occasions Mrs. Stetson would indulge in lectures on nationalism and she talked of Bellamy theories from daylight till the shadows of night fell over the earth."[62]

Such vivid prose, in a court document no less, made excellent copy just quoted verbatim, as newspapers in New York, San Francisco, Cincinnati, and Minneapolis did extensively.[63]

Repeatedly, press coverage revealed biases against women attempting to have both career and family, and attributed the trouble in the Stetson marriage to radical political influences. The *Los Angeles Times* saw Gilman as a crass careerist, speculating that her aims were actually being furthered by the ongoing divorce case: she would "soon be properly equipped, so far as advertising is concerned, to take the lecture platform and tell people how the universe should be run and human nature changed to conform with our nineteenth century civilization, from her standpoint."[64] The *San Francisco Examiner* struck a more earnest but no less critical pose: "There are not many women, fortunately for humanity, who agree with Mrs. Stetson that any 'work,' literary, philanthropic or political, is higher than that of being a good wife and mother."[65] A notable piece in the *Boston Herald* considered whether Nationalism was behind the divorce, as Walter's divorce papers appear to allege. Amid some effort by the Boston Nationalists interviewed to distance their proposals from anything touching upon the sanctity of marriage, there comes the admission of the president of the First Nationalist Club that "if Nationalism were to become an accomplished fact, and woman was economically the equal of man, man would approach a woman on the subject of marriage differently from the way he does at present . . . . [T]he equality of woman, in an economic sense, would render her wholly unlikely to marry for the sake of support."[66] This was, in fact, a sound statement of Nationalism, and Gilman's attitude toward marriage represented a reasonable effort to live out that principle within the messy, antiegalitarian world. In the view of the public, however, Gilman was an unnatural mother, an unfaithful wife, even perhaps a defective woman.

After all the derisive press coverage, it must have come as a bitter pill to Gilman that the charges against her, so compelling in the court of public opinion, were not legally sufficient. For Charlotte and Walter as for Meta and Upton, the first divorce suit was denied. It was deeply ironic, given Gilman's championing of women's economic independence, that the charge that ultimately proved successful before the California courts in 1894 was Walter's "failure to provide."[67] Of course it was true that Walter had failed to provide for his wife and daughter. But as we have already seen in some detail, it was also the case that late nineteenth-century society scarcely provided sufficient opportunity for bourgeois women to support themselves. In Gilman's story, indeed, it becomes clear that women's lack of independence, the shortage of career opportunities sufficient for women's self-support, had its effect upon same-sex as well as opposite-sex partnerships. Although the narrative of bourgeois ideology mainly concerns heterosexual romantic relations, it also has implications for Gilman's brief, intense relationship with Adeline Knapp in the mid-1890s.

Knapp, referred to as "Delle" and sometimes "Delight" in Gilman's diaries, as "Dora" in her autobiography, represented to Gilman an alternative possibility for romantic and economic partnership: "woman supporting woman," was Gilman's phrase.[68] All of the details that can be gleaned suggest that Gilman saw the relationship as a potential Boston Marriage, with all the enigma that the term implies. The case is made effectively by Gilman's first major biographer, Mary Hill, who recounts Charlotte's romantic and exclusive attachment to Adeline evinced in Gilman's diary entries dating from the spring of 1891: for example, "Miss Knapp near supper time. We are very happy together"; "My girl comes"; and "Take a moonlight ride, first with [daughter] Kate, then only with each other." As Gilman acknowledged many years later in her autobiography, Knapp was a "friend with whom I had sincerely hoped to live continually." When she later discussed potential marriage with George Houghton Gilman, she told him candidly that certain letters she had written to Delle might surface that he could find discomfiting. The letters to Adeline, Charlotte admitted, revealed "most fully the really passionate love I had for her. I loved her, trusted her, wrote her as freely as I write you." And later she put Houghton definitely on notice about the nature of the correspondence: "I told you that I loved her that way. You ought to know that there is the possibility of such letters being dragged out some day."[69]

As it happens, neither Gilman's letters to Knapp nor Knapp's to Gilman are extant, so there is minimal immediate documentation of the relationship. The limited evidence of the *Diaries* admits of the interpretation that Gilman and Knapp were perfectly compatible romantically but otherwise not well matched for a long-term partnership. We can say with some definiteness from this source that money and professional issues were the key points of tension. In short, the same issues of professional rivalry upon which the relationship of Walter Stetson, struggling artist, and Charlotte Perkins Stetson, aspiring social reformer, foundered also seem to have been quite enough to undermine the relationship of Charlotte and the professionally ambitious Adeline Knapp. In the *Living*, Gilman admits that she was Knapp's debtor in literal terms of cash exchanged: "She certainly did love me, at first anyway, and had been most generously kind with money." Clearly wishing to balance the scales, Gilman recalled that her contribution to the partnership was a matter of professional connections and intellectual labor. It was an exchange in which Gilman regarded herself as the exploited party: "My return was mainly in service, not in making a home for her, but in furnishing material for her work. She was a clever writer, and later I learned that she was one of those literary vampires who fasten themselves on one author or another with ardent devotion, and for the time being write like them."[70] Rancor still burned in Gilman some thirty years after the fact, although we may reasonably surmise that Knapp felt herself the loser in the exchange, for she had contributed money to the household whereas Gilman had offered the less tangible benefit of her literary eminence—perhaps an asset slightly inflated by Gilman in retrospect.

In any case, while Mary Hill seems inclined to idealize the benefits of "woman supporting woman," the details of the Gilman-Knapp partnership so far as we can discern them reveal another facet of their situation. Professional jealousy in a two-writer household was not necessarily any less fierce than in Gilman's first marriage pitting artist against writer-activist. The difficulty was certainly compounded by the fact that *both* members of the household were women competing in professional marketplaces unfriendly to career women. Even had there been domestic concord, there was plenty of stress for each woman simply in seeking to make a living in a male-dominated society.

It was difficult enough making a living on her own. When soon after her divorce Gilman sent her daughter east to live with her father and his new wife, Gilman's living expenses were reduced to self-support only. Over the next five years, life on the road as an itinerant speaker appears to have lessened the economic strain considerably, as in addition to her speaking fees (often meager enough) her room and board were usually provided by her hosts. Here Gilman's autobiography kicks into Horatio Alger, up-by-the-bootstraps mode, as she speaks of how she "paid all those San Francisco debts sooner or later. I remember how astonished the Oakland land-lady was when I turned up, some years after. She opened the door, and stood, staring blankly, as I calmly remarked, 'I've come to pay the rent.'"[71] Her major biographer, Margaret Lane, is inclined to follow suit, explaining that between 1898 and 1900 during her engagement to George Houghton Gilman (he went by "Houghton") Charlotte expected to establish "a steady income from writing and lecturing." In 1899 Charlotte made "elaborate plans about her income to be certain that she would not be financially dependent on Houghton," Lane explains, the issue being *not* financial security, for Houghton earned a steady and adequate income as a lawyer, but rather "Charlotte's need for economic independence."[72] In spite of the hardships thrown up by capitalism, Charlotte Gilman wished to live out, with Houghton, the socialist dream of a free and equal partnership founded upon professional and economic independence. And Lane reports Charlotte's success by the beginning of 1900 and therefore her readiness to marry, citing her first letter of the year to Houghton wherein she reports debts of $2,030 but an expectation of a $4,000 income that year.[73] But planning to pay debts and actually paying them are distinct acts, and Lane sidesteps Gilman's history of scheming but then failing to clear debts and of overestimating her projected earnings. In December 1899, just before the more hopeful projections cited by Lane, with royalties from *Women and Economics* coming in and her marriage to Houghton just a few months away, she writes in her final diary of the year: "Get well—get well—get well. And do good work! Pay all debts if possible."[74] By the time Gilman began publishing *The Forerunner* in 1909—at the very latest—she had given up all pretense of supporting herself.[75] Charlotte Perkins Gilman's intellectual and personal accomplishments in her lifetime were many, but financial independence was not one of them. Freedom from economic want she owed to her marriage to Houghton Gilman.

We may regard Gilman's intellectual work as benefiting considerably—in quantity, at least—by the economic and emotional support that the marriage to Houghton provided.[76] The first years of her marriage saw a flurry of book publication: In 1900 *Concerning Children* appeared; in 1903, *The Home: Its Work and Influence;* and in 1904, *Human Work.* Still more, Gilman's most ambitious venture in writing and publishing, her periodical entitled *The Forerunner,* would have been unthinkable without the unstinting support of Houghton. The journal ran from 1909 through 1916 and was written and edited entirely by Gilman, permitting her to publish virtually every word she wrote in these years without troubling over hostile editors, fickle readers, or author's fees. In the *Forerunner* she published poetry, essays, short stories, longer serialized nonfiction studies, and serialized novels (typically, one longer study and one novel running concurrently). Income raised by reader subscriptions (no commercial advertisements were solicited or accepted) never matched the costs of printing. And so *The Forerunner,* which yielded among other works the important utopian novels *Moving the Mountain, Herland,* and *With Her in Ourland,* serves as the ultimate reminder of Gilman's financial insolvency and the dependency of Gilman's intellectual work upon her husband's financial wherewithal. The fact that she was the beneficiary of an egalitarian-minded husband does not change the fact of her being an economic dependent—precisely the sexual-economic role she had argued against in her writing and sought so diligently to avoid in her professional and personal life.

What we find, then, in the relationship of Charlotte Perkins Gilman and George Houghton Gilman is a pattern that does as much to confirm the gender asymmetries we have observed as to challenge them. To be sure, Charlotte and Houghton were able to achieve something that eluded Upton and Meta, Hamlin and Zulime, and Will and Nina: a happy, companionable marriage in which both partners were able to engage full-time in their chosen careers. Their marriage ended with the death of Houghton in 1934, just about a month shy of their thirty-fourth anniversary; Charlotte followed in death little more than a year later. Yet Houghton and Charlotte lived within an economic relation in which—as in the other marriages—the male partner was the principal breadwinner, the female economically dependent.

There is much that can be gleaned, finally, from these various efforts to establish romantic (primarily heterosexual) partnerships that followed the socialist ideal—these various failed attempts to challenge "the family as an economic unit" with the patriarchal male at the head. To begin with, we may say that the failure of the various marriages here surveyed testifies powerfully to the ways that existence, after all, precedes essence: that the institutional structures and the habits of thought established under patriarchal capitalism, or capitalist patriarchy, are so deeply imbedded as to thwart even the best-faith efforts to circumvent them. On this count, the earnest but futile efforts of Upton Sinclair to live according to the law of "free love" and open marriage, as well as the spectacular contradiction between W. E. B. Du Bois's words and his actions, provide the most compelling evidence. All of these writers spoke of the need for capitalist structures of economic inequality to be dismantled in order for women and men to live truly in equality with one another, in their romantic partnerships as in their other social relationships. All of them—quite unconsciously—demonstrated this need through the asymmetries of their relationships with their lovers and spouses. That Du Bois may have been burdened with guilt when he wrote of "The Damnation of Women" would testify all the more strongly to the immediate relevance of the prescription he there offered: "The present mincing horror at free womanhood must pass if we are ever to be rid of the bestiality of free manhood; not by guarding the weak in weakness do we gain strength, but by making weakness free and strong."[77] If it was the "bestiality" of his own "free manhood" that he was unconsciously thinking of, then all the more compelling is the charge for wider social intervention to "make" women "free and strong." To the individualistic moralist who would say, "Physician, heal thyself," Dr. Du Bois testifies by both word and action that—under modern conditions, at least—the doctor cannot administer anesthesia to himself, cannot perform the operation upon him- or herself, cannot develop all the antibiotics that might ensure survival and speed recovery.

The opening premise of *Women and Economics,* and for that matter a key tenet of socialism more generally, held that women must be economically independent in order to be free and equal. But whereas Nationalism, Fabianism, and many strains of Marxism saw the independence of women either as a matter merely of legislation or the inevitable and happy result of the abolition of the profit system, Gilman envisaged bourgeois domestic ideologies as fatally undermining any such legislative or revolutionary transformation. The implications of this insight were profound among socialists and other progressives. Many sought to establish their own relationships with romantic partners on new terms of freedom and equality, among them Hamlin Garland, Upton Sinclair, and Charlotte Perkins Gilman herself. The results were not encouraging: certainly not in personal terms; probably not in political ones, either. To varying degrees, Garland, Sinclair, and even Gilman ultimately rejected partnerships founded upon relations of fairly symmetrical equality, choosing instead relationships that were asymmetrical, less economically equal, and seemingly all the more companionable, for that. Still more troubling was the course chosen by W. E. B. Du Bois, in which freedom in romantic relationships was apparently abetted by Du Bois's "progressive" attitude toward gender equality but, in fact, compounding the inequalities of power in his intimate relationships.

In any case, the frequency with which other socialists sought, but failed to live out, the kind of free, equal partnerships that Gilman called for may have brought into doubt the current feasability of such partnerships. If such failures and doubts did not erode the ultimate desirability and necessity of gender equality, they may have contributed to its becoming less central to socialist agitation; it may have come to seem a less daunting proposition to reconstitute the economy of the United States on terms of equality than to reinvent personal relationships across gender lines on those terms. Ironically, then, one of the legacies of Charlotte Perkins Gilman's subtle analysis of the family as an economic unit and of its attendant bourgeois ideologies may have been to erode the centrality of women's liberation as a driving issue within American socialism. A change in relations so revolutionary just seemed too difficult.

We must nevertheless remind ourselves that this erosion was relative; socialism remained progressive, not reactionary or misogynist, in its attitude toward gender equality. Moreover, the testimony provided by the partnerships we have here explored indicates the thoroughly dialogic interconnections between intimately personal and broadly political transformation, meaning that a transference of the struggle from intimately personal relations to labor, legislative, and legal arenas may represent an incomplete strategy, but not necessarily a tactically backward one. That Upton and Meta, Upton and Craig, Hamlin and Zulime, Charlotte and Adeline, and Charlotte and Houghton were not able to live out their egalitarian ideals, in spite of sometimes heroic efforts to do so, suggests after all the degree to which social and economic contingencies do place powerful limitations upon interpersonal relationships. A political response, therefore, to address these limitations by seeking macro changes in the economic and social order represents a reasonable response. So, in its own way, was Gilman's hopeful suggestion that the striving of women of all classes would lead eventually to economic parity with men and, hence, the foundation for social equality. Meanwhile, Gilman's analysis of bourgeois domesticity and the feminist-socialist commitment to transform personal relationships would remind socialists—at least those that continued to heed—that changes in economic relations, though necessary, were not necessarily sufficient conditions for the establishment of true human equality. Much work remained to be done, and on many levels.

CHAPTER FOUR

WITHIN THE VEIL: W. E. B. DU BOIS AND THE SECOND INTERNATIONALE, 1909–1919

Diverse and multiple as American socialism was during the period of the Second Internationale, racial diversity, and specifically African American diversity, was much less readily accounted for. In the *Jungle's* descriptions of the packinghouse strike of 1904 and the scabs who were used to break it, Sinclair's narrative focalized through his protagonist Jurgis Rudkus—himself working as a strikebreaker—plays upon the gamut of racist stereotypes of blacks as lazy, violent, and sex-crazed. While descriptions of the strike do make visible the roles of the hiring agents and the big capitalists who prey upon an underutilized black labor force, portrayals of black laborers code them as biologically and culturally subhuman: "The ancestors of these black people had been savages in Africa, and since then they had been chattel slaves, or had been held down by a community ruled by the traditions of slavery. Now for the first time they were free—free to gratify every passion, free to wreck themselves."[1] Sinclair's attitudes were not exceptional among socialists, either. Charlotte Perkins Gilman's biographers have documented their subject's racial and ethnic prejudices, which encompassed "blacks, Jews, and indeed most recent immigrant groups."[2] In a 1908 article published in the discipline-leading *American Journal of Sociology*, "A Suggestion on the Negro Problem," Gilman's opening statement of the problem is imbued with racist assumptions, as she states the problem of race as involving "the unavoidable presence of a large body of aliens, of a race widely dissimilar and in many respects inferior, whose present status is to us a social injury."[3] Although Gilman's theorization of parallel labor and women's movements provides a scheme onto which a semiautonomous, complementary movement for racial equality might readily be grafted, Gilman herself was not the one to recognize this possibility. Even socialists recognized for their lack of personal prejudice and racial egalitarianism were notable only for their relatively better stance on racial questions. Eugene Debs once announced that, compared to white workers, black workers were "not one whit worse off" and therefore concluded, "We have nothing special to offer the Negro, and we cannot make separate appeals to all the races."[4]

Racism has become part of the standard account of Second International socialism, often mobilized in the service of much more favorable estimates of the race policies of the Soviet-led Comintern. It explains, in part, why W. E. B. Du Bois's membership in the Socialist Party was so short lived. Du Bois joined the party in 1911 but left before the end of 1912, when he endorsed Woodrow Wilson for president over the Republican nominee Taft, the Progressive / Bull Moose candidate Roosevelt, and the Socialist standard-bearer Debs. Yet even as Du Bois shied away from Debs and severed his official ties with the Socialist Party, he nevertheless reserved his highest praise for Debs: "We can only say this frankly: if it lay in our power to make him President of the United States we would do so, for of the four men mentioned he alone, by word and deed, stands squarely on a platform of human rights regardless of race or class."[5] Du Bois's temporizing attitude toward socialism of the Second Internationale—admiring and affirming its ideals even while holding himself at arm's length from its institutions—was based upon factors more complex than a merely passing appreciation of socialist ideals or the influence of socialist colleagues upon the NAACP board, both of which have been highlighted by critics who have tended to dismiss Du Bois's socialism of the first two decades of the century.

A close reading of Du Bois's publications and pronouncements during this period reveals that Du Bois's engagement with socialist theory and praxis was substantial. Two trends that emerge during these decades were to characterize his work throughout the rest of his life. First, both before and after he was a party member, he articulated a philosophy that aligned closely with mainstream socialist ideology during the Second Internationale—neither on the far left of the movement nor, as some commentators have tried to suggest, on the far right wing. Second, he envisaged his role at the National Association for the Advancement of Colored People in a fashion later characterized during the Comintern as "burrowing from within," advocating for socialism inside an organization and constituency that he judged open to its values even while—much like the Nationalists or Populists in the 1890s—steering clear of the socialist label. Adopting one of Du Bois's signature metaphors, that of African Americans living "within the veil" of racism, we may say that Du Bois and other African Americans were not free of the veil in their relations with white socialists during the Second International (or under the Comintern, for that matter). But that veil did not prevent Du Bois and others from utilizing the analytical categories of socialism, particularly when Du Bois concluded that some of these categories aligned with black folk culture and African American practice rather than with imported European philosophies. Socialism provided categories that jibed with the practices and ideals of black American communities, even as those communities provided a potential model for socialist praxis—if only white socialists would take the chance to observe it.

FELLOW TRAVELER DU BOIS

> "Watch the Socialists. We may not follow them and agree with them in all things. I certainly do not. But in trend and ideal they are the salt of this present earth."

By dating Du Bois's association with socialism from the time he joined the NAACP and, simultaneously, linking his short-lived membership in the Socialist Party with the influence of socialists on the NAACP board, scholars of Du Bois have effectively downplayed Du Bois's early socialist commitments. In chapter 2, I have already disputed the argument that the class status of the socialists on the NAACP board predicates their subscribing to a conservative version of socialism. But this hardly settles the question of the particular variety of socialism that Du Bois subscribed to. Along these lines, Du Bois scholar Adolph Reed argues that the intellectual content of *socialism* at the time of the NAACP's founding was so "mercurial" as to demand a clear formulation of which "variety" of socialism Du Bois subscribed to.[6] Reed, however, dodges his own altogether reasonable question. Having just asserted the importance of identifying Du Bois's brand of socialist politics, he suggests that the precise variety of Du Bois's socialism was less important than his participation in an "overarching" American tradition of "collectivism."[7] Such a retreat might be defensible if it was, in fact, impossible to determine which variety of socialism Du Bois subscribed to. But it *is* possible to identify Du Bois's early links to socialism and to characterize his early socialist philosophy, because Du Bois both wrote extensively about socialism and used specifically socialist categories of critical analysis throughout his intellectual work.

These writings show not only that his philosophy was not particularly conservative but that it dates from the first decade of the twentieth century, before the NAACP was formed. There is some truth to the idea that Du Bois was encouraged in his socialism by members of the NAACP board who were Socialist Party members. Mary White Ovington, who was to become Du Bois's closest ally on the board, was especially assertive in her advocacy, which began in correspondence preceding the formation of the NAACP by five years.[8] By 1908 Ovington was urging Du Bois, practically chiding him, to join the Socialist Party: "Go on with your constructive work, with the effort to win the rights of manhood for every Negro in the country. And work with those who are fighting the same fight. You ought all to be done with bickering with Republicans or Democrats. There is a working man's party in the country. How can the Negro belong to any other?"[9]

Yet in 1904 as well as in 1908, unbeknownst to Ovington, Du Bois's thinking was already developing along the very lines suggested by her. At a convention of the American Missionary Association in Des Moines, Iowa, preceding Ovington's 1904 correspondence, Du Bois had declared racial tensions to be "but the sign of growing class privilege and caste distinction in America, and not, as some fondly imagine, the cause of it."[10] Sounded out by the Socialist I. M. Rubinow about whether his Iowa speech meant that he "considered the Negro question a part of the general social problem of distribution of wealth," about whether he concurred with Rubinow's view "as to the identity in the final analysis of the race problem with the whole social or labor problem,"[11] Du Bois averred, "I would scarcely describe myself as a socialist[;] still I have much sympathy with the movement & I have many socialistic beliefs." Du Bois's further explanation shows his analysis already inflected by socialistic reasoning: "I believe the Negro problem is partly the American Caste problem & that caste is arising because of unjust & dangerous economic conditions."[12] In 1908, but prior to Ovington's letter of that year, Du Bois had rebuffed another correspondent who touted the Prohibition Party, explaining that there was another third party that he preferred: "I think local option is a very good thing, but State Prohibition a very bad thing. . . . There is a third party, however, that I am very much inclined to support and that is the Socialist."[13]

In public pronouncements as well as in his private correspondence from the first decade of the century, it is already clear that Du Bois's vision of political economy was socialist. Two 1907 articles in the *Horizon,* the journal associated with the Niagara movement, stake out Du Bois's positions on debates *within* the socialist movement. In "Socialist of the Path," Du Bois's qualification that he did not believe in "complete socialization of the means of production—the entire abolition of private property in capital" described, in fact, the majority position within the Socialist Party. Only extreme communists held that all property should be held in common, and many socialists found small, owner-operated enterprises consistent with socialist reorganization. On two fundamental principles, meanwhile, Du Bois was absolutely in accord with practically all socialists: in his judgment that social progress would inexorably compel the socialization of industry, "greater ownership of the public wealth for the public good than is now the case"; and in his conviction that all the major industries ought to be collectively owned and managed: "Most of the human business called private is no more private than God's blue sky."[14] In the second *Horizon* editorial, "Negro and Socialism," Du Bois both reiterated his accord with overarching socialist ideals and postulated the shared interests of working-class blacks and whites in spite of their concealment by capitalist ideology:

> We have been made tools of oppression against the workingman's cause—the puppets and playthings of the idle rich. Fools! We must awake! Not in a renaissance among ourselves of the evils of Get and Grab—not in private hoarding, squeezing and cheating, lies our salvation, but rather in that larger ideal of human brotherhood, equality of opportunity and work not for wealth but for Weal—here lies our shining goal. This goal the Socialists with all their extravagance and occasional foolishness have more stoutly followed than any other class and thus far we must follow them. Our natural friends are not the rich but the poor, not the great but the masses, not the employers but the employees. Our good is not wealth, power, oppression and snobbishness, but helpfulness, efficiency, service and self-respect. Watch the Socialists. We may not follow them and agree with them in all things. I certainly do not. But in trend and ideal they are the salt of this present earth.[15]

While reserving judgment on the Socialist Party and the actions of particular Socialists, Du Bois's proclaimed philosophy is socialist through and through. Indeed, his analysis of black workers as "tools of oppression against the workingman's cause" concurs with Sinclair's representation of stockyard owners importing black workers as scabs.

Two other major publications whose composition preceded Du Bois's tenure with the NAACP shed further light upon his socialist philosophy in the first decade of the century. Although *John Brown* appeared in 1909 and *The Quest of the Silver Fleece* was published in 1911, a year after the founding of the NAACP, the later-published novel was actually begun before the biography, in the year following the appearance of *The Souls of Black Folk.* The evidence is clear that both *Quest* and *John Brown* were largely complete before Du Bois came north to become the NAACP's director of research and publication, and that they therefore reveal Du Bois's thinking before he came into frequent personal contact with Ovington, Walling, or other socialist board members. The books limn the two quite different conceptions of the path into socialism we have seen in tension with one another in the work of Sinclair and down through nineteenth-century socialist traditions: one path predicating a gradual, parliamentary movement into social democracy, another foreseeing a violent and precipitous revolution.

In *Quest of the Silver Fleece,* a multiplot novel set in both the cotton country of Alabama and the black bourgeois society of Washington, DC, Du Bois's primary vehicle for socialist ideas is his unlettered young black heroine, Zora. In an early encounter with Mary Taylor, a white teacher recently arrived from the North to serve at an all-black school founded during Reconstruction, Zora's well-reasoned unruliness offers a parable about alternative social values that might be cultivated outside capitalism. Confronted by Miss Taylor because one of her brooches has gone missing, Zora admits she has taken the jewelry and instigates the following dialogue on property ownership and theft:

> Still Zora appeared to be unimpressed with the heinousness of her fault.
>
> "Did you make that pin?" she asked.
>
> "No, but it is mine."
>
> "Why is it yours?"
>
> "Because it was given to me."
>
> "But you don't need it; you've got four other prettier ones—I counted."
>
> "That makes no difference."
>
> "Yes it does—folks ain't got no right to things they don't need."
>
> "That makes no difference, Zora, and you know it. The pin is mine. You stole it. If you had wanted a pin and asked me I might have given you—"
>
> The girl blazed.
>
> "I don't want your old gifts," she almost hissed. "You don't own what you don't need and can't use."[16]

Mary Taylor, representing the conventional view of property, owns her surplus of pins by virtue of belonging to a social class in which pretty adornments can be afforded with minimal regard for their cost or usefulness. In counterpoint, Zora introduces three key revaluations of property promulgated by socialism: products of human culture must be socially useful; they are to be distributed according to need; and if products are "owned" by anyone, they belong to those who actually make them (and then only for the sake of contributing to society those products that are useful and needed).[17] Soon after, the novel even develops the notion of alienated versus unalienated labor. Zora rejects Mary Taylor's suggestion of domestic service as an attractive wage-earning job, finding the idea of "helping" someone she "loves" incompatible with receiving a wage for it.[18] In contrast, her work with Bles Alwyn, the lover with whom she reclaims swamp land on which they raise a glorious crop of cotton, is literally and figuratively a labor of love.

Through the romance and the shared work of Bles and Zora, Du Bois also develops a vision of cooperative economics within black agricultural communities. This kind of community evokes the communal experiments of white socialists in the nineteenth century, although certainly Du Bois also has in mind the example of blacks living and surviving in cooperative micro-economies lodged within the predominant capitalist system (during slavery, under the peonage system, or at other times). Significantly, Zora leads the way—not the more cultivated Bles Alwyn, a kind of poster boy of the Talented Tenth, nor the white schoolmistress Miss Sarah Smith, Zora's mentor. Advised by Smith to bank a large sum of money received from a northern philanthropist, Zora asserts the need for a black community as independent as possible from the dominant economy: "'We pay off the mortgage, we get enough to run the school as it has been run. Then what? There will still be slavery and oppression all around us. The children will be kept in the cotton fields; the men will be cheated, and the women—' Zora paused and her eyes grew hard." To address the problem fundamentally, to root out the evil, there must be a new economic start: "We must have land—our own farm and our own tenants—to be the beginning of a free community."[19]

Zora insists that the cooperative colony that she has founded is only the beginning of a movement that must finally encompass white as well as black working people to be fully successful and secure: "Think of the servile black folk," Zora exclaims, "the half awakened restless whites, the fat land waiting for the harvest, the masses panting to know—why, the battle is scarcely even begun."[20] Cooperative colonies are to serve as a temporary sanctuary for exploited blacks, a stepping stone to the liberation of all the exploited masses, though the union of black and white proletarians can be envisaged only at a point in time beyond the scope of the novel. Yet according to the heroine

Zora (and presumably for author Du Bois), alliance within the working class is guaranteed in the long run by economic forces. Blacks can hasten its arrival by focusing upon their own group development, in order to "bring to that alliance as much independent economic strength as possible."[21] *Quest of the Silver Fleece* thus offers an embryonic plan for implementing socialism in the United States, and particularly a plan for black communities to exercise agency rather than merely wait for a revolution led by white labor.

On the whole, the socialist scheme laid out by Du Bois in *Quest* is nonviolent and gradualist. Zora buys the land for her cooperative community from the local white landowners. She successfully defends the community's ownership of the land in the existing courts. She and Bles recruit members of the community from the blacks in the neighborhood through rhetorical suasion, not compulsion. There is just one scene where Du Bois does offer a case for a limited kind of revolutionary violence—in defense of the integrity of the community when it is threatened by a rioting white mob. Yet because the plot is resolved by a virtual deus ex machina, as the white crowd proves almost comically inept when confronted by armed and determined black defenders, Du Bois sidesteps the question of how and when the use of force might be not only justified but effective. That was precisely the question Du Bois was compelled to take up when he turned to the biography of John Brown, his other major writing project in the years immediately preceding his tenure at the *The Crisis*.

For any American wanting to consider the use of violence to advance a social, political, and moral agenda, John Brown was the perfect subject. If any historical figure offers a case for illegal, even antigovernment, political violence in the United States, John Brown does. Who could condemn the motivation and the methods of John Brown after the Civil War had entered the national mythology, and the fight to emancipate the slaves had become the central moral justification for the national bloodbath? In 1904, the potency of the John Brown precedent had also been grasped by the neophyte socialist Upton Sinclair, who presented Brown as a heroic martyr in his Civil War novel, *Manassas*.[22] In spite of Sinclair's racial misunderstandings and prejudices, his budding socialism provided a stern rejoinder to the southern revisionists who argued that the war was about conflicting "ways of life," in which the genteel Cavalier culture of the South was the tragic loser. To a point, Sinclair agreed with the revisionists: the war *was* over competing ways of life. But the Southern cause consisted not of preserving a gracious agrarianism but of extending an economic system based on human enslavement westward and even, by imperial annexation, southward into Mexico. Therefore, in the famous conference between Brown and Frederick Douglass prior to Harper's Ferry, Sinclair puts into Brown's mouth an emphatic case in favor of armed insurrection, addressed to a hesitant Douglass: "You shrink from bloodshed—consider the blood of your brothers in Slavery! How many lives could be balanced against the continuance for one more year of this system, which makes every seventh woman of a whole race a harlot?"[23]

Du Bois's *John Brown* approaches the violence of Brown with more equivocation. Brown's actions in "bloody Kansas," Du Bois acknowledges, were but the active expression of abolitionism, the deed that fit the words of a rhetorician like William Lloyd Garrison: "He was the sword on which struggling Kansas and its leaders could depend, the untarnished doer of its darker deeds."[24] Early in his biography, Du Bois announces a preference for nonviolence when he asserts that Brown's efforts to foment an uprising were less efficacious than his martyrdom and his eloquence upon the scaffold. In the closing chapter, though, Du Bois revisits the question of political violence and reaches somewhat different conclusions. In this, the chapter freest in its interpretation of Brown, Du Bois joins (other) socialists in their portrayal of Brown as an incipient social democrat. Du Bois intuits "John Brown's own inchoate but growing belief in a more just and a more equal distribution of property." Even as such speculations have a limited historical basis, they illuminate Du Bois's own thinking upon social justice and the means of its achievement at this stage in his career. The socioeconomic egalitarianism that Du Bois imputes serves as a strong justification for revolutionary violence, for it underlies Brown's conclusion not only "that all men are created free and equal" but also "that the cost of liberty is less than the price of repression." As if to make perfectly clear that "the cost of liberty" might include bloodshed, Du Bois repeats the phrase later in the concluding chapter with a significant addition: "This then, is the truth: the cost of liberty is less than the price of repression, even though that cost be blood."[25]

Much as with Sinclair's comparative estimate of "bloodshed" versus "one more year of this system," Du Bois weighs the cost of bloody revolution against that of ongoing social inequality and finds that the latter may well be more grievous than the former. As in Sinclair's correspondence with Rockefeller, too, Du Bois's argument in *John Brown* notes that the choice of violent confrontation is often instigated by those in power, not those lacking it. Applying this observation to the color line, Du Bois asserts: "The present attempt to force all whites above all darker peoples is a sure method of human degeneration. The cost of liberty is thus a decreasing cost, while the cost of repression ever tends to increase to the danger point of war and revolution."

He does not see the spiral into violence as anything but regressive: "Revolution is not a test of capacity; it is always a loss and lowering of ideals."[26] Yet insofar as the effort to "force all whites above all darker peoples" is unmistakably the quest of white imperialists and capitalists, the world's ownership class, the question of violence is seen—regretfully—as their choice and not the choice of the downtrodden of the earth. For them and their representatives, whether they be John Brown at Harper's Ferry, Nat Turner and other antislavery insurrectionists, or contemporary proletarians, revolutionary violence may yet be the inevitable outcome to their social and economic environment.

As with Sinclair, Du Bois's contemplation of political violence placed him closer to the radical wing of the socialist movement than to the conservative wing. When Du Bois began his work at the NAACP and joined the Socialist Party in 1911, only one of his colleagues had offered anything comparable to his reflection on violent revolution occasioned by the John Brown biography. William English Walling had been working as a journalist in Russia during the failed revolution of 1905, and recognized that against the czarist repression violent revolution might be the only path to egalitarian transformation. But Du Bois's lack of congruence with the other, more conservative socialists on the NAACP board should hardly be surprising, given the evidence in *Quest of the Silver Fleece* and *John Brown* and other writings that Du Bois had developed his own socialist philosophy largely independently of them, prior to his assuming his positions as NAACP director of research and *Crisis* editor. Indeed, based upon the fact that *Quest of the Silver Fleece* was drafted by 1905,[27] we might reasonably conclude that Du Bois became a socialist well before 1911 when he joined the Socialist Party. A more likely year would be 1904 or 1905, placing his adoption of socialist convictions within a year or two of Upton Sinclair's more heavily and dramatically documented conversion to the cause.

SOCIAL DEMOCRACY AND DISENFRANCHISEMENT

> "I want to make votes tell."

Doubtless, once Du Bois came north and took up his posts with the NAACP, the new *Crisis* editor would have felt encouraged to join the Socialist Party given the number of NAACP officers who were also members of the party. At least six members of the founding committee of the NAACP were also active members of the Socialist Party of America. In addition to John Haynes

Holmes, Mary White Ovington, Charles Edward Russell, and William English Walling, the famous settlement house worker Jane Addams and the women's temperance leader Florence Kelley were also members. But the diversity of socialist attitudes among these NAACP leaders, noted earlier, ensured that they would not offer any particularly clear guide to integrating the movements for racial equality and for the abolishment of the class system. Given that the vagaries of race analysis by other Socialist Party members offered little guidance, either, it was largely up to Du Bois to hammer out the practical relationship between them, as he did, practically blow by blow, in his writing and editing in *The Crisis*. The process is most explicit in the first few years of his tenure, which correspond with his period of Socialist Party membership, but it continued throughout the years up to 1920.

Soon after joining the Socialist Party, Du Bois showed his recognition that the party was not necessarily the most enlightened radical group upon racial issues. In 1912 *The Crisis* reported positively upon the interracial organization of the Industrial Workers of the World—by then expelled from the party. In Texas, Louisiana, Arkansas, and Florida the IWW-affiliated Brotherhood of Timber Workers had organized "colored and white timber workers . . . in mixed locals, and this despite the fact that in some of the Southern States the laws prohibit public gatherings of black and white."[28] In contrast, in 1913 *The Crisis* noted that a leading labor organizer, though a regular member of the Socialist Party, was just as racist as representatives of the mainstream labor organizations: "Tom Hale, formerly business agent of Union No. 1, and a Socialist, declares that he will throw his vote away on the Democratic candidate rather than vote for a man who would not consent to employ white labor exclusively."[29]

From these items, it would appear that the problem with the Socialist Party was not that it was too radical for Du Bois, but that it was not radical enough—or at least maddeningly inconsistent—on questions of racial inequality. Here the immediate occasion of Du Bois's leaving the party, his 1912 endorsement of Woodrow Wilson for president instead of Eugene V. Debs, turns out to be a red herring—appearing, as it does, to repudiate socialist principle or at least to demonstrate Du Bois's affiliation with the most moderate of socialist creeds. All along, Du Bois asserted the rightness of socialist principles on racial as well as on class questions. In an October 1911 analysis of the women's suffrage, prohibition, and socialist movements, Du Bois declared, "Of all recent forward movements the Socialists have rung truest on the race question in their theoretical statements." Problems arose not in statements of principle but in the day-to-day organizing activities of the party. Less than a year into his membership in the party, Du Bois remarks critically that at theoretical statements "they have usually stopped. 'Why do not Negroes join the Socialists?' they ask. They do not ask such silly questions of white folks: They go and see why they do not join. They teach, agitate and proselyte; while among ten million Negro Americans they have scarcely a single worker and are afraid to encourage such workers."[30]

Much the same critique is offered by Du Bois in an article appearing in the 1913 *New Review*, a journal edited by William English Walling, probably the most radical of his socialist comrades on the NAACP board.[31] The article is notable both because it amounts to an apologia for Du Bois's departure from the party, and because it shows no departure at all from the socialist philosophy that had led Du Bois initially to join it. Proclaiming strict labor egalitarianism as a principle supposedly shared by socialists (himself included), Du Bois points out the inability of many in the Socialist Party to act according to it because of their underlying favoritism toward the interests of white workers over black. As a rubric to gauge socialists' success or failure to practice egalitarianism, Du Bois proposes "the test [of] the Excluded Class":

> If you are saving dying babies, whose babies are you going to let die? If you are feeding the hungry, what folk are you (regretfully, perhaps, but none less truly) going to let starve? If you are making a juster division of wealth, what people are you going to permit at present to remain in poverty? If you are giving all men votes (not only in the "political" but also in the economic world), what class of people are you going to allow to remain disfranchised?[32]

With a critique such as this, Du Bois raises the possibility that he could remain truer to socialist principles *outside* the party, vocally critical of its inconsistencies, than he would by staying within it and remaining relatively more silent. Better to be outside the Socialist Party, along with the IWW's Brotherhood of Timber Workers, than inside the party with Tom Hale.

Du Bois's reasons for keeping the party at arm's length had less to do with philosophical differences than with matters of practical leadership within the NAACP and of strategic calculation within American politics. As a practical matter, the unity of black America that Du Bois saw as a necessary condition to black political development—whether socialistic or otherwise—demanded that Du Bois should appeal to the gamut of black political views. Hence, *The Crisis* became a cheerleader of virtually all accomplishments by black Americans, whether they be academic honors, athletic exploits, successful businesses, or beautiful babies (the annual children's number was said to be the perennial best-seller).[33] As for Du Bois's aspirations to lead and to speak for the black masses, his socialist-informed analysis might tell him that white capitalists were as much or more at fault as working-class whites in the instigation of tension between white and black working people; but the immediate experience of black workers was that their friends were the white employers who gave them jobs, their enemies the white workers who barred them from unions, insulted them, and attacked them when they crossed picket lines. As Sinclair's ignorant expostulations on race difference show, and as Du Bois was well aware in the southern populist revolt, racism in insurgent democratic and anticapitalist movements was a matter of leaders' as well as followers' attitudes. In either case, if the editorship of *The Crisis* meant an opportunity to educate black Americans as to the benefits of socialism, it was one that would be maintained only if Du Bois approached the matter with deliberation and subtlety.

Du Bois's aloofness was strategic in relation to the Socialist Party, as well. Back before becoming a party member, Du Bois showed his recognition of the plight of third parties in the two-party U.S. system, which had bedeviled the People's Party and all other insurgents since the success of the party of Lincoln. As he had explained to a Prohibition Party interlocutor: "The only difficulty about supporting the third party is that you virtually throw away your vote, and this time I want to make votes tell."[34] The explanation remained virtually unchanged when Du Bois made his first presidential endorsement as *The Crisis* editor and, hence, exited from the party: "Because the Socialists, with their manly stand for human rights irrespective of color, are at present out of the calculation, the Negro voter must choose between these three parties"—that is, the Republican, the Democratic, and Roosevelt's Progressive Party.[35] In 1908, the problem of making black votes "tell" meshed reasonably well with a socialist-inspired ideal of progress, as Du Bois opted for an endorsement of the "socialistic" Bryan as opposed to Taft or Debs. With less hope than others had that the populist legacy of the Democratic Party initiated by Bryan would carry over into the candidacy of Wilson, Du Bois was forced to make a more fundamental choice between principle and pragmatism in the election of 1912.

If it is not surprising that he chose pragmatism given his still brief tenure as *Crisis* editor—recall that only a significant *minority* upon the NAACP board were Socialists—Du Bois's further reasoning for the Wilson endorsement reveals a political strategy fundamentally premised upon the voting strength—and voting weakness—of American blacks. The fact that this strategy did *not* coincide with that of the Socialist Party may be laid to the fundamental difference between the suffrage of the black masses and that of white workers. Whereas working-class and even poor white male voters as a class were largely enfranchised, the great majority of black citizens, concentrated as they were in the former states of the Confederacy, were not. In an obituary on the southern Populist and race-baiter Ben Tillman, Du Bois would write that the leader uniting poor southern whites and blacks "is not yet come" but "the real enfranchisement of the Negro will herald his birth."[36] With the power of the franchise, Du Bois reasoned, black citizens would wield power, making them valuable to their natural class allies, the poor whites of the South and the industrialized workers throughout the nation. As long as they were without that franchise, however, they were of little help to any insurgent party relying upon an electoral strategy, as the Socialist Party did.

What Du Bois was demanding, then, when he spoke of making black votes "tell," was that blacks use their vote specifically to gain suffrage rights for other black voters, making the votes cast by blacks in present elections multiply the number of blacks voting in future ones. The strategy most likely to win an expanded franchise soonest was to attempt to play the established parties off one another. It did not particularly matter that the Republican Party had been more assiduous in its patronage for black office-seekers. Suffrage was the central issue, and the Republicans had done nothing during their years in power to expand voting rights for blacks. Even as Republicans criticized the disfranchisement of black citizens in the Democrat-dominated South, Du Bois retorts that "without the consent of Republican Presidents, Republican Congresses and a Republican Supreme Court, Southern disfranchisement could not survive a single day." Theodore Roosevelt had not only lately been the head of that party, but his problematic presidential record had been capped by a Progressive nominating convention in Chicago that courted white southern support by refusing to credential black delegates, an outrage Du Bois referred to as "the Chicago disfranchisement." The Democratic Party was worthy of support, then, for little more reason than that it had not held the balance of national political power since 1892 and deserved a chance to improve upon the record of the Republicans. Accordingly, Du Bois's endorsement of Wilson seems perfectly willing to disavow the Democrats henceforth if they, too, failed to recognize the rights of black citizens: "It is better to elect Woodrow Wilson President of the United States and prove once for all if the Democratic party dares to be Democratic when it comes to black men."[37]

Waiting in the wings if the Democrats failed, meanwhile, was the Socialist Party and "their manly stand for human rights irrespective of color." That the Socialist Party remained the most reasonable ideological choice for black Americans all along became plain in 1916, with Du Bois's eleventh-hour recommendation of the SPA candidate, Allan Benson. Yet falling back upon the Socialist Party always carried definite risks. It meant, first, practically giving up on the short-term objective of increased suffrage. That meant, in turn, leaving ten million black Americans vulnerable to neglect by *all* political parties: not only the major parties, but a vote-hungry Socialist Party that, in spite of its fine ideals, might cater to the biases of the more fully enfranchised white proletariat. In short, Socialist affiliation without full suffrage rights might prove premature, preventing due consideration for black America in the Socialist Party when it rose to prominence, as Du Bois hoped it would.

Du Bois's emphasis on a voting strategy for gaining and ultimately winning power was not only quintessentially American but also typical of American socialism—something he shared both with the idealistic, articulate Debs and the whole range of pragmatic ward politicians who won elections and held office in the heyday years of the Socialist Party, such figures as Victor Berger, Meyer London, and Morris Hillquit. The socialist motive behind Du Bois's suffrage views was a durable part of his intellectual work, recurring many times in his writings in *The Crisis* and not only in his election-year endorsements. Consider Du Bois's lead editorial for November 1917, "The Oath of the Negro Voter," whose preamble declares the alliance of black Americans with the world's poor and proletariat even as it stresses the primacy of suffrage: "As one of the Earth's Disowned I swear to hold my Ballot as the sacred pawn of Liberty for all mankind and for my prisoned race." Whereas the "first and foremost aim" of voting was to be further gains in the suffrage itself—"the Enfranchisement of every citizen, male and female; and particularly the restoring of the stolen franchise to my people," the "second object" of black voting was to be "the division of the Social Income on the principle that he who does not work, be he rich or poor, may not eat; and that Land and Capital ought to belong to the Many and not the Few."[38]

If the implied threat to let the nonworking poor starve hardly seems beneficent by the standards of the modern welfare state, it is also a throwback to the obligation to labor that was among the responsibilities of citizenship in Bellamy's Cooperative Commonwealth. Insofar as the message was principally directed to a racial group that, practically without exception, already *had* to work to keep from starving, the threat to let the idle rich starve amounted to a revolutionary call to expropriate the expropriators. The call for "Land and Capital" to be owned by "the Many" rather than "the Few" sought to balance the immediate demands of small farmers and workers, the programs of the Single Taxers and old-time Populists with the program of the Socialist Party, suggesting at the same time that small-scale capital enterprises need not be eliminated to achieve a fair distribution of wealth. Precisely insofar as Du Bois's statement, like most pragmatic political platforms, caters to several interests simultaneously, it closely resembles the statements of a Socialist such as Sinclair attempting to balance the diverse factions and facets of American socialism.

CAPITAL, IMPERIALISM, AND THE GREAT WAR

> "The modern white laborer of Europe and America has the key to the serfdom of black folk, in his support of militarism and colonial expansion."

As early as *The Quest of the Silver Fleece,* Du Bois had given voice to his views that African Americans comprised a class uniquely singled out for capitalist exploitation and also, partly as a consequence, a class uniquely unified by group self-interest. It was the cultivation, education, and advancement of this group in the United States that comprised the core of his life work. During his first decade at the NAACP, though, Du Bois's researches into the black diaspora and his contacts with the Pan-African movement led him also to recognize the international dimensions of global capitalism especially as manifested in colonialism and, hence, to see the potential and real solidarity between people of color throughout the world. Anticolonialism and Pan-Africanism may be described as the second major trajectory of Du Bois's socialist analysis. Even as the Second Internationale crumbled at the beginning of the Great War, Du Bois's emphasis upon capitalist imperialism anticipated one of the key themes of the Third Internationale. It also led—ironically—to the same relational and relative view of racial categories that characterized his schemes for future black-and-white proletarian solidarity. Race was important, Du Bois found and maintained, because of its historical role in the process of economic and political disenfranchisement, and it would play a significant constructive role in reversing this process. Whereas for other socialists the Great War meant catastrophe, the sudden end of Socialist solidarity across European national boundaries, Du Bois took a quite different view, as he saw the war as the ultimate unmasking of the myth of white racial superiority and thus as a catalyst for a more genuine socialist solidarity across *all* national boundaries.

Meanwhile, white racism as expressed through both colonialism and capitalism had helped to break down class barriers among people of color. In Du Bois's *Quest of the Silver Fleece,* it is the singular solidarity of the African American community that underscores the viability of the cooperative economic solution envisaged in that novel. Throughout the nineteenth century the cooperative socialist movement had been bedeviled by the problem of group commitment. Unless held together by very strong cultural and social ties, as in the religious communities, communes were liable to disintegrate as soon as members recognized the difficulty of establishing cooperative economics while they remained surrounded by a hostile capitalist system. In Du Bois's view, however, the conditions of racist disenfranchisement and segregation in the United States potentially (and ironically) gave to black communities the coherence and stability that the nineteenth-century secular cooperatives had lacked.

Prewar issues of *The Crisis* spelled out the likelihood that enforced racial segregation, though morally repugnant, would result in a cohesive and semi-autonomous black community. In a *Crisis* editorial from 1913, "The Strength of Segregation," Du Bois predicted: "When the American people in their carelessness and impudence have finally succeeded in welding 10,000,000 American Negroes into one great self-conscious and self-acting mass, they will realize their mistake. . . . The physical intimidation of lynching cannot be kept up; the economic intimidation of exclusion cannot, with the present organization of Negro industry, be kept up after ten years. . . . After this—what? What can America do against a mass of people who move through their world but are not of it and stand as one unshaken group in their battle?"[39] An early 1914 issue of *The Crisis* excerpted various black newspapers on the subject of segregation, giving pride of place to a paper that described black America as "a nation within a nation" in which "We must have our own stores and not depend on the stores of other people." The *Afro-American Ledger* advised that blacks themselves "must provide for everything, from the birth of a child to the death of the great-grandfather. Boots, shoes, clothing, houses, lands, food, hospitals, schools, churches, orphan asylums, old folks' homes and what not." The editor of the *Ledger* suggested even that blacks must become investors in "bonds and mortgages of public utilities," "steamboats, street cars, railroads and everything else which takes public money to run," but not with the aim of becoming capitalists on a par with white Americans, but so as to exert maximum leverage in winning the rights for all black America.[40]

After the outbreak of hostilities in Europe, Du Bois kept at the theme of black unity, with economic cooperation among blacks being the critical element. In an August 1917 *Crisis* editorial he wrote that blacks "must enter American industrial development as a group, capable of offensive and defensive action, and not simply as an individual, liable to be made the victim of the white employer and such of the white labor unions as dare." While emerging as a nation within a nation, black America could—and must—maintain values that were collectivist rather than individualist, communistic rather than capitalistic:

> But how shall we enter? Shall we try the old paths of individual exploitation, develop a class of rich and grasping brigands of Industry, use them to exploit the mass of the black laboring people and reproduce in our own group all the industrial Hell of old Europe and America? No! This method has been advocated but it has been advocated by people who did not realize the new spirit that has come to the industrial world. Slowly and with great difficulty this new spirit is going to work itself out in the white world; but if we American Negroes are keen and intelligent we can evolve a new and efficient industrial co-operation quicker than any other group of people, for the simple reason that our inequalities of wealth are small, our group loyalty is growing stronger and stronger, and the necessity for a change in our industrial life is becoming imperative.[41]

Du Bois's optimism about progress in industrial cooperation arises in part *because of* the destruction of the war then raging in Europe. The unequivocal madness of the war showed, plainly enough, the bankruptcy of the old ways of doing business. "If sharpers and gamblers run the business and industry of the world," he writes soon after in another piece, "the result is the crop of mad jealousies that have made this present war." Hence, for the black community and the world alike, a new business ideal of "consecration" is plainly indicated: "We must oust the idea of selfish gain. We must try to teach the nations to earn a living by honesty, by efficiency, and along the paths of beauty." The only note of pessimism is that Du Bois is expecting no velvet revolution; the new commonwealth will emerge only "slowly and with great difficulty," and "the fine ideal of the Socialistic state" can be achieved only when "the consecrated business man" is cultivated in our children, "the people of the future democracy."[42]

The difficulties that might beset black America and others seeking a more egalitarian social order were made all the more apparent by wartime events on the home front. The war was a turning point for the very geography of black America, as industrial jobs that could no longer be readily filled by European immigrants were taken instead by black laborers from the South. The great migration, estimated in a June 1917 *Crisis* survey as 250,000 persons in the previous six months,[43] was generally considered a cause for celebration by Du Bois. It was certainly a happy development in the achievement of Du Bois's aim of greater black power in electoral politics, as blacks moved from southern districts that denied them the franchise to northen ones where their votes were assiduously curried. But the migration also intensified tensions between black and white labor, leading to conflicts of which the East St. Louis riot of August 1917 was only the most spectacular. Du Bois counted 125 killed in the riot, though later estimates put the number lower; and some 6,000 African American citizens lost their homes to rampage and arson. Thus it was only with the grimmest of satisfaction that Du Bois could assert that the riot had laid bare the racism of conservative labor: it was a "pogrom . . . engineered by Gompers and his Trade Unions." Black labor, the editor predicted, would remain defiant: it "continues to come North and ought to come North," a march that was, in Du Bois's imagery, the advance guard of black liberation. Not only supporters of the nation-state could employ the rhetoric of martial struggle and heroic self-sacrifice; so could Du Bois as an advocate of the black nation within the nation. "Despite the Trade Unions and the murderers whom they cover and defend, economic freedom for the American Negro is written in the stars," Du Bois predicted; "East St. Louis, Chester and Youngstown are simply the pools of blood through which we must march, but march we will."[44]

The acceleration of northward migration brought on by the Great War brought with it other, more subtle challenges for black Americans and leaders of the NAACP. The Great Migration and the greater urban concentration of black population would mean greater entrepreneurial opportunities for black businesspeople, and these opportunities would bring the temptation of emulating the individualistic behavior of white businesspeople. It was to this class, particularly, that Du Bois directed his plea for "the consecrated business man." The blandishments of white power revealed their allure, meanwhile, to the *Crisis* editor and NAACP director of research as well. Faced with the choice of making a stand against the war and facing persecution (as did the Socialist Party and the IWW), of taking a neutral stance and hoping for the best, or of supporting the racially segregated war effort and currying favor with the Wilson administration, the NAACP decided upon the third option, hoping to advocate for African American rights as well as possible within the wartime mobilization. The results were mixed. The NAACP succeeded in having black officers included in the new conscript army, but they were trained at a racially segregated camp and by white rather than black officers. Du Bois enjoyed a camaraderie closer than ever before with other members of the NAACP board, especially chairman Joel Spingarn.[45] In supporting the board's prowar position, he took the stance advocated by fellow socialists on the board William English Walling and Charles Russell. But Du Bois's "Close Ranks" editorial of July 1918, in which he seemed to announce a suspension of civil rights activism for the duration of the war, has been widely regarded as an embarrassing misstep, one of the low points in his career as a race leader.[46]

In the larger unfolding of Du Bois's career, however, the importance of his wartime excursion into patriotism was exceeded by his attention to European colonization and its countermovements occasioned by the war. This was not only a question of intellectual attention for the *Crisis* editor. It was also a matter of historical rupture and momentum, for the war both reshuffled the colonial deck, leaving areas formerly occupied by the Ottoman Empire or Germany under the control of Great Britain or France, and accelerated anticolonialist and nationalist movements throughout the world of "darker peoples," as Du Bois called them.

As far back as 1911, Du Bois had reported that his colleagues at the Universal Races Congress saw a parallel between colonial exploitation and the antebellum slave economy in the United States: "A strong, masterly argument was made to show that the economic foundations of imperialism were as weak as those of the slave barons of the South and as wicked."[47] In a 1913 editorial, Du Bois still more explicitly linked capitalism with imperialism—and presciently identified imperial rivalry as the prime catalyst of war: "The modern lust for land and slaves in Africa, Asia and the South Seas is the greatest and almost the only cause of war between the so-called civilized peoples."[48] When the war actually broke out, the self-destructive power of the colonial contest was available for all to witness. A Du Bois editorial from November 1914 could openly scoff at the notion that any of the combatants represented superior cultures, for all major combatants and several minor ones had been involved in an unholy scramble for colonies of which the war itself was a direct consequence: "To-day civilized nations are fighting like mad dogs over the right to own and exploit . . . darker peoples." Even brave little Belgium, whose "rape" had so outraged the world and mobilized American sympathy for the country, "has been as pitiless and grasping as Germany and in strict justice deserves every pang she is suffering after her unspeakable atrocities in the Congo."[49] In spite of their sufferings under colonial oppression, Africa and Asia were standing forth and showing their greater character and humanity. This Du Bois saw embodied, for instance, in the French Senegalese and British Indian soldiers that bolstered the Allied lines in the opening months of the fighting. A two-page illustration of Senegalese troops reprinted in the November 1914 *Crisis* still bears the caption supplied by its original publisher: "Out of Africa Have I Called My Son." But Du Bois's alternative caption reached the more direct and logical conclusion: "Black Soldiers from Senegal Fighting to Protect the Civilization of Europe against Itself."[50]

Most fundamental of the lessons reinforced for Du Bois by the events of the war and its immediate aftermath were those connected with two movements that transcended national borders: global anticolonialism and international socialism. These were concerns central to Du Bois's thought by the publication of *The Negro* in 1915. In this nonfiction work of history and cultural critique, Du Bois looked far beyond the late nineteenth-century race for colonies in locating the international tensions behind the European war, arguing instead that the impetus for colonization and possibly the catalyst for the industrial revolution lay in the transatlantic slave trade, which was "the first step in modern world commerce, followed by the modern theory of colonial expansion." But the Industrial Revolution carried within it another revolution in the organization and political awakening of labor, and so politically empowered labor, though only half consciously recognizing the threat to higher wages posed by slave labor within the southern United States, fought first to exclude slavery from the northern states, second to prevent the spread of the institution into the new western states, and third to defeat the South when the matter came to a head in the Civil War, thereby "suddenly and unintentionally" abolishing slavery. The growing power of labor, Du Bois then argues, was co-opted in a bargain offered by white captains of industry and accepted by white workers. "The new colonial theory" ameliorated the exploitation of the European working class, focusing instead upon a keener "exploitation of backward races under the political domination of Europe." This political domination was buttressed by (unequal) combination with the European and American working classes, all rationalized through racist distinctions, so that they were "practically invited to share in this new exploitation, and particularly were flattered by popular appeals to their inherent superiority to 'Dagoes,' 'Chinks,' 'Japs,' and 'Niggers.'"[51] The bargain was struck, Du Bois avers, soon after the American Civil War, so that the essential economic conditions for labor's identification with colonial enterprises preceded the race for formal annexation of colonies in Africa, which began in earnest only around 1875 with less than 10 percent of the continent under European control.

Du Bois's analysis does not focus only on what white workers and capitalists wanted from colored colonies, but also and primarily on what colored labor and leaders were doing in the meantime. Just as industrialization concentrated and educated a new proletariat in Europe, a few generations later it did the same for a new colored proletariat throughout the world, this one conscious of color as well as class as a source of a still more permanent and grinding caste exploitation. And so in *The Negro,* a book dedicated to the idea of Pan-Africanism, the term itself—not actually used until the book's conclusion—designates a specifically collectivist ideal of labor solidarity and of social transformation based on economic equality between all peoples:

> The Pan-African movement when it comes will not . . . be merely a narrow racial propaganda. Already the more far-seeing Negroes sense the coming unities: a unity of the working classes everywhere, a unity of the colored races, a new unity of men. The proposed economic solution of the Negro problem in Africa and America has turned the thoughts of Negroes toward a realization of the fact that the modern white laborer of Europe and America has the key to the serfdom of black folk, in his support of militarism and colonial expansion. He is beginning to say of these workingmen that, so long as black laborers are slaves, white laborers cannot be free. Already there are signs in South Africa and the United States of the beginning of understanding between the two classes.[52]

This analysis would remain essentially the same after the Bolshevik revolution, except that Du Bois's faith in the white working classes and in American Socialists was perhaps stronger in 1915 than after the war. Indeed, he foretells the kind of bloody revolution that later struck in Russia, even while suggesting that a choice remained: "In order for this colored world to come into its heritage, must the earth again be drenched in the blood of fighting, snarling human beasts, or will Reason and Good Will prevail?" In a reversal of his own interpretation at the conclusion of *John Brown,* and at odds too with various pronouncements of Upton Sinclair that the balance between violent reaction and peaceable progress lay in the hands of capitalists such as Rockefeller, Du Bois argued that the overwhelming majority of people of color would decide the issue: "The future world will, in all reasonable probability, be what colored men make it."[53] On the world stage as opposed to the United States, where people of color were in the minority, it was a straightforward matter of demographics: people of color, welded together into solidarity by race prejudice, outnumbered whites many times over. Writing in 1915 as the world war fomented by the European powers raged on, this hypothesis gave cause for relative optimism. At that juncture, Du Bois certainly saw reason to place greater faith in the patience, sagacity, and larger humanity of colored peoples than in the quality of white folks.

THE RED MENACE AND RACISM: 1919 AND AFTER

"Here is no simple question of race antagonism."

The Bolshevik revolution and the social unrest that swept the United States immediately after the war threatened to upset Du Bois's calculations as to the eventual triumph of the reason and goodwill of people of color. Whereas the March 1917 revolution that had toppled the czar and produced a Kerenski-led Russian Republic had been welcomed by liberals as well as revolutionaries in the West, the success of the Bolsheviks in November was viewed with considerable suspicion by all but the most radical, especially as it soon led to a separate peace with the kaiser and reinforcements of the weary German armies on the western front. Immediately after the November armistice, the United States and Great Britain sent a military expedition to Russia via Archangel in an attempt to assist the "White" counterrevolutionaries in turning back the "Red" Bolsheviks. Back home in the United States, Bolshevism became a convenient bogey with which to hammer the socialist and labor movements alike. Wartime gains in wages had swelled labor's confidence, while the patriotic necessity of staying on the job in wartime had kept grievances bottled up. The result was a year of strikes. There were over 1,000 in the summer of 1919 alone, and practically all steelworkers and coal miners went out. But nearly all were defeated, in large part because the new Red menace made it all too easy to paint mass labor action as the prelude to revolution.[54]

African Americans, including soldiers returning home, were by no means spared from the postwar reaction. In many cases, as had long been customary, they bore the brunt of antiprogressive violence. The carnage of East St. Louis and of other wartime riots had been terrible, but more people, black and white, were killed by race riots in 1919 than in all of the wartime years put together.[55] Most devastating was the disturbance in Chicago, which began with the stoning of a black boy who accidentally strayed into the water off a whites-only beach. For days after the killing, whites and blacks battled across well-demarcated lines separating white from black neighborhoods; the final tally counted some thirty blacks and fifteen whites killed, and many hundreds more wounded.[56] Significant riots took place in some two dozen other cities and towns in a wide belt across the Southeast, the border states, and reaching into the Midwest—places as varied as Washington, DC; Charleston, South Carolina; Knoxville, Tennessee; Longview, Texas; Elaine, Arkansas; and Omaha, Nebraska.[57] Most significantly, in 1919 the pattern of rioting began to change. Previous race riots had involved white-on-black violence almost exclusively, nearly all casualties and property damage being suffered by blacks, as in East St. Louis and in the infamous Wilmington, North Carolina, riot of 1898 (which had ousted the elected, biracial city government and served as the source for Charles Chesnutt's *The Marrrow of Tradition*). Now African Americans were fighting back.

If ever there was an occasion for Du Bois to embrace the rationale for violence cautiously advanced in his *John Brown* biography, the tumult of 1919 would appear to be that occasion. Barbara Foley's *Spectres of 1919: Class and Nation in the Making of the New Negro* asserts that antisocialist and racist reaction in the immediate postwar years, coupled with renewed socialist and African American militancy, constituted a unique opportunity for revolutionary activity in the United States. Among black activists as well as race-conscious white radicals, Foley argues, "those who espoused revolution" reached the conclusion that "capitalism, therefore, had to be supplanted, by either the ballot or the bullet, if racism was to be ended." While not citing earlier socialists who had made use of John Brown including Du Bois and Sinclair, Foley adds that in the immediate postwar years warrant for the "bullet" as well as the "ballot" was often provided by an appeal to John Brown, who was "frequently invoked as an insurgent ancestor—by African Americans and whites alike."[58]

Du Bois had, in fact, not only considered the implications of the John Brown precedent but had assessed the case for violent reaction at various times during the war, and well before the inspirations of the Bolshevik revolution of October 1917 or the declaration of the Third Internationale in 1919. Du Bois homed in repeatedly on the hypocrisy of the combatant nations justifying massive and indiscriminate violence in the name of patriotism while condemning the IWW and other radical, supposedly violent groups who advised their members not to fight. The theme contributed to an ongoing reflection about the reasonableness of force as a response to state repression and outright violence. If, as he had already begun to theorize in the pages of *The Crisis* prior to the war's outbreak, black America might be considered an oppressed nation within a nation, then what except the superior force of whites was to prevent black Americans from defending their de facto nationhood by self-defensive force? As long as black men fought for colonizer and capitalist, their military prowess was embraced; if they were to apply that prowess to self-defense, they would be condemned as traitors and treated as felons. "In America, in Europe and in Africa black men are fighting for the liberty of white men and pulling their chestnuts out of the fire," Du Bois observed in 1916; "One of these bright mornings black men are going to learn how to fight for themselves." Here it was not the socialist internationale but the Irish independence movement that offered the possible model for black action. Writing of the "foolish" Easter uprising of that year, Du Bois editorializes: "Would to God some of us had sense enough to be fools!"[59] Elsewhere it was the spontaneous militancy of blacks against simply intolerable conditions of class and race exploitation that provided the example for resistance, as in a March 1917 *Crisis* report upon "Direct Action" in an Alabama mine: "Two hundred striking Negro miners at the Banner Mines, near Birmingham, Ala., have refused to come out of the mines or to allow anyone to enter. The men are convicts and have quantities of dynamite. They complain of ill treatment." If there is any hint of socialist influence here, then the credit would go to the syndicalist methods of the Industrial Workers of the World, the one union bold enough to create interracial organizations in the South during this period.[60]

Most of all, it was the application of the military technique to black self-defense that alternately frightened and fascinated Du Bois. One key provocation for the *Crisis* editor was a bloody August 1917 incident involving black soldiers stationed in Houston. There, ill-treatment of black troops incited one hundred of them to go on a shooting spree at a police station: sixteen whites and six blacks were killed on August 23; before the end of the year, nineteen of the black soldiers were executed and another sixty-seven court-martialed and sent to prison, some for life terms.[61] The Houston uprising was a spontaneous reaction, and one to be deeply regretted, Du Bois had written in *The Crisis.* But the editor could not miss the fact that the Houston mutineers attacked the police station in the military formation in which they had been drilled. And representations of the men convicted to death sentences in the

Crisis emphasized their soldierly bearing and defiance to the end, suggesting their nobility as African American warriors.[62] The oft-quoted *Crisis* editorial "Returning Soldiers" is treated by David Levering Lewis as a revision of Du Bois's earlier (and still more often quoted) "Close Ranks" editorial, one that "would go a long way toward redeeming the perceived imprudence" of the 1918 editorial urging full African American support of the war effort.[63] Barbara Foley is also correct to see in it "a veiled threat" of black violence:

> By the God of Heaven, we are cowards and jackasses if now that war is over, we do not marshal every ounce of our brain and brawn to fight a sterner, longer, more unbending battle against the forces of hell in our own land.
>
> *We return.*
>
> *We return from fighting.*
>
> *We return fighting.*
>
> Make way for Democracy! We saved it in France, and by the Great Jehovah, we will save it in the United States of America, or know the reason why.[64]

But whereas Lewis emphasizes the way Du Bois's editorial appears to retract his earlier "Close Ranks" editorial, and whereas Foley links the 1919 editorial to a postwar revolutionary surge, the editorial is at least as remarkable for its continuity with Du Bois's earlier writings in which he had advocated fighting for democracy at home in the manner of the Irish nationalists, the Alabama miners, and the Houston mutineers. The very phraseology of Du Bois's denunciations of quiescent African Americans as "cowards and jackasses" echoes the earlier editorial on the Easter uprising, in which he calls them "fools."

Du Bois's fascination with antiracist violence in the wake of the war extends to one of the few instances in which the materials collected in his 1920 essay collection, *Darkwater*, differ from their original form of publication in *The Crisis*. In general, the fact that *Darkwater* remains relevant to postwar circumstances, in spite of the original publication of most of its essays during the war, attests to the perspicacity of Du Bois's wartime synthesis of race and socialist analysis.[65] In his reflections on the East St. Louis riot of 1917 included in his essay "Of Work and Wealth," Du Bois fabricates a more militant response among the black targets of white violence. In Du Bois's lengthy chronicle of the riot published in 1917, as in practically all other historical accounts, the blacks suffer abuse and murder as innocent, nonresistant victims. In Du Bois's account published in 1920, in contrast, the blacks strike back in self-defense: "The Negroes fought. They grappled with the mob like beasts at bay. They drove them back from the thickest cluster of their homes and piled the white dead in the street, but the cunning mob caught the black men between the factories and their homes, where they knew they were armed only with their dinner pails."[66] The invention is noted by biographer David Levering Lewis and characterized, reasonably enough, as "a famous paragraph describing a confrontation that never occurred" and an instance in which Du Bois "succumb[ed] to the temptation to romanticize the facts."[67] Nonetheless, if we understand Du Bois's essay to reflect upon—and represent by proxy—the more recent riots of 1919 as well as the conflict in East St. Louis, then we might add that this confrontation did not occur there, but it did later in Chicago, Washington, DC, and elsewhere—between the time that Du Bois initially reported the facts of East St. Louis and the publication of *Darkwater.* Ideologically, Du Bois's fictionalized description of the riot is in the spirit of Claude McKay's iconic postwar poem, "If We Must Die," which did follow the Chicago riot and implicitly comments upon it and other postwar incidents of black resistance. The repetition of specific ideas in common with McKay's poem, particularly the trope of being cornered "like beasts at bay," may even show an immediate influence of McKay upon Du Bois—just possible because McKay's poem first appeared in July 1919 and the final draft of *Darkwater* was not delivered to the publisher until September.[68]

Still, it must also be observed that neither Du Bois nor McKay represents racial violence as a portal to revolutionary change. Both suggest "ennoblement" in the fighters, certainly, but Lewis is also right in characterizing Du Bois's imagery as "desperate." So too is McKay's. Both scenes are ultimately futile in the sense that they represent historical and political cul-de-sacs. The point is underscored by McKay's opening conditional—"If we must die . . ." (but *must* we?)—as well as by the various references in the poem to certain and grim death, and the suggestion that the only object to be gained is "honor" in the eyes of white murderers. To be sure, not only in 1919 but for many years prior, in cities and counties across the country, African Americans found that McKay's desperate conditional described their lived experience all too well. Yet it did not describe the situation, or the state of mind, of all black Americans, and even in McKay's militant poem, it can hardly be said to describe the *desired* state of affairs. It is not, as Foley suggests with fervent optimism, a new international dispensation that is described but much the same old routine. This critical analysis of the murderous encounter is offered, but still more explicitly, in Du Bois's invention inserted into his historical account of the East St. Louis riot, wherein black Americans kill whites in defense of self and property at one point of conflict, but in which the general trend is for black workers to be killed by cowardly and "cunning" white mobs who attack them when and where their defenses are down. These scenes are neither recipe nor recommendation for a revolution.

In the crisis years of 1919 and 1920 and in years to come, more radical, usually younger, activists pressed Du Bois to come over to the Bolsheviks. A 1923 correspondent to *The Crisis,* John H. Owens, queried: "Does not the editor think that State Socialism, communism, or even the dread dictatorship of the proletariat, offers a better solution to the problems of the proletariat than any scheme suggested by the exploiting classes,—those who profit from the present system?"[69] Editor Du Bois in fact thought little of the schemes of the exploiting classes, but he also did not see the two options presented by Owens as the only ones available. Du Bois was willing to look to the Bolshevik revolution as a hopeful international development, to view the application of force and repression in the Soviets as perhaps a necessary response to centuries of czarist oppression. An editorial published in the September 1919 *Crisis,* then incorporated the next year into *Darkwater,* went so far as to declare that the Bolshevik ideal—"the vision of great dreamers that *only those who work shall vote and rule*"—might be the "one new idea" of the war, which in due course might justify all the carnage that produced it.[70] Du Bois was unwilling, however, to assume that the revolutionary model that had produced the Soviet Union necessarily applied to the situation in the United States. Alliances between black and white proletarians looked like the way forward in the United States as elsewhere in the industrialized world, but as long as the majority of white workers excluded blacks from their unions and were wont to lynch and riot, all the theorizing of the socialists would do black workers no particular good. Under these conditions, the use of force by black proletarians as called for by the Bolshevik paradigm would mean only desperate and futile, if heroic, self-sacrifice.

Du Bois continued to insist that a "great and real revolution" could be wrought in the United States by peaceful means using the parliamentary and legal procedures already available.[71] As contrasted with the Bolsheviks and their American exponents, Du Bois believed that physical force would be not only self-destructive to blacks but also unnecessary as long as democratic means remained available. Like earlier American socialists—Gronlund, Bellamy, Gilman—Du Bois insisted that socialism was the most rational system, demonstrably bringing the greatest good to the greatest number of citizens. Socialism would not only benefit the dispossessed, proletarians white and black, Du Bois explained; it was also the most logical system for all members of modern industrialist society in the sense that socialism worked out the contradiction between liberal democratic ideals and hierarchical capitalist practices. "Democratic control is everywhere limited in its control of human interests," Du Bois observes in one of the later chapters of *Darkwater,* "Of the Ruling of Men": "Mankind is engaged in planting, forestry, and mining, preparing food and shelter, making clothes and machines, transporting goods and folk, disseminating news, distributing products, doing public and private personal service, teaching, advancing science, and creating art." And yet "in this intricate whirl of activities," Du Bois continues, "the theory of government has been hitherto to lay down only very general rules of conduct, marking the limits of extreme anti-social acts, like fraud, theft, and murder." Supported by a variety of dogmatic assertions about the sanctity of property rights, "freedom of industry," and the "natural" laws of economics, the apologists of capitalism ridicule the possibility of democratic control of industry. All the while, Du Bois argues, most of the so-called natural laws of business are "clearly the dictates of self-interest laid down by the powerful private persons who today control industry." Indeed, in Du Bois's view, those private persons generally *know* that the industrial world has been made, and continually is remade, by their actions as well as the actions of many like-minded people going before them.

If the economic system has so demonstrably been constructed by an elite few for a privileged few, Du Bois reasons—working systematically through the logic of gradualist socialism—then that system can be transformed by the common sense of the nonelite, nonprivileged majority operating through the ordinary democratic process. "Of the Ruling of Men" can, therefore, conclude matter-of-factly: "Here it is that modern men demand that Democracy supplant skilfully concealed, but all too evident, Monarchy." Du Bois's account of the "clear" first steps in the democratic control of industry, moreover, does not need to invent a new revolutionary formula. It reads more like an assemblage of American socialist reforms going back to the Single Tax:

> the careful, steady increase of public democratic ownership of industry, beginning with the simplest type of public utilities and monopolies, and extending gradually as we learn the way; the use of taxation to limit inheritance and to take the unearned increment for public use beginning

(but not ending) with a "single tax" on monopolized land values; the training of the public in business technique by co-operation in buying and selling, and in industrial technique by the shop committee and manufacturing guild.[72]

Underlying Du Bois's conception is the notion of the producing classes, a notion that had been articulated by Charlotte Perkins Gilman (and others) in the early 1890s: even business managers might well be "producers" if they agree to operate upon cooperative rather than competitive principles. Also implicit in his formulation of cooperation across class lines was his understanding that the black community, with its common burden of racist discrimination cutting across class lines, could provide the model for the wider cooperative political economy to come.

All of these backward glances to the cooperative commonwealth, the cautions against acting rashly, the criticisms of the Bolsheviks whether direct or indirect, seem utterly anachronistic and misguided from the point of view of the Comintern, just initiated in 1919. But Du Bois was examining the present and looking to the future as well as connecting to the past. His position was responsive to—even if not much moved by—the radicals who looked forward to, and the reactionaries who feared, violent confrontation and sudden historical rupture. Even as Du Bois's own convictions of the race leadership of a Talented Tenth unmistakably parallel the intellectual leadership premised as necessary by Upton Sinclair (and Lenin, too), his position contemned the notion that a revolutionary vanguard of intellectual elites must take it upon themselves to foment social disruption and violence. If social conditions bred violence among the underclass, then that violence might well be defensible, based on the conditions. But actually to seek to catalyze and then direct violence—that would mean a "loss and lowering of ideals" (quoting Du Bois in *John Brown*) and regression rather than human progress. Du Bois and other American socialists had already seen evidence that parliamentary and democratic processes in the United States had moved the country toward greater public control over industry and a wider distribution of the national wealth. Du Bois had noted the "socialistic" direction taken by the Democratic Party through the national leadership of the party by William Jennings Bryan. Sinclair had seen further results in public oversight of food and drugs through the agency of the Republican Party as led by Theodore Roosevelt. Little though Gilman may have thought about suffrage for women in itself, 1920 had also brought the potential for a dramatic extension in the popular responsiveness of government, as the number of citizens eligible to vote more than doubled. I shall argue that the testimony of the future would also back Du Bois's position of patience and perseverance (adopted by Gilman and Sinclair as well) as opposed to the cause of social disruption and immediate revolution championed by the insurrectionists. For the tradition of socialist rhetorical persuasion and parliamentary change not only was to win the day within American socialism; it is also the tradition of socialist praxis that would, over time, be most responsible for the transformations to come in American political economy during the Great Depression.

PART TWO

LITERARY NEGOTIATIONS

CHAPTER FIVE

CALL AND RESPONSE: THE POLITICS OF LITERARY UTOPIANISM AND REALISM

The chapters of Part I have canvassed the writing of Gilman, Sinclair, and Du Bois broadly considered—published work, fiction and nonfiction, speeches in the case of Gilman, personal letters and other unpublished work. We have examined this writing with particular attention to what it says about American socialism of the 1890s and the two decades following: the period of the Second Internationale, and also the decades when the writers first declared themselves socialists and made their first efforts to leave their marks within the movement. Having established the shared commitment of these writers to economic egalitarianism and social democratic transformation, even within quite different political contexts, I shall now focus more narrowly on their literary work and, at the same time, extend the historical scope of the analysis more fully through the second and third decades of the twentieth century. This process will help to isolate a specific relationship between literature and politics: a poetics or aesthetics of American socialist literature during a twenty-year period that also happens to be associated with the rise of literary modernism in American literature.

Because for the triptych writers this process will continue to demonstrate correspondences between literary work and political action, we can also continue to trace the development of social-democratic politics as it confronted the series of challenges presented by the collapse of the Second Internationale in 1914, the rise of the Comintern in 1919, and the hegemony of capitalism in the 1920s. In spite of the significant differences between Populism, Nationalism, syndicalism, communist-anarchism, the Social Gospel, and social democracy, all were tolerated and even encouraged under the Second Internationale. How did writers and activists schooled in the polymorphous socialism of this earlier time come to terms with the changes initiated by the Great War and its repercussions? The question of the fate of American social democracy after the collapse of the Socialist Internationale can be addressed by studying the uses to which Gilman, Sinclair, and Du Bois put the realist and utopian literary modes, largely because those uses refracted debates over socialism, scientific and utopian, that had been staples of the movement for decades.

To establish the literary and political foundation for these questions, this chapter considers the way that the modes were brought together late in the first decade and in the second decade of the century in the fiction of all three of the triptych writers, at the very cultural moment that the social democratic movement in the United States reached its greatest popularity and just a few years before the Socialist Internationale would come to an unceremonious end. Even while realist and utopian literary modes, like scientific and utopian socialism, are defined by separate histories and by formal and ideological antinomies, their histories and conceptions are both intertwined and overlapping. Not only, for example, did Marx and Engels acknowledge the educational value of the French and English socialists that Marx also dismissed as idealists and Engels labeled "utopian," but Marxism along with other variants of socialism has gained authority by a utopian vision of a better world, a classless society defined by a higher code of ethics, as well as by a correct, scientific analysis of material and historical conditions. In nineteenth-century American literary history we may observe a parallel phenomenon. Alongside realism, subsequently considered the preeminent literary development in the later nineteenth century, American writers of the very same period were obsessed with utopian literature. Bellamy's *Looking Backward,* far from being an anomaly, merely fueled a trend within the fictional genre, as approximately twenty utopian fictions preceding Bellamy's novel were succeeded by some two hundred titles between 1888 and 1900, prompting one scholar to suggest that in the 1890s the utopian mode was the most popular of all American literary genres.[1] Although their procedures are almost diametrically opposed—the utopian form, by its very definition, describing a situation outside of social reality; the realist fiction describing social reality with the highest degree of verisimilitude possible—their cultural aims may be practically the same, for, as Thomas Peyser notes, realism and utopianism represent two facets of the same critical motive: "Both aim to displace social arrangements by revealing their self-contradictions and genealogy."[2] Certainly not all uses of realist or utopian modes comprised social democratic critiques of and alternatives to nineteenth-century society (in fact many of the sequels to *Looking Backward* were rejoinders to it), but nineteenth-century socialists did recognize the political potential of both modes. William Dean Howells, not only the foremost advocate of realism in American literature but an early convert to Bellamy Nationalism, wrote utopian as well as realistic novels expressing his views, *A Hazard of New Fortunes* and his other high-realist work being followed by *A Traveler from Altruria* (1894) and *Through the Eye of the Needle* (1907).

As far as socialist writers and readers were concerned, the literary discourses of utopianism and realism were always complementary; they were the métiers of socialist hope and capitalist critique. Yet considered apart from one another—they remained, after all separate genres—each mode had its besetting liability. The realist novel, after all, might be perfectly thorough in its account of the defects of market capitalism but (at best) only hint at what was to be done about these defects. This was in fact the complaint of Hamlin Garland about Howell's realism, which he believed left entirely unclear "what line of reform he thinks must be pushed next," and this very problem seems to have been critical in Howell's decision to turn to the utopian form after the publication of *A Hazard of New Fortunes.*[3] The utopian fiction, in contrast, might readily offer a detailed account of how its author believed society should be changed for the better yet founder entirely over how such an ideal society could in fact be actualized, given the very different reality of contemporary society. It is the very problem that Marx and Engels attributed to the utopian socialists: they were dreaming dreams with no possible foundation in really existing material conditions. Presumably, in the best of all possible political and literary worlds, the two modes would be brought together, so that each one's strength might serve as remedy for the other's liability. But how to accomplish this, when the very concepts of the literary forms are at odds with one another? From a political viewpoint, moreover, the separation was actually critical: for socialism to be a genuine alternative to capitalism, it must be asserted that there is some fundamental difference between the two political economies.

What writers needed was some kind of fictional pivot, which might plausibly and even causally connect the world of current reality with a future, better reality, while at the same time maintaining a real separation between the two. At close to the same time in the first decade of the twentieth century, Upton Sinclair, W. E. B. Du Bois, and Charlotte Perkins Gilman wrote utopian-realist fictions having definite socialist aims that introduced precisely this kind of pivot—and, as it happened, the same one. In likely order of composition, Sinclair's *The Jungle,* Du Bois's *Quest of the Silver Fleece,* and Gilman's *Moving the Mountain,* published in the *Forerunner,* discovered the same rhetorical figure and cultural resource to make the transition from the real to ideal credible: the experiences of religious conversion and commitment. Fittingly, each appropriated what amounted to the most widely available trope in American culture for an experience commonly assumed to lie beyond straightforward rational analysis; they sought thus to tap into a structure of feeling that was accepted as a basic reality by a great majority of Americans and, simultaneously, that tapped into their most idealistic aspirations for a good society and their own best ethical conduct.

SINCLAIR'S *THE JUNGLE* AND SOCIALIST REVIVALISM

> "It was the new religion of humanity—or you might say it was the fulfilment of the old religion, since it implied but the literal application of all the teachings of Christ."

Whereas *The Jungle* might be credited as the first major literary work to have happened upon the mixed mode—and conjoined plot—of a realist-utopian novel, the novel's narrative solution to the problem of actually linking, or pivoting, from one kind of story to the other is clearly delineated in a slightly earlier work by one of the other triptych writers, W. E. B. Du Bois's *Souls of Black Folk.* In the late chapter "Of the Faith of the Fathers," Du Bois records his observations of the southern black church, a singular revelation to the Massachusetts-raised scholar who went south of the Mason-Dixon Line for the first time during a college summer vacation. Although Du Bois focuses primarily upon African American religious experience, much of what he says may apply to American Protestantism generally.[4] Most significant for our purposes were those elements of religious revivalism identified by Du Bois as "the Preacher, the Music, and the Frenzy."

The "Preacher" Du Bois describes as the leading figure in the black community under slavery: "A leader, a politician, an orator, a 'boss,' an intriguer, and idealist,—all these he is, and ever, too, the centre of a group of men, now twenty, now a thousand in number." The "Music," originating in Africa, became "under the stress of law and whip . . . the one true expression of a people's sorrow, despair, and hope." As for the "Frenzy," Du Bois claims it as the element of religion "more devoutly believed in than all the rest," varying from "the silent rapt countenance or the low murmur and moan to the mad abandon of physical fervor,—the stamping, shrieking, and shouting, the rushing to and fro and wild waving of arms, the weeping and laughing, the vision and the trance."[5] The experience is wrapped in mystery even for the religious participants, Du Bois observes; it can be described only as an abstract theological assertion ("the Spirit of the Lord passed by"), an experience beyond rational or even ordinary psychological explanation ("seizing the devotee, making him mad with supernatural joy"), or the simple sum of its physical evidences ("without this visible manifestation of the God there could be no true communion with the Invisible"). Mysterious as the collaboration of preacher, music, and frenzy may be, the social impact of the church as more or less formal institution is plain enough and profound. Starting in slave times but continuing in large measure to the present, black churches "are really governments of men," Du Bois explains, and because such governments predated the establishment of monogamous family life, they tended toward "communistic" organization and morals. Although the late differentiation between classes of black Americans had led, in Du Bois's view, to a problematic diversity of religious styles ranging from "radicalism" to "hypocritical compromise," the persistence of the revival gave Du Bois hope for the social agency of black religion: "Some day the Awakening will come, when the pent-up vigor of ten million souls shall sweep irresistibly toward the Goal, out of the Valley of the Shadow of Death, where all that makes life worth living—Liberty, Justice, and Right—is marked 'For White People Only.'"[6]

Although Du Bois's tendency in *The Souls of Black Folk* was to downplay commonalities between black spirituality and American religious experience more generally, the central features that he identifies as essential to the black church are certainly also present—of course with allowances made for variations—in practically all forms of evangelical Christianity that flourished in the United States during the nineteenth century. Methodism, particularly, is notable for its connection with the working classes first in Great Britain and then in the United States, although, as with Du Bois's characterization of black religion, we may observe that the power of religious organizations for social mobilization encompasses all classes and might take any number of different political trajectories, from the communistic to the anarchic or cynically opportunistic. The connection between religious identity and progressive political activism that I am here suggesting in the triptych writers' fiction of the first decade of the twentieth century has, in fact, a very important precedent in socialistic and even openly socialist movements that took place in liberal U.S. churches in the 1890s, commonly known as the Social Gospel. One new element that Sinclair, Du Bois, and Gilman brought to bear upon the connection was an appeal to a more emotive, intense experience of conversion—which at the turn of the century, at least, meant broadening socialist appeals beyond the highly educated classes typically in attendance in liberal, high-church denominations. Another was the thoroughly secular reinterpretation of the religious experience: whereas the Social Gospel asserted that good Christians should be socialists, the socialist gospel according to Sinclair, Du Bois, and Gilman supplanted Christianity.

As it happens, all of the elements identified by Du Bois as key components of black religion are present in the pivotal scene of Upton Sinclair's *The Jungle*, the Socialist rally at which Jurgis is "saved" body and soul. Utterly disillusioned in his hopes for family life upon discovering that his cousin by marriage, Marija, has resigned herself to living as a prostitute, Jurgis is looking for a place to keep warm when he stumbles into a Socialist meeting. The response of the throng jamming into the hall has all the marks of a revival, of Du Bois's "Frenzy": "A tremendous roar had burst from the throats of the crowd. . . . Men and women were standing up, waving handkerchiefs, shouting, yelling."[7] Jurgis is initially drawn into the spirit of the meeting by the egalitarian and democratic spirit of the crowd. In contrast to an earlier Republican meeting held in the very same hall, where he was called a "bum," and from which he was ejected by police for falling asleep, at the Socialist meeting he is merely nudged when he dozes off, and then is encouraged to listen to the speaker by a fine young "lady" who addresses him as "comrade." While the class leveling obviously invokes the egalitarianism of socialist ideology, it also accords with the ethos of a revival meeting, especially that of the "decentralized and democratic Baptist faith" that thrived, Du Bois reports, under slavery, where every soul comes to the altar equal before God.[8]

Once Jurgis's attention is transferred to the speaker, he is held as rapt as anyone in the house. The Revivalist preacher, Du Bois says, was the descendant of the one surviving vestige of African social organization, the "Priest or Medicine-man" who "found his function as the healer of the sick, the interpreter of the Unknown, the comforter of the sorrowing, the supernatural avenger of wrong, and the one who rudely but picturesquely expressed the longing, disappointment, and resentment of a stolen and oppressed people."[9] The preacher's secular counterpart, unmistakably, is the figure Sinclair describes on the platform, a man who works the crowd like the peripatetic evangelist that he in fact *is:* "He was speaking rapidly, in great excitement; he used many gestures—as he spoke he moved here and there upon the stage, reaching with his long arms as if to seize each person in the audience."[10] As the oration continues, the socialist speaker assumes all the functions Du Bois identifies as belonging to the office of the priest: He draws from his own experience to express the frustrations of the common people; he demystifies the cause of those frustrations; he pronounces healing from the ailments of ignorance and powerlessness; and finally and consequently, he proclaims the rise of an agent of vengeance and justice, personified as "Labor." Just as Du Bois's black preacher unifies his congregants and empowers them for action, Sinclair's socialist orator represents a singular, unified "Labor" as attaining heroic powers: "Now a dream of resistance haunts him, hope battling with fear; until suddenly he stirs, and a fetter snaps—and a thrill shoots through him, to the farthest ends of his huge body, and in a flash the dream becomes an act! . . . he rises—towering, gigantic; he springs to his feet, he shouts in his new-born exultation."[11]

These rhetorical figures and turns of phrase constitute the socialist orator's "music"—the communicative medium to which Du Bois gives pride of place, in the black church and in American culture, to the slave or sorrow songs. Indeed, Sinclair ascribes musical qualities to the speaker's voice, at one point noting that "his voice was deep, like an organ."[12] Du Bois, however, notably sidesteps comparisons between the preacher's gifts as a speaker and his (or the choir's) gifts in song, merely suggesting their complementarity. And as it turns out, the most fruitful possibilities for comparison to the sorrow songs lie not in the quality of the speaker's voice but in the figurative language and themes of Sinclair's orator. Sinclair's speaker uses a number of key images from the historical trauma of black slavery and the struggle for emancipation in his speech. Repeatedly the orator refers to the workers as shackled or whipped, and several times these figures are combined, as for example: "the chains upon [workingmen's] limbs, the lash upon their backs, the iron in their souls." The common socialist usage of "wage-slaves" and capitalist "masters" is interspersed throughout the speech. Moreover, the oppression of "wage-slavery," just as of chattel slavery, is represented as many sided, abusing the spirit as well as exploiting the labor of the workers, so that they merely "plod on like beasts of burden." Consequently, the liberation of the "slaves" is twofold, involving first the freeing of their minds and subsequently their bursting their "shackles" or "bands."[13]

The closeness of Sinclair's discourse here to abolitionist rhetoric is enough to suggest a more direct link between the language of African American activism and that of socialism than I am otherwise arguing for. In general, I take Du Bois to be an able interpeter of the structures of evangelical Christianity simply because the southern black church that is his subject is a fit representative of the more general type, and I take the abolitionist echoes of Sinclair's rhetoric to stem from generic similarities between anti-slavery and anti-capitalist discourses. Sinclair's socialist discourse here, however, invokes the secularized conversion of Frederick Douglass's *Narrative*—a text with which Sinclair was almost certainly familiar from his Civil War research. Chattel slavery, Douglass recalls, did its worst not when it brutalized him physically but when it undermined his spirit, the essential sense of independent personhood that made him human. Battered by physical force and psychological abuse by a renowned slave-breaker, Mr. Covey, Douglass reaches the point where "the dark night of slavery closed in upon me, and behold a man transformed into a brute!"[14] When Douglass succeeds in besting Covey in a physical struggle, his triumph is offered up in explicitly religious and ecstatic terms: "I felt as I had never felt before. It was a glorious resurrection from the tomb of slavery, to the heaven of freedom. My long-crushed spirit rose, cowardice departed, bold defiance took its place; and I now resolved that, however long I might remain a slave in form, the day had passed forever when I could be a slave in fact."[15]

Sinclair's narrative similarly emphasizes the real-world implications of the conversion experience for individual liberation and empowerment. The final lines of the socialist oration that triggers Jurgis's ecstatic experience body forth the gigantic physical power of a proletariat that has broken its bonds and stands ready to battle its capitalist master just as certainly as Douglass stood defiant against Covey while yet a slave. Joined imaginatively to this proletarian colossus and, quite visibly, part of the masses in the meeting hall who rise as one to embrace this image of their collective personality, Jurgis experiences "an unfolding of vistas before him, a breaking of the ground beneath him, an upheaving, a stirring, a trembling; he felt himself suddenly a mere man no longer—there were powers within him undreamed of, there were demon forces contending, age-long wonders struggling to be born." Sinclair's chapter concludes with still more self-consciously religious language, even as his emphasis on physical description evokes Du Bois's account of the frenzy: "There was a falling in of the pillars of his soul, the sky seemed to split above him—he stood there, with his clenched hands upraised, his eyes bloodshot, and the veins standing purple in his face, roaring in the voice of a wild beast, frantic, incoherent, maniacal. And when he could shout no more he still stood there, gasping, and whispering hoarsely to himself: 'By God! By God! By God!'"[16]

In each case, the rebirth effected through the conversion experience (whether sacred or secular) functions as a critical narrative pivot and at the same time grounds it in an experiential reality. Du Bois describes the widely occurring revivalist experiences that he observed while working as a young teacher in the South. Douglass records the turning point in his biography, assuring his reader: "You have seen how a man was made a slave; you shall see how a slave was made a man."[17] Jurgis's experience is more thoroughly fictionalized, but the semiautobiographical *Love's Pilgrimage* cites Sinclair's attendance at a speech given by George D. Herron as an important milestone in his coming to socialism. Sinclair recalls in *Love's Pilgrimage* that once he was exposed fully to the ideas of socialist visionaries such as Herron, "The process of his 'conversion' was rapid."[18] The account that Sinclair supplies in his *Autobiography* of his "conversion" emphasizes both its ecstatic nature and the importance of socialist community: "It was like the falling down of prison walls about my mind; the amazing discovery, after all those years, that I did not have to carry the whole burden of humanity's future upon my two frail shoulders! There were actually others who understood."[19]

The trope of dramatic conversion grounded in experience—and not just the experience of these three writers, but of a great many people throughout the culture—is critical because it lends narrative and psychological credibility to the tremendous, seemingly irrational pivot from realism to utopianism—the shift in perspective that turns grim reality into a hope that is realizable as well as appealing. *The Jungle* did not invent this pivot; Sinclair's accomplishment in the novel was rather to identify, adapt, and highlight the already available conversion experience as a means to simultaneously separate and link the realist and the utopian.

The Jungle, addressing Marx's critique of religion as the "opiate of the people," counters the materialist suspicion of such spiritual epiphany by showing the social and political *results* of the conversion experience. Hence, Jurgis gains immediate psychological relief and hope for the future; he certainly reaps tangible, personal benefits: a meal and a warm place to stay on the night he attends the Socialist meeting, new and devoted friends, even a steady job with a socialist hotelier. He also turns his mountaintop experience swiftly to the practical service of the socialist movement; he becomes almost immediately an indefatigable proselytizer for the Socialist Party. The morning after his conversion experience Jurgis goes directly to his mother-in-law, the stepmother of his deceased wife, in order to "tell Elzbieta about the revolution!" In the days thereafter, Jurgis makes seeking new converts to socialism his habitual and virtually perpetual occupation. The evangelical mission of every member of the Socialist Party to spread its gospel was central to its political strategy; as Ostrinski explains, "The rule in America had been that one Socialist made another Socialist once every two years; and if they should maintain the same rate they would carry the country by 1912." In his evangelism, Jurgis adopts features of the orator-preacher, "acquir[ing] the reading habit" in order to develop more successful persuasive arguments to convert reprobates who persisted in the faith of "Individualism," and stepping out into the aisle of a Democratic meeting to denounce its speaker and exhibit the frenzy of inspiration: "He danced about and waved his arms in his excitement—and at the very climax he broke loose from his friends, and got out into the aisle, and proceeded to make a speech himself!"[20] Michael Folsom cites this passage as revealing Jurgis to be a "buffoon"; his friends appear to think so, as they "grabbed him about the neck and shoved him into a seat."[21] But the fault lies not in the quality of Jurgis's inspiration and insight—he duly backs up his denunciation of the speaker with facts—but rather in the overenthusiasm of a new convert who fails to recognize the necessity of not only the preacher and the music but also a community ready to receive the spirit.

It is precisely the value of a socialist community, both in the present and in the future, that dominates the novel after Jurgis's conversion. Almost unrelentingly didactic, only occasionally inspirational or dramatic, the closing chapters repeatedly tell about what the novel's final episode, the socialist rally celebrating election results, shows: the dynamic relationship between the socialist preacher-leader and congregant-party members. But the narrative turn wrought through the Socialist meeting and revival ripples not only forward through the utopian preaching and teaching of the final pages, but also backward through the realist action of the rest of the plot. Narratively and rhetorically, the conversion scene serves as the plausible hinge for unlikely, unexpected conclusions to what had begun as typical realistic plot lines.

The three hundred or so pages of narrative leading up to the conversion scene are organized by two major plot lines typical of the realist novel. The first is the domestic plot, which conventionally begins with the disruption of a particular family arrangement and ends with the institution of a new one. Fittingly for this novel, in which little goes well for nuclear families, the disruption occurs at the opening wedding scene, in which it soon becomes evident that, contrary to Lithuanian tradition, the wedding banquet is going to cost the family far more than they receive in cash gifts. In contrast to, say, the high-realist tradition of Dickens, where the orphan finds long-lost family and the down-and-out heroine finds a provident mate, the ensuing plot complications entirely defeat the Jurgis Rudkus family. Not only is his wife sexually exploited by her boss, but she dies in childbirth; the child for whom she gives her life falls off the sidewalk and drowns in a mud puddle. Still more offensive to conventional plot expectations, the story does not just end there in tragedy. Life goes on as Jurgis initiates another, second kind of plot, a species of bildungsroman: Jurgis takes off on a journey of individual discovery, a move from innocence to maturity. The middle chapters of *The Jungle* tend toward the picaresque, chronicling Jurgis's adventures on the road leading to the Socialist meeting. Insofar as Jurgis does survive his rough-and-tumble experiences on the road and in the city, the novel's bildungsroman plot ends comically, yet here too is an anomaly, for Jurgis does not find himself as an individual so much as he loses himself in a collective movement.

Sinclair's disruptions of conventional plot patterns are revealing, in themselves, about the novel's perspective on the social and ideological assumptions that undergird them. As the typical trajectories of the domestic novel and of the bildungsroman are fundamentally thwarted, Jurgis and readers discover that there is no hope for the American family under the conditions of capitalism, especially not for working-class families. An individual can survive in the capitalist system, as Jurgis learns when he becomes a petty thief and a political operative, but it is not possible to become a mature, socially responsible adult within that system. Sinclair's conclusion asserts that it is impossible for Jurgis to realize his ambitions for domestic happiness and self-development within the ideology of American individualism upon which U.S. capitalism so heavily depends.

But *The Jungle* has the audacity to go beyond these tragic disruptions. Its final pages not only offer utopian preaching and teaching; they also offer alternative utopian endings to realist *plots*. Hence the traditional, nuclear family that Jurgis has forever lost is replaced in Sinclair's novel with the socialist "family" and, ultimately, the human family. Comrade Tommy Hinds's hotel becomes "the new home in which Jurgis lived and worked," whereas in his relationships with his relatives it is said that "poor Jurgis was not very happy in his home life."[22] Moreover, Jurgis as an individual protagonist coming of age becomes absorbed into the collective protagonist of the Socialist-led proletarian movement. Jurgis's disappearance as the novel's central figure has particularly puzzled and frustrated more than one reader.[23] Yet this anomaly, offensive to virtually every plot convention, becomes comprehensible in light of the fact that in the socialist movement a strong individualist such as Jurgis is *supposed* to become subsidiary to the larger collective movement and a collective protagonist.

Another peculiarity of *The Jungle*'s ending—its several direct and indirect addresses to the reader—also catalyzes another kind of reflection upon the preceding realist narrative. Most insistently within the short utopian section, Sinclair hails his readers in ways that push them outside of the narrative itself, which bring the reader to consider a larger social purpose beyond the work of narrative fiction: socialist revolution. Even as the revivalist oration at the Socialist meeting launches the novel's utopian conclusion, the manner in which Sinclair inserts that oration serves to address not only Jurgis but also *readers* of the novel. Sinclair's repeated use of the second-person pronoun is initially directed toward a working-class audience: "You listen to these things . . . and you say, 'Yes, they are true, but they have been that way always.' Or you say, 'Maybe it will come, but not in my time—it will not help me.'" But the appeal also addresses all who would seek truth instead of following convention and expediency. By the time the orator moves toward a conclusion, he draws the class divide much where Charlotte Perkins Gilman and other Populist activists had drawn it in the 1890s, grouping together the "farmer," "miner," "weaver," "mason," "clever man [who] directs," "wise man [who] studies," and "inspired man [who] sings" and counterpointing the lot with "a thousand—ten thousand, maybe—who are the masters of slaves, who own their toil." Thus, when the speaker returns to his direct address of "you, workingmen, workingmen!" the group that he is inviting to identify with that label—whether fictional listeners to this speech or actual readers of the novel—appears to include anyone who would prefer not to be lumped with the ten thousand "idlers" and "parasites" of the capitalist owning class. It is, therefore, the clear majority of American hearers—and readers—that the speaker calls upon when he proclaims the agenda "that somehow, somewhen, the labor of humanity will . . . belong to humanity, to be used for the purposes of humanity, to be controlled by the will of humanity," and it is that great majority of readers who therefore are invited to be the agents of that agenda: "And if this is ever to be, how is it to be—what power is there that will bring it about? Will it be the task of your masters, do you think—will they write the charter of your liberties? . . . Can you not see that the task is your task—yours to dream, yours to resolve, yours to execute?"[24]

The narrative turn from realism to utopianism thus directs its appeal not so much to its central character, Jurgis, as to the novel's readership. We are apt, over one hundred years after the novel's original reception, to diminish the achievement and the impact of the novel's direct connection with its readers. In this connection, the genius of Sinclair's choice of subject matter can hardly be credited enough—or perhaps it was the genius of Fred Warren, who sent Sinclair to Chicago on assignment. For in demonstrating the actual physical corruption of the U.S. food supply, Sinclair had happened upon the most direct and visceral means of connecting a broad readership, including many middle-class citizens, with the particular proletarian lives of workers such as Jurgis, Ona, and Marija. The book did not just connect naturalistic characters tangibly to their audience, challenging the wall of difference normally separating the sordid people and places of naturalism from the majority, bourgeois audience. Nor is it merely notable for combining documentary with fiction in a way that anticipates the documentary realism, or the "admixture of journalism into fiction," that Barbara Foley heralds as distinctive of Communist writers of the 1930s. It is notable because it exposes, through precise (even) though fictional representation, industry's material corruption of the nation's food supply and so makes its challenge, literally, at gut level. The conditions that the novel described in the stockyards, born of the profit motive, struck home because they threatened the food of every reader as well as the lives of every worker in the yards. And thus, not only in the utopian concluding chapters of the novel and in the oration scene that brings Jurgis to embrace socialism, but also in the realist narrative that comprises the main body of the novel, Sinclair finds means to break down the barrier between reality and ideal as well as realism and utopianism. He appeals directly to his readers, calling them to a conviction of capitalist evils, showing them the salvation of socialism, and appealing to their active discipleship on behalf of the gospel of the earthly cooperative commonwealth. Sinclair hopes, thereby, to enact the role of preacher, to chant the music, and convert his readers by a frenzy to the gospel of socialism.

BLACK RELIGION AND "GOVERNMENTS OF MEN": DU BOIS'S *QUEST OF THE SILVER FLEECE*

> "God calls. Will you hear? Come to Jesus. The harvest is waiting. Who will cry: 'Here am I, send me!'"

The reception of W. E. B. Du Bois's novel *The Quest of the Silver Fleece* could hardly be more different than that of *The Jungle*. Whereas Sinclair's novel was the early twentieth-century equivalent of *Uncle Tom's Cabin* or *Looking Backward*, a tremendous popular success that also tangibly impacted American politics and society, Du Bois's novel was published in just a few thousand copies, was positively but not widely reviewed, and was not even fully recognized as a socialist book until the 1970s.[25] But the novel nevertheless testifies not only to the development of Du Bois's socialism from an early date—the line of analysis developed in chapter 4—but also to the dispersal of a utopian-realist formal practices among a range of U.S. socialist writers. And as with Sinclair, the chief narrative and cultural trope for bridging the gap is the scene of religious conversion, which appears in *Quest of the Silver Fleece* not at just one critical juncture but at three.

The utopian vision is developed through the unfolding of one of the two major plots of the novel, the romance between the young, southern blacks Bles Alwyn and Zora. In a novel otherwise featuring a familiar southern landscape, rife with racial conflict and exploitation, the representation of Zora and Bles as a utopian ideal depends upon a definite romanticism in their characterization and even more upon a distancing from that landscape. At the outset, Bles is a conventional Talented Tenth figure, the character able—and tempted—to consider a career in the upwardly mobile Washington, DC, pigmentocracy. Zora stands out more fully as a multifaceted prodigy: not only bewitchingly beautiful and charismatic, but able through private study to master Alabama law sufficiently to defend in court her community's title to their land. In the first half of the plot centering upon Zora and Bles, organized around the cultivation of a small field of cotton that they hew out of a swamp even as their romantic relationship blossoms, Du Bois's representation of character and setting is intensely idyllic, even mythic. Bles initially sees the island in the swamp as "a pretty tough proposition for clearing and ploughing," but Zora declares it to be the place "where the Dreams [*sic*] lives."[26] From this overtly idealistic and utopian starting point, the romance of labor and love in the cotton fields only deepens. The Edenic scene is markedly Afrocentric; African religion, rituals, and fertility symbols are prominent. In Africa, Zora's mother, Elspeth, was a conjure-woman, a religious priestess knowledgeable in all the secrets of communicating with the divine, healing disease, soothsaying, and planting a bountiful harvest. She it is who plants the field after Zora and Bles have cleared it, bringing forth "small, smooth black seeds" that she announces have been "sowed with the three spells of Obi in the old land ten thousand moons ago."[27]

For *Quest* as for *The Jungle*, however, the full flowering of the cooperative ideal is located in the future. If, on the one hand, the fact that an ideal community is present at the outset seems to ground its possibility more concretely in reality, and if, too, the depiction of this community throughout the novel allows it to function in counterpoint, all along, with the realist plot that serves up a particularly critical representation of northern capitalism and southern plantocracy working in tandem to exploit black and white labor alike, the grounding of a prototypical utopian community in the present also, on the other hand, appears to open it up to corruption from the real world and the realist plot. Even as, for example, Elspeth's religious rituals and power have been preserved with minimal corruption from their sources, her status as the preserver of a fertility cult has been terribly distorted by slavery, for under slavery and its postbellum reincarnations Elspeth has devolved into a procurer of black girls for the local white men. Significantly, it is the old economy of the "traffic in women" as well as the new economy of capitalism that conspire to ruin the utopian dream, presented simultaneously by the romance of Bles and Zora and the premarket economy of their miraculous cotton crop. The leading local perpetrator of these twin corruptions is, in fact, one and the same person. Soon after the cotton crop is harvested—two glorious bales of long-staple cotton—the biggest landowner in the vicinity, Harry Cresswell, asserts his property rights over the field Zora and Bles have carved from the swamp. Almost at the same time, Bles learns that Elspeth has pimped her own daughter, Zora, with the principal customer being none other than the same Harry Cresswell. The utopian, Afrocentric dream has apparently been an illusion. To underscore the intermingling of economic and sexual exploitation, the chapter in which Zora brings her cotton to market and is cheated out of its value is entitled "The Rape of the Fleece." Meanwhile, Bles Alwyn renounces his ties to Zora and heads off for Washington, DC, to make his way in the cynical but very real world of politics.

These incidents occurring at the novel's midway point mark key turns in both plot and thematic exposition, for here it is that the possibility of human relations based upon love and labor equality are challenged directly by a more grittily realist plot that features not only the machinations of the white plantocracy figured by the Cresswells and their white capitalist allies and kin (by strategic intermarriage), but also the pragmatic calculations of the individualistic and rapidly stratifying black urban community that Bles discovers in Washington. Even as the Cresswells, their northern allies, and the African American bourgeoisie seek to maintain and extend their privileges, Zora and the black proletariat appear doomed to fall further behind. After Harry Cresswell impounds the cotton, he also vindictively charges "back rent" for the squatter's cabin in the swamp where Zora and her mother have been living, placing Zora suddenly in danger of falling into a downward spiral of indebtedness and share cropping: "She was now penniless, and in a sense helpless. She was now a peon bound to a master's bidding."[28] Still, as she clings to the bale as one of her children, sneaking into the Cresswells' great barns at night, the bale signifies a real possibility of unexploited labor, of labor for love and productivity rather than power and profit: "One thing alone lay in her wild fancy like a great and wonderful fact dragging the dream to earth and anchoring it there. That was the Silver Fleece. Like a brooding mother, Zora had watched it. . . . To Zora's mind, this beautiful baled fibre was hers; it typified happiness; it was an holy thing which profane hands had stolen."[29] To put the matter simply, Zora seeks to own the full product of her labor. This ideal of unalienated labor will persist through the intertwined plots of the novel. How to render that ideal as a reality looms as a steep challenge, however, for under present hellish circumstances Zora's fantasy of labor ownership has far less foundation than Colonel Cresswell's boast to an admiring visitor: "Yes, sir, grown on my place, by my niggers, sir!"[30]

Whereas the split between realist and utopian modes in *The Jungle* is particularly sharply marked by the plot transition of Jurgis's conversion, the transition in *Quest*, figured in Zora's conversion to the gospel of economic and social cooperation, is more gradually shaded. Yet much like *The Jungle, Quest of the Silver Fleece* shifts, by its end, away from a traditional plot line focused upon individualistic success or failure to one concerned with collective aims. Zora, like Jurgis, is compelled to renounce her prospects for romance and family life before committing to the communal project that propels her through the remainder of the novel. After Bles leaves her, Zora finds work as a domestic for a wealthy white woman with whom she travels widely; it is from this woman that Zora learns that Bles is engaged to be married to Miss Wynn, an upwardly mobile socialite in black Washington, DC, society. In despair Zora wanders the streets; she assumes Bles is forever lost to her. The parallel to Jurgis is again uncanny, whose last ties to his former family seem to have been snapped when Marija announces her intention to remain a prostitute, after which Jurgis wanders out into the streets—and happens into the Socialist meeting. Much as with Jurgis, Zora is attracted to the church because "It looked warm, and she was cold."[31]

While the meeting that Jurgis attends is a Socialist rally that resembles a revival in an African American church, the meeting that Zora discovers is a revival in an African American church that resembles a socialist rally. Except for the color of his skin, the itinerant evangelist at Zora's meeting is practically interchangeable with the leader at Jurgis's: "He had the build and look of a fanatic: thin to emaciation; brown; brilliant-eyed; his words snapped with nervous energy and rang in awful earnestness." The preacher sounds a traditional Christian theme, at least initially: self-renunciation. But this is self-renunciation not for the sake of individual salvation in the sweet by-and-by, but for the sake of group advancement in the here and now, and thus it speaks both to Zora's immediate need and her long-term solution for her people. The preacher proclaims: "A single self as an end is, and ought to be, disappointment; it is too low; it is nothing. Only in a whole world of selves—only in their vast good is true salvation. The good of others is our true good; work for others; not for *your* salvation, but the salvation of the world." This is not what this particular congregation is accustomed to hearing from their regular minister. For Zora, however, who has been respectful but "untouched" by the Frenzy of the southern black church and appreciative but not especially moved by the "beauty of wall, window, and hymn" in the northern white church, the minister's call to worldly self-sacrifice and worldwise community-building is a soothing balm and a stirring challenge.[32] Zora alone walks down the aisle to accept the minister's charge. When Zora returns to the street and then to her employer, her outlook is radically transformed. Like Jurgis's story, the tale related by Zora and the narrator is clothed in religious language—"I've been converted," Zora reports—but the supernatural is just as decidedly naturalized here as it had been in Douglass's *Narrative,* Sinclair's *The Jungle,* and Du Bois's own closing injunction in "Of the Faith of the Fathers." For Zora in *Quest of the Silver Fleece:* "Above the doubt and beyond the unrest, rose the great end, the mighty ideal, that flickered and wavered, but ever grew and waxed strong, until it became possible, and through it all things were possible. Thus from the grave of youth and love, amid the soft, low singing of dark and bowed worshippers, the Angel of the Resurrection rolled away the stone."[33]

Still, the collective enterprise is merely initiated at the unconventional, secularized revival meeting in the northern city. The call and Zora's vision are to be realized in the South. It is to the South that she must return and win additional disciples to the gospel of cooperative labor and independent black community-building—and in the South where Du Bois provides not one but two revival-style meetings to get the job done. First, upon returning home to the South, Zora goes to a church meeting and succeeds in persuading two hundred of her neighbors to help clear land for an agricultural commune including, but also greatly adding to, the cotton field originally planted by herself and Bles. But the day appointed for the beginning of this project coincides with the date of a great revival meeting, and the jealous local preacher turns the congregation against her. In the eyes of the pastor and his followers, the problem with Zora's scheme is that it is too closely grounded in the Kingdom of Earth. Zora is suspect from the start, given her mother's allegiance to the altogether too-material, earth-centered practices of traditional African religion. It depends upon a second orator at the big meeting, an elderly man of longer-standing authority in the community, to bring out Zora's neighbors to lend her assistance. Significantly, his authority is fundamentally rooted in black Christianity. Being someone who "spoke their religious language and spoke it with absolute confidence and authority," this unexpected ally of Zora is able to counter the proclamations of the local preacher with a message blending a traditional altar call with a call to worldly action: "'God is done sent me to offer you all salvation,' he cried, while the people wept and wailed; 'not in praying, but in works. Follow me!'" As the transformation of the Saturday revival to an organizing meeting for another kind of revival occurs late at night—indeed, in the early hours of Sunday morning—Du Bois's symbolism is racheted up in intensity, for this means that the land-clearing takes place in violation of the Christian "sabbath" consecrated by rest and worship. By blending traditional Sunday imagery with the radically different labor of this particular Sunday, Du Bois indicates simultaneously the revolutionary potential of the church and the revolutionary change needed to realize it: "Before sunrise, tools were in the swamp, axes and saws and hammers. The noise of prayer and singing filled the Sabbath dawn. The news of the great revival spread, and men and women came pouring in. Then of a sudden the uproar stopped, and the ringing of axes and grating of saws and tugging of mules was heard. The forest trembled as by some mighty magic, swaying and falling with crash on crash."[34] Here, as in Sinclair, superhuman force is gained not by supernatural power but the massed force of a collective social body, here leveling an entire forest in a single day.

The revolution that Zora and her southern allies wreak upon the usual Sabbath is typical of both the plot turns and the themes enunciated throughout *Quest of the Silver Fleece.* Zora's determination to put the community first, her own self-interests second, extends to the romantic plot even after Bles returns South. A revolution must be initiated in gender and sexual as well as in class and racial relations. From Zora's point of view, there can be no more fundamental and important aim than to rewrite the sexual and romantic politics of the South—including the sexual-romantic politics of that primal relationship wherein she was the Madonna. Thus, when Bles returns to the South, disgusted with the cynical self-interestedness of the African American bourgeoisie in Washington, he recognizes that Zora is no longer the young girl whom he fell in love with but a mature woman and community leader. When he gathers the courage to ask this newly made woman to marry him, Zora initially turns him down and asks him instead to work alongside her at the rapidly expanding cooperative community. If in one sense this means a break from the union of work and love symbolized by the fleece, it is perhaps a necessary one in a world so callous about ideals. Now, too, the unequal masculine/feminine dichotomies of mind/body, experience/impulse, are decisively checked. His romantic attentions, indeed his whole relationship with her, are no longer essential to her happiness or her vision, as they had been. He is instead merely an important adjunct to the cooperative project; he is being asked "to be simply human, a learner and a follower," to accept "comradeship" in place of his erstwhile roles as guardian and lover.[35] Formerly, she had been forced to accept dependency upon men for economic support, whether the men in question were whites that made her a whore, or blacks able and willing to exalt and support her as an angel in the house. Now (in precisely the sort of rearrangement of socioeconomic roles that Gilman had called for), Du Bois envisions that the communal project gives women the psychological independence and economic self-sufficiency that allow them to meet men, black and white, as equals. Thus, although it has some of the trappings of a conventional romantic plot, *Quest of the Silver Fleece* works to challenge economic and social inequality on gender as well as racial and class lines.

The comprehensive social democracy envisioned by *Quest of the Silver Fleece* seeks, ultimately, to link up with the cooperative commonwealth being promulgated by Sinclair in *The Jungle* and by other white socialists throughout the movement. Zora and Du Bois have much bigger designs than the independence and integrity of black education or the success of a single cooperative community. For when Zora realizes they can save the school and Miss Smith suggests that "the battle's over," Zora immediately sees the school's assured independence as only the beginning.[36] As we have seen, *Quest* envisions black communes as a self-defensive stratagem, a stopgap until white workers achieve class consciousness, realize their common cause with blacks, and seek black workers as allies in seeking social democracy on a wider, national scale. But here, at its most expansive vision, the ending of the novel is simultaneously marked by a realist's understanding of limits. Only on rare occasions is such solidarity even glimpsed by other characters, as when the white mother of a child crippled by a mill accident, having just been denied her suit for damages in court, comments upon the next case in which a black child stands trial for petty larceny: "Durned if I don't think these white slaves and black slaves ought ter git together."[37] The mother's sentiments are seconded by a white mill worker down from the North (in all probability a labor organizer), who offers the following to his fellow white workers: "Get together with the niggers and hold up this whole capitalist gang. If you do n't get the niggers first, they'll use 'em for a club to throw you down."[38] But this particular worker has just been fired, probably blacklisted; this speech is his final word before getting on the train for the North.

In addition to the theoretical limits of Du Bois's socialist vision, articulated in narrative and philosophy, there are also the practical limits of audience reception and agency. The novel had only a fraction of the readers that *The Jungle* did, and only a fraction of those readers, white or black, were likely to act upon those suggestions. But in writing *Quest of the Silver Fleece*, Du Bois the first-time novelist did have one particularly important audience very close to his imagined reader, perhaps even an ideal reader, and certainly one who was well positioned to act upon the novel's realist recognitions and utopian plans: himself. If the immediate reception of the novel was modest, its impact was uniquely extended and amplified to the degree that Du Bois used it as a template for an agenda that he was subsequently to articulate in *The Crisis* and sought to act upon as a leader in the NAACP. As *Crisis* editor, Du Bois had the opportunity to record and to encourage developments in economic cooperation and social equality with a highly receptive audience and over an extended period of time—more than twenty years. The importance of women's rights as a corollary and necessary condition of equal rights for blacks; the significance of labor agitation among whites and sporadic attempts toward cooperation between white and black labor; the value of the black church as a source of racial organization and solidarity—all of these were featured regularly in the pages of *The Crisis.* Featured more intermittently, though often enough to make the editor's ongoing interest clear, were reports and recommendations regarding the specific anticapitalist remedy of cooperative economics in the black community. In 1917 and 1918, for example, following his appeal to the "consecrated business man," the editor published a series of articles about economic cooperation among blacks that culminated in a substantial dialogue with nationally known co-op authority J. P. Warbasse and in Du Bois's convening a conference on cooperation and even founding the "Negro Cooperative Guild" in the fall of 1918.[39] To be sure, such recommendations did not always find a very tractable audience among readers of *The Crisis*—but this reception was prognosticated by the realism of the *Quest of the Silver Fleece*, even as the necessity of a persistent vision of the cooperative commonwealth was acted out though its utopianism.

"NEW RELIGION" AND THE SKEPTICAL BROTHER: *MOVING THE MOUNTAIN*

> "A topsy-turvy world, wherein all one's most cherished ideals are found to be reversed, rearranged, or utterly gone; where strange new facts are accompanied by strange new thoughts and strange new feelings—the pressure becomes terrific."

Given Charlotte Perkins Gilman's strong roots in the Nationalist movement, it is hardly surprising that when she turned to novel writing it was the utopian form popularized by Edward Bellamy that she adopted as her primary mode. Yet her first full-length utopian novel, *Moving the Mountain,* was actually less sanguine than either Sinclair's or Du Bois's realist-utopian novels about the speed and ease with which American society might be able to make a transition into socialism. Perhaps the key factor was her comrades' newness to the movement. Whereas they were fresh converts in the first decade of the twentieth century, she had been affiliated with socialism for two decades. She had seen too much about how the Nationalist enthusiasm had quieted, and the Populist movement diverted, to be overly confident about any particularly hopeful predictions. In most respects the novel fits the utopian mode precisely, for the dominant impression of her representative citizen-narrator of 1910, removed abruptly from the modern world and then returned to it suddenly thirty years later, is his wonderment at the changes that have taken place by 1940. Gilman's utopian scenario is just as far fetched as that of any other writer in the mode, as she postulates an informant who is lost on a Himalayan expedition, loses most of his memory, and is cared for by a remote Tibetan tribe until recovered by his enterprising younger sister, now all grown up and a college president. Yet the imperative that lies within the very premise of the book—to make society much better within half the span of a person's life—foregrounds the difficulty of such a transformation, even bringing to light dystopian possibilities elided by Sinclair's and Du Bois's narratives. Highlighting the difficulty is that this novel, while again using religious experience as the central paradigm for expressing and negotiating religious experience, uses as its narrator-protagonist a most reluctant and skeptical inquirer into the new religion of social cooperation.

Although Gilman's religious references are more aligned with austere Congregationalism than passionate Methodism, Gilman's narrative is immediately framed in ways that both highlight the importance of religion and liken the passage into socialism to a religious experience. Just before John Robertson, the novel's narrator-protagonist, is separated from his expedition party in Tibet, the group lays hands on a six-month-old American newspaper announcing the death of Mary Baker Eddy, founder of Christian Science, and reporting upon a new religious enthusiasm sweeping the United States: "Another religion had burst forth and was sweeping the country, madly taken up by the women."[40] The novel subsequently treats religion—not politics—as the principal model for how social democracy is promulgated and understood. When on the voyage home John first confronts his sister Ellen, or Nellie, about the new society he will be returning to, he begins with what seems to him the worst of all possibilities: "Come—Have we adopted Socialism?" Nellie calmly replies that socialism has indeed been adopted twenty years before and has become so fundamental a part of social organization as to cease to be in any way controversial. More important to the social transformation—and more fully part of the ongoing work of the society—is the "New Religion." John is manifestly uninterested in *this* explanation; from observing their father, a highly religious man, he had concluded that religion was a "joke," "a patent fire escape" for arranging things for the next life and a racket for getting money in this one. He wonders: "Did you have another Incarnation of any body?" John's flip question is the furthest thing from the conversion experiences of Jurgis and Zora—and for good reason, because he is not yet converted and continually proves a difficult student of the social democratic catechism.

In our other socialist conversion narratives, human bodies when massed and organized collectively become larger than life; they become the gods of a fully naturalized supernaturalist humanism. In *Moving the Mountain,* John's skeptical retort seemingly prevents his sister Nellie from being more direct in naming the "Incarnation" that inspires the new religion: "'You might call it that,' Nellie allowed, her voice growing quietly earnest, 'We certainly had somebody with an unmistakable Power.'" It presently emerges, however, that the "somebody with an unmistakable Power" is the collective social body—just as in Sinclair and Du Bois—wherefrom it follows that the religion of humanity consists in nothing more or less than the collective life of humanity. Thus, the experience of religious conversion, in this instance, is effectively the same one expressed through the collision of realist and utopian plots in *The Jungle* and *Quest of the Silver Fleece*—the struggle between individual aspirations and the collective good. In *Moving the Mountain,* though, the clearest account of the conversion is not an individual one but a collective enthusiasm for socially productive labor. Nellie's account explicitly compares the spread of the new social gospel to religious proselytizing, although, in keeping with her (and Gilman's) attitude throughout, the rapid dissemination is characterized not so much by a frenzy as by a deep earnestness that fails to stimulate much of a response in John:

> "A Social Service Union was formed the country over; it was part of the new religion. Every town has one—men and women. The same spirit

that used to give us crusaders and missionaries now gave plenty of enthusiastic workers."

"I don't see yet how you got up any enthusiasm about work," said I.

"It was not work for oneself." Nellie explained. "That is what used to make it so sordid; we used really to believe that we were working each for himself. This new idea was overwhelming in its simplicity—and truth; work is social service—social service is religion—that's about it."[41]

The most comprehensive religious image for understanding the novel's view of socialism—and its efforts to render socialism in familiar and widely acceptable terms—is the one suggested in the novel's title itself. "Moving the Mountain" alludes to Jesus's rabbinic conundrum about faith being able to move mountains. One passage in which it appears is Mark 11:23, which promises that followers of Christ will be able to command mountains to throw themselves into the sea. The more familiar and still more paradoxical form of the saying is found in Matthew 17:20, where Jesus tells his disciples that with "faith as small as a mustard seed, you can say to this mountain, 'Move from here to there' and it will move. Nothing will be impossible for you."[42] The sense of both of these original passages highlights the necessity and power of supernatural intervention into human affairs: if the disciples of God incarnate can, after all, muster up only the faith of a mustard seed, then clearly the differential in force between that and the power to move mountains must be supplied by a force outside immediate human resources.

Characteristic of both Gilman and her fellow socialists at this historical moment when socialism was still on the rise, Gilman's handling of this metaphor and theme thoroughly naturalizes it, brings it definitely within the scope of human power while still retaining the sense of grand potentiality, of being able truly to "move mountains." In Gilman's view, the problem is not that the physical mass of the mountain is so terribly obdurate, but that the usual state of mind and lack of faith, which says it cannot and shall not be moved, *is*. One of John's guest tutors, a doctor of sociology, explains that "ideas are the real things, sir! Bricks and mortar? Bah! We can put brick and mortar in any shape we choose—but we have to choose first! . . . We had every constituent of human happiness, sir—except the sense to use them. The channel of progress was obstructed with a deposit of prehistoric ideas."[43] Equally important to Gilman's robust and materialistic conception of idealism is her insistence upon collectivism. The faith of the "mustard seed" looks small because it is presented as singular, and any kind of real change—

whether it involves literally moving mountains or transforming social relations—is inconceivable without its being held by many individuals en masse. This is precisely the explanation that John's informants offer for the rapidity with which society has changed during the thirty years while John has been away. Brother-in-law Owen explains to John that the very bricks and mortar of society have been rearranged, the channel for progress opened swiftly and permanently, because of the swift and nearly universal "lateral transmission" of education: "You conceive of it as being done in one place after another, instead of in every place at once."[44] When the fundamental logic of the new social ideas is presented to and grasped clearly by practically all people, they are able together to challenge and change the most recalcitrant of social, including material, circumstances.

All of this does not mean that the drama and trauma of the conversion experience from capitalism to socialism, individualism to collectivism, pragmatism to idealism, are absent in the cerebral and didactic world of *Moving the Mountain.* Truly, the rhetorical virtues of *The Jungle* and *The Quest of the Silver Fleece* stem largely from their being able to keep in view the various pitfalls and structural inequalities of capitalism for long enough, or at least frequently enough, that the socialist conversion is largely experienced as a relief. The cost of the conversion—the loss of individuality, the suspension of individual advantage for the sake of the collective good—is either largely submerged or posed as a minor inconvenience in comparison to the trauma of the protagonists in a brutal realist plot. With that realist plot largely absent in *Moving the Mountain* and with conversion a foregone conclusion, Gilman's utopian novel—like practically all other novels in the mode—delves more deeply into utopian design, at the price of exposing more fully its potential pitfalls. Without a realist plot helping to secure the idealism of the social democratic utopian vision, the narrative opens other oppositional possibilities, so that the utopian vision inevitably brings into relief its dystopian double.

Our guide to the alternative dystopian vision, narrator and protagonist John Robertson, signals his discomfort almost from the outset. John expresses it strongly at the moment of sudden transition from his "realistic" old-world existence to the utopian new world of America, circa 1940, which is narrated within the first two pages of the novel. Although not definitely flagged as a religious conversion experience, John's account shares many of the features of this experience as described by the other writers, beginning with the sensation of having been dead (or presumed dead in Tibet, in John's case) and of awakening to a new life:

> When one comes to life again like this, and has to renew acquaintance with one's own mind, in a sudden swarming rush of hurrying memories—that is a good deal of pressure for a brain so long unused.
>
> But when on top of that, one is pushed headlong into a world immeasurably different from the world one has left at twenty-five—a topsy-turvy world, wherein all one's most cherished ideals are found to be reversed, rearranged, or utterly gone; where strange new facts are accompanied by strange new thoughts and strange new feelings—the pressure becomes terrific.[45]

Just as with Jurgis, Frederick Douglass, and even Zora, the awakening to new life occurs after a period in which the brain has slumbered, John having been reduced to an existence of little more than physical survival while away in Tibet, just as the rest of the world was awakening to new social connections and responsibilities. Furthermore, John describes his experience as consisting in a complete revolution in perspective that results in both physical and mental tumult. Yet the very pivot that functions as a dramatic, positive, religious conversion for Sinclair, Douglass, and Du Bois is merely traumatic for John.

Eventually John, the visitor from the old world, is persuaded to accept the advantages of the new. But the debate in *Moving the Mountain* is framed in terms that the novel's readers might not be quite so willing to go along with. John's objections are relatively harmless. He tends to resist most strenuously those points on which Gilman's arguments are the strongest, as when he fusses about few women behaving with the demure femininity he recalls as so flattering to his male ego. But his reluctance gestures to the possibility of resistant readers, some of whom may find highly problematic points to which John raises no particular objection, points that appear to reflect Gilman's own prescriptions (and, all too often, prejudices). Considering that in Gilman's time restrictions upon immigration were widely popular, and considering that nowadays Gilman's ethnic and racial prejudices have been well documented, readers might not be surprised at the ramped-up program for the cultural education and assimilation of new immigrants that Nellie touts when she and brother John make landfall at New York City. Generous readers might even find a constructive, progressive element in the various national gates of entry that are exalted as "splendid arches with figures on them, like the ones they used to put up for Triumphs." There are gates both for those immigrants favored and for those disfavored by popular proposals that sought to limit immigration and culminated in the infamous Immigration Restriction Act of 1924: "There's the German Gate, and the Spanish

Gate, the English Gate, the Italian Gate—and so on." But the realistic details invented by Gilman are disquieting: before even embarking for the United States, the emigrants must "be antiseptically clean, they and all their belongings" and upon arrival—just to be sure!—"There is physical examination—the most searching and thorough—microscopic—chemical."[46] The details are hardly incidental; Gilman's proposed immigration policies reflect a central strategy for transforming society: the application of the methods of scientific management and industrial efficiency to human beings.

Moving the Mountain is disarmingly direct about the possibility of applying principles of scientific selection and industrial management at the point of reproduction. One of John's informants, a transportation expert, explains to him: "You will remember the dawning notions of 'scientific management' we began to have in the first decade of the new century. . . . It occurred to us to apply it to ourselves—and we did." Thus does Gilman slip eugenics into her mix of utopian/dystopian projections. "Any woman can be a mother," Nellie elsewhere tells John, "if she's normal," a conditional clause put in casually—and all the more alarmingly for that—which makes clear a woman's fitness to give birth is determined in advance by medical experts. Equally scientific and systematic are the measures that *Moving the Mountain* projects for managing unsuitable individuals already born and living as citizens in the United States. The process is framed as an issue of the necessary and necessarily painful moments of conversion from the old capitalist society to the new social democratic one. A prominent social historian of 1940 explains to John Robertson, "Our first step—or one of our first steps, for we advanced like a strenuous centipede—was to check the birth of defectives and degenerates. Certain classes of criminals and perverts were rendered incapable of reproducing their kind." Finally, a professor of ethics—a man cured of the dissipation of his youth—explains to John that to create proper social conditions, "We killed many hopeless degenerates, insane, idiots, and real perverts, after trying our best powers of cure." The directness and brutality of these declarations must necessarily undercut the good doctor's reassurance that "it is really astonishing to see how much can be done with what we used to call criminals, merely by first-class physical treatment."[47] From our latter-day perspective, even Gilman's choice of a time frame for her narrative is eerie. For in forecasting the world of 1940 as well as in embracing elements of eugenics, she unavoidably evokes the specter of Germany's National Socialism, the Nazis. Can it be merely a heaping on of unfortunate historical-linguistic coincidence that the movement within which Gilman was schooled in socialism was called Nationalism?

There can be no simple answer to this question, whether historically, ethically, or politically. Although it reflects no particular credit on Gilman either as a novelist or as a humanitarian that *Moving the Mountain* seldom offers any evidence of irony, let alone criticism, of the minute social engineering anticipated in the United States of 1940, it is peculiarly fitting that from passage to passage it is almost impossible to decide whether the novel should be read as utopian or dystopian. We can find no firm standpoint either to celebrate the novel's egalitarianism or to condemn its authoritarianism. Expressed in terms of literary modes and political binaries, the issue may usefully be framed by the observation that no generic mode, linguistic expression, or even ethical stance can be completely pure, utterly unmixed. The most immediately realistic depiction evokes some idealistic projection. The most consistently utopian projection calls for some form of realism. Utopian narratives, however idealistic or futuristic they may be, must after all be moored in the experience of their writers and readers, and this mooring means that utopian texts always remain connected to the contingencies—and the possibilities—of their social situation, reflecting their limits even while imagining the possibility of changing those limits.[48] The most rigorously idealistic projection of all can, at times, warrant the most brutally realistic praxis of all. Capitalism can—and every day does—justify the most barbaric behavior, whether in the name of a principle or for the sake of pragmatism. Socialism can do—and has done—the same.

For Gilman and other socialists, the problem for any social democratic society was that no utopian blueprint—no matter how perfect—could be drawn upon a social tabula rasa. In their societies, capitalism had already been there first. This is the major premise underlying Nellie's apologetics for mercy killing of "hopeless degenerates," compulsory sterilization of "a large class of perverts," and asylums for "blind and crippled" syphilitics: "One of our inherited handicaps was that great mass of wreckage left over from the foolishness and ignorance of the years behind us."[49] To a large extent in Sinclair's account of the socialist conversion experience, and to a smaller yet still significant extent in Du Bois's account, the apparent sharpness of the dividing line between *before* and *after* nurtures the illusion that the whole society as well as the individual's perspective can be transformed just like that, at a stroke. The sustained focus of Sinclair's and Du Bois's narratives upon realist, anticapitalist critique permits the utopian, socialist alternative to appear more ideal than it could ever be in embodied reality. By concentrating on the period *after* the liberating experience of conversion, and by describing with frankness the process of consolidating and institutionalizing the "new religion," Gilman's narrative attacks that illusion at its root. Recognizing the risks of projecting a utopia too far into the future and losing plausible contact with current reality, Gilman chose to situate her new and improved society in *Moving the Mountain* just thirty years into the future. Because she also recognized that such a short period was insufficient to bring about the transformation of an entire society—and because she could not anticipate all of the ways future readers would recognize the limitations of her utopian vision—she called it reasonably "a baby Utopia, a little one that can grow."[50] *Moving the Mountain* thereby forges an uneasy balance between the affirmations of its utopian vision—the abolition of poverty, attention to the welfare of all individuals—and its allowances for a necessary social pragmatism. Early on, when John attempts to establish the straw-man argument that socialism promises plenty for all without labor, Nellie avers that of course "Socialism did not alter the fact that wealth comes by labor."[51] The novel subsequently proceeds in the most direct terms to suggest that a social democracy must continue to have laws, jails, asylums, and various restrictions upon individual liberty enacted for the common good.

Gilman's novel also anticipates the limits imposed upon human societies by the finite material resources on earth. For all of the ways that Gilman's utopian projections may strike latter-day readers as off the mark—even as flirting with dystopianism—Gilman's environmentalism anticipates what amounts to the final argument for a political economy of egalitarian distribution as opposed to capital accumulation. Intriguingly, the utopian environmental vision of *Moving the Mountain* uses as its point of departure the realist critique of Sinclair's *The Jungle.* Of the several catalysts of social democracy described by Gilman, including the enthusiasm for the new religion, the one described in the most detail and pinned down with the greatest historical specificity is linked directly to public outrage over impurities in food and public measures seeking to remedy those impurities. Nellie recalls for John that the movement had already been afoot when he had disappeared into Tibet in 1910: "The world was ill-fed. . . . People sold poison for food in 1910—don't forget that! You may remember the row that was beginning to be made about it."[52] The allusions to *The Jungle* and to the pure food and drug legislation that followed it are unmistakable—as is the implication (shared by Sinclair, as it happened) that the legislation marked not an end but a beginning for the social democratic movement. From this factual starting point, the fictional narrative that Gilman spins out emphasizes women's leadership in demanding—and supplying—safe and healthful foodstuffs. Immediate domestic concerns over food consumption soon spiral outward to systemic changes in production, social organization, and resource management.

As on other topics, Gilman's utopian vision for environmentalism sometimes seems almost calculated to offend. The 1940 world described by Gilman has accepted as settled policy the extermination of nuisance species—and has eliminated any number of species already. Not only has the world been rid of the "gipsy moth" and the "elm beetle," but Nellie announces proudly that tigers, wolves, and most "big game" have been systematically exterminated.[53] But to such offenses against environmental preservation, Gilman adds expectations of clean and renewable energy sources and a far more healthful environment. The harbors of New York City are clean enough to swim in, and the air, too, is clean: "The Jersey shore shone clear," John reports, "no foul pall of oil smoke overhanging."[54] Coal is no longer burned in cities but at the mines, where it generates electricity that is transmitted elsewhere. But apparently the need for nonrenewable sources of energy has been greatly decreased, for sister Nellie reports: "New York has enough water power, you see. The tide mills are enough for this whole region."[55] Elsewhere, *Moving the Mountain* speaks of wind, geothermal, and solar energy as being widely tapped. Meanwhile, the countryside—which we might imagine having been despoiled by the new coal-burning generators—is portrayed as a well-manicured parkland, "old beauty cultivated in every direction," with particular attention to the preservation and cultivation of vegetation: "You don't see so many bald spots. A healthy, permanent world has to keep its fur on."[56] Arboriculture is especially valued as it increases the surface available to photosynthesis and resists more effectively the loss of fertile soil to erosion.[57]

Still, Gilman's vision of an anthropocentric and minutely engineered nature is the kind of thing that might further stir up fear of totalitarianism. This is Thomas Peyser's observation on the arboriculture of *Herland,* one of whose male visitors describes its cultivated forests of edible seed and fruit-bearing trees as "a truck farm." The quotation of Zygmunt Bauman that Peyser applies to the Herland forest, "a gardener's vision, projected upon a world-size screen," applies all the more fully to the continental landscape of *Moving the Mountain.* And what of Bauman's assertion, applied to Gilman by Peyser, that this gardener's vision reflects "the grimmest totalitarian enterprises of the twentieth century"?[58] Readers' suspicions might be increased all the more when they understand that Gilman countenances eliminating not only wild predators but cats and dogs: "We've changed our view as to 'pets' and 'domestic animals,'" sister Nellie explains placidly; "We ourselves are the only domestic animals allowed now."[59]

Yet it is precisely at a point such as this, where Gilman's future society seems almost pettily dystopian, that the standpoint of *Moving the Mountain* cuts through the ideological sentimentalities of modernity. There are real costs in the socialist conversion, but some things that seem valuable are almost purely the sentimentalities of an individualistic, bourgeois culture that deserve largely to be debunked and rejected. The maintenance and reverence of wild nature, posited by Peyser as the antithesis of Gilman's heartless "mastery of nature," are largely the concerns of a bourgeois society with the luxury to maintain large tracts of land as nonproductive wilderness. Gilman's emphasis on agricultural productivity looks rather different from the point of view of poor people who are starving but might not be, if only agricultural wealth were distributed more evenly. For all her anthropomorphism, Gilman's attitude toward pets cuts through the hypocrisy of modern humans' attitudes toward nonhuman animals: the same U.S. society that lavishes more care and sentimentality upon millions of dogs and cats than upon millions of fellow human beings, also breeds, houses, and feeds millions of cows, pigs, chickens, turkeys, goats, fish, geese, and horses for the sole purpose of slaughtering and eating them. The future society represented in *Moving the Mountain* is *not* entirely vegetarian. Yet the vicious warehousing and industrialized slaughter of modern society, reported in visceral detail in *The Jungle,* is also in critical view when Owen reports that "meat eating . . . is decreasing every day; but the care and handling of our food animals improves even more rapidly." Meanwhile, the industrial principles of efficiency and productivity predicate vegetarianism as the final goal. "We have a magnificent system of production and distribution," explains John's niece, Hallie, a food inspector, "with a decreasing use of animal foods."[60]

Gilman's environmental principles postulate, first, that higher productivity (including maintenance of the environment and the nutritional efficiency of vegetarianism) will make possible the elimination of human poverty and starvation. Second, however, is the postulate of global limits. Unlike today's free-market advocates of higher agricultural productivity, for whom faith in constant technological innovation makes population control a relatively unimportant question, Gilman asserts a definite carrying capacity of the world's resources. Thus, *Moving the Mountain* sees as essential not only the maintenance of the productive power of the land—"Now a man would no more think of injuring the soil, the soil that feeds him, than he would of hurting his mother," a specialist in productivity remarks—but also the conscious limitation of human population: "We increase a little too fast now, but see every hope of a balanced population long before the resources of the world are exhausted."[61] In reply to the criticism that the trope of the garden represents an insatiable will to power, *Moving the Mountain* works effectively to contextualize the trope even while reaffirming it: Human beings *do* indeed cultivate the world for their use; to deny this is to evade the primary material condition of human life. Human beings *are* numerous and omnivorous enough to press against the earthly limits of life, and in so doing they threaten other forms of life. If such a recognition of the interdependence of all life, and thus the necessity of maintaining life through conscious effort, means reasserting the trope of the garden, then that trope certainly does look like the proper conceptual framework for our historical moment. If, still more, a recognition of life upon earth as fenced in by the boundary of the lower atmosphere means accepting the trope of the garden, the recognition should certainly provoke self-conscious analysis among us all. But this analysis should certainly not be organized along the lines of the binary choice suggested by Peyser, between dehumanizing totalitarianism and human freedom, but rather over *how* to wield the conscious authority that human beings already have over themselves, the world around them, and each other, without which modern human societies would not be possible and could not long survive.

Perhaps the most fundamental conclusion to be drawn from *Moving the Mountain* is its insistence, sometimes made in spite of its own utopian designs, upon the absence of historical guarantee for any political economic scheme, however righteous and rational in its conception. The point is hammered home directly and repeatedly with respect to capitalism and its core ideology of individualism. To hail the power and the value of the individual, as capitalist liberal democracies do, does not guarantee the empowerment or the well-being of real, live individuals. The novel also makes much the same point regarding social democracy. Through her novel Gilman, probably unconsciously, shows that the logic of egalitarianism can be (and we know, certainly has been) perverted to justify very unequal, unjust, and murderous policies. Simultaneously and more consciously, Gilman homes in upon the work that must be done to achieve a more equal society—and the material limits of human society that ensure all political economies will fall short of unfettered plenty and absolute freedom. In this, Gilman addresses perhaps the most utopian and misleading of all human dreams, shared alike by many adherents of most world religions and by many proponents of capitalism and socialism: the assumption that human beings have limitless time and inexhaustible resources to get their relationships and societies right; the promise otherwise of eternal life. She thereby challenges the desire, harbored by both free-market capitalism and socialist anarchism, to eschew all limits and all discipline, whether self-discipline or socially administered discipline. *Moving the Mountain* pushes beyond the moment of conversion writ large—the moment of proletarian liberation, when the sensation of complete freedom, divine power, and life eternal are suddenly opened up to the socialist acolyte. It explores—beyond that moment—the perilous and uncomfortable decisions that individuals in any society must face if they wish to be honest with each other and realistic about the world in which they live.

CHAPTER SIX

UTOPIA AND APOCALYPSE: SOCIAL DEMOCRATIC FICTION AND THE GREAT WAR

More than the average citizen or statesman, socialists had foreseen the Great War. Capitalism had not only pitted class against class but nation against nation; mass, industrialized warfare was but the most open expression of day-to-day reality in a society riven by class conflict. In a 1913 editorial in *The Crisis,* Du Bois offered what amounted to a prediction of war, given unresolved issues in the scramble for empire: "The modern lust for land and slaves in Africa, Asia and the South Seas is the greatest and almost the only cause of war between the so-called civilized peoples."[1] In *The Man-Made World: Our Androcentric Culture,* published alongside *Moving the Mountain* in the *Forerunner* for 1911, Gilman asserted that in an androcentric world the principal model for politics is competition and combat, which in international relations inevitably leads to the kind of arms race and military alliances evident in Europe: "It tends to make each man-managed nation an actual or potential fighting organization, and to give us, instead of civilized peace, that 'balance of power' which is like the counted time in the prize ring—only a rest between combats."[2] Still more astonishingly specific—and in certain key respects, accurate—was Upton Sinclair's prognostication in his 1907 treatise *The Industrial Republic: A Study of the America of Ten Years Hence.* There he predicted economic collapse and social revolution within the next decade—unless a major war were to intervene. He identified the catalyst of such a crisis in the contest between imperialist capitalism and social democracy in Germany, wherein "an irresponsible military despot in absolute control . . . knows that his only chance to put off the revolution is to pick a quarrel and beat the war-drum," and therefore, when the despot calls "the masses to the defence of the honour of the Fatherland, upon the Social-Democratic Party of Germany will fall the task of saving civilisation."[3]

But though socialists might predict the sharpening of colonial rivalries, the strife of patriarchal politics, and the inevitability of nationalist wars, their predictive powers did not necessarily lead to an advance of social democratic political economy. Indeed, the electoral and reformist strategies favored by Second Internationale socialists were no more likely to succeed in times of rupture and uncertainty than in periods of continuity and stability, when prosperity might make a larger share of the producing classes, including elements of the bourgeois, willing to contemplate a wider distribution of the common wealth. The uncertainty that the Great War produced in socialist calculations is clearest in Sinclair's hedging of his otherwise bold and prescient predictions in *The Industrial Republic.* In the United States, Sinclair suggested that war might postpone social revolution for ten years; or then again, it might lead in the direction of "a political empire," "an engine of war to be wielded by a military despot," resulting in an empire to rival the Romans in longevity and oppressiveness.[4] But then when the war became not a matter of hypothesis but reality, Sinclair and other socialists entertained still another possibility: that the war would greatly accelerate international social revolution. In either case, however, instability and uncertainty were the rule, and the clear, geometric progression calculable by Comrade Ostrinski's rule of thumb—if "one Socialist made another Socialist once every two years"—was replaced by the political equivalent of chaos theory, something like Gilman's notion of sudden, society-wide transformation occurring "in every place at once" but without any certainty whether the result would be the cooperative commonwealth or a totalitarian dictatorship.

The changes found expression in social democratic narratives, as well. Before the war, the narrative arc from realism to utopianism could be charted as a logical, almost ineluctable progression, as exposure of capitalist iniquities led to the clear remedy provided by social democratic virtues. The conversion scene at the crisis of this plot might be read as an allegory of the internal contradictions of capitalism reaching a crisis, then propelling the social body from the trauma of alienated labor into the new harmony of cooperative economics. During the Great War and its immediate revolutionary aftermath, the narratives of Gilman, Sinclair, and Du Bois are traversed by forces not only beyond intentional human control but also outside clear explanatory categories—including especially those categories of rational, orderly, and nonviolent social change embraced during the Second Internationale. Not least of these irruptions is the war itself, which makes an appearance either directly or indirectly in the major works of fiction written by our three writers between 1915 and 1919: specifically, Gilman's *Herland* and *With Her in Ourland* novels, Sinclair's *Jimmie Higgins,* and W. E. B. Du Bois's "The Comet." In these fictions, it is not the conversion experience but the apocalypse that defines the narrative crisis or crises, and it is the apocalyptically destructive—and potentially recreative—energies of war and revolution that must be contained, negotiated, or otherwise passed through.

HERLAND AND NATIONAL DEFENSE

> "But this succession of misfortunes was too much for those infuriated virgins. There were many of them, and but few of these would-be masters, so the young women, instead of submitting, rose, in sheer desperation, and slew their brutal conquerors."

Herland and its sequel, *With Her in Ourland,* continue Gilman's dialogue with social democracy. They also frame a definite response to the world war. These points are often lost upon critics, perhaps because they often read *Herland* in isolation from its sequel, and this novel happens never to mention socialism explicitly and is set almost as far as possible from the European battlefields.[5] But the separation of *Herland* from *With Her in Ourland* is a product of the novel's subsequent publishing history, for the novels were serially published without interruption in the 1915–16 *Forerunner*—and nowhere else until *Herland* was published separately in 1979. Not only is *With Her in Ourland* labeled as "Sequel to *Herland*" on its first page, but the final scenes of *Herland* set up explicitly the continuation of the narrative in a sequel, as Ellador, the spouse of the novel's protagonist-narrator, Van, is selected by the Herland leaders to act as an ambassador to visit the outside world and assess the feasability of establishing international relations. The connection between the novels is integral enough to both that I would like to suggest a coinage expressing that relation: a *duology,* on the analogy of *trilogy,* and embracing the sense of the "duologue," a dramatic conversation involving two voices. By reuniting the two novels, we restore Gilman's overall narrative and rhetorical scheme, for as Lisa Ganobcsik-Williams rightly states, the sequel "moves Gilman's model of a feminist democracy from Herland to test its applicability in what she portrays as the wider world of the early twentieth century."[6]

With the link between *Herland* and *With Her in Ourland* again recognized, it becomes practically impossible to miss the interconnections between gender equality and socialism in Gilman's narrative. Socialism, implicit throughout *Herland,* is named in *Ourland* as being at least coequally important with the women's movement. Examining the progress being made in the contemporary United States, Ellador cites "your women's movement and labor movement" as equally significant, and she suggests that the two may be interpreted for one another and coordinated with each other by an overarching socialism: "The most inclusive forward-looking system is Socialism, of course."[7] Reconnecting the two halves of the duology is significant in terms of narrative structure as well, for doing so reveals the same mixed realist-utopian mode that was prevalent in the prewar fiction—albeit in this case inverting the more typical order by putting the utopian vision first, the realist critique second. As with the prewar instances of this fictional form, the plot is organized in part by a conversion narrative, as Van and his fellow adventurers Terry and Jeff become acquainted with Herland and are gradually led to choose between living there and living in the outside world, in Ourland. The moments of greatest crisis, including the most important turning points in the plot of the duology, come from another source, however: irruptions of violence and irrationality that must be contained so as to preserve the integrity of the social democratic vision.

That the matriarchal society of *Herland* is meant as an alternative to the masculine world of military conflict is inscribed in the novel's plot—slender though it may be. The scenario of the novel initially evokes any number of elements in common with a juvenile male adventure tale. The location of the region to which the three principal characters travel, which, though unnamed, is readily enough identifiable as a wilderness somewhere in the upper reaches of the Amazon, recalls the scenes of some of the most celebrated and dangerous expeditions. To take the most famous example, in 1913 former president Theodore Roosevelt had completed a treacherous, deadly, and widely publicized journey up one of the tributaries of the Amazon, the hitherto-uncharted and aptly named River of Doubt.[8] Terry, the moving force behind the Herland excursion, is a wealthy, worldly young man who supplies the requisite technology, notably a portable float plane that enables the male adventurers to reach the mountain fastness of Herland, and meanwhile helps to make a key thematic tie between capitalist accumulation and androcentric power. Once in Herland, the narrative continues in its parody of juvenile boys' fantasies, as the men almost immediately find themselves approached by attractive young women, one for each, who stay teasingly just out of reach of them. When the men are taken into custody, they escape using a rope ladder and make a dash for freedom over several nights of cross-country trekking and days of lying in concealment. The adolescent adventure comes to a sudden and anticlimactic halt, however, when the Herlanders subdue them not by a pitched, violent confrontation but by the concerted strength of many powerful, middle-aged women that Terry grimly calls "the Colonels."[9] From this point, the men's Great Escape tale transforms suddenly into the Big Tutorial, as the men are treated not as prisoners so much as "truants" and, realizing both that resistance is futile and that Herland is an interesting place to learn about after all, the men submit to their lessons. The novel shifts into familiar utopian territory: three male strangers being schooled by three specially chosen tutors. The men can hardly complain of ill treatment, either, for their tutors are motherly and endlessly patient, and eventually they are paired off romantically with the three young women whom they had met upon their initial landing.

In spite of the calm orderliness that appears to guide the Herland polity, the narrative structure of *Herland* also highlights irruptions of violence, happenstance, and irrationality that stand in some contrast to the parallel features in *Moving the Mountain.* In the novel of 1911, the historical events that set off the social democratic transformation are centered upon a new religion among women: a movement of religious enthusiasm, to be sure, and yet a concerted effort to reform and then remake their society. And what are the historical events parallel to these in the novel of 1915, those that lay the foundation for Herland society? From the annals of the land, the visitors learn that some two thousand years before, it had been a much larger kingdom, "bi-sexual," polygamous, and slaveholding. But over a period of years its population and especially its men were "decimated by war" and gradually retreated toward their mountain stronghold. When a massive landslide cut off virtually all the freemen from their country, the slaves revolted, killing all the remaining men and boys and many of the older women as well. These revolutionaries, however, were met by an equal counterrevolutionary movement, as the"infuriated virgins . . . instead of submitting, rose, in sheer desperation, and slew their brutal conquerors," to the last person.[10] Thus it is that war, revolution, and counterrevolution set the stage for the miracle of virgin birth, and then of ongoing parthenogenetic reproduction continuing to the present.

While the chaotic origins of Herland stand thematically in contrast to its systematic progress thereafter, the facts of the narrative introduce the possibility that the tumult of war and revolutionary violence might actually be socially creative. As a response to contemporary events in 1914–15 and as an anticipation of the revolutions to sweep Europe in 1917–19, Gilman's narrative may be seen as contemplating not only the political path favored by the Second Internationale social democrats but also the path charted by the revolutionaries of the Paris Commune and touted by some of the more radical Marxists and direct actionists. While, on the whole, Gilman remains committed to the former, the narrative considers the latter as well, and the plot even intertwines the two, so that peaceful, maternal progress actually depends upon a sharp, violent, revolutionary break from the past, when the "desperate" and "infuriated" virgin avengers slaughter their male oppressors.

Furthermore, *Herland* does not represent its utopian society as a realm of freedom apart from coercion and even occasional, necessary force. The fact that Van, Terry, and the third in their party, Jeff, come to accept the terms of their confinement and even to love their captors may downplay the significance of the fact that they are not free to come and go as they please, but it does not altogether conceal it. Toward the end of *Herland,* at a time when the three men are finally at liberty to explore the country at will and their relationships with their soon-to-be wives are well established, Van reports that still "we were always under a certain degree of watchfulness. When Terry burst forth to tramp the streets at night he always found a 'Colonel' here or there; and when, on an occasion of fierce though temporary despair, he had plunged to the cliff edge with some vague view to escape, he found several of them close by."[11]

Not only the male visitors but the Herlanders themselves submit to a high degree of regimentation and conformity. Most do this willingly enough, but threats of coercion and ostracism lie just beneath the surface to deal with any outliers. Van discovers, for example, that for the sake of population control the majority of Herlanders have only one child and "those held unfit are not allowed even that." Later expanding on the latter point, Van's appointed tutor, Somel, explains that in order to eliminate antisocial individuals, the Herlanders had embarked upon an aggressive program "to breed out, when possible, the lowest types." Thus, "If the girl showing bad qualities had still the power to appreciate social duty, we appealed to her, by that, to renounce motherhood. Some of the worst types were, fortunately, unable to reproduce. But if the fault was in a disproportionate egotism—then the girl was sure she had the right to have children, even that hers would be better than others." In such cases, Somel solemnly expounds, the authorities were sure to make certain such mothers would not be permitted to be caregivers to their children. Van reports being unconvinced of the wisdom of this measure, an instance in which the kind of genuinely credible, skeptical narrator found in *Moving the Mountain* is reintroduced, and indicates a point on which Gilman appears to know all too well her readers' points of fiercest resistance.

On matters of reproduction, *Herland* steps back from the draconian measures described in *Moving the Mountain,* suggesting either that Gilman had changed her mind or, at least, that she had become more rhetorically savvy in the interim. When, for instance, Van raises the possibility that population control might be effected through abortion, Somel responds with horror, her response showing that this is so far from the Herland mind-set that she cannot conceive of someone of her gender terminating her own fetus: "Do men do that in your country?" she wonders.[12] Yet even as the most invidious features of social engineering promulgated in *Moving the Mountain* have been revised out of *Herland,* the collectivist ethos of individual sacrifice for the sake of the group is a constant, and as such the novel retains elements of the hard lessons of the earlier novel about the sacrifices that must be made by, and may be demanded of, the most privileged members of society—individuals such as the wealthy playboy Terry.

Thus, even as the plot of *Herland* asserts its preference for peaceful, systematic social evolution, it also reveals its preference for a particular style of institutional discipline and proactive policing over overt social conflict. Such discipline is always, ultimately grounded in violence—wielded rarely, but always held in reserve, and definitely threatened at the crisis of the novel, the expulsion of Terry that both brings the *Herland* narrative to a conclusion and launches the *Ourland* narrative. The elements that conclude the *Herland* plot stand in significant contrast to the concluding episode of Gilman's prewar utopia, *Moving the Mountain.* John Robertson gradually slips away from the formal instruction of his tutors, choosing to see his revamped homeland for himself and finally, feeling homesick for "some neglected-looking land, some ragged suburbs," returns to the decrepit, backward home place of his Uncle Jake, Aunt Dorcas, and Cousin Drusilla.[13] There the crisis, such as it is, involves his wooing of Drusilla, who after marriage to John finds that the social mores of the New Religion are to her liking, on which basis her chivalric husband accepts the new ways also. The closing episodes of *Herland* are focused on romantic desire as well, but here the critical event is a far cry from the gentle wooing of cousins, as the macho Terry attempts to rape his Herlander wife, Alima. As with the founding of the Herland republic some two thousand years before, the outbreak of masculine violence is met neither with feminine submission nor with pacifist nonresistance, but by a precisely calibrated application of force, as Terry is swiftly restrained first by a symbolically appropriate kick to the groin by Alima, and then by a superior contingent of matronly home guards.

In these final episodes of *Herland,* perhaps even more than elsewhere in the novel, Gilman's presentation repeatedly shows how issues of gender and sexuality are connected to economic relations. In the discussions the couples share as they prepare for their Herland marriages, the relation that the women utterly refuse is the economic one of "possession." This, Terry insists, is the relationship signified when a woman assumes her husband's surname: "It was a sign of possession," he explains to his wife-to-be: "A wife is a woman who belongs to a man."[14] Jeff immediately puts in a plug for the equality of the marriage relation, "And a husband is the man who belongs to a woman," and yet the legal system in "our country" was as likely to side with Terry as with Jeff, as U.S. laws as well as social conventions tended to give husbands control over both their wives' money and their wives' bodies.[15] What the men from outside mean by the proper economic relation between husband and wife is detailed by Van in an expository paragraph in the final chapter, one in which he finds his own culture's reckoning of women's *value* as particularly impoverished:

> We value them, sincerely, for their perverted maternal activities which make our wives the most comfortable of servants, bound to us for life with the wages wholly at our own decision, their whole business, outside of the temporary duties of such motherhood as they may achieve, to meet our needs in every way. Oh, we value them, all right, "in their place"; which place is the home, where they perform that mixture of duties so ably described by Mrs. Josephine Dodge Daskam Bacon, in which the service of "a mistress" are carefully specified. . . . But—that combination of industries, while convenient, and in a way economical, does not arouse the kind of emotion commanded by the women of Herland. These were women one had to love "up," very high up, instead of down. They were not pets. They were not servants. They were not timid, inexperienced, weak.[16]

The multifaceted picture of woman as worker is of a piece with Gilman's analysis we have seen in *Women and Economics,* and as it appears elsewhere: in some instances women's work resembles wage labor, especially when the sexual economics of marriage parallel the economics of prostitution; in others it resembles slavery, especially when domestic labor is performed in exchange for material maintenance. In either case, though, the women of Herland are workers too intrepid, experienced, and strong to countenance any such roles.

Within the Herland society that does not pay wages or differentiate at all in the remuneration allotted to the various professions, Terry's effort to possess his wife registers primarily as an effort to enslave. This is altogether fitting for a society whose only record of labor exploitation in its history is, in fact, slavery—at the time of the wars and earthquake that separated the women from their men, they were "a polygamous people, and a slave-holding people," like the Roman and Greek societies of the same era.[17] As his marriage approaches, Terry, the most atavistic of the men, retreats from the capitalist mode of "possession," or commodity culture, to the precapitalist modes of "conquest" and "mastery." "There never was a woman yet that did not enjoy being *mastered,*" Terry boasts, then sings a snatch from the bawdy Rudyard Kipling verse that mixes racial, gender, and economic domination: "I've taken my fun where I found it, / I've rogued and I've ranged in my time, / . . . The things that I learned from the yellow and black, / They 'ave helped me a 'eap with the white."[18] Ultimately, there is simply no common social or economic understanding between Terry and Alima that admits to ideological negotiation, no possible "exchange" whereby they might organize their relationship. With no social relation of production available to them, it is almost inevitable that their relationship will erupt into violence. Indeed, given the ways that Gilman's presentation of Terry and Alima associates each with a particular political-economic system, their showdown is not an individual contest but a reenactment of Herland's founding conflict between two inimical ways of life.

The resolution of the conflict in the trial, conviction, and eventual expulsion of Terry reinforces the fact that Herland society does not eschew force, or even violence entirely, but rather offers a radically different conception of violence. For Terry, competition, struggle, and violence are intrinsic to human growth and progress. The laws and customs of the outside world that he represents, moreover, institutionalize certain unequal power relations, including the right of husbands to conjugal relations with their wives. For the Herlanders, in contrast, cooperation, compromise, and nonviolence are the norms promoting the progress of the human race, and their laws and customs strictly protect the weaker members of their society from the stronger. The difference is highlighted clearly in a passage late in *With Her in Ourland,* in which Ellador rages against the American bias against government intervention preventing the strong from doing harm to the weak: "'That is what government is for isn't it?' she replied. 'To preserve justice, to prevent the selfish and ambitious from harming others, to see to it that production is increased and distribution fairly carried on.'"[19] With these great differences in view in *Herland,* as well, we might not be surprised that the "local Over-Mother" who hears Terry's case sides with him insofar as she recognizes the fundamentally different ideas that obtain in the outside world. She finds that his fault lies in acting according to customs that are foreign, not universally evil or illegal. Therefore, his actions constitute a kind of grievous breach in diplomatic relations, like the criminal acts of a diplomat, and therefore the appropriate punishment can only be expulsion and banishment.

Terry's confrontation also serves to reveal the otherwise largely hidden role of coercion in Herland society. They believe in the rightness of their harmonious existence, in which a difference in political economy is foremost, and they are willing to defend that existence with force, including deadly force if necessary. Again, a later explanation offered by Ellador in *With Her in Ourland* is useful. Decrying the political system in the United States for its tendency not to protect the weak but to enrich the powerful, Ellador the forester applies her attitude toward agricultural pests to the parasites of democracy: "It is time you were severe on them, Van. I'm no Buddhist—I'm a forester. When I see trees attacked by vermin, I exterminate the vermin if I can. . . . You have got to see that for a man to rob another man is bad enough; for a man to rob the public is worse; but to rob the public *through the government* is a kind of high treason which—if you still punished by torture—would be deserving of the most excruciating kind."[20] Much the same attitude is on display in the final, climactic scene of *Herland.* In response to Terry's outburst, which is tantamount to a declaration of war against Herland, the high council of Herland replies swiftly and in kind, asserting that the leniency of the previous legal decision and the very rights of Terry as an individual are necessarily trumped by national security. "'Then,' they said quite calmly, 'he must remain an absolute prisoner, always.'" Terry backs down with equal swiftness, for he knows firsthand the effectiveness of the Herland system of countrywide surveillance and involuntary confinement. Moadine, who has been Terry's tutor, urges the punishment of the sort meted out by Ellador to agricultural pests: "Anesthesia would be kinder."[21] It is, therefore, the further threat of a death warrant as well as the prospect of lifetime imprisonment that secures the restoration of diplomatic relations, the uneasy conclusion of *Herland,* and the segue into *With Her in Ourland.*

For all their peaceableness and cooperation, the Herlanders thus show a surprising willingness to consider capital punishment and torture as well as a demonstrated expertise for policing. If such a suggestion removes some of the luster from Gilman's utopian vision, it has the virtue of bringing it down to earth, of locating her conceptions of a society that is orderly and egalitarian—and *can* be egalitarian, in part, because it is well ordered—within the realm of human realizability. As long as characters such as Terry pose a menace, then the state, however democratic and liberty-loving it may be, must reserve force and compulsion as necessary powers of last resort. In these capacities, the state does nothing more or less than represent the people as a whole in the enforcement of equality and the commonwealth among themselves, and nothing more or less than the organization of the people in their defense of the same from foreign invaders. Just as significantly, the Herlanders reserve the right to police ideological and cultural boundaries: to judge the value of attitudes and forms of social organization that are offered, even strongly advocated, by the emissaries from another world, and to reject those they rule to be incompatible with their prosperity, harmony, and equality.

Whereas *Moving the Mountain* projects a much better utopian society in the United States of thirty years hence, *Herland* seems less sanguine about American social progress. We might well consider this as an explanation for the far greater geographic distance between the *Herland* utopia, at an undisclosed location high up in the South American mountains. Still, the *Herland/Ourland* duology is set in the immediate present; *With Her in Ourland* almost immediately reminds us that the European war in all its terrible familiarity is raging in Europe. And the situation of Herland curiously parallels that of the United States of 1915 and 1916 in several respects. At the time Gilman began writing and publishing *Herland* at the beginning of 1915, the kind of matriarchal pacifism that holds sway in Herland had a real influence in U.S. politics. The most popular song of that year, "I Didn't Raise My Boy to Be a Soldier," was released in January, the same month that the Woman's Peace Party was founded with over one hundred thousand members. In May of the year Woodrow Wilson issued a proclamation for the first time recognizing Mother's Day as a national holiday, dubbing it a "Mother's Day to Promote Peace," and a few days later his response to the sinking of the *Lusitania* was to declare the United States "too proud to fight." The next year Wilson would win reelection under the slogan "He kept us out of the war."

Yet by the end of 1915 as well as throughout 1916 Wilson was also formulating a program of war preparedness, and so it is fitting that the *Herland/Ourland* duology offers a justification for the use of force, even extending to the restriction of civil liberties. In 1916, Wilson promoted "one-hundred-percent Americanism" as a campaign theme, a proscription of cultural difference that set the stage for the enforced unanimity of the wartime mobilization in 1917. More constructively, Wilson articulated principles that sought to define a specifically American understanding of war, justifying the use of force solely for the defense of essential American values and institutions, warranting only such force as would be necessary to overwhelm their adversaries, and demanding justice and tolerance toward those adversaries, once subdued.[22] That such a set of policies, if implemented by the United States, might actually make that nation an ally in the pursuit of social democratic schemes had already occurred to Gilman, judging from the nonfiction pieces she was writing and publishing in *The Forerunner*.[23] It had already occurred to Upton Sinclair as well, and eventually even to W. E. B. Du Bois. In effect, the state that these social democrats was intent upon capturing appears to have been more valuable intact, operating with a nominally progressive national and international agenda, than it would be despised, discredited, or in ruins. Yet for Gilman at the end of 1915, the conclusion remains a tentative one, for after all the Herland republic had risen from the utter overthrow by war and revolution of its anthrocentric, slaveholding predecessor—and *Herland* remained only the first half of an as yet uncompleted duology.

PROGRESS AND PERIL IN OURLAND

> "They began to plan, slowly, wisely, calmly, making no haste."

Whereas *Herland* lays out the rationale for an assertive national defense—of Herland and even, by extension, of the United States—the opening chapter of *With Her in Ourland* offers a more specific analysis of the European war in 1916. Because in the novel's opening chapters Ellador and Van arrive in Europe via England, Ellador is practically guaranteed seeing the circumstances and causes of the war from an Anglo- and Francophilic perspective. When, for instance, Ellador does background research on the war, she does so in an English library whose holdings focus upon the alleged German atrocities in Belgium. But if Ellador's point of entry into Western civilization helps to secure a definite sympathy with America's most likely allies in the event of intervention (and to signal Gilman's own international sympathies), it by no means ensures an endorsement of the social, political, and military systems that she witnesses in Europe. Nor does it lead to advocacy of an early American intervention in the war, which by 1916 was publicly touted by former president (and Amazonian adventurer) Theodore Roosevelt. Terry's eagerness for battle signals most clearly the narrative's cautious attitude about getting too closely involved in the conflict, for this trait is obviously of a piece with the reckless masculinity that made him so dangerous in Herland. When Ellador asks whether the war represented some kind of aberration in androcentric history, Terry replies blandly, "It's only bigger than usual, as most things are now." In the Christian era, Terry expounds, there have been no more than three hundred years of peace, and only "here and there, scattering," which to him serves as proof that war is not only "normal" but ultimately beneficial: "Bad as it is, it is evidently human nature to do it. Nations advance, the race is improved by fighting. It is the law of nature."[24] Ellador finds this manifestly insupportable, for the historical record of Herland shows that war *cannot* be human nature. And Terry's wholehearted endorsement of the pointless carnage of the battlefields of 1915 and 1916 stands as the clearest of cautions against Americans joining the fray anytime soon.

Ellador's encounter with the Great War marks the third time in the *Herland/Ourland* duology that an apocalyptic event, a catastrophic irruption of irrationality and violence, disturbs the generally placid progress of the utopian narrative. The historic Herland catastrophes of earthquake, revolution, and counterrevolution had had a happy outcome, secured in the annals of Herland books and in hundreds of years of social progress since. Terry's attempted rape of Alima was unprecedented in Herland, yet if Terry's case was beyond Herland law, the Herland tribunal as well as the nation's police force proved sufficient, and Terry's actions could reasonably be interpreted as an atavistic aberration, an outbreak that does not seriously challenge the Herlanders' philosophy. In contrast, the Great War challenges Ellador's, and Herland's, suppositions about the world at their very core, raising fundamental questions about human nature, moral agency, and social organization. Her observation of the war leads her to a near breakdown. Although Ellador's and indeed all of the Herlanders' conceptions of human nature and progress are based upon their experience of an all-female society, their interrogation of their male visitors has repeatedly sought to challenge the men's presupposition of hard-and-fast differences between male and female; thus, Ellador's encounter with the annihilation of millions in the European war is not something she can immediately distance herself from as men's work. Given the interconnections between history, society, and religion within Herland, her breakdown in the face of the Great War resembles a crisis of faith or a spiritual dark night of the soul, a faltering of her assurance in the "great central Power," "the River of Life" that she has imagined to course throughout all humanity.[25] At issue, in the Herlanders' humanistic faith, is the question of human progress.

Whereas Europe represents the very apex of world culture according to the lights of Van and his companions, Van recognizes that quite the contrary is true based upon the evidence of the war. He therefore urges Ellador to "say it all. Say the very worst. Say—'This world is not civilized, not human. It is worse than the humble savagery below our mountains.'"[26] Such a stance, with which Ellador reluctantly concurs, challenges directly her certainty about human progress and its irreversibility. It also destabilizes received knowledge about civilization and savagery—specifically, about which cultures represent which. It begins to help Ellador out of her difficulty as well, for it affirms that if she cannot trust in the certainty of progress, she can at least trust the truth of her own observation. The one affirmation that emerges from Ellador's crisis of faith is the fitness of her own senses and intellect to make judgments. The irruption of the irrational and the violent can shake her faith in the assured supremacy of rationality and nonviolence to guide and guarantee human progress, but it does not ultimately challenge the possibility and the necessity of making rational judgments about social organization and practices, and of seeking all the more diligently to organize—and reorganize—society according to those judgments.

The encounter with the world war marks, further, the definite entry of Gilman's duology into the realist mode, after which all social conventions, political institutions, and economic practices of any world cultures that happen to fall in Ellador's path are open to scrutiny and critique. Truly, Ellador's critical evaluations about Ourland proliferate as she travels around the world. In North Africa, she is impressed by the "whole system of irrigation and its enormous benefits" for agriculture in an arid land, but she is critical of "the immeasurable futility of the fellaheen, still using the shadoof after all these ages of progress." In China, she criticizes overpopulation and overfarming, "shocked beyond words at the vast area of dead country; skeleton country, deforested, deshrubbed, degrassed, wasted to the bone, lying there to burn in the sun and drown in the rain, feeding no one."[27] And she fastens upon the practice of footbinding among women as not only a violation of human rights but also an indication of dysfunction and lack of progressivity in the nation as a whole. In Japan, with its clear limitations of arable land, Ellador is still more appalled at the lack of foresight in refusing to use birth control, and finds the subordinate status of women linked to its crisis in overpopulation. Just as the women in Herland had seen the definite limits upon their agricultural base and acted accordingly, Ellador postulates that "surely the [Japanese] women could see . . . how many people to a mile can live healthfully and pleasantly," but then she learns of the limitations upon the "status of women in Japan," which render women's viewpoint entirely irrelevant to the social, political, and military policy of the nation—clearly heading toward the same androcentric solution of imperial expansion being tried so disastrously in Europe.[28]

Such snap judgements based upon a tourist's acquaintance with these non-Western nations would appear to give fodder to the long-standing criticism of Gilman as ethnocentrist and racist. The impression is further reinforced when Ellador arrives in the United States and renders prejudiced judgments on the situation of both African Americans and Jewish Americans. It hardly excuses Gilman, either, to point out that her views of black Americans (apparently voiced via Ellador) were shared by Sinclair, and that her views on Jews were shared by Du Bois. Only in the 1953, fifty-year anniversary edition of *Souls* did Du Bois think to remove eight derogatory references to Jews as heartless financiers, deceivers, and sharps, including one suggesting—along lines offered by fellow sociologist Gilman—the cultural or biological transmission of racial characteristics, insofar as "the defence of deception and flattery, of cajolery and lying," supposedly typical of Jews in the Middle Ages, "left its stamp upon their character for centuries."[29] That the problem of racialist and racist thinking apparently besets many Second International socialists, though it may partly explain Gilman's prejudices, makes the fault all the more grave for socialism of this era.

Yet if *Herland* and *With Her in Ourland* cannot and should not be read with complete affirmation of their views of racial difference, the novels' conceptual framework does more to challenge than to affirm customary assumptions about cultural, including racial, hierarchies. The *Herland* narrative implicitly challenges notions of white supremacy and racial kinship between the Herlanders and the male adventurers, insofar as the Herlanders—in spite of an apparently "Aryan" lineage—assert the difference of their society from the outside world, while observing the similar behaviors of all races of people in "Ourland" in spite of being acquainted with "the broad racial divisions we had told them about."[30] The challenge to Western cultural superiority is an ongoing and explicit theme throughout *With Her in Ourland.* Indeed, the novel undercuts the very dichotomy between savagery and civilization (not incidentally, the term *savagery* is Van's, not Ellador's). For example, Van imagines that the Herlanders see their difference from their own near neighbors in the same kind of racist and imperialist terms with which white citizens of the United States regard Native Americans; he describes them as "savages, like those in the forests below your mountain land, though more advanced in some ways." But in this he is greatly mistaken; cultural difference, even seeming cultural superiority, cannot for Ellador serve as the basis for genocide and expropriation. Ellador's questions about how Euro-Americans managed to "arrange" with the Native Americans while taking their land leads to the following dismaying admission by Van: "I hate to tell you, Ellador. You see you have—a little—idealized my country. We did not arrange with those savages. We killed them."[31] When Van and Ellador's voyage across the Pacific is broken by a stop in the Hawaiian Islands, newly annexed as U.S. territory, additional awkward questions follow. After Van attempts to ameliorate the national guilt for the colonization of the islands, referencing the value of Western civilization and claiming historical inevitability, Ellador cuts him short, rejecting as indefensible any civilizing mission that demands the destruction of its subjects. Among several lines of argument employed, a critique of conventional religion as well as Western culture is prominent: "Do you think Christ would have had the same effect on them?" Ellador asks; "And does civilization help dead people?"[32] Just as prominent is an analysis that treats the U.S. acquisition of Hawaii in terms of political economy, an example of capitalist exploitation of labor and expropriation of land.[33]

As *With Her in Ourland* proceeds from West to East, then back to the West via the Pacific Ocean, the narrative exercises critical judgment on *all* world cultures, in one way or another. The project is far from being cynical, nihilistic, or deconstructive, however. The novel's procedure, in the tradition of literary realism, seeks to follow analytical reason. Sometimes adeptly, sometimes incompletely but suggestively enough, it limns a process of separating that which is beneficial to humanity from that which is not. The most obvious case in point is Ellador's embrace of modern ideals of women's rights and her condemnation of women's inequality wherever she finds it, which makes utterly no allowance for various forms of patriarchy just because it happens to be part of a treasured indigenous culture. She also universally values contemporary knowledge and technology related to population control and environmentalism, cutting no slack for the societies of South and East Asia where overpopulation has contributed to poverty and starvation.

Ellador (and by extension, Gilman) also values modern industrial development, even to the point that capitalism *may* represent a system preferable to others—patriarchal feudalism, for example. *Ourland*'s qualified critique of modernity is of a piece with practically every modern manifestation of socialism including the most revolutionary Marxist creeds. Modern production has reduced labor time and made possible the mass production of food and other goods. If such production has gone hand in hand with capitalism and private profit, that does not necessarily negate the value of its products. The difficulty is not one of productive technologies, but rather of who controls production and how production is distributed, the questions of whether industry is democratically or autocratically directed, and of whether workers receive the full product of their labor or profits are taken by private owners. The issue is illustrated when Ellador takes Egyptians to task for irrigating by means of the shadoof when a mechanical pump might be used. Still near the beginning of her journey, Ellador assumes the unity of the human race; her world tour is interested in investigating "what [the different cultures] have done for one another, and for the world," operating on the premise that those cultures freely share their contributions to humanity. Thus, her only explanation at this point in her journey is intellectual dullness among the men of the region.[34] She eventually comes to understand the degree to which various cultures are not interested in doing anything "for one another, and for the world," but are concerned rather with what other cultures, and the world, can do for *us.* Only later, when, for example, she sees the brazen expropriation and exploitation of the native Hawaiians is she in a position to recognize that peasant farmers in North Africa who use a hand-pump instead of machine power are not necessarily ignorant or obstinate; they lack the capital to buy the machines from Western developers who will not, after all, share them free of charge.

Some of the very lines of analysis that are deprecating toward cultures that have not been at the forefront of industrial modernization turn out to be even more sharply critical of those "advanced" groups who have sought to exploit them. Consider, for example, Ellador's inquiry into open immigration policies. Americans have accepted unrestricted immigration as exemplary of American democracy under the guise of an ideology of individualism: in effect, by the entirely specious notion that because some poor and unlettered men have become wealthy, therefore, the poor and uneducated have as much opportunity as the wealthy and learned do. What Ellador points out, however, is that recent immigrants' faith in this very principle of equal opportunity makes them ready targets for political demagoguery and economic exploitation. Many immigrant laborers are "deliberately imported . . . victims, poor ignorant people scraped up by paid agents, deceived by lying advertisements, brought over here by greedy American ship owners and employers of labor." As for their capitalist masters, those who profit from their labor and proclaim American freedom, they are no more ready to practice true democracy, justice, and equality than the most recent and uneducated of immigrants. The development of social democracy is thus hindered just as much by many U.S. citizens of long standing, "Sons and Daughters of the Revolution who are aristocrats, plutocrats, anything but democrats."[35]

The *Herland/Ourland* duology—and not least Ellador's critical examination of world cultures—does imply throughout a consistent, ideal standard of judgment that remains intact even when Ellador's (and Gilman's) application of the standard is wayward: it is the core ideal of social equality, understood as founded fundamentally upon economic equality and as superseding gender, racial, ethnic, and other forms of difference (particularly when these are used to warrant or perpetuate inequality). At the same time, that Ellador's prescriptions are provisional, after all, is signaled by the fact that she has been on a fact-finding mission; it is actually the job of other, wiser and more experienced Herlanders to determine the manner, time, and place of their contact with the outside world. Both the constancy of this scale of judgment, and the narrative's uncertainty over precisely how to apply it to a world run amok, may be seen in the lack of a serious crisis toward the conclusion of *With Her in Ourland.* There are some sharp, closing judgments in Ellador's analysis of American society: her statistical account of the extraordinary profit reaped by the railroad through its rates for a single Pullman car; her even grander analysis of the gross domestic product of the United States, showing that the salaries of capitalists are fourteen times greater than those of white-collar employees, and thirty times those of the average blue-collar worker; and a remarkable fulmination against the conservative economic shackles placed upon American society by the U.S. Constitution, a document whose commerce clause has been used to insulate from public intervention a variety of capitalist vermin: "You have your oil-suckers and coal-suckers, water-suckers, and wood-suckers, railroad suckers and farm-suckers—this splendid young country is crawling with them—and has not the intelligence, the energy, to shake them off."[36] But there is no sharp crisis—no irruption of violence as we find at the closing of *Herland* or the outset of *With Her in Ourland*—that might either propel a definite intervention of the Herland values into the outside world or require a further challenge to the core validity of those values. Ellador leaves the ultimate course of Herland policy up to the Herland collective, especially as represented by the Over-Mothers.

As for herself, though, Ellador does decide that she cannot in good conscience bring a child into the world as currently constituted, and therefore, after she returns to Herland and presents her report to her elders, she will remain there. Van, in turn, chooses to join his wife in Herland, and it falls to Ellador and Van to become the parents of the first male child born in Herland for two thousand years. This conclusion is inconclusive not merely because it lacks in drama, either. On the one hand, that a boy is born in Herland, and that heterosexual unions are accepted there, comprise symbolic steps of Gilman's utopia toward the real world, ratifying the interpretation that Gilman does not imagine that Herland must be populated only by women to be ideal. On the other hand, the necessity for Ellador to retreat from Ourland—even from the still as-yet peaceful United States—underscores the sharpness of the novel's criticism of America's current social reality. There are too many bloodsuckers clinging to the body politic, it seems.

To the extent that the *Herland/Ourland* duology is a parable of social democracy, the importance of separation, of keeping socialism apart from the contaminations of capitalism and politics-as-usual, is not quite trumped by the value of intercultural engagement, keen as that need may be in a world being torn apart by conflict. So it is that the wisest heads of Herland, though eager to help Ourland, find themselves also seeking to maintain ideological and practical distance: "They began to plan, slowly, wisely, calmly, making no haste; sure above all, that they must preserve their own integrity and peace if they were to help others."[37] In these novels that, as much as anywhere in Gilman's work, contemplate the possible value of sudden and violent revolution, the Herlanders find the best course still lies in holding back from the usages of the world at war. To the extent that the duology also offers a parable of America's relation to the conflagration of the war, the lesson is cautious uncertainty. For even as the dramatic ending of *Herland* postulates the notion of defending and enforcing peace and order by force when urgent circumstances so dictate, the ending of *With Her in Ourland* suggests the need for neutrality and peace to help the war-torn world. If this is an unsatisfying ending, it may well be because *With Her in Ourland* and *The Forerunner*, both coming to an end in December 1916, concluded at a peculiar historical moment both for the social democratic movement and for the United States. The United States had just reelected a president in large part for his success in keeping the United States out of the war but who, meanwhile, had prepared for war by a xenophobic propaganda campaign. Internationally, the socialist movement had lost practically all faith in the efficacy of Second Internationale parliamentarianism, and the new effort to be catalyzed by the Bolshevik revolution and the Third Internationale lay ahead. Not only were the Herlanders planning slowly, wisely, and calmly; as it happened, Lenin and his confederates were biding their time in the mountain fastness of Switzerland while the world war swirled around them. Nationally, socialists were deeply divided over whether to hold to the antiwar stance that had been universally disregarded by Europe's socialist parties in 1914, or to lend support to the ostensibly progressive Wilson administration, whether it continued to keep us out of, or brought us into, the world war. The years immediately ahead would not give any clearer bearings as to which response was better, either.

FROM MILITARIST TO MARTYR: *JIMMIE HIGGINS*

> "Never, never could this battle be truly won! Never could the body be wholly forgotten, its clamorous demands wholly stilled!"

For Sinclair, the one of the triptych writers most closely aligned with the mainline socialist movement, the coming of war presented the deepest of crises, for the failure of the socialist parties to impede the war mobilization seemed a grave shortcoming in principle, in power, or in both. Even when the war was only a hypothetical possibility, though, Sinclair's correspondence with other socialists shows that the obvious party-line response—univocal opposition to capitalist-imperialist wars—was by no means a foregone conclusion. The purest of social democratic principles had backed Sinclair's 1909 publication of "War: A Manifesto Against It" in socialist periodicals in the United States, England, and Australia, in which Sinclair asked socialist labor leaders throughout Europe to pledge themselves in advance to a general strike in the event of war. But the German theoretician and Social Democratic Party leader Karl Kautsky flatly refused to sign Sinclair's manifesto; in fact, he refused even to have it published in the party press. Kautsky's explanation was twofold: On the one hand, "The German government is much too strong, to let us try an insurrection, when it prepares war"; on the other, "I hope, *after* a war, after the debacle of a government we may get strength enough, to conquer the political power."[38] Kautsky's rationale for nonsupport of Sinclair's manifesto succinctly anticipates the impact of war and revolution upon the best-laid plans of parliamentary socialists. War had the potential to halt, in its tracks, the gradual conversion of the masses to socialism; in the hands of a majority antiprogressive government, nationalism inflamed by war represented the most powerful of political weapons, readily wielded to crush antiwar dissent. But war also might have as its sequel revolution, and thus the terrible and irresistible historical engine of war, seemingly beyond any form of conscious political agency, might turn against its capitalist and imperialist maker. Either contingency suggests the necessity for a new socialist strategy in the face of the kinds of irrational, violent energies that left their mark upon Gilman's utopian/realist duology of 1915–16. It may be particularly fitting, then, that the Marxian socialist Kautsky and the non-Marxian Gilman assumed similar attitudes as the storm of war approached: if the leading forces of capitalism, imperialism, and autocracy seem inclined toward self-immolation, then it might be best thing for socialists to stand back, and as far away from the flames as possible.

The crisis of the war, as it finally engulfed the United States in 1917 and 1918, marked the most nearly complete hiatus from professional writing in Gilman's entire career; only in the years before her coming of age in the Nationalist movement and in the last years of her life did Gilman publish less frequently. The nearly perpetual writing and publishing machine of *The Forerunner* having been brought to a halt at the end of 1916, Gilman published only five pieces of nonfiction and no fiction or poetry at all during 1917 and 1918. This is all the more astonishing given that in 1919 once again Gilman cranked up her prodigious output, publishing 246 journalistic pieces primarily but not exclusively through the *New York Tribune* syndicate.[39] It is as if Gilman personally identified with the resolution of the Herlanders to plan in seclusion, to remain aloof, lest the contagion of war should touch her "integrity and peace."

Meanwhile, however, fellow moderate socialists were actively pursuing the other course that had been suggested in the Herland duology, the possibility that a vigorous national defense might be compatible with the progress of social democracy. In the years of American neutrality, Upton Sinclair was among these. Even as Sinclair had been instructed by Kautsky about the possibility of pragmatic socialism taking a course quite different from—even entirely contrary to—apparent socialist principle, the now more worldly-wise Sinclair took his turn to assert this possibility to some of the younger, more idealistic progressives. When Tracy Mygatt wrote to Sinclair in mid-1915 requesting his public support for the Anti-Enlistment League, her appeal combined the pacifist feminism of the Woman's Peace Party and the idealistic socialism that in 1909 had led to Sinclair's own antiwar manifesto. Mygatt wrote to Sinclair surmising, reasonably, that "as a Socialist" he would also be "an anti-militarist." Interestingly, Sinclair references Kautsky's letter of 1909 in order to explain why, in 1915, he was contemplating support of American intervention on the side of the Allies as constructive, possibly even essential, to the advancement of socialist aims. If, as Kautsky testified, the power of Germany's autocratic rulers was so complete as to prevent the circulation of an antiwar manifesto in peacetime, and if, as Kautsky opined, the only hope for social democracy in Germany was the overthrow of the government, then the best way for socialists in the United States to offer assistance would be to help in the utter military defeat of Germany. In his lengthy response to Mygatt, Sinclair argued that "until that barbarian caste is overthrown, and the body, mind and soul of Germany delivered from its dominion, there can be no peace anywhere in the world, and all talk of social reform is wasted breath."[40]

This social democratic logic depended, naturally, upon the assumption that military victory for the United States and the Allies would not mean the triumph of reactionary forces there. It counted, even, upon the proposition that the inevitable social dislocations of the war mobilization might exert a definite push toward socialism in the United States. Without presuming to have any extraordinary political power, and all along closely following the policies enacted by the Wilson administration, Sinclair and other prowar socialists meanwhile did what they could to pull the United States in the direction of social democracy. In contrast to Gilman, Sinclair threw his writing into the maelstrom of 1917 and 1918, with the result that his wartime novel *Jimmie Higgins* registers every twist and turn in his attitudes toward the war. Most conspicuously, having initially identified social democracy with the victory of the Allies, the serial novel shifts, in midcourse, to worry over the consequences of that victory, leading Sinclair to the brink of despair over parliamentarianism and toward hope in out-and-out revolutionism.

The novel's opening chapters evoke nostalgia for the prewar Socialist Party, which could hope to grow by the peripatetic campaigning and persuasive rhetoric of its leaders, and an ever-widening circle of individual conversions and commitments to the social democratic creed. Almost reverential is the episode at the very beginning of the novel in which "the Candidate," unmistakably the perennial socialist presidential candidate Eugene Debs, plays "hooky" from his party obligations for an afternoon, going with the archetypal grassroots party worker, Jimmie Higgins, to the local swimming hole instead of resting up for his evening speech.[41] Although discouraged by reports of impending war in Europe, the Candidate is refreshed by his afternoon with Jimmie, who reminds him that "our movement is rooted in the hearts of the people!"[42] Published in the fall of 1918, after U.S. troops were fully engaged at the front and after Debs had been sent to federal prison on sedition charges for his opposition to the draft, the opening scenes contrast all the more fully the wartime reality with the peacetime one, associating the relatively united, steadily growing, and ideologically secure prewar party with the innocence of the final peacetime day of summer. As ever with nostalgia, though, Sinclair's representation has a polemical undercurrent. His portrayal of Jimmie in particular indicates a nativist bias, as if recent immigrants had not been a critical part of the Socialist Party all along. Insofar as the generic, prewar party-worker Jimmie could not "recall a word of the foreign language he had spoken at home, nor did he even know what that language was,"[43] the opening of the novel pointedly suggests that the party owed its past success to an all-American identity and a nativist organizing emphasis. The animus in *Jimmie Higgins* is especially directed against the German faction within the party. Plot events in the novel go well out of their way to represent the antiwar faction as part of a pro-German conspiracy. When the war's outbreak is reported in Leesville, the novel's primary American setting, a socialist crowd hears the German Social Democrats have heroically resisted their nation's war mobilization. A few days later, however, the citizens of Leesville learn that this was only a trick of German propaganda, designed to goad Allied social democrats to follow suit with their own general strike and so hand victory to Germany. Subsequently, Jimmie gets a job at a German American–owned bike shop that turns out to be a front for a plot, bankrolled by Germany, to "[make] explosives and [plant] them all over the country."[44] Still later, when the Russian soldiers and workers succeed in their uprising and the German soldiers have an opportunity to follow suit, only a brigade revolts, an action swiftly and brutally put down (a reference to the January 1918 revolt in which Rosa Luxembourg and Karl Liebnecht participated). The rest of the German army obediently marches forth to occupy Russia, "fir[ing] upon the red flag, as they would have fired upon the flag of the Tsar."[45] Such treachery, such apostasy to the cause of international socialism, leads Jimmie to enlist with the U.S. Army in hopes of teaching the faithless German soldiers a lesson.

Behind these fictional incidents—the accounts of actions in Germany being more or less based on fact, those of conspiracies in journalism and sabotage in the United States being almost altogether fabricated—was a bitter fight of Sinclair and his allies with German American party leaders over the proper Socialist response toward the U.S. declaration of war in April 1917. Although recognizing, as Sinclair had in 1909 and 1915, that socialist principle stood unequivocally against capitalist wars, Sinclair and other leading non-German socialists suspected something other than this principle to be behind the German American leaders' foursquare support for an antiwar resolution. National leaders such as Victor Berger and Morris Hillquit had throughout their careers been the most pragmatic and careful of social democrats: to this Sinclair could attest personally, given Hillquit's refusal to support the Ludlow mourning pickets. Among the minority of socialists who resigned from the party in the spring of 1917 when the antiwar resolution was passed, it was widely assumed that the underlying reasons for the suddenly principled socialist stance of Berger and Hillquit was affinity for their homeland and responsiveness to their German American electoral base. Algie Simons, a party member in Wisconsin, the epicenter of German Americanism in the party, wrote despairingly to Sinclair: "Unfortunately any influence we might exert is discounted by the German intrigues within the party. This has apparently damned us to everlastingly [*sic*] impotence among intelligent people."[46] Charles Edward Russell wrote scathingly of Sinclair's hopes for a partywide referendum on the war: "What is the use of bothering about the referendum (if there is one) or the minority report (if there is one) or anything else connected with the damned party? It is going to hell and let it go and I should judge by what I hear of it that the sooner it got there the better."[47]

The various innuendos about German disloyalty and conspiracy published in *Jimmie Higgins* were only a part of the novel's agenda, as stated by Sinclair at its inception: that Jimmie Higgins, the archetypal socialist grunt, could be loyal to both his country and international socialism, helping to win a victory for American democracy and social democracy simultaneously by dying on the battlefield in France. The identity of national and socialist interests appears complete in Sinclair's précis, which, though appearing with the first chapter of the serial in October 1918, gives away the ending in order to make precisely this point: "Jimmie Higgins Votes for democracy—this last line meaning that he gives his life on the battle-field."[48] And so it happens that within just a few months Jimmie miraculously goes from humble mechanic in Leesville, United States of America, to the front lines in France. Because Jimmie is a motorcycle repairman, and because such repairmen are in short supply among the Allies, he arrives in France just in time to participate in the tide-turning battles of late spring 1918. Remarkably, he just happens to be on a motorcycle delivering messages to the front lines as the climactic stage of battle is reached, just happens to arrive at a key machine-gun position when the last soldier there is struck dead, and just happens to man the machine gun and successfully repulse the German assault on this post, which just happens to be the linchpin of the entire Allied line, before he himself is gravely wounded. This, we learn, is what a single person committed to the ideals of democracy and freedom can do. It is a sequence of plot improbabilities worthy of Sinclair's early days writing of the exploits of Mark Malory, U.S. Army cadet, and Clif Faraday, U.S. Navy ensign, and woven of the same ideological fiber as these stories penned during and soon after the Spanish-American War.

There is, at the same time, something almost *too* cartoonish, something too flagrantly campy, about Jimmie Higgins's extraordinary timing and uncanny heroism—not that Sinclair was incapable of unintended, entirely unself-conscious, campiness. In any case, Jimmie Higgins does not, as had been announced months in advance, give his life fighting for democracy in France. He survives, recovers, and is promptly sent to Russia to serve with the British and American expeditionary force fighting an undeclared war against the Red Bolsheviks and in support of the "White" Russian counterrevolutionists. Between the time Sinclair had conceived his plan for the novel and the time came for Jimmie to die, Sinclair found he had other plans for him and another important political and historical theme to treat: the revolution in Russia.

Bitter as his attitude remained against the chiefs of the Socialist Party, Sinclair had not found his adventure in wartime collaboration with the Wilson administration, or even his foray into building a new, nativist party of "Industrial Democracy," to be particularly satisfying or fruitful. Already back in May 1917, while Sinclair and the prowar faction were trying to hammer out the agenda for their alternative social democratic organization, Sinclair had disputed with the others about whether to differ from the wartime policy of the Wilson administration. In particular, Sinclair believed the socialists should demand that Wilson immediately declare his war aims, which, with respect to Germany, should call only for the overthrow of the kaiser and, with respect to the United States and its allies, should pledge no territorial annexation. Support for the Wilson administration, Sinclair reminded his colleagues, was not an end in itself but a means to social democratic ends: "We wish to assist the revolutionists, not merely in our own country, but in the enemy countries. We do not wish to further or advocate any program in our own country which would make unnecessary difficulties for the revolutionists in the enemy countries."[49] While not disputing Sinclair's principles, the others would not press any demands upon the Wilson administration. Efforts to turn Industrial Democracy from a paper to a flesh-and-blood organization faltered almost immediately; prowar socialists such as Charles Edward Russell and William English Walling devoted far more energy to the task of bringing other groups into the progressive, prowar fold, including notably the National Association for the Advancement of Colored People, on whose board both served.

Later in 1917, Sinclair began yet another of his presidential letter-writing campaigns, this time protesting to Woodrow Wilson the suppression of radical journals, particularly those that opposed American involvement in the war. Repeatedly referring to the president's own wartime appeal to make the world safe for democracy, Sinclair declared himself in sympathy with Wilson's position but informed the president that his lieutenants were playing fast and loose with freedom of speech and rights of due process: "Is it utterly impossible to conduct a war in a democratic way? Is it impossible to deal with the opponents of war at home with the weapons of democracy, which are reason and fair play, instead of the weapons of autocracy, which are the policeman's club and jail?"[50] Still later, arguing on much the same grounds, Sinclair wrote in protest of the administration's legal prosecutions of antiwar dissenters.[51]

From the very beginning of that portion of the novel relating Jimmie Higgins's experiences in Russia, Sinclair's narrator sheds whatever sympathy had remained for the Wilson administration's wartime conduct. Sinclair's account of the war as represented in *Jimmie Higgins* at first had lagged behind actual events by more than four years; his historical account of the war's beginning in July and August 1914 appeared in October 1918, just a month before the war ended. By the time Jimmie was dispatched for Russia, however, the serial had almost caught up with real-life events, so that the novel's arch commentary upon Wilson's participation in the botched peace treaty followed the announcement of its terms by mere weeks. Whereas the Versailles treaty was a major disappointment to Sinclair, the Archangel expedition was an outright betrayal. Jimmie, the narrator reports, "had swallowed [the government's] propaganda, he had filled himself up with their patriotism, he had dropped everything to come and fight for Democracy. . . . And now they had broken their bargain with him, they had brought him here and ordered him to fight working-men—just as if he had been a militiaman at home!" The U.S. Army, Jimmie learns, is in Russia to "wipe the idea of Bolshevism off the map," all for the sake of the French government and French bankers offended because the Bolsheviks had repudiated the czar's millions of francs in war loans.[52] Contacted by a Jewish American socialist who has returned to his ancestral home to assist the revolution, Jimmie pledges never to kill any soldier of the Red Army and to distribute among the troops copies of an antimilitarist pamphlet. For these acts of sedition, Jimmie is imprisoned, tortured, tried, sentenced to twenty years, and placed in solitary confinement. Out of solidarity with his comrade, Jimmie refuses, however, to identify the source for his pamphlets.

Sinclair's narrative is full of portentousness, but the torture scenes—as graphic as anything before written in American literature—are imbued with a seriousness of treatment equal to their material. Today progressive Americans are appalled by accounts of "waterboarding" of detainees in U.S. military custody; over ninety years ago, Sinclair exposed the horrors of the same torture, then identified by the still more deeply ironic euphemism of the "water cure."[53] Of this method of torture, the final test of Jimmie before he goes before the court-martial tribunal, we hear that the subject is laid on the ground, his hands handcuffed behind his back and under him, whereupon one torturer sits on his feet, the second on his stomach, and the third pours water down his throat with the help of a funnel: "Jimmie had to swallow, of course; he had to gulp desperately, to keep from being choked, and pretty soon the water filled him up, and then began the most fearful agony he had yet endured. . . . Jimmie could not scream, but his face turned purple and the cords stood out on his forehead and neck; he began to strangle, and this was worst of all; every convulsion stabbed him with ten thousand knives."[54] Following an unvarnished account such as this, the melodramatic proclamations of the narrator may perhaps seem a pardonable literary offense: "In the soul of Jimmie Higgins was heard that voice which speaks above the menaces and commands of tyranny: which says: I am Man, and I prevail. I conquer the flesh, I trample upon the body and rise above it. . . . I am Freedom, and I break all laws, I defy all repressions, I exult, I proclaim deliverance!"[55] Moreover, such spiritual transcendence is immediately qualified by Sinclair. His chief interrogator, though thwarted, gives orders that another crew of torturers should repeat the water cure every two hours: "And Jimmie lay and moaned and wept, all by himself, quivering now and then with the perilous ecstasy, which does not last, but has to be renewed by continuous efforts of the will, as a tired horse has to be driven with spur and whip. Never, never could this battle be truly won! Never could the body be wholly forgotten, its clamorous demands wholly stilled!"[56]

That Sinclair sees this terrible conflict as the real war for democracy is signaled by the fact that the chapter describing Jimmie's final torture is given the chapter title originally projected for the climactic battle scene in France: "Jimmie Higgins Votes for Democracy." To a significant degree, Sinclair transfers the heightened individualism of Jimmie's triumph over the Germans at Chateau-Thierry to Jimmie's struggle with his American tormentors in Archangel. In the face of a degrading incarceration and trial, even knowing that his Jewish American comrade has by now almost certainly fled to save himself, Jimmie refuses to name his confederate. This refusal, which seems only a matter of personal honor and leads him finally to be tortured into madness, turns out to be critical, for the Russian Jew from New York City returns to the camp to post placards exposing Jimmie's supposedly secret court-martial and torture, thus sharpening questions about the U.S. mission to Russia in the minds of Jimmie's soldier-comrades. The narrator reports that similar questions, meanwhile, are being asked back home in the U.S. Congress: what right did the United States have in "sending troops into a country against which war had never been declared"? And the statements of the president are not of much help to the guardians of law and order, either. Although late in the novel Sinclair indicates that it is the president's idealistic words, not his deeds, that are progressive, it is nevertheless inconvenient for the U.S. military forces "trying to put down those Russians who were in revolt against 'economic serfdom'" that the U.S. president had recently traveled to the convention of a major U.S. labor organization (presumably the American Federation of Labor) and denounced "economic serfdom" whenever and wherever suffered by U.S. workers.[57]

If the individual action of Jimmie is critical, it becomes widely significant only because he is working in concert with others, and they with him. The hyperbole of Jimmie holding the line against "the whole Hun army" becomes, in the Archangel episode, a more realistic assessment of the limits of individual action and possibilities of group coordination and collective organization—the kind of balance between individual conversion and collective political power that Sinclair had formulated in the closing pages of *The Jungle.* Part of the rhetorical power—and realism—of the ending of *Jimmie Higgins* is that Sinclair could not write of the end of the British-American expedition to Russia, for it had not reached a conclusion either when *Jimmie Higgins* appeared in book form in late spring 1919 nor when the serialized publication wound up in the *New Appeal* of August 9, 1919.[58] Sinclair could not write the end of that counterrevolutionary intervention, nor could he write with any certainty the outcome of the Bolshevik revolution. And what he could say, and predict, about the social democratic movement was less assured than it had been at any time since he had become a socialist: less than in 1906 when he published *The Jungle* and exclaimed "Chicago will be ours!" far less certain than in 1907 when he published *The Industrial Republic* and predicted a parliamentary revolution by 1912, and even less predictable than in 1917 when he had placed faith in the progressive trajectory of the U.S. war mobilization.

In his open letter applying for readmission to the Socialist Party of America in July 1920, Sinclair spoke frankly of the dimmed prospects for social democracy in the United States: "We, who have dreamed the beautiful dream of a peaceful social change, of the birth of a new order without bloodshed and waste—we see our chances growing slimmer, our hopes fading day by day."[59] But if Sinclair was bowed by the setbacks of the war years, he could also speak with defiance of the lesson of "no compromise" learned once again from hard experience. Writing at the conclusion of *Jimmie Higgins* the year before, he appeals to his readers to write their own ending to Jimmie's narrative, and not only in pressuring their government to bring the troops home from Russia (something that did in fact happen, perhaps a recommendation for the virtues of representative government, after all) but also in fighting with renewed ferocity for the rights of labor and social equality in the United States. There is in that conclusion the same sorrowful note that dominates his letter of 1920: "Poor, mad Jimmie Higgins will never again trouble his country," the narrator reports. But because the story of Jimmie is not solely an individual one but a collective one, and because this is not yet a story with an end as long as there are comrades—and readers—to remember and act upon his story, the narrator can also prognosticate, "Jimmie's friends and partisans, who know the story of his experiences, cannot be thus lightly dismissed by Society. In the industrial troubles which are threatening the great democracy of the West, there will appear men and women animated by a fierce and blazing bitterness; and the great democracy of the West will marvel at their state of mind, unable to conceive what can have caused it."[60]

To the key question of the moment—what to make of the Bolshevik revolution in Russia—Sinclair gave a more positive and enthusiastic answer than many who had been participants in the Second Internationale. Most of the other prowar socialists were as swift in denouncing the Bolsheviks and Communists as they had been in renouncing the German American leaders of the party.[61] In contrast, Sinclair's letter seeking readmission to the Socialist Party advocated, unmistakably, a policy informed by the example of the Soviets and suddenly cool toward parliamentarianism: "So I ask to come back to the Socialist Party; to help as far as I can in the task of persuading the workers both of hand and brain, the wage-slaves of the factory and the white collar slaves of the office, to educate themselves and organize themselves and make democracy a reality, not merely in politics, where it counts for very little, but in industry, where it counts for almost everything."[62]

Still, the resolution of *Jimmie Higgins* recalls in notable ways the irresolution of the ending of the *Herland/Ourland* duology, completed less than three years before but in historical terms seemingly an aeon earlier. Perhaps the clearest evidence of qualification in Sinclair's endorsement of the Bolshevik revolution is that Sinclair takes as his hero not an agent of revolutionary violence but a martyr of counterrevolutionary violence. His secondary hero, too, the Jewish American Bolshevik who collaborates with Jimmie, does not conspire to commit acts of sabotage but merely to dispense information—and not even, initially, propaganda against the American presence in Russia but simply copies of revolutionary appeals left by Russian soldiers for the advancing German ones. The distinction between martyr and militant might seem narrow, particularly when the one so often calls for, and seems almost naturally to demand, the other. Sinclair seems, moreover, to testify to the limitations of the martyr's call in his brutally realistic depiction of Jimmie's torture: simply put, the heroism required is of an extraordinary sort. It may be within the grasp of any human being to proclaim as does Jimmie in his soul, "I conquer the flesh, I trample upon the body and rise above it," but it is the condition of humanity, too, to be subject to the involuntary needs, passions, and responses of the body, and thus the narrator also reports of Jimmie's continuing agony: "Never could the body be wholly forgotten, its clamorous demands wholly stilled!" Besides being an excruciating depiction of the bodily pain of torture, the remark may also be readily enough applied to the social democrats' long-standing efforts to change society by challenging ideologies and political structures using rational argumentation and appeals to conscience, when what matters is the ongoing, underlying struggle of physical power and psychological will. When the body fights back involuntarily, when the natural response to the ruin of a good man is to wreak retaliatory ruin, is it not after all the realistic path to turn to revolutionary violence? Sinclair's defense of the Bolsheviks suggests that revolutionary violence is warrantable and perhaps inevitable. Yet as he stands poised to lay aside "the beautiful dream of a peaceful social change, of the birth of a new order without bloodshed and waste," it is clear that Jimmie's struggle is heroic because he refuses to lay aside the beautiful dream; he *does* after all succeed in submitting the demands of the body to the convictions of the mind.

In 1920, Sinclair would rejoin the same Socialist Party that he had left in 1917—or at least the rump of the wartime party in which Hillquit and Berger remained leaders and which chose not to affiliate with the Soviet-led Third Internationale. Had the party's commitment to parliamentarianism no longer mattered to him, it would have been far more likely and easy for him to join the Workers (Communist) Party—the new American party aligned with the Internationale that drew off a majority of the old Socialist Party membership. If, more than ever before, the wars and revolutions of 1914–20 had injected the possibility that violence and social chaos would attend social democratic revolution, it remained critical to Sinclair that the seemingly utopian ideal of nonviolent action, even approaching and including martyrdom, should be the standard for socialists. Have the socialists work for revolution through labor unions, elections, and legal action; let the capitalists fire the first shots when their private wealth is expropriated for the public weal, and let the violence be counterrevolutionary. Then the power of the state—the police, the courts, the military—might be wielded against the counterrevolutionaries, as with Gilman's mighty Herlander "Colonels." Sinclair would advocate this formula for legal revolution, counterrevolutionary violence, and police power repeatedly during the 1920s and 1930s. It kept faith with the tenets of the Second Internationale, took into account the violent and chaotic new realities catalyzed by the war, and found its tentative start in the twists, turns, and uncertainties of *Jimmie Higgins*.

DOWN TO EARTH WITH "THE COMET"

"Low on the horizon lay a long, white star—mystic, wonderful!"

The apocalyptic episodes that we have observed in Gilman's and Sinclair's fictions—variously represented as tragedy, warning, or opportunity—become in W. E. B. Du Bois's short story "The Comet" the stuff of fantasy. In many ways, this was in keeping with Du Bois's quite different perspective on the war: the comeuppance of Europe, including the failure of European socialism, had been cause for a certain grim satisfaction for the *Crisis* editor. The wish that Western civilization might be laid utterly waste, leaving behind practically a blank slate upon which to rewrite the human story from the beginning, forms the central premise of Du Bois's story. And why not? The year 1920, when the story was published as the closing piece of *Darkwater*, was not one of ongoing reckoning with the final toll of destruction and death from the Great War, and the year when the single remnant of Wilson's idealistic hopes for a just peace, the League of Nations, was rejected by the U.S. Senate even as the lame-duck president was laid low by mortal illness. It was also, as we have already explored in chapter 4, the year of reckoning for the U.S. labor movement and another grim and murderous season for race relations in the United States.

There are elements of revenge fantasy touching on practically all of these historical issues in the catastrophe described in "The Comet." Given the symbolic as well as actual importance of American finance both in bankrolling the world war and in backing the conservative political and economic offensive of 1919–20, it is fitting that Wall Street is the scene of the most fantastic scenes of death and destruction when the titular comet spews its poisonous gases over the earth and (apparently) wipes out almost every oxygen-breathing being. In the entrance to one bank there lie the bodies of "a hundred men and women and children . . . crushed and twisted and jammed, forced into that great, gaping doorway like refuse in a can—as if in one wild, frantic rush to safety, they had crushed and ground themselves to death."[63] That such carnage, evoking the mass slaughter in the no-man's land of the western front, is visited upon businesspeople and civilian women and children may be read as a commentary upon the interconnections between the war and America's business interests, and also as the suppressed wish of the soldiers who were sent to the front and suffered at the urging of the safe, patriotic, and often complacent civilians on the homefront. In any event, although the catastrophe described by Du Bois is a natural disaster, the fact that the comet deals death by a plume of poisonous gases enveloping the earth must be read as deeply connected to the recent world war, in which poison gas was among the new terrors and a powerful symbol of the war as an indiscriminate modern industry of death.

Most immediately and explicitly, though, the revenge fantasy is about the comeuppance of racist white America. When the story's principal black character, Jim, is preserved from the comet because his job as a bank messenger has sent him on an errand to a subterranean vault considered "too dangerous for more valuable men," he is at first frightened when emerging from the vault to discover everyone in the bank has been killed. His assumption is that the bank has been robbed and he will be held to account. Soon, however, realizing that everyone in the streets is dead also, he acts in ways that previously had been forbidden. Though surrounded with corpses, virtually frozen in attitudes of life, he enters a Fifth Avenue hotel and serves himself at its exclusive restaurant, "seiz[ing] a tray from dead hands" and eating the food "ravenously": "'Yesterday, they would not have served me,' he whispered, as he forced the food down." Soon he borrows a car and reconnoiters the city with a freedom heretofore never experienced, though with the necessity of detouring to Park Avenue "to avoid the dead congestion" on Forty-second Street.[64] Most transgressive of all is Du Bois's choice of the second main character in "The Comet," a rich white young woman whose willingness to accompany Jim and, ultimately, to consider him a suitable social and sexual partner, flouts the most incendiary of racist taboos.

The relationship between Jim and the young woman—unnamed until the end of the story—swiftly becomes the vehicle for the utopian vision that rushes to fill the void created by the apocalyptic revenge fantasy. "The Comet," more forthrightly than either Sinclair's *Jimmie Higgins* or Gilman's *Herland/Ourland* duology, imagines present catastrophe as a vital opportunity for social progress. Significantly, Du Bois is emphatic about how the vision involves economic as well as racial equality. In the first interchange between the black man and white woman, it is their former difference in wealth that is articulated first:

> "Have you had to work hard?" she asked softly.
> "Always," he said.
> "I have always been idle," she said. "I was rich."
> "I was poor," he almost echoed.
> "The rich and the poor are met together," she began, and he finished:
> "The Lord is the Maker of them all."

Only after this benediction, effectively proclaiming that the apocalypse has ushered in a new heaven and a new earth, do the two major characters make reference to the racial difference that has also previously separated them, and then rather more indirectly than their previous reference to class distinction. "How foolish our human distinctions seem—now," says the woman, to which Jim replies: "Yes—I was not—human, yesterday." Then, in another allusion to Hebrew scripture, specifically the successful cross-cultural relationship between Ruth and Naomi, the young woman concurs: "And your people were not my people."[65]

The new beginning for humanity, embodied literally as well as figuratively in this partnership between Jim and the rich young white woman, is most fundamentally an assault upon class differences under capitalism, which are completely obliterated by the destruction of modern industry and society. Gender difference remains prominent; the woman becomes a kind of female fertility goddess: "She was primal woman; mighty mother of all men to come and Bride of Life." Racial difference is also highlighted in Du Bois's account, especially prominent in a description of Jim, which recalls the glory of African and Mesopotamian kings: "He arose within the shadows, tall, straight, and stern, with power in his eyes and ghostly scepters hovering in his grasp. It was as though some mighty Pharaoh lived again, or curled Assyrian lord."[66] Class is evoked explicitly in this reference to dark-skinned nobilities, but precisely to emphasize the degree to which the former social relation between these two characters has been obliterated; they are now equally regal.

The singular importance of sexual reproduction between these two individuals immediately demands comparison with the situation at the end of *Herland,* in which the birth of Alima and Jeff's child is eagerly anticipated, and at the conclusion of *Ourland,* in which the birth of Ellador and Van's son is heralded. Given that Du Bois frequently conceptualized the parallels between gender and racial inequality and, hence, stressed the potential for collaboration between race activists and feminist ones, we might reasonably hypothesize that Du Bois's archetypal figures for the rebirth of humanity are a feminist woman and a race-conscious man. Certain seemingly incidental facts about the main characters in "The Comet" substantiate this line of interpretation. Besides the immediate facts that the woman is young, white, and formerly rich and pampered, she is notable for skills and activities not associated with conventional femininity. She is a woman of modern technical and artistic inclinations, as she was saved from the comet because she was working in her own hermetically sealed darkroom developing photos. Her representation as a progressive new woman is further reinforced by the fact that she is able to drive an automobile. Whereas Jim must find a Ford in order to drive, she volunteers to chauffeur Jim to Harlem in one of her family's fancier, faster, and trickier-to-drive makes (an ironic reversal of usual socioeconomic roles). What Du Bois idealizes here, then, is a collaboration across lines of gender and racial as well as class difference. To the parallel, mutually reinforcing labor and women's movements extolled by Gilman, he adds, and represents as coequal, the movement for racial equality.

That Du Bois means for the relationship between the young woman and Jim to represent an ideal synthesis of racial, gender, and class equality is signaled, unmistakably, by one of the archetypal scenes of utopian fiction: the materialized prospect, literally from a great, commanding height, of the better world to come. The convention is evident in *Herland* both through the initial flyover that Van and his companions make of the well-manicured Herland civilization, and by the setting of Herland upon mountain heights overlooking the rest of the world. It is evident in a utopian-apocalyptic fiction by Sinclair, *The Millennium,* an apocalyptic fantasy in which a radium experiment gone wrong leaves eleven human beings alive on earth, ten of whom are able to form a commune commanding a vision of the future from John D. Rockefeller's repurposed Pocantico Hills estate. Standing at the head of this utopian tradition is the panoramic prospect of Boston from the roof of the Leete home in the final year of the twentieth century, in which the outline of the Charles River and the contour of Boston Bay, each of its islands in the right place, are the principal facts that assure Julian that the dreamlike city he sees below him—broad avenues, verdant public parks, magnificent public buildings—is indeed Boston. In Du Bois's version, the transcendent vision from on high, provided courtesy of the skyscraper housing the business offices of the young woman's father, emphasizes not the particulars of the country and city of the future but rather the apocalyptic agent of transformation:

> Dark-purple clouds lay banked and billowed in the west. Behind them and all around, the heavens glowed in dim, weird radiance that suffused the darkening world and made almost a minor music. Suddenly, as though gathered back in some vast hand, the great cloud-curtain fell away. Low on the horizon lay a long, white star—mystic, wonderful! And from it fled upward to the pole, like some wan bridal veil, a pale, wide sheet of flame that lighted all the world and dimmed the stars.[67]

This is the moment of revelation, positioned between the woman's "Annunciation" and the man's reincarnation as "Assyrian lord." Straightforwardly and explicitly, it recasts the engine of the apocalypse as a scene of transfiguring beauty. Even as its imagery rises far above the civic grace of Bellamy's Boston to the level of the Romantic sublime, "The Comet" embraces and transforms the image used by Bellamy's narrator, Julian West, to express his worst fear for the nineteenth-century civilization that he represents: the possibility that "the parabola of a comet was perhaps a yet better illustration of the career of humanity. Tending upward and sunward from the aphelion of barbarism, the race attained the perihelion of civilization only to plunge once more to its nether goal in the regions of chaos."[68] At the moment when Jim and the young woman, Julia, glimpse this comet, the "plunge" into "the regions of chaos" is precisely what they hail:

> They cried each to the other, almost with one voice, "The world is dead."
>
> "Long live the——."[69]

Bellamy's fiction deals with the threat of chaos with fear—and with the refusal to admit the necessity of scrapping the old world to start over anew. Du Bois's fiction embraces the apocalypse, and admits that scrapping the old world might indeed be necessary and desirable.

But this is not the end of the story for Du Bois, for the beautiful vision of apocalyptic destruction and complete reconstruction is, after all, too beautiful. The couple breaks apart from one another when they hear the honking horn of the young woman's father's car. Soon they learn that most of the young woman's family as well as most of the rest of the world outside of New York City has been spared. The abrupt shift back to reality is marked by a sudden reversal of how proper names are used: the young white woman, formerly nameless, is called "Julia" and "my darling" by her father. Jim is referred to as a "nigger" by the white male characters when they suspect him of improper relations with Julia, as "my good fellow" by the father when Julia vouches for his good character, and as "Jim" by the father, with undue familiarity, when Jim introduces himself as "Jim Davis."[70] Although Julia credits Jim for her rescue, she acquiesces to the divide of racial inequality, reinforced by the myth of white female sexual purity, insofar as the narrator records that "she did not look at him again." The color line thus having been firmly reestablished, the rich father reinstates its economic underpinnings, paying Jim for services rendered by "a roll of bills from his pockets" and offering both paternalistic encouragement and the opportunity for wage labor: "I've always liked your people. If you ever want a job, call on me."[71]

If, owing to the difference wrought by world war and revolution as well as by his more widely inclusive utopian vision, Du Bois can much more readily conceive of cataclysmic change positively than could Bellamy some thirty years previous, he also finds in "The Comet" that real conditions cannot yet admit of such a course. This may be good news, for the world is perhaps not so unredeemable as to demand absolute destruction, but it may equally be bad news, insofar as the world is certainly not ready to sustain an egalitarianism as complete as that which Du Bois envisions. Coming down from the heights, the narrative's emphasis would seem at first to be on the latter point, for at the end of "The Comet" the obstacles of economic inequality, racism, and sexism that have reasserted themselves appear to be as intractable as ever. Yet the fantasy does not quite end in despair when it returns to a social situation somewhat corresponding to America in 1920. For not only has Julia's family survived; so has a portion of Jim's. His child has died, to be sure, a reminder of the heavier price typically exacted from people of his class as opposed to Julia's, even by natural disasters. Jim's wife appears on the roof of the Metropolitan Building as well, "brown, small, and toil-worn" but unaccountably still alive, and when she cries out "Jim!" she restores his familiar name to the proper familial context. There is, therefore, both a symbolic and a realistic satisfaction in the final line that records the restoration of Jim's relationship with his African American wife: "He whirled and, with a sob of joy, caught her in his arms."[72] Jim turns, then, from the great task of repopulating a biracial earth to the more modest work of rebuilding Harlem—and with some relief that the apocalypse has not actually happened and that it might not actually be necessary.

To a large extent, then, "The Comet" reaffirms the course that Du Bois had been laying out for a decade before the world war. For Du Bois, the groundwork for the egalitarian commonwealth, glimpsed so seductively in the story's fantasy, had to be done first and for the foreseeable future within the black community. The story reaffirms a certain separation from the wider social democratic movement. At the same time, though, the world war and revolution did leave their mark upon Du Bois's work and thought, just as on Sinclair's and Gilman's. "The Comet," like *Jimmie Higgins* and the *Herland/Ourland* duology, imagines concretely—and even realistically, at least within the parameters of the mixed utopian-realist mode—the possibility of violence and revolution doing the job of social transformation, if ordinary and nonviolent processes prove unequal to the challenge. Yet "The Comet" also joins with Sinclair's *Jimmie Higgins* in recommitting to the reality of actually existing socialism, however different that might be from the socialism of the Second Internationale or from the ideal socialism of utopian imagining and desire. It is Gilman's *Herland/Ourland* duology that remains more aloof, and holds out for a more perfectly egalitarian social organization. Whether tilting toward realism or toward utopianism, Du Bois, Sinclair, and Gilman joined in preaching patience and perseverance to social democrats. Recognizing the risks of attempting perfect equality all at once by embracing total revolutionary change, all three continued to opt for social transformation through already established cultural and political channels, even if those channels were merely a flawed Socialist Party crippled by internal strife and persecution, a single-author journal with limited circulation, or a still-fledgling civil rights organization (and not one, by any means, univocally dedicated to social democracy). On this point, their message for American socialists was a shared one: Strive for equality now, where you are. Better—in spite of the seductions of apocalyptic grandeur—to avoid the cataclysm and go to work to prevent its necessity.

CHAPTER SEVEN

HEAVEN AND EARTH: REVELATIONS AND DOUBT IN THE SACCO-VANZETTI DECADE

The revolutionary moment of 1919 passed rapidly, a consequence both of the government's stern repression of left-wing activity and of Left activists' unreadiness, or unwillingness, actually to undertake the revolutionary violence the government accused them of plotting. Membership fell precipitously in both the Socialist Party of America and the several, successive Comintern-aligned parties that splintered off from it.[1] Even as problems multiplied for socialism in the United States, those who remained committed to the movement were alternately tantalized and inspired by promising developments internationally. Parliamentary socialists could look to the success of Great Britain's Labor Party, which in the 1920s rapidly overtook the Liberal Party as the primary rival of the Tories and counted members of the Fabian Society among its most important leaders.[2] Militant revolutionaries had still more to celebrate and seek to emulate: actually existing socialism in the Union of Soviet Socialist Republics. For many freshly minted communists, a trip to the USSR was something akin to a pilgrimage, inspiring rhapsodies such as the one Michael Gold penned in 1924 to his comrade and literary mentor Upton Sinclair:

> One feels so normal and strong in Russia; and all the things one only theorizes about here and feels a little bitter and savage in defending, are so simple and real in Russia. It's a great new amazing place, everything beginning, life young and hopeful and strong. There are some things one doesnt like, for it is not Utopia by a long shot; it is the earth and not heaven; the earth in the throes of the birth of a new race of giants. Since

I have come back here (about three or four days ago) I have found myself thrust into many arguemnts [*sic*] with liberals, anarchists, Socialists etc. and I am not used to it yet. They argue about shadows, most of them; and after one has seen the reality, with its good and evil, one doesnt know how to answer the dialecticians. You must certainly get over there, Upton. I saw nothing in Europe or in America or Mexico that stirred me so much as hum-drum Russia at its business of bringing in Communism. A trip to Russia searches one's soul; strips away sentimentality and nonsense; makes or breaks one.[3]

In the main, Gold's panegyric lays claim to the real, the material actuality, as contrasted with the ethereal, the "shadows" of theory and an ideal but impossible "utopia." This binary seeks to separate the Communists from their socialist and liberal comrades and, by the same token, to separate the prewar social democracy from the harder-headed postwar communism. But of course this very binary opposition is itself deeply rooted in socialist debates going back some seventy years, in which Marx and Engels and their more moderate comrades took turns claiming the science of their socialism and charging their rivals with utopian wishful thinking. Moreover, Gold's text is shot through with forms of religious expression that, we have noted, also played a central role in the prewar socialist narratives of Gilman, Sinclair, and Du Bois. Not only does Gold invoke straightforwardly the favored metaphor of conversion when he speaks of an experience that "searches one's soul," "makes or breaks one," but he frames the ideal of a natural supernaturalism with the same figure of the emergence of a colossal, collective proletarian body favored by his social democratic predecessors: "the birth of a new race of giants." The more that Gold seeks to hail a new socialist millennium, it seems, the more he repeats the tropes by which socialism had defined itself dating well back into the previous century.

On these points, moreover, there is a curious homology between postwar discourses in radical politics and in the arts. The received version of literary modernism treats the Great War as a kind of historical continental divide. Just before the war, Ezra Pound had proposed "Make It New" as the credo of a poetry making a dramatic, even revolutionary, break with the past. And lo, once the high passes of war and revolution were traversed, there was no going back. Anyone clinging to the old ways of doing and seeing things was lost in nostalgia and irrelevance, however appealing some of the prewar hopes and methods might seem. Willa Cather's *One of Ours* might beat out John Dos Passos's *Three Soldiers* for the Pulitzer Prize for 1923, but the younger generation of writers and their advocates merely took this as clear evidence of their avant-garde status. And the critical dismissals of Cather's idealistic war narrative practically coincide with Gold's dismissal of socialists dealing in "shadows"; H. L. Mencken suggests, for instance, that the triumph of Cather's novel over Dos Passos's pointed to the unhappy day when "fancy achieves the inevitable victory over fact."[4] Yet repeatedly, the criteria set forward to assert the superior epistemology of the modernists amount to no more or less than the reassertion of the values that had been hailed as the foundation of realism, a generation or more earlier. Mencken insists upon the superiority of "fact" over "fancy." Pound argued for the validity of imagist principles by recourse to recent findings in cognitive psychology, while T. S. Eliot formulated his understanding of the poetic image, at its best, as the realization of an "objective correlative." Still more directly appealing to objective, material reality as the basis for the best art was William Carlos Williams's formulation: "No ideas but in things." We may even observe, furthermore, that the kind of ecstatic, utopian inspiration that marks Gold's text, and which in the utopian narrative mode serves as the double to realism, appears also in the modernists. Williams's formulation by no means disclaims ideas, but rather insists upon a properly material basis for them. Pound's imagist manifesto argues that the poetic image, when rightly executed, "gives that sense of sudden liberation; that sense of freedom from time limits and space limits; that sense of sudden growth, which we experience in the presence of the greatest works of art." The materiality of the modern city and of Western literary culture, even when reduced to its most basic elements by being fragmented to bits in Eliot's *Waste Land,* forms the basis for the transcendent, spiritual striving of that poem's closing.

Granting that much of the new art was, in truth, quite different from its predecessors—just as I would grant that the socialist movement was certainly changed by the Bolshevik revolution and the red summer of 1919—I would also observe that the tropes for making valid arguments and for idealizing one's preferred cultural formations remain surprisingly similar across the supposed "revolutionary" breaks in the arts and in international socialism.[5] Such an understanding is substantiated, I will argue, by work of Gilman, Sinclair, and Du Bois in the decade of the 1920s.

At a time when atheism was the official, hard-and-fast line of the Comintern and yet the language of religious faith imbues writing about the revolution, at a time when Charlotte Perkins Gilman's indifference to the directions taken by international socialism reached new heights, her final book-length piece of cultural analysis, *His Religion and Hers: A Study of the*

Faith of Our Fathers and the Work of Our Mothers (1923), mounted an important critique of the abuses of religion, secular as well as sacred, and a compelling vision for how the human impulse to spirituality and the socialist goal of material equality might be integrated. When artists of the "New Negro" Renaissance urged W. E. B. Du Bois to believe black equality might be realized through arts and culture rather than politics, the *Crisis* editor fired back that he did not care for arts or culture except so far as they served the political ends of social equality for all people of color. When black Communists pressed Du Bois to join the party, he affirmed that the slower, steadier path of black independence and solidarity could be adapted to the ever-increasing international integration of economic and political relations, showing just how in his second novel, *Dark Princess.* And about the time it seemed Sinclair's naive realism and his hope for a coalition politics transcending radical party lines had proven altogether passé, along came the cause of the Italian anarchists Nicola Sacco and Bartolomeo Vanzetti to unite radicals and liberals alike and to provide Sinclair with a story for which his style of documentary realism was demanded and which—precisely by being told in this style in his 1928 novel *Boston*—revealed the epistemological limits of realism. These were performances that revealed their relevance to the conditions of modernity, to modernism, and to postrevolutionary socialism in large part by remaining stubbornly committed to a methodical, nonviolent, and democratic socialist praxis.

RELIGIOUS FAITH AND REVOLUTIONARY COMMITMENT

> "Seeing God as within us, to be expressed, instead of above us, to be worshipped, is enough to change heaven and earth in our minds, and gradually to bring heaven on earth by our actions."

In her attitudes toward the modernist revolution in the arts as well as the militant direction of the Third Internationale, Gilman was the most contrary of the triptych writers. Although her widely known "Yellow Wall-Paper," first published in 1892, utilizes a stream-of-conscious narration that anticipates the technique of James Joyce, Virginia Woolf, and William Faulkner, Gilman did not make such narration her practiced mode; indeed, the story's stylistic sophistication is utterly untypical of the author's oeuvre. This was a matter of quite deliberate authorial choice. In her autobiography she proclaimed, mixing self-deprecation and defiance: "I have never made any pretense of being literary. As far as I had any method in mind, it was to express the idea with clearness and vivacity, so that it might be apprehended with ease and pleasure."[6]

While quietly indifferent to modernist artistic and literary developments, she loudly criticized postwar trends in international socialism. Immediately after the war Gilman rejoined the cultural conversation with a dramatic upsurge in her writing output. Having published only a handful of articles in the years when the United States was at war, she began producing and distributing daily editorials through the *New York Tribune* syndicate beginning in March 1919 and kept at it into April of the following year. Among the periodicals that bibliographer Gary Scharnhorst has cataloged, the *Louisville Herald* printed Gilman's editorials almost every day, and the *Buffalo Evening News* and the *Baltimore Sun* published her releases regularly as well, so that altogether 313 different pieces by Gilman were distributed by the syndicate in approximately thirteen months.[7] Although this return to public prominence coincides interestingly with the postwar upsurge in radical activity, Gilman's themes and attitudes were hardly endorsements of dramatic revolutionary change. She continued with many of the same subjects that had always been her métier: women's progress in social freedom, advances and setbacks in municipal government, fashions in women's clothing, the labor movement. The problems of class as well as gender inequality remained part of her agenda, but the presence of a newly aggressive labor and radical movement is hardly evidenced in her writing—except as she occasionally took a swipe at the revolutionaries in "Anarchists and Jokes" or "Exiling Dissenters."[8]

Racial and ethnic prejudices crowded into her work as well, as articles in the *Tribune* syndicate such as "The Peoples of America" and "Real America" expounded upon some of the more disturbing theses of *Moving the Mountain*—that social solidarity depends upon common culture, and that some American ethnic groups have collective histories and characteristics at odds with such a common culture in the United States.[9] In the multiethnic reality of New York City, her home during much of her marriage to Houghton, she found a harbinger of doom, "the rapidly descending extinction of our nation, superceded by other nations who will soon completely outnumber us," for as she solemnly explains, "with the majority rule of democracy . . . our grandchildren will belong to a minority of dwindling Americans, ruled over by a majority of conglomerate races quite dissimilar."[10] This amounts practically to a grotesque parody of the old dream of the Second Internationale, to transform American political economy altogether through the ballot box. The collation of ethnic and racial otherness with political menace almost inevitably carries over into the final characterizations of international socialism in her career, for in the autobiography she complains, "Socialism, long misrepresented and misunderstood by the violent propaganda of Marxism, has been fairly obliterated in the public mind by the Jewish-Russian nightmare, Bolshevism."[11]

As scholarship has shown for some time now, such attitudes about racial difference—far from placing Gilman at odds with other modernist writers—actually suggest a kinship between her and other prominent modern writers including Wyndham Lewis, T. S. Eliot, Ezra Pound, Ernest Hemingway, F. Scott Fitzgerald, and William Faulkner.[12] Such a correspondence between Gilman's views and the racial and ethnic fears of her white, male peers is primarily cautionary: a reminder that the social discipline, individual self-sacrifice, and collective identity necessary for social democracy to work can become oppressive if not balanced by tolerance, democratic participation, and protections for individual liberty. Yet there remain elements of Gilman's postwar writing that remained relevant to the socialist movement of her time—largely by being constructively critical of it.

Gilman's long-standing idée fixe—that the line of gender was the fundamental fact of social organization and social dysfunction—effectively demanded a balance in socialist theory and practice that had long been undermined as the class struggle came to feature contests of force between male capitalists and male proletarians that sidelined the exploitation of individuals defined via other axes of power. Moreover, through the Second Internationale and into Third, the class struggle had become reified into the class line through a particularly doctrinaire interpretation of Marxist theory, with the social relations of proletarian and bourgeois hardening into specific class identities, working-class versus middle-class. This Gilman had challenged in *Women and Economics* and continued to challenge in *His Religion and Hers.* For Gilman, the origin of the class struggle did not even lie in the rise of capitalism, with its accumulations of profits in the hands of the bourgeois, but in the far earlier emergence of patriarchy, with the ownership of wives and concubines providing the template for ownership of slaves and then, much later, wage-slaves.[13] Ever since the primordial marginalization of women, social development has been warped by sharp conflicts between men, whose tendencies toward competition and combat have sown the seeds of social dysfunction and morbid inequality. The remedy lies not through the latest class conflict between proletarian and bourgeois but in the reintegration of the conciliatory and harmonizing tendencies of the world-creative sex, women, into the human community. Far from embracing this remedy, however, political agents across the political spectrum rarely even recognize the core problem: "We are so used to the strange aborted position of the house-bound woman, living in the great world as if she were by nature only a servant and a prisoner there, that we do not yet being to appreciate what the world has lost by losing its mother."[14]

Gilman's maternal analysis thus issues a challenge to really existing socialism as well as to capitalism. No more impressed by the economic activity spurred by the Soviets' five-year plans than by the great aggregate wealth of the United States, Gilman saw equality in distribution as well as in production as the test predicated by the principle of motherhood, the most rigorous test of human progress. In spite of the clear, "primal duty" of motherhood "to provide for the coming race," Gilman complains that "we find in the human race such wide-spread poverty that millions of children are so born, so reared, as to degenerate instead of improving, to die instead of living." Such outrage is clearest where it concerns children, but Gilman finds no excuse for poverty among anyone at all in a modern, industrialized world where there is sufficient production to supply the wants of all. Directing her attention first to the United States and other capitalist countries, Gilman notes, "Our distribution is so grossly disordered that we find a state of unwholesome congestion among the rich, and a general pernicious anaemia among the poor." Looking to Soviet Russia, Gilman cuts no slack for the Bolsheviks in their ongoing battle against the former royalists, landed gentry, and various bourgeois, for the architects of the planned economy merely "substitute some arbitrary system of their own, based on various fallacies, still governed by the masculine impulse to combat, postulating a war between classes, urging hate and violence," with the results to be seen in the continuing hardships of the Russian people. Clearly not reading the same accounts that Michael Gold as well as Sinclair and Du Bois were then consulting when they hailed the steady progress of Russia toward prosperity, she writes of "the most conspicuous and ghastly failure of artificial distribution . . . shown by those who prey on slaughtered Russia." Gilman's characterization of the Bolsheviks as a new variety of power-hungry parasites—carrion-eaters—must be reckoned as apt enough when the planned starvation subsequently orchestrated by Stalin is considered.[15]

The central topic of Gilman's *His Religion and Hers* not only extends by self-conscious reflection the prewar tendency to cast socialist commitment as religious conversion; it also critiques postwar efforts to submerge this tendency by disparaging it. Whereas Social Gospelers had been an important part of the prewar socialist movement, the attitudes of postwar socialists tended to assimilate more thoroughly the Marxist aphorism denouncing "the opiate of the people." Thus, even as Gold's celebration of the Russian revolution is imbued with the language of eschatology, he contrasts the verifiable material progress of Russia with the merely idealistic and therefore phantasmagoric projections of the old-school theorists. The diametrical opposition and relative values of the two modes of thought are also evident in a 1931 exchange between Emma Goldman and Upton Sinclair over the virtues of the Soviet Union. The famous anarchist's autobiography, *Living My Life,* had been highly critical of the Soviet regime and especially its treatment of anarchists. Because early in 1920 Goldman had been deported to Russia during the Palmer raids, she could claim firsthand knowledge of Soviet repression when writing to chide Upton Sinclair over his fellow traveler's defense of Soviet Russia: "Your desire to see in every Soviet move the hand of god has somewhat effected [*sic*] your literary values. That is as it must be with people who rrmain [*sic*] true to the church whatever its faults. But I am a heathen and have always been, hence it was impossible to write about the wonders of the Five Year Plan." Sinclair's reply attempts to turn the tables on Goldman. Economic reports from 1931 had shown that Soviet production had surpassed France and Great Britain, and was third behind Germany and the United States. "The essence of superstition," Sinclair declared, "is a refusal to face facts, and if the Communists have solved the problem of production and you refuse to admit it, you are the one who has a church and is relying upon the hand of God."[16] Back and forth the socialist antagonists go, agreed on practically nothing except for the undesirability of religious faith and the value of empiricism.

Gilman's *His Religion and Hers* exhibits something of the same critical attitude toward religion. Her critique of religion, following lines mapped out in *Moving the Mountain,* is that virtually all religions have pursued a dream of eternal life beyond this world while ignoring the firmly established reality of eternal life all around us—that is, the potential for a virtually perpetual endurance of the life of the human species through constant reproduction and collective development. Practitioners of conventional religion have committed this error in spite of the fact that the various altruistic good works preached by all religions *should,* in fact, be conducive to a better life for their children as well as to a heavenly personal reward. As Gilman observes, "Even the teaching of Jesus, heart-warming, truth-filled doctrine of 'God in man,' of 'Thy kingdom come on earth,' of worship in love and service, was soon swamped by the resurgence of the death-idea, and became a mere short cut to the 'other life.'"[17] This amounts to the standard socialist criticism of religious otherworldliness as the destructive delusion of the masses, understood alike by the Wobbly folk singer Joe Hill scoffing at "pie in the sky when you die" and the early nineteenth-century theorist Moses Hess, whose *Communist Confession of Faith* (1846) asserted that "the Christian imagines the better future of the human species . . . in the image of heavenly joy"; "We, on the other hand, will have this heaven on earth."[18]

Unlike her adamantly atheistic comrades, though, Gilman ultimately took an agnostic stance upon religion, no doubt recognizing the past importance of Social Gospelers to the socialist movement and hoping to conciliate religious believers of all kinds. Among her introductory comments is a concession to traditional religionists that could not be brooked by those who had made atheism the state religion of the Soviet Union: "It should be definitely understood that no denial is made of the future life of the individual soul after death; but that exception is taken to our disproportionate interest in that prospect, to the neglect of the future life of the race on earth."[19] Her further comments make clear, moreover, that the Soviet state should be numbered among those institutions that exhibit the masculine principles of sharp division and bitter conflict, so evident in the wars of religion down through history. While offering a forthright feminist critique of traditional religion, that critique also confronts the logic of the bourgeois/proletarian binary that was being applied to such murderous long-term effect in Soviet Russia. In spite of her differences with conventional religion, therefore, Gilman's *His Religion and Hers* is much less in sync with the Communists' relentless purging of czarist and bourgeois influences from the new Russia than with the traditional religious virtues of altruism, charity, and equality. Like the Social Gospel before, Gilman works self-consciously to harness long-standing religious convictions and institutions rather than attacking them.

Gilman's position on religion seeks to balance two forms of pragmatism: an empiricist insistence upon the reality of this material world, where facts might be determined and theories tangibly brought to bear; and at the same time a realistic understanding of the importance of spirituality and the power of religious institutions, both of which might be used rather than challenged by socialists. Gilman thus adopts the traditional language of religion in describing an alternative, maternal religion—as thorough a natural supernaturalism as any materialist could hope for. "God," Gilman avers, "is the Life within us, the Life of the world, to be worshiped in fruition." Quite simply, she proposes a religion based upon birth instead of death. In her scheme, reliance upon a higher power beyond this earth is displaced by reliance upon the endurance of earthly life, so that the responsibility for "eternal" life falls with existential completeness upon the shoulders of the religious adherents alone: "Whether our own children and grandchildren will be benefited much, depends on us, now; on our immediate conduct."[20] We may readily doubt whether such a vision would actually appeal (or *did* appeal) to adherents of any traditional religious faith, many of whom still found (and find) important the securities of an ultimate deity beyond human agency and of a life beyond this one, however robust their social mission may be. Yet Gilman's message might well find inspiration from, and an audience among, those Protestant denominations—Unitarians, Congregationalists—where the Social Gospel flourished largely because traditional comforts of an afterlife and supreme deity had been fundamentally questioned.[21]

Gilman also appeals to those who are not affiliated with any traditional religious group but may wish for the kind of wider connections formerly supplied by religion—connections to a community wider than a locale and a history longer than individual human life. In short, she renders self-consciously, and appeals to, the religious and spiritual elements of socialism that Michael Gold expresses even as he and other comrades sought ruthlessly to deny them. The appeal is especially clear in a passage in the closing chapter of *His Religion and Hers* that riffs on Moses Hess's 1846 invocation of "heaven on earth":

> Seeing God as within us, to be expressed, instead of above us, to be worshipped, is enough to change heaven and earth in our minds, and gradually to bring heaven on earth by our actions. Seeing human life as one unbroken line, visibly immortal, readily improvable, takes off the weight of discouraged ages, sets us on the broad, bright, upward road. No straight and narrow path, like a turnstile into a park, to squeeze into heaven by,—each for himself and the devil take the hindmost,—but an open way, always broadening as we grow, up which we can help one another.[22]

Such an understanding of religious faith not only connects to the socialist spiritual tradition marked out by Hess and others in the nineteenth century but also is entirely consistent with the materialist, empirical analysis of the Third Internationale socialists. Gilman, however, does not suppress or disparage the impulse toward spirituality, and she does not replace one dogmatic authority (the traditional church) with another (the Internationale), which manifestly is what adherents to the Third Internationale were in the process of doing. The "open way, always broadening as we grow," hardly describes the various "five-year plans" or "lines" already being prescribed from the high seat of the Kremlin. While explicitly linking to the more overt religiosity of earlier socialist manifestations, Gilman also reemphasizes the longstanding convictions of the prewar socialism that violence and force are counterproductive to true social progress, and that a "heavenly" commonwealth is achievable through collective, rational, orderly action—and *not* by sudden and complete revolutionary upheaval. At the moment that Gilman's ethnocentrism and anti-Marxism placed her further and further at the margins of the movement, her foregrounding of religion as a socialist theme comprised a salutary corrective to the suppression of religion among her erstwhile comrades. Her unwavering focus upon the values of a maternal socialism served as a rebuke to fellow socialists whose obsession with winning the class war had led to neglect of certain segments of society marginalized by and from power. Her insistence upon nonviolence and rational progress as the paths into socialism constituted a similar challenge to socialists of the rising generation. Capitalist exploitation and war had changed the world for the worse, but why should socialists let them change the course of socialism as well?

BACK TO THE FUTURE WITH THE DARK PRINCESS

> "In 1952, the Dark World goes free—whether in Peace and fostering Friendship with all men, or in Blood and Storm."

In contrast to Gilman, W. E. B. Du Bois was close to the cultural, literary, and political cutting edge in the 1920s. Under his editorship, *The Crisis* could claim credit for having debuted the work of many of the literary lights of the Harlem, or "New Negro," Renaissance: Langston Hughes, Jean Toomer, Countee Cullen, Georgia Douglas Johnson, Arna Bontemps, even Alain Locke, who would become Du Bois's rival for the role of impresario of the renaissance. Although it was Locke who coined the appellation "The New Negro," Du Bois may claim credit for originating the "Renaissance" label, predicting in a published 1920 exchange with Claude McKay that "a renaissance of American Negro literature is due; the material about us in the strange, heart-rending race tangle is rich beyond dream and only we can tell the tale and sing the song from the heart."[23] As for Du Bois's political position, although in 1921 he and his associates had heard both of "splendid results" in Soviet Russia and of "other things that frighten us,"[24] virtually all of his reservations were swept aside when in 1926 he visited the Soviet state. On the one hand, he reported in an editorial wired from Russia, his fears about the U.S.S.R. had not been confirmed by his experience, which is not quite to say they had been disproved: "I did not see the Russia of war and blood and rapine. I know nothing of political prisoners, secret police and underground propaganda." On the other hand, what he had seen, what he could testify to, had hugely impressed him: "I stand in astonishment and wonder at the revelation of Russia that has come to me. I may be partially deceived and half-informed. But if what I have seen with my eyes and heard with my ears in Russia is Bolshevism, I am a Bolshevik."[25]

Only slightly less enthusiastic were Du Bois's editorial statements when he returned home. His defense of the Soviet Union against charges of authoritarianism, published in *The Crisis* of February 1927, hewed close to the mark set by American Communists. The Russian Communist Party, Du Bois argued, held as its ultimate principle the democratic control of society by all citizens; only the backwardness of the Russian peasants and the recalcitrance of the bourgeoisie made a temporary dictatorial control of the state necessary. Frightening as this might be to Americans proud of their "freedom" and "rights," Du Bois asserted bluntly that liberal democracy was but a vehicle by which the oligarchs held sway in the United States: "This is nothing new. In this [American] government 'of the people' we have elaborate and many-sided arrangements for ruling the rulers."[26] The bottom line for Du Bois was that liberal democracy, for all its apparent advantages of openness to reform and responsiveness to the people, had largely failed in actually empowering the people, whereas the authoritarian rulership of formerly backward Russia was succeeding: "Not manhood suffrage, woman's suffrage, state regulation of industry, social reform nor religious and moral teaching in any modern country have shorn organized wealth of its power as the Bolshevik Revolution has done in Russia. Is it possible to conduct a great modern government without the autocratic leadership of the rich? The answer is: this is exactly what Russia is doing today."[27]

Neither in politics nor in art was Du Bois inclined to follow the party line entirely, however. Rather than offering a clear model, the Soviet Union provided a useful foil for lack of political progress in the United States and the limitations of the "New Negro" Renaissance alike. Du Bois's sudden effusiveness about Soviet Russia jibes provocatively with his analysis of the "New Negro" Renaissance as it had developed—and as his attitudes had evolved toward it—by the mid-1920s. Du Bois was critical not only of any government led by rich autocrats but of the literary aristocracy of the Renaissance. It was in 1926, near the very peak of the movement and just before his departure for the Soviet Union, that Du Bois had declared that he did "not care a damn for any art that is not used for propaganda."[28] He argued not only that the success of black arts and literature mattered to him only if it contributed to racial progress in all areas, and for all black Americans, but also that the opportunity for any and all citizens to experience aesthetic pleasure was itself a measure of progress—and one in which the "New Negro" Renaissance had failed, regardless of how much its artists drew their subject matter and forms from black working-class culture. Even in aesthetic matters, the socialist economy of abundance is just below the surface, and is immediately placed in implicit counterpoint with the capitalist economy of scarcity, for Du Bois reports that "today the mass of human beings are choked away from it [beauty], and their lives distorted and made ugly. This is not only wrong, it is silly. Who shall right this well-nigh universal failing? Who shall let this world be beautiful?"[29]

Du Bois was also independent in his political views. While praising Soviet progress, his *Crisis* editorials stopped short of advocating a Bolshevik-style revolution in the United States. His experiences in the Soviet Union as well as his observation of the "New Negro" Renaissance suggested that his vision for black America needed to be updated. But he as well as the Bolsheviks had been thinking for some time about the limitations of Western-style democracy, and he had become too well acquainted with the particulars of race and economics in the United States not to insist upon a revolutionary plan carefully fitted to those particulars. His vision was also international, like that of the Comintern, but it centered not in the Soviet Kremlin but among the economically exploited people of the darker world and in their capitals often directly subject, via colonization, to the capitalist powers of the Western world. Hence it was, inspired by the Soviet example but also determined to have his say, that on ship returning from the U.S.S.R. Du Bois began to write his second novel, fifteen years after the publication of *Quest of the Silver Fleece. Dark Princess* was completed within months of his return to the United States and published in early 1928.[30]

In its breadth of setting, international cast of characters, and articulation of a transnational socialist strategy, *Dark Princess* registers clearly the transformation of international socialism after the Bolshevik revolution as well as the impact of the war upon American culture. The milieu of the postwar expatriate is immediately signaled in the plot's inciting incident, in which the Talented Tenth protagonist, like so many other American intellectuals of the 1920s, seeks Europe as a refuge from American intolerance. Matthew Towns, a brilliant medical student, is denied a medical degree because white hospital administrators refuse to give him a residency in which he might be called upon to make obstetrical examinations for white women. The balance of the novel's first section, "The Exile," both reflects upon the comfort Du Bois had found as a doctoral candidate living abroad in the 1890s—for Towns goes not to Paris but to Berlin, where Du Bois had studied—and signals his own recent, revelatory experience in Bolshevik Russia. The Indian "dark princess" of the novel's title, Kautilya, has traveled through and been impressed by the U.S.S.R. on her way to a meeting of the leaders of the nonwhite world, held secretly in Berlin. What she learns there comes as a surprise to the other leaders, for in Bolshevik Russia she has heard "reports—careful reports of the world's masses," including the "astonishing" report on black America that "they are a nation today, a modern nation worthy to stand beside any nation here."[31] These reports reflect the current prevailing wisdom of the Comintern, formulated by rising party insider Josef Stalin, which stipulated that ostracized ethnic or racial groups within capitalist countries should be regarded in the same light as colonies subjected to imperial domination; black America was a "submerged" nation, or nation within a nation, that must be delivered first to independence, whereupon it would be free to pursue its own best interests (preferably and presumably by adopting socialism). Du Bois thus credits the racial enlightenment of the Comintern, even as in other venues he had praised its leadership of international socialism.

The introduction not only of representatives of the colonized world but also of the socialist leadership of the Soviet Union practically ensures that *Dark Princess* will offer an expanded international understanding of what must be done to remedy racial and class exploitation. From the outset, however, the novel's intellectual framework establishes both Du Bois's intellectual and political independence (and that of the colored world) and the importance of continuity between the prewar and the postwar social democratic vision. It is notable that the cultural and political integrity of black America, though unrecognized by the nobles of East Asia, South Asia, and Africa until taught them by the Bolsheviks, is known intuitively by Matthew Towns. Towns asserts the moral and cultural value of the African American masses, tested and proven by slavery, peonage, and domestic service, and as specimen of that value reels off, impromptu, a performance of "Go Down, Moses." If there is a subtle adjustment in Du Bois's earlier conceptions of the Talented Tenth—from the best educated and best heeled of black Americans, to whichever black Americans have shown their mettle in the crucible of racism—Du Bois's emphasis is upon what he, the author of *The Souls of Black Folk* twenty-five years hence, has been preaching to black and white America alike for that period and longer. Moreover, the composition of the cabal to which the princess belongs stresses that the subject and submerged nations of the world are independent from the Internationale. The princess's conference with the Bolsheviks as well as the addition of Matthew, representing the African diaspora, brings in a necessary component of class consciousness, but otherwise the group including leaders from Japan, China, Egypt, and India is presented as sufficient unto itself. The claim, implicit but clear enough particularly for any readers familiar with Du Bois's championing of Pan-Africanism from before the war, is that the Comintern might have its role to play in bringing anti-imperialism to the attention of the West and in raising the class consciousness of the East, but that anti-imperialism and national independence movements among people of color did not require the invention of international socialism.

The very literary form of *Dark Princess* suggests Du Bois's continued faith in the soundness of socialist and racial equality movements that had originated before the war, for *Dark Princess* sticks to the prewar social democratic literary script—realist critique of social problems counterpointed with utopian socialist solutions—and repeats many of the same character types and plot features of *Quest of the Silver Fleece.* Once again, Du Bois's utopian vision is embodied in the relationship between a strong, dark-skinned woman and a vacillating black man, whose rejection of another romantic partner, a cynical social climber in the African American pigmentocracy and Illinois politics, becomes the pivotal moment in the narrative and thematic development of the novel. Although the novel's scope is international, *Dark Princess* like *Quest of the Silver Fleece* trains its critique primarily upon conditions in the United States. The longer, middle sections of the novel take up, in turn, most militant and most pragmatic political options for black Americans, analyzing them carefully in order to supply, as Eric Sundquist suggests, "an anchor for Du Bois's visionary critique."[32]

Part II, "The Pullman Porter," deals specifically with the question of political violence, showing an awareness of the increased currency of militancy among African Americans and insisting, at the same time, upon the formula articulated before the war in *Dark Princess:* violent resistance might be ethically defensible, but it is not practically feasible. Fittingly, given the black and white violence in city streets during the summer of 1919, the continuation of the reign of lynch-terror in the South, and the radicalism of small but vocal groups such as the Hamitic League of the World and the African Blood Brotherhood (ABB),[33] Du Bois gives the case for antiracist violence a fuller hearing in *Dark Princess* than in the earlier novel. When the princess assigns Matthew the task of researching the readiness of black America to participate in a worldwide uprising against racist rule, he picks as its most likely American leader Perigua, a Jamaican-born Harlemite. Although Matthew is skeptical about Perigua's methods, Du Bois gives some of the best lines to the militant leader. When Matthew notes that, after the sobering destruction of the world war, few American blacks have any inclination to resort to violence, Perigua storms back in sharp counterpoint: "We think that the blows of white men—of white laborers, of white women—are blows for us and our freedom! Hell! you damned fool, they have always been fighting for themselves. Now, they're half free, with us niggers to wait on them."[34]

Yet by 1928, Du Bois could proclaim with considerable confidence the impracticality of carving a black nation from the United States by main force. The groups led by leaders resembling Perigua had either virtually disappeared or imploded. Groups such as the ABB, to which Perigua's organization bears the closest resemblance, were never particularly viable as mass political organizations.[35] Marcus Garvey's Universal Negro Improvement Association, which was militant in rhetoric if not in action and had been prominent and rapidly growing in the early 1920s, had been thoroughly discredited, its leader Garvey imprisoned on charges of fraud and tax evasion. Yet the novel is not uncritical of the efforts of black Americans in the direction of nonviolent activism, either. Part II of *Dark Princess* describes the movement to unionize among the Pullman porters as every bit as moribund as the effort to mobilize black Americans to strike back with violence against lynching—one of the principal stratagems proposed by the African Black Brotherhood. When the porters with whom Matthew is working fail to put up even a gesture of protest against the lynching of one of their number,[36] Matthew in desperation joins with Perigua in a sabotage plot and suicide pact, as he agrees to remain on the train carrying the spineless porters (and also, they learn, a special car bearing Klansmen home from their national convention) and to distribute propaganda in the cars just in advance of Perigua's bombing of the road that will result in a massive train wreck. The fact that Matthew's mind is changed only by the most improbable of deus ex machinas actually underscores the reasonableness of violent direct action. Matthew is deflected from his resolution only because the princess happens to be on this train, and because Matthew happens to discover this just before the train arrives at the trestle dynamited by Perigua. In effect, the compelling logic of revolutionary violence and martyrdom appears to be derailed by a romantic motive of the most personal and arbitrary kind. As presented in the narrative, Matthew had decided to become Perigua's accomplice because of a careful analysis of social and political factors. In contrast, Matthew pulls the bell-rope and stops the train simply because the princess, with whom he has been enamored from the first time he set eyes upon her, bids him to.[37]

Whereas Part II is racked by ambivalence about political violence, Part III, "The Chicago Politician," offers little qualification at all in its critique of everyday politics in capitalist America and social climbing among the black bourgeoisie. It is in this section of the novel that similarities of structure, narrative, and character between *Dark Princess* and *Quest of the Silver Fleece* are most apparent—not perhaps a testimony to Du Bois's novelistic talent, but nevertheless evidence of consistency in Du Bois's cultural critique as well as a testament to continuity in the capitalist, racist structures of cultural and political power. Like Bles Alwyn, Matthew Towns parlays his good education and fine manners into a promising political career. Like Zora, princess Kautilya drops out of sight throughout much of the section that recounts the hero's rise in fortunes, even as, like Zora, she operates at the margins to construct the radical alternative to political opportunism. The counterpart to *Quest's* social-climbing Caroline Wynn is the Chicago political insider Sara Andrews. The main difference between the plots is that Matthew actually marries Sara and gains political office, a seat in the state legislature that is to be his stepping stone to the greater power and wealth of election to the U.S. Congress. Thus, Matthew's revolt against political opportunism is all the more dramatic—and offensive to social convention—when he forfeits his impending nomination to Congress and forsakes his marriage vows to take up with Kautilya, who has been laboring among the humblest of proletarians and raising the Communist-aligned box-makers' union to international prominence.

When arm in arm Matthew and Kautilya march through the dinner party Sara has arranged to clinch Matthew's nomination for Congress, Du Bois shows himself capable of sudden and seemingly unabashed melodrama. This scene, particularly, functions as the kind of narrative and thematic pivot from realism to utopianism that we have seen performed by the conversion experience in earlier fictions. In other words, it serves a definite ideological function even as it provides fodder for aesthetic criticism (David Levering Lewis, for example, mentions "grandiosity of plot, walking antitheses, and deus ex machina devices" in his catalog of the novel's deficiencies).[38] While Part I of *Dark Princess* establishes an international frame for the problem of inequality and suggests the importance of black America in assessing and addressing the problem, and Parts II and III describe and ultimately reject two black American responses—violent revolutionism and status quo opportunism—it remains for Part IV of the novel, "The Maharajah of Bwodpur," to thresh out an alternative response. As is the case in the concluding chapters of other specimens of the mixed utopian-realist genre, the tension in this section lies not in the final turns of the plot but in the negotiation between various political and philosophical positions. The suddenly blossoming romance between Kautilya and Matthew is the turning point into utopian exposition. Part IV begins with a lush, extended romantic tryst between the couple at Matthew's handsome Chicago flat. In between their sensual pleasures—lovemaking, gourmet dining, playing records (classical, though mostly inspired by themes and melodies from the black world)—the utopian discourse begins in earnest.

That discourse shows Du Bois's willingness to enter into conversation with the Bolshevik leaders of the Third Internationale, yet Du Bois continues to insist upon the autonomy and even preeminence of the darker world in solving the worldwide problems of inequality. When, for a time after their romantic tryst, Matthew and Kautilya go separate ways, Kautilya's visionary monologue becomes a dialogue in the correspondence between herself and Matthew. Within this dialogue, Matthew voices the more pessimistic and puritanical attitude about social democracy—a point of view that chimes especially well with Bolshevik positions. Support for the Bolshevik line is perhaps clearest when Matthew delineates the real political grounds that comprise the stepping-off point toward a better society: "We cannot choose between monarchy and oligarchy or democracy—no—we can only choose the objects for which we will enthrone tyrannical dictators," whether a dictatorship for the sake of czarist "aristocrats," for the American "millionaires," or for Soviet "factory workers and peasants." In order for industrial modernity to be preserved—and thus for there to be plenty available to be distributed to the masses—there must be centralized authority and bureaucracy, for "always, everywhere, massed and concentrated power is necessary to accomplish anything worth while doing in this muddled world, hoping for divine Anarchy in some faraway heaven." The argument is essentially the same one articulated a year before in Du Bois's *Crisis* editorial, "Judging Russia." Given the evident similarity between American oligarchs and Russian czars, Matthew is led to wonder whether armed revolution might be necessary after all, as it had been in czarist Russia: "I am afraid that only great strokes of force—clubs, guns, dynamite in the hands of fanatics—that only such Revolution can bring the Day."[39]

It is up to Kautilya, consistently given the last word by Du Bois, to qualify Matthew's militant tendencies. To Matthew's proffered maxim, simultaneously puritanical and Bolshevist, "Work is God," the princess directly counters with higher principles of human community and delight: "Love is God and Work is his Prophet." The princess recasts Matthew's "dictatorship for the factory workers and peasants" somewhat as well, suggesting the importance of leaders coming *from* the masses as well as ruling *for* their benefit. One sentence in Kautilya's letters particularly stands out, as if it were an extended title for a position paper at a Communist Party congress: "Only Talent served from the great Reservoir of All Men of All Races, of All Classes, of All Ages, of Both Sexes—this is real Aristocracy, real Democracy—the only path to that great and final Freedom which you so well call Divine Anarchy." Finally, Kautliya has an answer to Matthew's revolutionary impatience. Quoting from Matthew's "mother's Bible"—"A day unto the Lord is as a thousand years, and a thousand years as one day"—Kautilya enjoins him, "Do not be in a hurry," for "all that we need, and need alone, Time; the alembic, Time. The slow majestic march of events, unhurried, sure."[40]

Although in *Dark Princess* becoming a socialist is more like falling in love than having a religious conversion, the very final pages of *Dark Princess* also turn to religious experience to ratify the socialist vision—and with a grandiose vengeance. Kautilya is quoting from Matthew's mother's Bible because, during her mysterious absence, she has taken refuge with his mother in rural Virginia while she awaits the delivery of her baby, conceived in her union with Matthew but unbeknownst to him. The scenario, with its resulting preachments of millennial patience and the inevitable march of progress, is evocative of the feminine and maternal religion advocated by Gilman. By novel's end, both plot and setting prove as romantic and improbable as any creation from this decade that saw the rise of the spare, ironic modernist novel in American literature. When the baby turns out to be a boy, Matthew is summoned to Virginia to attend the coronation of the "Maharajah of Bwodpur"—whom he discovers to be none other than his own son—and royal ceremony is joined with nuptial celebration, as Kautilya and Matthew (recently divorced by Sarah) are married by an old black preacher. They then burst forth in a spontaneous rendition of a spiritual, delivered in four-part harmony with the assistance of the preacher and Matthew's mother. Then the coronation "pageant" ensues: "A score of men clothed in white with shining swords" appear on the scene, emerging from the woods (waiting in the wings, so it seems) to proclaim the newly born maharajah in rites mixing Hindu, Buddhist, and Christian elements.[41] Whereas *Quest of the Silver Fleece* had ended merely with a marriage between hero and heroine, showing that love and work are compatible after all, *Dark Princess* ends with a marriage, a birth, and a coronation, indicating that romance and world salvation might go hand in hand. The utopian grandiosity of it all is duly noted by Eric Sundquist, who describes the "Christ-Buddha child" as "an embodiment—or better, an incarnation—of the mysterious idea of race-nationhood transcending geography and time that Du Bois's Pan-African aesthetic could achieve only in the fictive moment of prophesy."[42]

Yet if the novel's closing scene is undeniably far out, the novel's final section makes clear that it has a more definite plan than just the "idea of race-nationhood transcending geography and time." Not only do the invocations of world religions suggest the constructive, real-world functions of religious belief (asserted by Gilman as well), but Du Bois's choice of May Day as the wedding day also indicates the potential complementarity of religious conviction and political radicalism, uniting as it does the inauguration of the month of Mary, the Blessed Mother, with the traditional day of spring fertility celebrations and the internationally recognized Labor Day. Still more, the repetition of common elements in the conclusions of *Quest of the Silver Fleece* and *Dark Princess*—the scenes infused with religious imagery and rhetoric, the fulfilled promise of romance, and the powerful affirmations of hope, order, and progress that result from both—point to the degree to which the ideals articulated in the novels were not merely the invention of an overheated fictive imagination but the considered political program of a consistent, principled, and patient political activist. The international scope of *Dark Princess* is new, but the specific social democratic logic that stands behind Kautilya's proclamations continues the program followed by Du Bois years before the Bolsheviks had ever been heard of in the West, and thus continues also to parallel the analyses of Sinclair and other Socialists unwilling to disavow the strategies of the Second Internationale. In the United States, Matthew asserts that black Americans "must help overthrow the rule of the rich by distributing wealth more evenly first among themselves and then in alliance with white labor, to establish democratic control of industry." In India, Kautilya envisions the necessity of an anti-imperialist, national independence movement as a precursor to industrialization and democracy. Even then, the liberation of India and other colonies depends upon the action of white workers in the industrialized world.[43] There are others in the princess's cabal who do not believe that her "path of Peace and Reason" is practicable—whether because the color line will hold fast, or because the stratagems of international capitalism are too many and complex—but she succeeds at least in persuading this faction to assume a twenty-five-year timeline for liberatory struggle, during which the last word on violence is to be spoken not by the leaders of the darker world, nor by the darker masses, but by the white, capitalist world that now holds the power: "Ten years of preparation are set. Ten more years of final planning, and then five years of intensive struggle. In 1952, the Dark World goes free—whether in Peace and fostering Friendship with all men, or in Blood and Storm—it is for Them—the Pale Masters of today—to say."[44]

Such prognostications might well have seemed the crowning fantasy at the time the novel was published in 1928. In hindsight, however, 1952 as a benchmark year of colonial liberation was an excellent forecast, overshooting by just two years the independence of Kautilya's India and by three years the success of the Communist revolution in China (Chinese revolutionaries being among the most active members of the princess's cabal). It underestimates by only two years the liberation of Vietnam from French colonial rule. Although it misses by a decade the official declarations of independence in Algeria, Egypt, Ethiopia, Nigeria, Kenya, and virtually all the rest of Africa, by the early 1950s anticolonialist parties in these countries had indeed picked up enough momentum to make eventual independence almost certain. Most critical of all is Du Bois's recognition of the autonomy of anticolonial struggles throughout the world and his insistence that independence is possible through peaceful agitation if the colonial power does not actively choose "Blood and Storm"—as in fact happened in India and most other British colonies. For all of its improbabilities in plot, implausibilities of character, and grandiosity of rhetoric, *Dark Princess* may meet and even exceed the final test of the modernism of any particular literary work: a critical synchronicity with modernity. For *Dark Princess* is not only moored in the sociopolitical circumstances of the 1920s—the debate over revolutionary violence given impetus by black nationalism, the inspiration provided to radicals by the Soviet Union, the exploitation of people of color throughout the world—but the novel also uncannily anticipates anticolonial militancy and the postcolonial period itself. This was not a matter simply of guessing on Du Bois's part, either, but a plan of work in which he would continue to bend his intellectual and political labors, and through which he would continue to have some success in influencing the direction of African American, and even to some extent Pan-African, political culture.

REALISM AND TRUTH-TELLING IN *BOSTON*

> "Always it happened, sooner or later, that everything turned out as Vanzetti had figured out and predicted!"

Perhaps no one typified the predicament of American socialism in the 1920s—nor the persistence of a social democratic vision in U.S. politics—better than Upton Sinclair. He virtually embodied the disunity and confusion of the socialist movement in the years immediately following the Red Scare. Not entirely trusted by his Socialist comrades when he rejoined the party, he was criticized by the Communists with whom he had expressed sympathy in *Jimmie Higgins* but whose party he would not join. Meanwhile, the indifference of the wider culture toward socialism was signified by Sinclair's sudden obscurity in the early 1920s. Sinclair was practically invisible in publishing circles, apparently because his customary literary-political mode was rendered passé by modernist experimentalism.

Sinclair's response was to keep his nose to the literary and political grindstone. During much of the twenties, he kept busy with a series of journalistic exposés in various fields of American cultural and economic production—most of them self-published. Sinclair called these books, collectively, the "Dead Hand" series, a play upon the "invisible hand" of the marketplace so named and supposed to be beneficent by Adam Smith. He had established the "Dead Hand" paradigm with a wartime book, *The Profits of Religion* (1918), which had studied the effects of the profit motive upon contemporary religion. In the 1920s five additional studies swiftly followed: *The Brass Check* (1920), on capitalist control of the "free" press; *The Goose-Step: A Study of American Education* (1923), focusing upon capitalist domination of higher education; *The Goslings* (1924), moving down to the primary grades; *Mammonart* (1925), critiquing the influence of economic power over artistic production through the ages; and *Money Writes* (1927), assessing critically the same factor in contemporary literature. Through the work of producing these books, Sinclair was also able to gauge the survival of radical and progressive activism at a time when the eclipse of the Left was (and has since been) widely assumed. The first five of these six books were published by Sinclair himself rather than being taken up by any commercial publisher, so Sinclair knew firsthand that the principal organs of popular opinion and cultural production considered socialism irrelevant. Yet he was also aware of an active, radical readership not accounted for in the major publishers' calculations of marketability and legal liability. Not only did these books have thousands of readers dedicated enough to buy them directly by mail from Sinclair, but the books were compiled with the assistance of scores of collaborators, as Sinclair's method of research involved contacting correspondents both to check his facts and to solicit their personal narratives of capitalist malfeasance.

When he was not immediately engaged in writing books, Sinclair's occasional political forays into direct action both tested more directly the lengths to which the state would go to repress radical ideas and explored the possibilities that might remain for collaborations between radicals, social democrats, and progressives. When in the early 1920s remnant locals of the Industrial Workers of the World were harried by prosecution under California's criminal syndicalism laws (passed during the war but still in effect), Sinclair and other activists founded the Southern California branch of the ACLU to defend them. As their inaugural action, Sinclair and two colleagues first got themselves arrested for public speaking at the location where Wobblies had recently conducted one of their free-speech fights, then conducted a wide-ranging publicity campaign that held up Long Beach and California officials to national ridicule. Sinclair and his collaborators thus tapped into resources of cultural and political resistance showing that the constituencies of prewar radicalism and Progressivism had not wholly abandoned the scene. To the editors of the *New Republic,* Sinclair's arrest was one of a number of recent events—including the banning of their own magazine from library shelves—that showed the "actual freedom of thought" in the United States was more circumscribed than "in any other important country in the world, including even Russia."[45] Yet the very fact that the *New Republic* and others were speaking out suggested that agents for progressive change—including institutions and publications—had either remained intact or were being rebuilt since the war. Neither the *New Republic* nor the ACLU was going away, however unfavorably they were viewed by state and national authorities.

Any suggestion that Sinclair was fighting merely a rear-guard action, as well as any thought that literary success lay only in his past, was premature. With *Oil!* (1927), his novel of the petroleum industry that was his first publication in ten years with a major national press, Sinclair scored a success with both mainstream readers and his left comrades. The book shows only glimpses of anything like modernist fictional technique—a rare example being the concluding montage tripping between Republican celebrations of electoral victory, jazz music, and the deathbed of a Communist martyr. But the novel was hailed widely as renewing Sinclair's reputation as a novelist and recasting a nineteenth-century tradition of socially observant and politically self-conscious realism. The reviewer in the *Nation* had to issue the obligatory cautions about the propagandist and moralist in Sinclair, but at the same time compared Sinclair's art favorably with the great moral and social reform writers of former times: "This overwhelming knowledge and passionate expression of specific wrongs are more stirring, more interesting, and also more taxing than the cynical censure of Fielding and the sentimental lamentations of Dickens."[46] Mainstream recognition served only to increase Sinclair's stature on the far left. The *New Masses* review of *Oil!* marveled that Sinclair could win over bourgeois readers even while skewering their "Babbitry": "The exasperating good sense of the man, his propagandistic ability, his practical way of expounding rudiments to the unschooled masses are offensive to every rightly constituted mind when facing genius."[47] The one complaint in a 1928 special issue of the *New Masses* dedicated to him—the Upton Sinclair fiftieth anniversary issue—would be that he had not switched over from the Socialist to the Communist Party.

Not only *New Republic* progressives and individual radicals like Sinclair remained active in the 1920s, but socialists of various hues were regrouping throughout the decade. It might have seemed that radicals had been crippled by the postwar repression, that the revolutionary flare-up was ultimately a flameout, as Barbara Foley asserts. But Foley's conclusion that "the production of literature inflected with revolutionary politics had slowed to a near-trickle by the last half of the decade"[48] simply—and unaccountably—omits the radicalizing and galvanizing effects of the Sacco and Vanzetti case. On the contrary, the trajectory of radical politics in the decade would be better understood as moving in quite the opposite direction—with radical fervor at its ebb relatively soon after the war, in the wake of the Palmer raids and Red Scare, but then slowly regathering intensity as the decade unfolded. At first Nicola Sacco and Bartolomeo Vanzetti were defended only by the small circle of Italian anarchists who were most directly concerned when their comrades were arrested and charged with the robbery and murder of the paymaster and his guard at a Braintree, Massachusetts, shoe factory. But the trials and legal appeals of Sacco and Vanzetti rallied liberals as well as radicals by the time of their execution in August 1927. From the outset, the case traversed the most invidious features of the period of so-called normalcy: arrested near the height of the Red Scare that helped to launch the reactionary, procapitalist retrenchment of the 1920s, they were persona non grata for their Italian ethnicity as well as for their political views. During the early years of their imprisonment and initial court appeals, new, draconian restrictions on immigrants gained legislative favor, culminating in the federal Immigration Act of 1924. The inability of the Massachusetts legal system to provide Sacco and Vanzetti with either a fair trial or a just appeal was palpable: the trial judge permitted both ethnic and political slurs against the defendants, and he repeatedly coached the prosecution; then, by the genius of Massachusetts jurisprudence, the appeals judge who denied Sacco and

Vanzetti's complaint of bias turned out to be none other than the trial judge who had been guilty of the bias.[49]

Some of the defenders of Sacco and Vanzetti had been radicals long before the case. Arturo Giovannitti, an IWW organizer in the second decade of the century and an official of the International Ladies Garment Workers Union in the 1920s as well as a noted poet, had served on the Defense Committee from early on. Upton Sinclair initiated contact with Bartolomeo Vanzetti in 1922, visiting him in June and soon thereafter publishing a glowing testimonial to Vanzetti's character in the *Appeal to Reason* that was widely reprinted.[50] Another public critic of the Sacco and Vanzetti case was W. E. B. Du Bois, who as early as 1922 wrote of "two Italians . . . sentenced to death for a crime which has never been properly proven against them." Du Bois was moved enough by the tragedy of these two Italians—and the potential importance of their fate to black Americans as well as to American radicals—that he drew up a prospectus for a play he considered writing about the pair.[51] Other writers became radicalized by their exposure to the Sacco-Vanzetti judicial travesty, or at least were willing to affiliate themselves with the Italian anarchists, phenomena documented by Daniel Aaron's *Writers on the Left.* Among the protesters identified by Aaron were liberal intellectuals such as Walter Lippmann and John Dewey, distinguished jurists including Felix Frankfurter, the widely respected historian Arthur Schlesinger, and the acerbic and radical writer Dorothy Parker. John Dos Passos joined the cause in 1926. A veritable flood of literary and political support came still later, Aaron notes, when it became apparent that ordinary legal appeals were bootless. As the execution date of August 22, 1927, approached, scores of American writers joined demonstrations in Boston. Those arrested for protesting in the streets included Gold and Dos Passos; playwrights John Howard Lawson and Ruth Hale; novelists Grace Lumpkin and Katharine Anne Porter; and poets Edna St. Vincent Millay and Lola Ridge. Those denouncing the execution included Edmund Wilson, Malcolm Cowley, Babette Deutsch, and the many poets appearing in *America Arraigned!*—a collection edited by American anarchists Lucia Trent and Ralph Cheyney and published in 1928.[52] Sinclair's novel *Boston,* also published in the year following the execution, was merely one of scores of publications at once denouncing the execution and characterizing it as a watershed, revelatory moment about the nature of American capitalist (in)justice.

Upton Sinclair's novel *Boston* was exceptional among the protests of the Left not only by its sheer bulk—over eight hundred pages—but by its epic ambition, for in the novel Sinclair set out to tell the truth of the case on behalf of all the radicals who took the most active interest in it. On the very night he had heard of Sacco and Vanzetti's execution, Sinclair recounted in his preface, he had formed a resolution to tell their story, a motion soon seconded by his loyal cadre of radical readers: "It seemed to the writer that the world would want to know the truth about this case, and his judgment proved correct, because there began a flood of cablegrams and letters from five continents, asking him to do the very thing he had decided upon."[53] Such faith in the truth-telling function of realist fiction seems particularly quaint in comparison with the attitudes and technique of the foremost writers of the rising modernist generation: their intensely subjective narrators or, alternatively, third-person narrators able only to describe the external actions and speech of their characters; their poetic experiments in collecting fragments of knowledge that might be pieced together only by force of will, and then only imperfectly; their representation of different, conflicting voices or consciousnesses as the only and uncertain foundation of knowledge. Paradoxically, though, Sinclair's very methods conspired to produce a novel that was forced to acknowledge concretely the limits upon achieving either objective knowledge of present society or a clear path to the future cooperative commonwealth.

Had *Boston* sought to tell the truth merely about capitalism and the forms of its political and legal legitimization—commonly known as liberal democracy—then the only epistemological gap would have emerged on the familiar chasm between proletarian and bourgeois, revolutionary and status quo. But Sinclair hoped also to tell the truth about the liberal-radical coalition mobilized to save Sacco and Vanzetti—what Daniel Aaron describes as "a disparate group of Communists, anarchists, well-meaning old ladies, idealistic students, writers, lawyers, newspaper-men, labor officials, liberal Bostonians, and Harvard professors."[54] In particular, Sinclair felt he knew something about the differences between anarchists and socialists, and between revolutionary and liberal activity. So it happened that, in the process of hailing the grand coalition mobilized to save Sacco and Vanzetti, the distinctions that he made between the various actors and parties on the left practically ensured that within the novel itself, as well as in its reception, conceptions of the truth would fragment along multiple ideological lines.

Sinclair was on relatively safe ground with his left comrades when he emphasized the breadth of the coalition of reasonable citizens who allied with one another in the Sacco-Vanzetti campaign—even when the principal voice of reason, and Sinclair's central character, is a sixty-year-old matriarch from Brahmin society. In his portrayal of Cornelia, who after the death of her financier-husband breaks away from her highly respectable family to see how the other half lives, Sinclair integrates a moment of intense idealization within his very characterization. Cornelia's championing of the anarchists Sacco and Vanzetti symbolizes the very broadest extension of the center-left coalition that Sinclair had been, for years, arguing for. But improbable fictively as it was for a character such as Cornelia to take up work in a cordage factory and befriend the Italian immigrant and fishmonger "Bart" Vanzetti, the notion of an alliance between blue-blooded Boston ladies and condemned anarchists was well grounded in the facts of the Sacco-Vanzetti defense. A dozen or more such society women were active in the defense almost from beginning to end, and moreover, in the novel's preface Sinclair claimed that one of his California neighbors was in fact a "runaway grandma" much like Cornelia, who had spurned her respectable Boston family at age sixty and immersed herself in working-class life. (Later, in his autobiography, Sinclair named her as a Mrs. Burton.)[55] Cornelia importantly assists in Sinclair's idealization of another key character, Bartolomeo Vanzetti. If making Cornelia his heroine might have seemed dubious to his Communist and anarchist colleagues, Sinclair risked alienating his mainstream audience by making Vanzetti his hero. Sinclair addressed both perils simultaneously by bringing the characters into friendship and their philosophies into close comparison, with the result that anarchism is presented as a natural extension of the religious and political ideals of the revered Pilgrims. When on a picnic to Plymouth, Cornelia describes the "Pilgrim fathers" as "really quite wonderful" pioneers who came to a "wilderness," lost half of their number the first winter, and yet refused to return home when boats came from England the next summer: "That showed what kind of people they were." Bart's response respects Cornelia's account of the Pilgrims and goes straight to the heart of the anarchist message, a message that in the particular phrasing provided by Sinclair also speaks to America's supposed ideals: "Shoore," said Vanzetti, "greata people—ribelli—fighta priest, fighta king—come for joostice, come for liberty. But get liberty for self, no give for odder. I say liberty for all."[56]

Almost inevitably, the comparison of Cornelia to Vanzetti demands some articulation of contrast between the characters. Some of the differences between them result in the novel's sharpest criticism of class difference and ethnocentrism in American society. The multiplot structure of Sinclair's novel counterpoints the alleged crimes and the punishment of Sacco and Vanzetti with the proved crimes and the nonpunishment of members of Cornelia's well-to-do family. The men of Cornelia's family are among the Massachusetts bankers and lawyers convicted of conspiracy to defraud an upstart business competitor whose factories are proving all too efficient and competitive in the capitalist free market. Sinclair here represented, under a thin layer of fictionalization, an actual crime roughly contemporaneous to the robberies and murders of which Sacco and Vanzetti were convicted—the Willet case of 1921.[57] The Supreme Court of Massachusetts would refuse to lay aside the Sacco and Vanzetti verdicts even when provided with abundant evidence of prejudice in the original trials, claiming they could rule only on points of procedure, not fact. But the high court had been ready enough to ignore both facts and procedure when intervening on behalf of the Willet defendants and overturning their conviction. The contrast provided Sinclair with the perfect object lesson in unequal justice: "When it was a question of protecting the property of bankers, the court had not hesitated to set aside the verdict, and to declare that the jury had been unjustified in drawing the conclusions it had seen fit to draw."[58]

But the Cornelia-Bartolomeo friendship also draws out other points of difference that dismayed Sinclair's comrades on the left when they saw the drafts Sinclair shared with them or when they read the novel's early installments in *Bookman,* in which the novel began to appear serially in February 1928. For Cornelia, telling the truth seems to be a straightforward matter of rendering facts; from her point of view and that of the real-life women who involved themselves in the Sacco-Vanzetti case, the travesty of justice in the Massachusetts courts lay in the courts' indifference toward the facts of the case. From the point of view of social outsiders—recent immigrants in a time of xenophobia, anarchists in a season of red-baiting, proletarians in a society riven by class struggle—the telling of "truth" is firmly in the grasp of the powerful and often twisted by them to their own ends. From the outsider's point of view, the telling of lies may be seen as an excusable tactic of war—and so might violence and other behavior regarded as lawless by the social insiders. One of Cornelia's acquaintances, a French Communist newspaperman named Pierre Leon, thus cautions Cornelia: "Don't be shocked if you should some day learn that some workers commit what the bourgeoisie calls crimes in the struggle against the exploiters." It is possible, Leon suggests, that Vanzetti and his friend Sacco are not only genial anarchists of a philosophic bent but also militants able, by that very philosophy, to justify banditry and murder. Says Leon, "Set this down for certain at the outset—all militant anarchists believe in bombs. Not all make them—any more than all Christians sell their goods and give to the poor. . . . But the faith calls for it." And as for lying to a sympathetic soul like Cornelia with puritanical notions of right and wrong: "It goes without saying that anybody who will fight will try to deceive the enemy."[59]

Just as he had done for the "Dead Hand" series, Sinclair's method in writing *Boston* involved consulting as many inside informants as possible—a process that honored the collectivity of the Sacco-Vanzetti story and, at the same time, opened up the novel to a great diversity of partial truths about the case. It also exposed Sinclair, early and often, to harsh criticism from others on the left who wanted their own particular line on the Sacco-Vanzetti case to be presented. Above all, the great majority wanted Sinclair to join them in vigorously professing faith in Sacco and Vanzetti's innocence. Within a month of the executions—also exactly a month into Sinclair's work on the novel—rumors began to surface that Sinclair was uncertain of their innocence. While in the final stages of preparing the Sinclair fiftieth anniversary issue, Gold wrote in a postscript to one of his letters, "I have been hearing rumors again, (one only last night) that in your book & private talk you spread an impression that you think Sacco & Vanzetti were really guilty of the payroll murder." Gold wrote that he doubted the rumors but wished nonetheless that "for my private peace of mind . . . you will drop me a postcard saying—nothing to It."[60] Sinclair did not offer any reply—no postcard, no letter—for months, quite manifestly because there *was* something to "It."

Gardner Jackson, a member of the Sacco-Vanzetti defense committee, told Sinclair flatly that "your handling of Vanzetti and the gun question" "touches my anarchist friends to the quick and makes them fear that, after all, you are going to end up in this book as a specific propagandist."[61] The "gun question" was serious because one of the more incriminating pieces of information at trial had been that Vanzetti and Sacco had been carrying guns at the time of their arrest, and because expert ballistics testimony (fraudulently used) had played an important part in their murder convictions. Sinclair had had the temerity to portray Vanzetti as carrying a gun not only at the time of the arrest but also on a daily basis during the period of the Palmer inquisition, even on a picnic with Cornelia and Betty, Cornelia's granddaughter and kindred spirit in rebellion against staid Boston culture. Robert Minor, a Communist Party activist and longtime associate of Sinclair, had become so alarmed by the early *Bookman* installments and Sinclair's evasive responses to queries that he laid plans to travel from New York City to Pasadena solely to confront Sinclair in person. He was deterred only when Sinclair resorted to a combination of dilatory tactics and concessions: refusing to communicate directly with Minor himself but communicating through his partner, Lydia Gibson, that "I am only interested in facts" (hardly reassuring); promising there would be plenty of time to discuss the facts via written correspondence, with at least a month before the installment indicating guilt or innocence would be due at the *Bookman;* and even offering to permit Minor to see the proofs before publication.[62]

Sinclair achieved a truce with his Communist friends by retreating from his earlier boast that *Boston* would get to the bottom of the Sacco-Vanzetti case. Regarding knowledge of the basic facts, he would ultimately profess merely agnosticism. When Sinclair finally replied to Mike Gold, fully half a year after Gold's anxious inquiries of September 1927, he was not fully reassuring in his attitude toward Sacco and Vanzetti's innocence, yet his response also reveals the compromise he had decided upon, and why he felt compelled to make it: "I am not going to say that I know they were innocent, because I do not know that. But I am certainly going to say that they were not proved guilty, and I am going to show the facts of what actually happened to them, and the kind of men they both were, as far as I can find it out."[63] Part of Sinclair's difficulty in "finding out" lay in the fact that comrades further to the left did not trust him enough to confide fully in him. Sinclair had, for example, tried and failed to get Robert Minor to pump his Communist comrade Elizabeth Gurley Flynn, a confidante of the anarchists' inner circle by virtue of her partnership with Carlo Tresca.[64] The greater part of the difficulty, though, lay in the Massachusetts court system—after all, the only arbiter that could establish guilt or innocence in the only way that counted. Because the court did not care to examine its biases, it rendered the facts and therefore the fundamental basis of a guilty or innocent verdict impossible to attain. In the postscript of a February 16 letter to Robert Minor, in which Sinclair delves into the question of Sacco's guilt or innocence, he states that the only positive knowledge possible under the current legal system is a negative one, that the court did not and could not provide a fair trial: "I have not been planning to say in my book that Sacco was guilty. I do not consider that I *know* that he was guilty. I have only second hand and third hand evidence. I can certainly say that he was not proved guilty and that he did not have a fair trial."[65]

Volume 2 pivots dramatically from criticism of the anarchists to criticism of those who imagine they *could* have a fair trial in capitalist courts. The targets of Sinclair's analysis include not only open backers of capitalism but also those liberal allies in the Sacco-Vanzetti coalition who saw their conviction as an aberration. In the world outside the novel, these would include prominent jurists such as Felix Frankfurter who believed the case cried out for legal reform but certainly not social revolution, as well as the society ladies who were among the most indefatigable supporters of the defense. Their point of view is amply represented in *Boston* by Cornelia Thornwell, and the graveness of her misguided faith in the courts and in the virtue of truth-telling itself is reflected in the plot of the novel, for these are the fatal flaws that are presented as ultimately dooming Cornelia's friend, Vanzetti, and his anarchist comrade, Sacco. At the close of volume 1, nearing the end of the defense argument, Cornelia is presented with the proposition that the defense can be saved if only she will fabricate an alibi for Vanzetti. Although on the day of his alleged crimes Vanzetti had delivered fish to a score of immigrant households, any number of which should be able to vouch for him, the defense has reason to believe that the testimony of all the Italian housewives in Boston will not equal a single word from a Boston blue-blood, who had not, after all, seen Vanzetti on the day of the payroll robbery and murder. At the outset of volume 2, Cornelia gives her answer: she cannot commit perjury, cannot lose faith in the power of truth-telling, and cannot admit that the courts and other apparatus of existing society are beyond hope of reform. That faith and hope doom the defendants, and from that point on—as in the third-act crisis of classic Greek tragedy—the outcome is never really in doubt. The revelations to come involve only the fuller unfolding of knowledge about how misguided Cornelia's liberal views are.

In volume 1, Sacco and Vanzetti tend to be portrayed as idealistic dreamers. In volume 2, it is the lawyers and the liberals, increasingly joining the fight to save the condemned, who become the unrealistic dreamers: they believe, somehow, that their efforts should make a difference. Sinclair's narrator exclaims: "Pitiful the plight of hard-working and law-abiding lawyers, who had made all the proper moves, and won the chess-game a dozen times over—and now their opponents would dump the board and throw the chessmen into their faces!" To the panic of the lawyers and their allies, the calm foresight of the condemned stands in stark contrast. Again and again, Vanzetti's perspective is vindicated, as Sinclair puts it melodramatically: "[It] was exactly as Vanzetti, lying through those endless hours in his prison cell, had figured out and predicted. Always it happened, sooner or later, that everything turned out as Vanzetti had figured out and predicted!"[66] From the first, Sacco reads his case as a clear-cut instance of the class war; as a sworn enemy of the state now in its power, he "never let himself be fooled by hope. 'They have got us, they will kill us.'"[67] And so it happened just as Sacco had predicted, as well.

Far from repudiating the philosophies of the Communists and anarchists, the ending of the novel goes a long way toward actually vindicating the philosophies of these most radical of comrades. Cornelia's granddaughter Betty, who in the course of the novel moves from being an apolitical social rebel, to budding socialist, to fervent young Communist, declares unequivocally that the execution of Sacco and Vanzetti demonstrates the bankruptcy of liberalism. Minutes before their deaths, she declares: "Don't you see the glory of this case—it kills off the liberals! Before this, it was possible to argue that injustice was an accident, just an oversight—in a country that was so busy making automobiles and bathtubs and books of etiquette! But now here's a test—we settle the question forever!" All of the state's most eminent politicians, businessmen, and even "our most cultured university president," Betty exults, take their orders from a single supreme authority: "They all obey the great capitalist drill-sergeant, and not a man deserts to the enemy—not one single man!" To which her grandmother Cornelia can respond only, "Bart and Nick were right about it all along. . . . They knew more about Boston than we did."[68]

Sinclair's most radical readers were as enthusiastic about the novel's ending as they had been wary of its opening. The clear majority of Sinclair's Communist and anarchist readers felt that their brand of revolutionary socialism and the central truth of class struggle had won out, after all. To be sure, the anarchist *Road to Freedom* published a critical assessment of *Boston,* to which Sinclair fired back a scathing, aggressive reply that returned to his theme of the errors of anarchism: "Would you like me to contribute to your columns an article of intimate revelations on the subject of 'Anarchists I have known and their attitude to dynamite.'? Among the Anarchists I have known were Caron, Hansen, and Berg, three boys who blew themselves up with a dynamite bomb they were making."[69] But Carlo Tresca suggested that an Italian translation of *Boston* could and should be made in Italy, even at risk of persecution by the Mussolini fascists; he wished also to order two thousand copies immediately, "to be sold by me to the Italians in this country, provided the conditions are not too hard"—the latter reference suggesting Sinclair's book too might be "mental dynamite" that might be open to censorship.[70] Mike Gold's *New Masses* published a piece by Joseph North that was less a book review than a call to arms. North even strikes Sinclair's favorite theme as a writer of historical fiction: "Every word is true, as thousands of pages of testimony, of newspaper accounts will attest." Still more, however, North located the truth of the book in its focus on raising class consciousness:

> The execution of Sacco and Vanzetti branded an indelible scar on the forehead of the masses, in good old Puritan fashion. It branded class consciousness into a hundred million workers thruout the world.
>
> In Upton Sinclair's book you can see that process.[71]

Much as it seems that Sinclair had swung around to a hardline, class-war representation of the case, those Communist readers who felt certain Sinclair was about to come over to their party showed a certain degree of wishful thinking, and their readings of the novel as definitely supporting a Comintern line were constructing an interpretation that the textual facts might warrant—but not exclusively. Communist readers would naturally gravitate toward the interpretation of the executions offered by the young Communist Betty, but her interpretation is, after all, only that of a single fictional character, and her exulting over the executions because they vindicate so clearly her own political philosophy might seem callow to non-Communist readers. For Cornelia, who unlike her granddaughter has known Vanzetti as a personal friend, there can be no such exuberance over his extinction. Her weary reply to Betty is an endorsement of Sacco and Vanzetti's personal perspectives, not of a party line, and the truth claim she makes stresses Cornelia's and Betty's *lack* of knowledge as much as Sacco and Vanzetti's fullness of knowledge. As if to stay consistent with that premise, Cornelia does not presume to announce in positive terms what the two anarchists actually *did* know. Though Cornelia announces that "Bart and Nick were right about it all along" and confesses that "they knew more about Boston than we did,'" she does not—or cannot—name the specific content of that knowledge. The distinction marks a definite shift from the possibility of realist social knowledge, which Sinclair had purported to offer at the outset of the novel, to the necessity of a modernist epistemology that testifies to the impossibility of any such knowledge. The obfuscation of the Massachusetts courts made it impossible to tell what the truth about Sacco and Vanzetti had been; therefore, the only kind of positive knowledge that can be offered is, of necessity, partial: the power of capitalism (and perhaps, the sharpness of the capitalist-socialist binary) to obscure the most basic of facts, and therefore its illegitimacy in presuming to rule upon them. From the critique in *Boston,* as in the critique of so many unequivocally modernist texts, Sinclair and his readers mostly come to know what they do not know.

This hardly means that *Boston* abandons utopian idealization, any more than it wholly abandons either realistic narrative technique or the realist insistence upon a material world beyond delusion and obfuscation. But the form that Sinclair's utopianism takes under the pressure of historical circumstances, including both the conflicting diversity of his various audiences and the antiepistemology of capitalist modernity, is a far cry from the definite blueprints of Gronlund's cooperative commonwealth, Bellamy's millennial city, or for that matter Sinclair's own industrial republic. It presents, instead, a kind of Rorschach blot for radicals. The key rhetorical flourish in the novel's penultimate paragraph, for example, might be read by Communists as attesting to the key theoretical pronouncements of Lenin and Stalin supplementing Marxism, whereby these Bolshevik leaders articulated the differential status of subject and submerged nationalities under colonization and thereby included their particular demands within the international socialist program. For the anarchists, however, the key fact about this passage was that it positioned their representatives, *their* comrades Sacco and Vanzetti, at the center of a worldwide, spontaneous revolutionary movement:

> A hundred million toilers knew that two comrades had died for them. Black men, brown men, yellow men—men of a hundred nations and a thousand tribes—the prisoners of starvation, the wretched of the earth—experienced a thrill of awe. It was the mystic process of blood-sacrifice, by which through the ages salvation has been brought to mankind!
>
> A hundred million workers, shackled and blind, groping in a poison fog manufactured by their masters, learned that two of their fellows had been put to death for lifting the banner of freedom. In spite of all the wrangling of the radical sects, that was a fact the meaning of which could never be obscured; a fact which shone like a pillar of fire in the workers' night.[72]

The passage's remarkable slippage from Italian American anarchists to people of color throughout the world also opens up the socialist possibility articulated at length by Du Bois's *Dark Princess:* that now the socialist movement gathers strength, intelligence, and impetus from colonized people of color throughout the world. The degree to which these masses appear to be self-mobilized seems to pull them free from Bolshevik inspiration and direction, and Sinclair's representation of lighter-skinned European ethnics as the center of the international revolutionary movement was precisely the formulation that Du Bois had offered earlier that year: the stance of the white workers of Europe and North America would determine whether revolution would come with tumult and violence or with order and calm.

In the end, the apotheosis of Sacco and Vanzetti in itself tends to undermine their affiliation with any particular sect. The rhetorical presentation of Sacco and Vanzetti in specifically religious terms—as religious martyrs who "had died for" the colonized peoples of the world—also contributes to their unique capacity to bring socialists together—or, at least, make socialists believe they have been brought together. The religious imagery is rampant, and explicitly commented upon by the narrator, who is keen to explain "the mystic process of blood-sacrifice." The beginning of the following paragraph combines a contemporary allusion to the poison gases used against soldiers in the world war with a biblical one to Samson, which in turn dovetails with Sinclair's own representation of the powerful proletarian body as well as African American representation of the shackled but strong black body under slavery. This is immediately followed by an explicit reference to the unifying power of the blood sacrifice, in which the various factions of socialism are compared to religious splinters, and the testament of Sacco and Vanzetti is akin to the leadership of God gathering the Israelites and leading them out of Egyptian slavery. The martyr's death suits the need for a unifying political discourse because it is the story, par excellence, of apparent ending that is really an entirely fresh beginning: and a nearly perfectly blank beginning at that, a tabula rasa, or empty signifier that is all the more empty and waiting to be filled because its authors are absent and unable to speak any more for themselves. Sacco and Vanzetti had indeed provided the unifying narrative of the Left, uniting the various social democratic factions ranging from anarchists to progressive fellow travelers, and doing so while (and because of) drawing a sharp demarcation between the capitalist and socialist visions of society. Yet as we have seen in the case of Jimmie Higgins, the death of these suffering, heroic political prisoners maximizes sympathy—they are killed rather than killing—while by the very same token minimizing specific political direction. As with Jimmie and religious martyrdom generally, it is the strength as well as the weakness of Sacco and Vanzetti that their meaning and purpose depends entirely upon what those who follow *make* of them.

Whereas Sacco and Vanzetti could be admired universally in part because they were almost entirely powerless, socialism by whatever path would require the conquest and the wielding of power, and the question of power admitted no simple solution, whether posed in utopian, realist, or modernist terms. Even as it unifies, Sinclair's melodramatic borrowing from religious traditions seems, for the most part, to suspend facing the question of power. Yet Sinclair's handling of religion is precisely one of the points at which Sinclair stuck with the longer standing, pre-Communist social democratic tradition that welcomed adherents of the Social Gospel as belonging under the big tent of socialism. Just a few years earlier, another old-time social democrat, Charlotte Perkins Gilman, had posited plainly that the life-sacrifice of people dedicated to the principles of real freedom and equality in this world should not be understood merely as analogous to that of Jesus Christ or any of the other world-transformative religious figures. Their lives given for the collective, ongoing life of humanity are the very essence of religion. In Sinclair's view, if not necessarily Gilman's, Sacco and Vanzetti were such figures. As with the meaning of Sacco and Vanzetti's martyrdom, however, a broad reformulation of religion within the context of future human life on earth, the "beyond" about which some degree of scientific knowledge is possible, does not stipulate any specific plan. But it does define an important collectivist tendency just at the cusp of a key historical moment, when radical politics in the United States would gain unprecedented momentum as the New York Stock Exchange crashed and the world economy began to slip into the Great Depression. For even as the Depression expanded the social malaise of the modernists into a widely popular structure of feeling, Upton Sinclair, W. E. B. Du Bois, and other social democrats were the radical sect with the clearest articulation of the possibilities and the pitfalls of collaboration among the range of skeptics and believers who looked, almost out of historical necessity, to changes in the national government for the way out of capitalism and into the cooperative commonwealth.

PART THREE

POLITICAL INTERVENTIONS

CHAPTER EIGHT

ONCE MORE UNTO THE BREACH: SOCIAL DEMOCRATIC ADVANCE AND RETREAT IN THE RED DECADE

In the narrative of American literature, socialism, and political change that we have been tracing, when we enter the 1930s and the Great Depression we approach the crisis. This narratorial understanding concurs with those scholars who have specialized in the Left and Communist-affiliated literature in identifying the 1930s as the historical moment of decision. But it also sharply disputes their singular focus on that decade and on the Communist Party, suggesting instead the importance of the story's beginning in the pre–World War I years, when the socialist movement gained definition and grew under the auspices of the Second Internationale, and the story's middle in the war years and the 1920s, when the socialist movement was thrown into confusion and was maintained by a remnant, only some of whom were Communists.

The tempo and trajectory of social democratic activism necessarily changed when the great economic collapse of the 1930s suddenly made the circumstances of many more Americans much more desperate, thus giving socialism in its various forms a much wider and more sympathetic hearing and government intervention in the economy all the more urgency. Here and now, the investments of the previous decade made by socialists in terms of political commitment, intellectual work, and ethical integrity began to pay off. Socialists had something to say, they had plans, and they could point to years of careful thought about precisely the issues of economic instability and inequality that had only recently been impressed upon the majority of their fellow citizens.

For the eldest of my triptych writers, Charlotte Perkins Gilman, there would be scant opportunity to join in the upsurge of socialist activity. In her seventies, she was completing her autobiography but was not in good health; she lost her husband, Houghton, to a cerebral hemorrhage in 1934, and she herself was diagnosed with breast cancer that year. She died by her own hand in 1935. Still, her death like her life was wrapped in a social cause, for in an article appearing posthumously in *Forum* and *Reader's Digest* she defended her impending choice to die not merely as an individual right but as a social obligation: as she had no further contribution to make to society, she refused to accept life-giving medical attention that might be better expended on others.[1] For the other two triptych writers, however, both of whom would live into their nineties, there remained much working and fighting to do. They were in the very thick of events within their respective political and literary spheres during the 1930s. W. E. B. Du Bois was first thrown into the middle of an interorganizational struggle between the NAACP and the Communists over defense of the Scottsboro Boys. Then he was the principal instigator of an intraorganizational conflict within the NAACP over the degree to which economic issues were to become part of its agenda. Meanwhile, Upton Sinclair was campaigning for the governorship of California on the Democratic ticket, winning a stunning August 1934 victory in the Democratic primary and then losing by a landslide in the November general election.

One of my key conclusions, argued in the final chapter, is that a number of the social democratic developments Gilman, Du Bois, and Sinclair had fought for were on the verge of being implemented by the federal government, and that all three writers had a hand in defining the political terms and shaping the ethical appeals that made the New Deal and ancillary transformations possible. The more immediate story, told in this chapter, is less affirming, for both Du Bois and Sinclair pushed for greater social democracy sooner than most of their colleagues or fellow citizens could countenance, and both therefore endured keen personal losses even as the fuller social democracy they envisioned was being partially realized. Americans were getting the social democratic message, but first they had to shoot the socialist messenger.

THE SCOTTSBORO BOYS AND THE NICEST ASSOCIATION FOR THE ADVANCEMENT OF CERTAIN PERSONS

> "It deserves from Russia something better than a kick in the back from the young jackasses who are leading Communism in America today."

In 1934 Countee Cullen published a poem in which he proclaimed that "Scottsboro, Too, Is Worth Its Song (*A poem to American poets*)." Referencing the burst of activist literary production by writers mobilized in response to the Sacco and Vanzetti case, he expressed disappointment that the Scottsboro Boys had not elicited a similar reaction: "Surely, I said, / Now will the poets sing. / But they have raised no cry. / I wonder why."[2] Cullen had a point; whereas Sacco and Vanzetti had been defended by many individuals who were not Italian Americans or anarchists, the defenders of the "Boys" came from a more limited set of constituents. Yet Cullen was not alone among black poets in joining the cause. Langston Hughes, for instance, had published not merely a single poem about the Scottsboro Boys but a book of poems and a verse drama, *Scottsboro, Limited,* already in 1931. And the efforts of the Communist-affiliated International Labor Defense had rallied white writers and intellectuals—if not white poets—by the scores. Among the signers of petitions on behalf of the Scottsboro Boys were John Dos Passos, Sherwood Anderson, Theodore Dreiser, Lincoln Steffens, Thomas Mann, H. G. Wells, and Albert Einstein.[3] Although Upton Sinclair did not consider writing a drama based on the Scottsboro Boys as Du Bois had thought to do on Sacco and Vanzetti, Sinclair too was among the signatories. Indeed, for the taste of most leaders in the NAACP, the Communists had been altogether too successful in involving white folks in the Scottsboro case.

Nominally, perhaps, the NAACP could claim to have been the first outside group to aid in the defense of the nine young men accused of raping two young white women on a freight train that had departed Nashville, Tennessee, on March 30, 1931, bound for Memphis. On that train a fight had taken place between groups of young hoboes, white and black, over control of a gondola car, and the whites, losers of the fight, had lodged charges of assault. At the train's next stop, just over the Tennessee-Alabama line, the sheriff and his deputies in Paint Rock, Alabama, found nine black men on the train as well as two white women, Ruby Bates and Victoria Price. On cues provided by the sheriff, the women accused the young men of rape, and thereupon the men were arrested, charged, and jailed at the county seat at Scottsboro, Alabama, which provided them with the collective name by which they were ever after known: the "Scottsboro Boys." Because the defendants' court-appointed attorney received assistance from an attorney employed by the Interdenominational Colored Ministers' Alliance of Chattanooga, and because one of the members of the alliance was also an NAACP member and wrote the national leadership about the case, NAACP general secretary Walter White could subsequently claim that the NAACP had been on the case before the Communist Party. But the NAACP's efforts on behalf of the Scottsboro defendants almost immediately went from token to farcical. Uncertain whether the association should throw its limited resources behind the defendants on the chance that they were, in fact, guilty, White requested that his Chattanooga correspondent have a transcript of the trial made and sent to him in New York City. Then White waited, read the newspapers, and waited some more, learning only two weeks after his request that a transcript had never been made because the Ministers' Alliance had run out of money and their attorney could not pay the court stenographer.[4]

By the time White sent a check for $24 to correct the problem, the Communist Party had already moved decisively to fill the legal vacuum left by the NAACP. On the day after the defendants had been pronounced guilty, the International Labor Defense (ILD)—the legal defense arm of the Communist Party, USA—voted to mount an appeal on behalf of the convicted "Boys" on the basis of reports sent by Communist organizers who had attended the trial.[5] The Communists treated both the defendants and their parents with greater respect than they had ever been shown by white people, providing them an access to political agency that they had never before imagined: before the year was out, several of the mothers would tour the country as guest speakers of the party. In contrast, when Walter White and other NAACP officials finally showed up, they struck most of the parents as pretentious and condescending.[6] In private, White wrote to field secretary William Pickens, "I think I ought to warn you in advance that you have probably never before encountered such ignorance as you will find here"; in public, he called them "humble folk . . . [with] few opportunities for knowledge."[7] Consequently, the ILD was supported by a clear majority of the young men and their parents, the latter being especially critical because a majority of the defendants were legal minors. The conclusion of Mamie Williams Wilcox was widely shared by the other parents and their children: "We are not too ignorant to know a bunch of liars and fakers when we meet up with them and [we] are not too ignorant to know that if we let the NAACP look after our boys, that they will die."[8]

In point of fact, the ILD deserves credit for having saved the Scottsboro Boys from execution. The ILD took the lead in winning stays in advance of their July 10, 1931, execution date. It was the ILD, too, that won a landmark 1932 decision before the U.S. Supreme Court ruling that the Scottsboro defendants had been denied due process because of the incompetence of their court-appointed counsel. The ILD also won a second precedent-making appeal before the High Court, which in 1935 ruled that race must be admitted as a factor in empaneling a "jury of peers." Even while taking its legal defense to the highest court in the land, the Communist Party carried on a relentless publicity campaign, including massive letter-writing campaigns to the Alabama governor and presiding judges and street protests in the North and extending to the capitals of Europe. On this point the Communist Party strategy probably did as much long-term harm as good. Although the results of this confrontational strategy were not fully apparent for a number of years, the no-holds-barred publicity campaign contributed to a practical deadlock in achieving justice for the Scottsboro Boys. Certainly none of the Scottsboro defendants were ever executed, but the Alabama courts continued to hand down death sentences regardless of the exculpatory evidence presented and doubts raised by the U.S. Supreme Court, and successive governors of Alabama denied appeals for parole and clemency. The ILD's public ridicule of Alabama before the nation and the world helped to ensure that the state would relinquish its hold on the Scottsboro "boys" only on its own terms, and thus the defendants all grew into adulthood within Alabama's debilitating and vicious prison system before any were free men.[9]

The party's public campaign among black Americans sought not merely to gain support for the ILD's representation of the Scottsboro defendants but to supplant the NAACP as the leading voice of black America. In the class-war conception offered by the Communist Party, the NAACP was necessarily a part of the problem because it did not acknowledge the party as the undisputed leader in social transformation. Robert Minor wrote of "The Negro and His Judases," which lambasted Walter White and the association's field secretaries. Eugene Gordon, writing in the *New Masses* of July 1931, deemed the NAACP to be an acronym for the "Nicest Association for the Advantage of Certain Persons." The leadership offered by the association, Gordon declared, had been "weak, vacillating, hypocritical, ignorant, venal, and self-seeking. It is all these things in its very nature. It could not be anything else and exist as a part of the capitalist system and a defender of that system." Therefore, the race leaders of the NAACP had "as much to do with the black masses of workers and share-croppers as any similar group of scented, spatted, caned, and belly-filled parasites have to do with the white masses."[10]

White and most of the other association officers reciprocated the Communists' contempt, giving no quarter in their fight with them.[11] From the beginning of the Scottsboro struggle, however, Du Bois offered a more nuanced response. He had been laboring for the better part of twenty years to articulate a socialist vision for black America; he could and did critique the Communist Party, but consistency with his earlier positions also demanded that he share common ground with the party. In "The Negro and Communism," Du Bois's major statement on Scottsboro appearing in the September 1931 *Crisis,* Du Bois sought to break down the stark us-versus-them binary offered by the party and reinforced by many in the NAACP. Acknowledging, as he had before, the importance of the Russian revolution, "the greatest event in the world since the French Revolution and possibly since the fall of Rome," and noting as well that the recent economic collapse had shown the shortcomings of capitalism, Du Bois held out for a middle course between the mainstream parties and the Communists. While on the one hand the Republicans and Democrats offered merely some "new legislation, better administration and better aid," and on the other hand the Communists "propose an entire sweeping away of the present organization of industry," the Progressives and Socialists would provide a safer and saner *via media:* "increased government ownership of land and natural resources, state control of the larger public services and such progressive taxation of incomes and inheritances as shall decrease the number and power of the rich."[12]

Of course, it counted for relatively little that Du Bois shared the Communist Party's views on the bankruptcy of U.S. capitalism. Because he proposed other groups as the parties of social transformation, he was compelled in "The Negro and Communism" to make his critique of the party foremost. In Du Bois's view, the Communists in charge in the United States offered a ridiculously rigid application of socialist theory to American conditions. The U.S. Communists' charges against the NAACP leadership lacked understanding of the class origins of the black leadership class, for class differentiation had not become so sharp among black Americans as to undermine wholly a shared experience of exploitation at the hands of white, capitalist industry. Those black Americans that *had* become bourgeois had done so, in most cases, within their own lifetimes, so they largely retained the ideology of the working class even as they remembered the experience of poverty. The smear campaign directed against the NAACP, Du Bois explained, could only be effected by "deliberate misrepresentation of friends who are fighting for the same ideals as the Communists"; the NAACP, he concluded, "deserves from Russia something better than a kick in the back from the young jackasses who are leading Communism in America today."[13]

But according to Du Bois, the Communists' misrepresentation of the NAACP was only the beginning of their errors. Socialist theory as interpreted by the Communist Internationale stipulated "a revolutionary dictatorship by the working class" as the necessary path to socialist revolution.[14] What exactly would a dictatorship by this particular class look like in the United States? Du Bois wondered. In the North, white workers had excluded blacks from their unions and then attacked them when they took jobs as strikebreakers. In the South, they "formed the backbone of the Ku Klux Klan and have furnished hands and ropes to lynch 3,560 Negroes since 1883." Du Bois allowed that the Communist Party was "courageous" in admitting black members and involving blacks in their "strikes and agitation," but if American blacks were to act as the Communist Party urged them—joining the party, organizing, and agitating against conditions in the South, all in the expectation that white workers would follow their example and thus bring about a general insurrection—Du Bois foresaw a result just short of suicide:

> American Negroes do not propose to be the shock troops of the Communist Revolution, driven out in front to death, cruelty and humiliation in order to win victories for white workers. They are picking no chestnuts from the fire, neither for capital nor white labor.
>
> Negroes know perfectly well that whenever they try to lead revolution in America, the nation will unite as one fist to crush them and them alone. There is no conceivable ideal that seems to the present overwhelming majority of Americans higher than keeping Negroes "in their place."[15]

This drew upon a long history of Du Bois's refusing to sacrifice the immediate demands of black Americans to the long-range interests of larger causes. The memorable idiom about chestnuts was repeated from an early Du Bois observation about the willingness of colonial troops to fight in the Great War, even as the wider argument about black violence inevitably calling forth a still more violent white response went back to *Quest of the Silver Fleece*. Moreover, just as he had suggested in *Darkwater* that white labor must act to liberate black labor, Du Bois insisted that the much greater numbers and power of white workers called for them, not black laborers, to take the lead in both radical activism and interracial cooperation: "There is no doubt, then, as to the future, or as to where the true interests of American Negroes lie. There is no doubt, too, but that the first step toward the emancipation of colored labor must come from white labor."[16]

That Du Bois was correct about the white response to black collaboration with the Communists was not only supported in the long run by the legal deadlock over the fate of the Scottsboro defendants; it was also borne out shortly thereafter by events on the ground in Alabama. In June 1931, four white Communists and a black comrade came down from Chattanooga to Tallapoosa County, Alabama, with the aim of organizing blacks into a sharecroppers' union. The four whites stayed briefly; the black man remained, concentrating his efforts on farmers in the vicinity of the small town of Camp Hill. Besides bread-and-butter issues—higher wages for picking cotton, better winter provisions for croppers—Scottsboro was the organizer's rallying cry. On July 16, some two hundred blacks gathered at a church near Camp Hill to write a letter to the state's governor protesting the Scottsboro verdicts. Acting on a tip from an informer, the county sheriff, Camp Hill police chief, and two deputies traveled to the meeting. On the road they confronted a young black man armed with a shotgun, Ralph Grey, apparently stationed as a guard for the meeting, who fired upon them; they returned fire and wounded Grey. Immediately the representatives of the law returned to Camp Hill and deputized some five hundred additional white citizens, who subsequently arrested scores of blacks, some of whom were charged with murder, others with carrying concealed weapons, and many with conspiracy. Some of the deputies found the house where Grey was being sheltered, killed the wounded man, and displayed his bullet-riddled body in front of the county courthouse; they also burned to the ground the church in which the stillborn sharecroppers' union had met. The presumed black ringleader of the Communist cell was taken from jail by a mob and never seen again.[17]

That Du Bois was right about the inflexibility and callousness of the Communist Party theory as it applied to African Americans was borne out, likewise, by the party's response to Camp Hill. One man had died for certain, another in all probability, several others were wounded, the black community for miles around was terrorized, and neither the sharecroppers' union nor the Communist Party was established in the region. No matter. To the general secretary of the Communist Party, USA, these were apparently the harbingers of revolution. Earl Browder, writing in the April 1932 *Communist,* wrote with unmitigated confidence:

> In the midst of the Scottsboro campaign we made another political step forward, in the struggle of the Negro share-croppers in Camp Hill. This battle was the first struggle directly resulting from our penetration of the Black Belt, of the agrarian population. It brought out the basic question of the Negroes as a nation, the question of the land and land-tenure, the question of the agrarian revolution, the overthrowing of the semi-feudal

agrarian relationships. While immediately Camp Hill was only a struggle for certain partial demands, and correctly so, it threw a bright light upon the basic problem of the land, and thereby became a political milestone in the development of our Negro work.[18]

Perhaps the murders of two black Americans looked relatively unimportant if Browder was indeed following the Comintern line and the Bolshevik model. Even so, it is difficult to see just for whom "a bright light" was thrown upon "the basic problem of the land." Doubtless, Camp Hill proved to Browder and the sectarian audience he addressed in *The Communist* that revolt was brewing among black farmers in the South. But if Camp Hill cast any light whatsoever on the matter among the black Americans who were slated to do the revolting, the truth revealed was the inadvisability of having anything to do with the Communist Party.

Like the Communists, Du Bois realized the desperate situation of black farmers in the South. In a June 1933 *Crisis* editorial, Du Bois would note that out of 700,000 black tenant farmers in the South, 400,000 were sharecroppers, whose "economic condition, under the laws and usages of the South, is but little removed from slavery."[19] But Du Bois realized, in addition, the futility and self-destructiveness of armed black resistance in the South. While not naming Camp Hill, Du Bois alluded directly to the events there as he went on to analyze the Communists' efforts to organize the black croppers in the South: "Without plan or apparent forethought, the Communists sent agitators down into a rural county of northern Alabama, and induced the wretched Negro sharecroppers to form a 'Union.' The result was an immediate clash with the authorities: the communist organizers ran away, and a half-dozen black men face a term in the penitentiary." Whereas Browder, following the Stalin-originated line, asserts the importance of black "national" agitation and sidesteps the question of white working-class reaction, Du Bois focuses upon the critical question of white psychology in the South, which made the great majority of poor white farmers all too eager to squelch any movement of poor black farmers toward organization. "It may well be that this attitude on their part is the result of silly ignorance and instigated directly or indirectly by the land holders and capitalists," Du Bois allows, "But whatever its cause may be, it is a fact, and to ignore such a fact is stupid and wrong."[20] Du Bois intuited clearly the "bitter expense" to southern blacks for any move toward armed resistance. And his reckoning of the social position and power of poor southern whites is acute, on a point where the understanding of Browder and other party theorists was remarkably dull.

The failures of the Communists in response to Scottsboro particularly and race agitation generally produced more negative knowledge than it did positive knowledge—not how to proceed in interracial and anticapitalist agitation, but how *not* to proceed. Du Bois's critique of the Communists' position turned, at bottom, on the question of leadership in black America: Who could best lead? White Communists following a line promulgated by the Comintern, half a world away? Or black leaders emerging directly from the masses of Aframerica? Surely, Du Bois reasoned, the NAACP deserved the benefit of the doubt based on its past performance, its "honesty, earnestness and intelligence . . . during twenty years of desperate struggle." As subsequent writings would make abundantly clear, Du Bois's search for a middle way demanded critique of his own organization, as well. If black leaders were to continue to merit their positions of authority and influence, they needed to make adjustments to reach out to the black masses who were suffering all the more acutely because of the Depression. They needed, too, to study what the Depression was showing about the instability and inequality of American capitalism, and they needed to formulate a program that would allow African Americans to share fully in the more carefully planned economy and democratic control of industry that were almost certain to characterize the government's response to the crisis. In short, the NAACP and black America both needed socialism more than ever, and Du Bois resolved to supply the need to whatever extent it lay within his power.

SELF-SEGREGATION AS REVOLUTIONARY STRATEGY

> "What are we really aiming at? The building of a new nation or the integration of a new group into an old nation?"

While in 1931 Du Bois gamely defended the NAACP in its struggle with the Communist Party and the International Labor Defense, arguing for the independence of black America from the direction supplied by the party, in 1932 the *Crisis* editor presented more fully the positive content of his proposed agenda for black America, which sought to promulgate its independent development apart from capitalist direction and ideology. This further campaign of education and persuasion led him squarely into conflict with the traditions of the NAACP and the philosophies of most of its other leaders. The strategy of self-directed social democracy for black America, and by extension for people of color throughout the world, had been developed long in advance in *The Quest of the Silver Fleece*, *Dark Princess*, and various *Cri-*

sis editorials. But to proclaim it once again at this moment in the organizational life of the NAACP, when the stresses induced by the Depression and the challenge posed by the Communist Party seemed to demand organizational solidarity, meant that Du Bois was not only stirring philosophic debate but precipitating an organizational crisis.

Du Bois entered this particular fray with the odds within the NAACP against him. Walter White had been appointed permanently to the general secretaryship only in January 1931, a few months before the Scottsboro crisis broke. Yet when in the fall of 1931 Du Bois and others in the NAACP office sought to have White removed from office, charging that funds designated for *The Crisis* had been diverted into the association's general fund instead, the association's board merely reprimanded him and proceeded to back him with a vote of confidence.[21] Du Bois henceforth found himself with fewer allies on the board than ever before. Even longtime supporter and socialist Mary White Ovington complained in a memo to a fellow board member that Du Bois was "growing increasingly incompetent. As a choice between him and Walter White, Walter is worth ten times as much to us."[22]

Outside the highest levels of NAACP leadership, however, the rising generation of black leaders looked to Du Bois's work and his brand of social democratic economics as foundational. Even while lambasting the "young jackasses" who were directing Communist Party policy, within the NAACP and black America more generally Du Bois took sides with the younger, more radical leaders. Abram Harris, an economics professor at Howard University, had been in correspondence with Du Bois for over a decade. *The Black Worker* (1931), coauthored by Harris and Sterling Spero, had been written with the assistance of Du Bois's accumulated files on the subject of cooperative economics, and its argument essentially ratified the Du Boisian position that because white workers comprised the larger and more powerful proletarian faction, interracial cooperation and radicalization depended upon them, not the minority of black workers.[23] Harris was just one of a number of young activists at Howard University who, to a greater or lesser degree, shared Du Bois's convictions that the NAACP should review and adjust its mission to meet the emergency of the Depression. Characterized by David Levering Lewis as the "Young Turks" of the NAACP, these included Sterling Brown, poet and professor of literature; Charlie Huston, dean of the law school; Ralph Bunche, chair of the political science department; and E. Franklin Frazier, a sociologist on the faculty.[24]

It was therefore with some sense of being in the vanguard not only of political-economic history but also of intellectual trends within the black community that Du Bois began in 1932 a new initiative to educate black American readers of *The Crisis* about socialism. The campaign was inaugurated with a *Crisis* survey of the black press's attitudes toward Communism, with results published in the April and May 1932 issues. Although half of the editors who responded to Du Bois's survey—seven out of fourteen—definitely advised their readers *against* Communist involvement, five editors directly or indirectly endorsed it, and two gave such equal representation of the Communists' virtues and vices that they might be counted in either—or both—camps. Even in those cases where the editors urged their readers to stay away from the Communists, they could not deny the appeal of the Communist program for black America. One of the opponents, William Kelley of the *Amsterdam News,* feared the possibility that if the Communists had their way, a proletarian dictatorship would put into power "the same ignorant white working class which forms the backbone of every lynching mob" (echoing an argument he might have seen previously in the pages of *The Crisis*), yet he also suggested that communism was merely the secular manifestation of Christian ideals presented in the first-century Acts of the Apostles.[25] Du Bois himself, while withholding endorsement of the Communist Party, unmistakably advocated socialism as the means to address and redress the capitalist legacy, and closed the series with a recommendation of books on the subject. Du Bois's reading list was decidedly eclectic, listing Henry George's *Progress and Poverty* immediately after Karl Marx's obligatory *Das Kapital,* endorsing the Soviet experiments in planned economics as described in Ilin's *The Five-Year Plan,* and featuring American socialists Norman Thomas and Harry Laidler alongside the Communist Scott Nearing.

Already in January 1932, Du Bois had announced that the discussions of the coming year would constitute a "New Racial Philosophy." *The Crisis* for 1933 presented the rapprochement between black America and socialism still more systematically. In the January issue, Du Bois announced twelve general topics to be covered in successive monthly installments. He made the socialist and Marxian tilt of the inquiry particularly clear in a February precis of the coming issues: the March number, on the topic of "Work," would offer as subtopics "Depression, Capitalism and Karl Marx"; May, on "Income," was slated for "The 'Class Struggle' of the Black Proletariat and Bourgeoisie"; June, on "Government and Law," would consider "Revolution in America by vote and action"; July, on "Crime and Indigence," would take up "Punishment, Charity and the Black Proletariat"; and September, on "Race Discrimination," would continue the theme, covering "The Dictatorship of a Black Proletariat."[26] The first issue of 1933 could already offer a clear preview of the eleventh issue, focused on "Social Contacts," whose rhetorical questions defined the crux of class and race relations: "Is the method of advance among colored people today a building up of social classes so that the educated, the rich, the well-to-do and the moral can separate themselves from the poor, the ignorant and the criminal? Can this class-building technique of civilization be ignored in our case and something better substituted?"[27]

In 1933, too, Du Bois was able to turn the NAACP's second Amenia conference into a referendum upon the politics of the association. Unable to make any headway in challenging the institutional structure of the association from within its offices, Du Bois was able to stage a kind of temporary ideological coup through his considerable input into the list of guests invited to the Spingarn estate in Troutbeck, New York. The first Amenia conference hosted by Joel and Arthur Spingarn, longtime mainstays on the NAACP board, had been held in 1916 in the wake of Booker T. Washington's death and was an occasion to consolidate the NAACP's leadership of black America.[28] That the second conference hosted on the grounds of their opulent ancestral home would hail the inevitability of state intervention into the economy and the desirability of race-conscious cooperative economics was undoubtedly not anticipated by the Spingarns, who were personally close to Du Bois but far more conservative politically.[29] With faculty from Howard at the forefront, the thirty-two conferees passed resolutions announcing that "individual ownership expressing itself through the control and exploitation of natural resources and industrial machinery had failed in the past to equalize consumption with production," and asserting that "the interests of the Negro cannot be adequately safeguarded by white paternalism in government." In language unmistakably influenced by Du Bois and probably also crafted in part by him, the resolutions proceeded to call for a program of black activism fostering the "increased *economic independence*" of blacks. "No matter what artificial class difference may seem to exist within the Negro group," the conferees insisted, "it must be recognized that all elements of the Race must weld themselves together for the common welfare."[30]

In the months after Amenia, Du Bois kept up the drumbeat of black social democracy, all the while moving more pointedly toward a direct criticism of the NAACP that put him on a collision path with his fellow leaders. "On Being Ashamed of Oneself: An Essay on Race Pride," published in September 1933, is haunted by the NAACP's shortcomings in response to Scottsboro. Passages such as the following are difficult not to read as a palimpsest of Scottsboro, distinctly echoing the Communists' criticisms of the "Nicest Association for the Advancement of Certain Persons":

> When . . . in offense or defense, the leading group of Negroes must make common cause with the masses of their own race, the embarrassment or hesitation becomes apparent. They are embarrassed and indignant because an educated man should be treated as a Negro, and that no Negroes receive credit for social standing. They are ashamed and embarrassed because of the compulsion of being classed with a mass of people over whom they have no real control and whose action they can influence only with difficulty and compromise and with every risk of defeat.[31]

Du Bois's editorial went on to take a far wider swipe at the specific philosophy espoused by the NAACP, including its long-standing opposition to segregation and idealization of integration. As Du Bois saw matters, the unspoken desire of the leading African Americans was to escape "blackness," as if African parentage were a "stigmata of degradation." The path of escape was, in fact, available in some measure for the most gifted, the best educated, the least marginalized and the lightest in color. But the opportunity and the willingness of Talented Tenth blacks to make this escape meant wider and deeper class stratification, and such stratification ultimately meant that the struggle for civil rights was not, in fact, a fight for the equality of all black Americans. The NAACP's integrationist goals and strategies had seemed both practical and idealistic, but in the real world, Du Bois argued, they sustained scrutiny on neither of these grounds. "What are we really aiming at," Du Bois wondered, "the building of a new nation or the integration of a new group into an old nation?" While noting that the "latter has long been our ideal," Du Bois at the end of 1933 tilted toward the former. "A new plan must be built up," the editor proclaimed; "It cannot be the mere rhodomontade and fatuous propaganda on which Garveyism was based. It has got to be far-sighted planning. It will involve increased segregation and perhaps migration." The new plan Du Bois envisaged was to be facilitated by a propaganda for racial pride. It could only be possible through racial solidarity, and particularly an immediate halt of Talented Tenth flight from the black masses. Its key instrumentality—and immediate goal—was increased black economic independence: "A new organized group action along economic lines, guided by intelligence and with the express object of making it possible for Negroes to earn a better living."[32]

Though he had defended the NAACP's leadership gamely in 1931, by 1933 Du Bois's social and political views had become practically indistinguishable from those of the NAACP's chief antagonist, the Communist Party. Not only had he used the Communist Party as an ideological foil to press his case for a stronger economic agenda within the NAACP, but his strategy of racial self-segregation, articulated with ever-increasing stridency, was sounding more and more like the position promulgated by the Comintern. Among other matters dealt with at the Sixth World Congress of the Communist International, convened back in 1928, the party line defining African Americans as a superexploited national minority was laid down. Working from the writings of Lenin and Stalin on imperialism, delegates theorized that American blacks were in fact a "nation within a nation," analogous to the ethnic minorities of the old czarist Russian empire that had formed the basis for the individual republics of the new U.S.S.R.[33] As explained by Jos. Prokopec in the May 1930 *Communist*, the party's U.S. theoretical journal, the official line of "Negroes As an Oppressed National Minority" asserted that black Americans might form an independent nation, centered in a "Black Belt" extending across portions of the Deep South states where three million black Americans already comprised a majority. Because they were subjected to precapitalist forms of exploitation, southern blacks were not yet fully formed as a proletariat, and therefore would need to fulfill their nationalist ambitions before proceeding to a true proletarian revolution.[34] The Comintern line on black American nationhood—or the "49th State," as it soon came to be called—was promulgated by the U.S. party throughout the 1930s, and was the underlying foundation of its agitation surrounding the Scottsboro tragedy.

From one perspective, the position taken by the Comintern and the apologia made by Prokopec was based on simplistic analogies between the Soviet and American situations. From another perspective—a perspective not far removed from Du Bois's—there was a shrewd common sense to Prokopec's argument. Independence was necessary in the first place, Prokopec had argued, because only through self-sovereignty would it be possible to guarantee the equality so earnestly sought by African Americans; without this, "'equality' is practically meaningless. . . . an empty phrase." With a far broader and deeper empirical basis for judgment, Du Bois argued practically the same thing, noting that tremendous increases in black literacy and education had resulted not in the acceptance of blacks as equals but the further exclusion of blacks from equal social, economic, and political opportunity. In "On Being Ashamed of Oneself," Du Bois thus concluded:

"Notwithstanding this [increase in literacy and education], the Negro is still a group apart, with almost no social recognition, subject to insult and discrimination, with income and wage far below the average of the nation and the most deliberately exploited industrial class in America." All effective advances in social and economic life "in the last quarter century," Du Bois argued, had come through "segregated . . . institutions and efforts," whereas on the larger national scene of industry and the professions "we have fought battle after battle and lost more often than we have won."[35] Moving toward his final assertion that "*The next step, then, is certainly one on the part of the Negro and it involves group action*," Du Bois could have been elaborating upon Prokopec's assertion that the "bourgeoisie and the Social Democracy are willing to grant abstract 'equality' to a minority, but when it comes to carrying this out to its logical conclusion, then they use every 'democratic' means to keep these people subjected and oppressed." For in September 1933 Du Bois concurred, "There seems no hope that America in our day will yield in its color or race hatred," for "we have no physical nor economic power, nor any alliance with other social or economic classes that will force compliance with decent civilized ideals in Church, State, industry or art."[36] The single difference between Du Bois's "New Racial Philosophy" and Prokopec's racial "separation" and "segregation" is that Du Bois urged "new organized group action along economic lines" without demanding the establishment of a political unit, the "49th state" called for by the Comintern.

Prokopec's "Negroes As an Oppressed National Minority" even converges intriguingly with Du Bois's philosophy insofar as Prokopec tacitly accepts interclass cooperation along separate racial lines. Although Prokopec indicates clearly enough that the most desirable leaders for the "national revolutionary movement" would in fact be black proletarians, Communist Party members, or both, the party line as explained by Prokopec is essentially compatible with Du Bois's policies of black self-segregation, nationalist development, and "watchful waiting." In one passage Prokopec scoffs at the "captaincy promised to the then militant Du Bois" as a buyout by American capitalism during the world war, but Prokopec accepts the "Negro peasantry, the petty and middle bourgeoisie" as the "driving force" behind black nationalism and thereby effectively accepts the leadership of Du Bois himself and even—if the offer of self-determination is really to be taken seriously—of the other petit bourgeois blacks in the day-to-day leadership of the NAACP. In the end, Prokopec permitted the same blurring of distinctions between the middle-class black leadership and the black masses that Du Bois made, and for precisely the same reasons offered by Du Bois: that blacks held a "class" grievance and interest in common, and therefore had a shared revolutionary agenda, insofar as all blacks regardless of class suffered from color discrimination.

The imperative need for interclass cooperation between black leaders and the black masses was precisely the issue that Du Bois was seeking to drive home with his "Segregation" editorial of January 1934. In the words of David Levering Lewis, the editorial was the intellectual and organizational equivalent of "lobbing a concussion grenade": a shock to "his overwhelmingly surprised readers" as well as to NAACP chief Walter White.[37] Yet the intellectual path to this astonishing and controversial editorial had been well paved over the previous two years, and far from being an exaggerated expression of Du Bois's "periodical indulgence of black nationalist nostrums," as biographer Lewis suggests, the claim that black America should not only seek racial solidarity but, as far as possible, economic and political independency stemmed from a long-standing exploration of African American social democracy that had been sharpened by, but certainly had not originated during, three years of intellectual fencing with the Communists. Indeed, if "Segregation" took Du Bois's readers fully by surprise, they could not have been reading very closely either *The Crisis* or Du Bois's novels. The pith of the argument was practically Du Boisian boilerplate, little different from his many other editorial statements on social democracy among black Americans: "It is the race-conscious black man cooperating together in his own institutions and movements who will eventually emancipate the colored race, and the great step ahead today is for the American Negro to accomplish his economic emancipation through voluntary determined cooperative effort."[38] Even the polemically charged rhetoric directed against the NAACP itself was merely the extension of arguments already made in "On Being Ashamed of Oneself."

Du Bois had concluded by the beginning of 1934 that the leadership of the NAACP needed a major overhaul both in philosophy and in personnel. In January of that year he wrote in private to Abram Harris indicating that he was committed to a program in cooperative economics with or without the NAACP. "I should like to talk to you and a group of our way of thinking," Du Bois suggested, "concerning the possibility of a movement inside or outside the N.A.A.C.P. to start the Negro race on a proper economic program."[39] As Du Bois saw further evidence of the philosophical intransigence of the association's fellow officers, he became all the more reckless both in his editing of *The Crisis* and in his dealings with those officers. In April, among an additional four articles on segregation, Du Bois's lead editorial, "Segregation in the North," trained his rhetorical fire directly upon the executive secretary of the NAACP: "Walter White is white. He has more white companions and friends than colored. He goes where he will in New York City and naturally meets no Color Line, for the simple and sufficient reason that he isn't 'colored.' . . . It naturally makes Mr. White an extreme opponent of any segregation based on a myth of race. But this argument does not apply to Schuyler or Miller or me."[40] Du Bois certainly had a point; in his early days with the NAACP, White had been able to conduct lynching investigations by traveling to the scenes of the crime, passing for white and thereby freely mingling with and listening to gossip from white witnesses.[41] Yet Du Bois's argument also amounted to a clear and vicious ad hominem, as many in the association immediately protested. George Schuyler, no doubt smarting over being named in the editorial, declared in the *Pittsburgh Courier* that Du Bois's attack on White amounted to an admission of defeat: "Imagine the Top Sergeant of the Talented Tenth fouling like a punch drunk pugilist despairing of victory." Using essentially the same boxing metaphor, Joel Spingarn wrote to Du Bois privately that the attack against White amounted to "hitting below the belt."[42]

Given Du Bois's continued prestige, efforts to extract him from the *Crisis* editor's chair were fairly protracted, even if Du Bois's removal had become inevitable after his "White is white" editorial. In the meeting of the board of directors in January 1934, Du Bois had actually succeeded in seating two new members strongly inclined to his way of thinking on political economy: Abram Harris and Rachel Davis Du Bois (no relation to W. E. B.). Yet even then Du Bois knew where the balance of power lay; lacking support he had formerly counted on from Ovington and Joel Spingarn, he observed in a letter to Harris that the radicals remained "a hopeless minority within a group of elderly reactionaries."[43] When important votes on policy and personnel came along, the NAACP board made rhetorical concessions to Du Bois even while firmly repudiating the editor's racial-economic philosophy and systematically stripping him of organizational power. The May meeting brought the kind of proposal that Du Bois had long dreaded: action by the board that would rein in his journalistic freedom, making *The Crisis* a mouthpiece of the association as opposed to Du Bois's oracle. More than once Du Bois had fended off efforts of this kind. But now with Ovington and Spingarn helping to form a majority supporting Walter White, a motion was passed forbidding any NAACP staff member to "criticize the policy, work, or officers of the Association in the pages of *The Crisis*" and declaring the journal to be the "organ of the Association."[44] Within days of this decision Du Bois offered his resignation, though it took two more board meetings—and a threat of resignation from Walter White—before the board gave up all hope of reconciliation and accepted it.[45]

There might have seemed to be a glimmer of hope that Du Bois's social and economic philosophy would live on within the association beyond its architect's tenure. At the very July 9 meeting at which Du Bois's resignation was finally accepted, Abram Harris was appointed the chair of a Committee on Plan and Program of the Association and the Future of *The Crisis*. With the rest of the committee strongly inclined toward socialist political economy as well, including Mary White Ovington, Rachel Davis Du Bois, and Sterling Brown on the seven-person committee, the report was likely to recommend—just as Du Bois had wished—that the NAACP emphasize economic development and shift its focus from Talented Tenth issues to the broader problems of the black masses. Among the programmatic proposals made in the preliminary draft, the committee recommended "workers and farmers councils," which would engage not merely in education of black labor but in "actual participation in strikes, lockouts and labor demonstrations." James Weldon Johnson, who found himself in the conservative minority on the committee, was outraged by this and virtually all language with an economic slant. Above the phrase "prevailing economic and social conditions," part of a sentence characterizing the NAACP as erroneously accepting such conditions, Johnson put a question mark above every word except for "and" in his copy of the preliminary report; in the same draft, exposition of the faults of liberalism demanded a marginal question from Johnson about whether the report was proposing the "abolishment of property."[46]

Such resistance extracted a number of concessions in the final committee report: references to workers' and farmers' councils, for instance, were removed. Moreover, although the report was accepted by the NAACP board in September and adopted at the NAACP's annual convention in June 1935, it was essentially neutralized by the association's choice of leaders for its implementation. The same convention that approved the report on "Plan and Program" gave Walter White extensive, indeed virtually exclusive, control over putting the new NAACP program into action, a control that ensured that the NAACP's involvement in labor, radical politics, and economic issues, in general, would be minimal.[47] Furthermore, with the editorship of the *Crisis* being assumed by Roy Wilkins—who had confided to White that "only a small minority is at all concerned with the question of integrating the race into the economic and political pattern of the day"[48]—there was no officer in the association to act as a radical counterweight to White, and the potentially transformative aspects of the proposal were no more than a hollow, rhetorical shell.

While in coming decades White and Wilkins focused the NAACP's energy upon a legal strategy for winning black equality—certainly not a strategy lacking in concrete, progressive results—Du Bois returned to Atlanta University, as he embarked upon a highly productive period of research and publication in the second half of the 1930s. *Black Reconstruction in America,* an argument extending his analysis of political economy in *The Crisis* to a historical interpretation of black social democratic agency after the Civil War, appeared in 1935. The most extensive biographical work of his career, *Dusk of Dawn,* came out in 1940. During this period he also labored indefatigably upon his longtime ambition to edit a massive encyclopedia on all people and things pertaining to Africa and the African diaspora, which then had the working title of "Encyclopedia of the Negro." These academic activities failed, however, to exert the leverage upon black American culture and politics that he had had in his twenty-five years as *Crisis* editor and NAACP officer; Du Bois had been cut adrift from any institutional platform suitable for implementing his findings and philosophy. Again and again in the last two decades of his life, Du Bois would persistently, and for the most part futilely, seek an adequate and trustworthy vehicle for bringing his social democratic vision into reality.

Notably, Du Bois would not embrace the Communists until positively driven into their arms by Cold War politics in the 1950s. There were two primary reasons for his reluctance. First and foremost, as he articulated from the beginning of the Scottsboro struggle, he was convinced that the task of social democratic transformation among African Americans would be led best by African Americans. The fact that Communist policies in the United States were guided, on very many points, by the Comintern dominated by the Soviets and convened in the U.S.S.R. made Communist leadership in black America fundamentally dubious—even if Du Bois concurred in general terms with the Stalinist line of an independent black nationalist movement. The Comintern's notion that the white American proletariat was to be the historical instrument liberating black America was just one too many improbabilities, as far as Du Bois was concerned. The second reason for Du Bois's refusal to fall in line with the Communists was his unshakable perception that open insurrection stood at the heart of the Communist strategy and his equally unshakable judgment that any such insurrection, necessarily involving violence, would inevitably bring ruin to black America. In an editorial titled simply "Violence" published in May 1934, Du Bois responded to the questions of "a certain group of young, American Negroes, inspired by white Radicals," who wondered why the circumstances of American blacks were much different from those of the colonists at the time of the American Revolution, the black slaves of Haiti, or the peasants of the French Revolution. His replies were straightforward: African Americans lacked the superior numbers enjoyed by the Haitian slaves, and with the barrier of the color line and their minority status in the United States, they lacked the opportunities for political persuasion available to the American rebels and the French peasants. "With the same tactics that Hitler is using in Germany, [white Americans] would seek to annihilate, and spiritually, even physically, reinslave black folk of America," Du Bois explained; "Of this, there is no reasonable doubt, and it is, therefore, our clear policy not to appeal to force until clearly and evidently, there is no other way."[49] In Du Bois's view, the short-term remedy to racial inequality was not direct confrontation but strategic retreat, voluntary and organized self-segregation, group solidarity and development. Du Bois's individual retreat in the 1930s, however involuntary, also bore the character of a strategic calculation—a calculation that neither the NAACP nor the Communist Party was prepared to lead black America reliably toward economic and social equality. Lacking the right leadership with the right philosophy, black Americans—Du Bois testified—were better off treading water than forging ahead at all costs, a judgment that many black Communists including Langston Hughes, Ralph Ellison, and Richard Wright would reach only a number of years and considerable hard experience later.

EPIC AND THE MAKING OF A SOCIAL DEMOCRATIC MAJORITY

> "I have believed in the people, and the one thing you can do for me tomorrow is to vindicate that faith, out of which the life and the books of Upton Sinclair have been made."

Upton Sinclair, like Du Bois, found that the circumstances of the Great Depression both opened up new opportunities for social democrats and dictated changes in socialist tactics. Explaining his decision to enter the California governor's race as a Democratic candidate in the fall of 1933, Sinclair suggested that in times of prosperity he had had the leisure to preach utopian idealism from the sanctity of his study and the high pulpit of pure-and-simple socialism. But times of crisis compelled pragmatic action and ideological compromise:

> For thirty years I traveled around the United States, and wrote books urging people to work for a beautiful dream, which I called the co-operative commonwealth. It was going to be a perfect society from which had been abolished poverty, crime, etc. I talked to audiences, and they received me with enthusiasm, but they went away and never did anything about it.
>
> In this present crisis, seeing our civilization tottering on the edge of an abyss, I sat down and tried to figure out what was the matter. I had thought I had about thirty years more, but I realized that I had less than thirty months, or maybe thirty weeks, in which to do something. I decided that what I had been saying was too perfect to believe in. People said, "Yes, that is lovely, but it won't come in our time. Maybe in a thousand years." So I decided to drop all Utopias and to concentrate on one definite, concrete job.[50]

That "one definite, concrete job" was, merely, to end poverty in California. Sinclair's campaign to "End Poverty in California," soon to be known by the acronym "EPIC," was a practical campaign only relatively speaking, not utopian only when compared to that "beautiful dream" of a fully formed cooperative commonwealth. Yet in troubled economic times formerly utopian dreams might become practical, because urgently needed and politically feasible, policies. And the very audacity of Sinclair's idealism was unquestionably central to the appeal of his candidacy for governor; the fact that he had long been schooling himself in alternatives to capitalist political economy—through some thirty years of political ups and downs—gave him bedrock credibility.

Fittingly, the campaign was inaugurated by the writing of a novel. In late 1933, not long after changing his party registration to Democratic, Sinclair formally kicked off his campaign with the publication of his immodestly titled tract *I, Governor of California, and How I Ended Poverty.* Subtitled *A True Story of the Future,* the novel is in the socialist tradition of futurist fiction headlined by Bellamy's *Looking Backward.* Unquestionably, it was the overwhelming response of Americans to Bellamy's novel that Sinclair had in mind when he wrote *I, Governor.* Yet the circumstances of the author, his book, and its readership hardly seemed auspicious for duplicating the success of *Looking Backward.* Sinclair had run for statewide office in California twice before on the Socialist ticket, his candidacy generating minimal interest; both times he had won fewer than 10,000 votes whether running for governor or U.S. senator. The novel generated even less plot suspense than

Looking Backward, its title giving away pretty much all the key narrative elements. Still more, with its regional focus and shorter time frame, predicting what would happen in the next twelve months as opposed to 127 years, the novel presumably appealed to a much narrower base of potential readers and threatened to strain their credulousness to even more extreme lengths. Establishing utopia by the year 2000 was an easier task, surely, than ending poverty in California by 1935. Nevertheless, the first edition of the book, published in October 1933, sold its 10,000 copies in barely more than two weeks. In January 1934, Sinclair reported to a key political ally, progressive Republican senator Bronson Cutting of Nebraska, that the EPIC plan "is going here like wildfire" and that 93,000 copies of *I, Governor* were in print.[51] A total of ten print runs of between 20,000 and 30,000 brought the total number of copies to 255,000 by September 1934.[52] Meanwhile, the number of EPIC Clubs studying *I, Governor* kept pace and soon outstripped the number of reading groups that had read *Looking Backward* in the heyday of Nationalism, when some 150 Nationalist clubs were distributed over twenty-seven states. Already in February 1934, there were 300 EPIC clubs spread across California, from Alturus in the far northeast to Chula Vista south of San Diego.[53] Within the next few months—far more rapidly than Bellamy's clubs had transformed into the political agency of Nationalism—EPIC clubs were not only studying the End Poverty plan but organizing for the election: soliciting campaign contributions (one dollar per month being the standard); distributing campaign literature, windshield stickers, and stamps; canvassing neighborhoods; working to register new voters as Democrats committed to EPIC; and recruiting EPIC candidates in every precinct in the state.[54]

Californians found in *I, Governor* pretty much what they might have expected from a writer who had made his living by critiquing capitalism and touting socialism, and who had been registered as a member of the Socialist Party of America up until a few days before embarking upon his gubernatorial campaign. Sinclair's philosophy as laid out in the novella was unmistakably socialist in the traditions of the American party and the Second Internationale. Thus, the first two of Sinclair's "Twelve Principles of EPIC" read like a cross between the opening of the U.S. Declaration of Independence, Henry George's *Progress and Poverty,* and Marx and Engels's *Communist Manifesto:*

1. God created the natural wealth of the earth for the use of all men, not of a few.
2. God created men to seek their own welfare, not that of masters.

From these two a prioris, Sinclair deduces the following two assertions, which echo Edward Bellamy's rationale for industrial democracy under modern economic conditions:

3. Private ownership of tools, a basis of freedom when tools are simple, becomes a basis of enslavement when tools are complex.
4. Autocracy in industry cannot exist alongside democracy in government.

The principles continue through a variety of more focused items, some phrased as socialist adages ("When some men live without working, other men are working without living"), others referencing conditions specific to the 1930s (in point 10, the "destruction of food," then part of the New Deal agricultural policy, is labeled "economic insanity"). They conclude with two points that reframe the industrial aim and political method that Sinclair had articulated as the fundamentals of socialism since *The Jungle:*

11. The remedy is to give the workers access to the means of production, and let them produce for themselves, and not for others.
12. This change can be brought about by action of a majority of the people, and that is the American way.[55]

The last bit about "the American way" may read like political palaver, except that Sinclair like Du Bois had maintained this commitment in the face of intense criticism from their Comintern-affiliated colleagues for some fifteen years. And now he was backing up his words with action by putting himself on the ballot and running an all-out election campaign.

Like Sinclair's overarching rhetoric, the practical details of the EPIC plan were fundamentally socialist. Beginning with the core socialist principle of "production for use, not for profit," which was to become one of the key slogans of the EPIC movement, Sinclair's *I, Governor* proposed that the unemployed of California should work to support themselves in a separate state-sponsored and cooperative economy. Manufacturing as well as agricultural "colonies" were envisioned by Sinclair, both of them engaging in efficient and modern production methods facilitated by up-to-date technology and expert advice, and both being social and economic units complex enough to demand the services of managers, teachers, physicians, and other white-collar and professional workers as well as manual laborers. The farm-colony system, Sinclair explains in *I, Governor,* "will guarantee a living at the outset, and when the colonies have got fairly under way, it will guarantee comfort."[56] Of the factory colonies, he enthuses: "Let us construct a complete industrial system, a new and self-maintaining world for our unemployed, in which they will live, having as few dealings as possible with our present world of speculators and exploiters."[57]

Although Sinclair touted his plan as highly practical, oriented to the "one definite, concrete job" of eliminating poverty, he was equally clear from the outset that he hoped the EPIC colonies would ultimately become the vehicle for the coming of the cooperative commonwealth. This was plain from the inception of the campaign in *I, Governor,* in which Sinclair wrote of the wonderful progress of EPIC and of its new state agencies, the California Authorities for Land, Production, and Money (CAL, CAP, and CAM), within a year of his election:

> The process of EPIC was like that of a swiftly flowing river eating into a sand bank. Private industry began to crumble; and as quickly as any productive enterprise failed, it was made over into a public institution. Nothing could withstand the current of co-operation.
>
> By midsummer [1935], when the new crops began to come in, the system was flourishing. There was food for everybody, and word spread that California was paradise, and all over the United States caravans of automobiles were heading for the Golden State. Nobody worried, because it was known that each of these newcomers would bring a pair of arms and a head.[58]

Even when, late in the campaign, Sinclair sought publicly to reassure middle-class voters by downplaying this revolutionary trajectory of EPIC, Sinclair wrote privately to his socialist colleagues to insist upon it. To his son David, who pleaded with Sinclair to return to the Socialist fold, he responded, "I am still a Socialist and I tell everybody that this is the case and I am limiting myself to a definite program in this emergency. . . . While we are [implementing EPIC] the profit system may continue as best as it can. If our plan succeeds, we will gradually undermine the profit system, as I have explained in the book, but that is a later development."[59]

As a social democratic plan submitted to the voters for their endorsement, EPIC was always as much a political scheme as it was an economic plan. As such, it sought to follow the producerist script written well back in the nineteenth century: the plan to End Poverty in California was meant to appeal broadly to bourgeois as well as proletarian and unemployed Californians. While EPIC's appeal—and lack of appeal—with the middle classes was to become the crux of the fall campaign, the primary race began by mobilizing a core of working-class stalwarts—whether employed, unemployed, or underemployed—and only later proceeded to reach out to the middle classes. Although the most comprehensive study of Sinclair's California campaign, Greg Mitchell's *Campaign of the Century,* claims that EPIC "was not, despite what many thought, a poor people's movement" and cites the number of leaders who were "middle-class and middle-aged," Mitchell's account nevertheless indicates that Sinclair's support in the fall general election campaign was at least evenly divided between the middle and working classes, as he notes that a typical EPIC audience at the Los Angeles Shrine Auditorium in September 1934 "came from every strata of society." Mitchell also observes that "men on relief provided a solid core of workers to distribute campaign literature."[60]

Still less equivocal evidence of EPIC's core working-class constituency emerges from an oral history project conducted in commemoration of the fiftieth anniversary of the movement. Mort Newman, in 1934 an EPIC campaign worker who was otherwise "generally unemployed" had been able to stay off of relief by occasionally working as a helper at a print shop and (pace Mitchell) by selling EPIC literature. His recollection stresses that the supporters drawn to the EPIC campaign first, and the most loyal at the last, were "the unemployed, the needy, who were critical of the social and economic situation as they saw it [and were] not treated seriously by the opposition." Recalling errands Newman ran when he worked for the printer, Newman shows Sinclair's overwhelming support among working-class people as well as the unemployed: Newman had to make deliveries with the boss's car, which had a Merriam sticker on its windshield, many times traveling into "commercial areas or working class areas or in places where the unemployed gathered." Consequently, Newman recalls impishly, "I knew that a car with a Merriam sticker might develop a flat tire very early, or it might even have a rock thrown through a windshield. So as a favor to the owner, I put a Sinclair sticker on top of his Merriam sticker, and the car always came through untouched."[61]

Even as the Communist Party continued to deprecate the NAACP in its Scottsboro publicity, representatives of the party in California relentlessly hammered Sinclair and the EPIC campaign as socialist democratic pretenders. Yet party workers recall that their efforts to undermine the Sinclair campaign were often ambivalent, and that the working-class people they sought to reach were energized by the Sinclair campaign. Fifty years after the campaign in which he ran for state treasurer on the Communist ticket, Archie Brown remained critical of Sinclair's noncommital attitude toward the San Francisco labor disturbances that broke out in the summer of 1934, in which Communist activists were heavily involved and which Governor Frank Merriam, newly ascended to the governor's office, had worked to crush. But he cited the United Front strategy initiated soon thereafter as an implicit acknowledgment that the party had been too "sectarian" in its attitude toward Sinclair.[62] Louise Lambert, a Communist organizer in Los Angeles County in 1934, offered still more startling evidence of the party's postmortem assessment of the EPIC campaign. Lambert reported that at the grass roots Communists worked alongside, and within, the EPIC organization during the campaign, even casting their votes for Sinclair alongside Communist Party candidates lower on the ballot. Still more remarkably, she recalled that Robert Minor of the national party leadership had visited the Sinclair campaign headquarters on the day of the election, where he had "a fantastic eye-opener." In the Sacco and Vanzetti struggle, Minor had been apoplectic when he heard Sinclair was considering the possibility that Sacco was guilty. In the ILD's confrontation with the NAACP, he had been the no-holds-barred author of "The Negro and His Judases." When he met with Communist Party operatives in Los Angeles the day after Sinclair's loss at the polls, however, Lambert found him a "very chastened man":

> He said, now he went to the headquarters there, and as the returns came in, you know, some of the returns were quite significant, and he observed the workers, who were there by the hundreds, thousands. They all turned [out] because they were ready to celebrate. He saw them, and he could, you know, perceive their feelings, which were highly emotional naturally, and when the defeat came, people cried, wept. And then when reporting this to the board, he said, he shook his head and he said, we've made a big mistake, you know—it came on real fast—and he said we've made a big mistake. He said we never addressed ourselves to those people, which was true. He said we didn't *know* them, we didn't *get* to know them.[63]

Sinclair and EPIC, Lambert asserted, *had.* Early on, the Sinclair campaign gained the support of the majority of working-class and poor people, and it never lost that support. They saw the election of Sinclair, whatever the risks of putting an undercover Socialist in office, as far better for their interests than the election of Merriam. The political radicals, whether in one of the socialist parties or outside them, also knew precisely what Sinclair was up to:

among the Communists even then at work among the San Francisco longshoremen, it was called "burrowing from within." The key question among them was not whether Sinclair was a social democrat or a turncoat, but whether he could in fact gain enough middle-class support to bring about social democratic revolution through the Democratic Party.

Sinclair had sought the middle class from the very outset of the campaign, following the long-standing theory and practice of American socialism going back to the prewar Socialist Party, the People's Party, and Nationalism. In *I, Governor of California,* he said forthrightly: "My plan proposes to divide the voters into two classes—those who would benefit by the program and those who would lose by it. The former outnumber the latter ten to one, so it is a question of whether we can get the people to realize their own interests. I seek the votes of all the unemployed; of owners of homes and ranches of less than $3,000 assessed value; of all who would benefit by old age and widows' pensions."[64] Other details of the initial statement of EPIC assured readers that the shift from a profit system to "production for use" would obliterate neither the bourgeois professional and class identities of middle-class people who were unemployed nor the bourgeois aspirations of those who had previously been blue-collar workers. In an echo of Bellamy's labor "army," Sinclair wrote in *I, Governor* that, as a recently inaugurated governor, he would address each governmental appointee "as to the commander of an army."[65] And a commander would need lieutenants. *I, Governor* suggested that they might be some of the very managers now serving in capitalist enterprises; after the collapse of capitalism, Sinclair observes, "There were jobs for all—even for those who had managed capitalist industries, because there was managing to be done in EPIC."[66] Sinclair's supplementary explanation of EPIC entitled *EPIC Answers,* a compilation of Q&A columns originally published in *EPIC News* and published in the summer of 1934, was specifically designed to reassure "small farmers, small merchants, small independent professionals." Farmers were told that EPIC would permit them to exercise their expertise without the need to worry over making mortgage payments. Merchants were told that EPIC would need shopkeepers, accountants, and inventory specialists to mind the community stores. Doctors and teachers would be needed in EPIC, as would clergy, except now they might get somewhere in their trade: "For the first time in history it will be possible to practice the Golden Rule in daily affairs."[67] Sinclair had an answer for virtually every professional except for "capitalists"—stockbrokers, land speculators, factory owners, and a few assorted hangers-on like real estate agents and salesmen, who under EPIC would need to find other, socially productive occupations. Only there did Sinclair draw the line, lest working-class audiences with any pride or radicals with any principle should find Sinclair's social egalitarianism entirely eclipsed in the effort to corral votes.[68]

One of the milestones in the EPIC campaign came in May 1934 when Sheridan Downey dropped out of the race for the gubernatorial nomination and chose instead to run for lieutenant governor as Sinclair's running mate. That an ambitious, professional politician would not only concede to Sinclair but join his campaign as a subaltern helped to legitimate EPIC. Downey, a district attorney in Wyoming at age twenty-two, had worked more recently as a lawyer in Sacramento, served on a senate-appointed committee investigating corruption in Republican governor Rolph's administration, and published two books that showed ideological congruence with Sinclair's views, *The Coming Crisis* and *Forward America.*[69] But Downey had joined forces with Sinclair only after considerable behind-the-scenes negotiation, which resulted in a campaign that became more conventional in substance as well as style. Just the presence of Downey as a running mate (which wags immediately dubbed the "Uppie-Downey" ticket) encouraged Sinclair to imagine that he might actually win, and therefore prompted a realistic assessment of what they could and could not do if actually called upon to govern. So long as he was in the realm of utopian fiction, he could freely postulate that bonds would be sold, farms and factories bought or rented, and the unemployed be put to productive and self-sustaining labor. But Downey pointed out the implausibility of selling bonds to capitalist financiers that Sinclair proposed in the long haul to render redundant. He also told Sinclair that the state's books wouldn't balance if he implemented all of his tax-cutting proposals at once: in particular, he mentioned that teachers could not be paid their salaries without the help of the sales tax.[70] *Immediate EPIC,* published after Sinclair's nomination to spell out the initial steps to be taken if he were elected, included several elements representing a scaling back of the ambitious plans articulated in *I, Governor.* Sinclair was forced to concede, for instance: "The clever politicians have fixed it so that the school teachers are dependent upon the sales tax for their salaries. . . . We will not repeal the sales tax until we have found another way to get the money. We may have to start by repealing the sales tax on food."[71]

A good many of Sinclair's most ardent supporters were disappointed at the shift toward pragmatism. Mort Newman lamented fifty years later that EPIC as it evolved through the course of the campaign was "not really" socialist but a program of "reform." Still, EPIC never asked for middle-class votes except with the expectation that, in voting for EPIC, they would not only be pursuing their own best self-interest but also allying themselves with the interests of the working classes and the poor. At the high point of EPIC fortunes, in his radio addresses just before and just after the primary election, Sinclair's message powerfully meshed a utopian appeal, retaining the socialist division between the exploited and the exploiters, with a realist assertion, insisting upon the practicality of the EPIC program. Sinclair wondered, why could the highly educated people in charge of California business and regular politics not see the practicality of putting the unemployed to work in "self-sustaining . . . productive labor"? Why, indeed, did "the whole power of vested privilege [rise] up against it?"

> The answer is: because they are afraid of the precedent. They are afraid the plan will succeed, and show the unemployed how to produce for use instead of for profit. It will put into the minds of the unemployed the idea of getting access to land and machinery by the political method, by the use of their ballots. And if they once get access to good land and modern machinery they will produce so much, they will make such comfort and plenty for themselves, that they will never again be content to support the parasites of Wall Street.[72]

The class war remains the central framework for Sinclair's political vision, even as the evolving particulars of the EPIC plan had come to make various practical allowances for industrial discipline, labor specialization, tax policy, and federal-state cooperation. Whatever their rank or class pretensions, voters who cast their ballots for Sinclair were allying themselves with the unemployed and against the "parasites" of capitalist industry and politics-as-usual.

The verdict among Democratic primary voters was emphatically for class warfare: for giving government by Sinclair and EPIC-pledged candidates a chance. In the August primary, Sinclair won a vote of 436,000, beating his seven Democratic rivals by a plurality of some 40,000. Sinclair's prospects for the November general election looked good not only because he won an overwhelming endorsement within the Democratic Party, but because new voter registrations garnered largely through the EPIC movement had brought the party into the majority for the first time, with 330,000 new voters pushing the Democratic registration to 1,494,000, slightly exceeding the Republican figure of 1,419,000. The rising tide of Democratic voters was also reflected in the numbers of ballots cast in the primaries: 832,000 on the Democratic side as compared with 814,000 on the Republican, with sitting governor Merriam winning the Republican nomination by gaining a plurality of 346,000 votes in the four-candidate race.[73] After his victory, Sinclair headed east to pay visits in Washington, DC, New York City, and at Franklin D. Roosevelt's upstate country home in Hyde Park. The trip took the character both of a victory lap and of an opening parley between the soon-to-be social democratic governor of California and the reigning captains of U.S. economic and political power.

CAMPAIGNS, INC., AND THE UNMAKING OF A SOCIAL DEMOCRATIC MAJORITY

> "It is impossible that the voters will elect a man who has written that!"

The EPIC campaign, I have suggested, was built upon Upton Sinclair's labors as an author and socialist. In the primary race, especially, Sinclair's credibility built up over years of prophetic witness against the evils of capitalism suddenly paid off. In the general election, however, Sinclair's long-accrued assets as a socialist writer were still more suddenly turned against him. To be associated with socialism while Bolshevism continued to seem a menace, to have critiqued conventional religion, American education, patriotism, journalism, and literature as ideological apologists for capitalism, and to have done so repeatedly over the years in numerous published books—these were assets just too rich to place into the hands of skilled political adversaries. If the Republican candidate and sitting governor Frank Merriam was not a particularly effective campaigner,[74] there were others, including many in the film industry and a key pair of political entrepreneurs in the fledgling political-consulting business, who knew all too well both a class-enemy to their power and the means to destroy him as a political candidate. Consequently, too, Sinclair's victory lap following the primary turned out to be politically disastrous as well as premature, for Sinclair's hubris and his equivocal reception by the powers-that-be and particularly by the president were swiftly turned against the Democratic nominee.

That Sinclair had garnered a large number of votes from the ranks of the middle classes and poor as well as the working classes and unemployed could not be denied. During the short eight-week general election season, it was the task of the Republican Party and its allies to drive a wedge between these voting blocs; they sought, quite simply, to affirm once again the interests of the bourgeois and the employed with the wealthy and powerful. While the sitting but unelected Republican governor, Frank Merriam, was a notably lackluster campaigner (he had ascended to the office just that summer, after the sudden death of governor James Rolph), a host of Republican activists resolved to make up for their candidate's liabilities by rhetorical ingenuity and relentless attacks upon the recent socialist Upton Sinclair. Leading the charge were Clem Whitaker and Leone Baxter, who were just starting up their political consulting business, Campaigns, Inc., and saw in the Sinclair candidacy a ripe opportunity for making their reputation. It took Whitaker and Baxter little more than a long weekend of reading in early September, skimming through Sinclair's life works and compiling a card catalog of quotes, to amass enough material to illustrate scores of inflammatory pamphlets and fill the front pages of California newspapers for the rest of the autumn. Other Republicans throughout the state got much the same idea, Greg Mitchell notes. Charles Teague, the biggest citrus grower in the state, headed up the fund-raising campaign against Sinclair among big business owners in Southern California, forming a front organization called the United for California League to collect their donations and retaining an ad agency with instructions to comb through Sinclair's works for damaging quotes. The arch-conservative *Los Angeles Times* editorial staff was soon also poring over Sinclair's novels and nonfiction, an endeavor assisted by an anonymous man who showed up one day at the *Times* with a file box crammed with quotations transcribed on index cards.[75] Within a few weeks of Sinclair's nomination, the United for California League and another group based in northern California called the California League Against Sinclairism—the primary client of Whitaker and Baxter—were churning out pamphlets condemning the longtime Socialist and author by his own words. One or another of them, and in some cases practically all of them, were sent to every Californian with a mailing address.[76]

The *Los Angeles Times* put its Sinclair quotes to extensive use as well. From September 22 to election day, the *Times* featured a quote-a-day placed prominently in a text box, typically somewhere on the bottom of the front page. When the first of the quotations appeared shortly after the conclusion of the state Democratic convention, Sinclair supporters were sanguine. Had not Sinclair, their author-politician-savior, predicted incendiary attacks against his campaign in *I, Governor of California,* and had not the candidate in the novel nevertheless won in a landslide? But Sinclair the real-life candidate had a quite different reaction: "It is impossible that the voters will elect a man who has written that!"[77] Mostly the quotations avoided the topic of economics: only six of the boxed quotes in the *Times* presented Sinclair's views on this topic, as compared to twenty-six on religion, education, the professions, and sundry other topics. In the midst of the Depression, the editors of the *Times* as well as the politicos at Campaigns, Inc., and United for California apparently judged it to be far less expeditious to argue economics with a socialist than to change the subject and focus instead on the socialist's unconventional social mores. *The Profits of Religion,* published by Sinclair in 1918, proved to be a particularly rich lode, providing material for text boxes and pamphlets that revealed Sinclair attacking the Catholic Church, Christian Science, and the Seventh-Day Adventists as well as Christianity in general.[78] There were many damning sources in the Sinclair oeuvre, though: judged by how often they were quoted, most useful were the semiautobiographical *Love's Pilgrimage,* the fictional *100% The Story of a Patriot,* and the books of the Dead Hand series. Sinclair had said vicious things about the "A.E.F., the R.O.T.C. and the Boy Scouts" as well as the "University of California *and* U.C.L.A.," which he had called "The University of the Black Hand." Sinclair was not only a "Dynamiter of All Churches and All Christian Institutions" but also an "Active Official of Communist Organizations," and "the Man Who Said the P.T.A. Has Been Taken Over by the Black Hand." Finally, Sinclair had disparaged "the Home, the Institution of Marriage *and* Advocate[d] Free Love."[79]

On those relatively infrequent occasions on which the *Times* or the anti-Sinclair organizations treated economic issues, their publications were at least as revealing about capitalist ideology as they were about Sinclair's plans for the governorship. In a pamphlet entitled "What Sinclair's Epic Means to You" representing the views of the "Young Liberal League"—affiliated with the California League Against Sinclairism and hence another conduit for Whitaker and Baxter[80]—the arguments were founded upon two competing and indeed contradicting logics about the workings of capitalism. Neither was particularly flattering about capitalism, but both asserted, sometimes with alarming nakedness, that there was nothing anybody of modest means could do to change it.

On the one hand, Californians were told that capitalism reflected fundamental laws of economics; to tamper with these laws as EPIC hazarded to do, the pamphlet explained, was either altogether impossible or would wreak utter ruin upon the state's economy. This was the explanation negating those provisions of EPIC that sought to extend the social safety net—beneficent measures offering pensions for the elderly, the disabled, and widowed women with children. Calculating that perhaps half of the state's population aged over sixty would be classified as needy—286,853 people—the pamphleteers estimate that pensions for the elderly would cost the state $14,300,000 per month. "Where is Sinclair going to get the money?" they implore. "There just isn't that much money." To counter EPIC property tax proposals, the Young Liberal League simply assumes the financial necessity (and right) of property owners to profit from their holdings; any government effort seeking to tap into their profits will inevitably fail and automatically result in higher costs for consumers, in this case renters: "Remember, the landlord simply passes his costs on—the tenant pays."[81] Another bit of folk wisdom turned to political use by Baxter and Whitaker further reveals their—and the culture's—capitalist mind-set. "You cannot create employment by destroying employers," their pamphlet assures us, as if the divide between bourgeois and proletarian was the permanent condition of human relations.[82]

On the other hand, Campaigns, Inc., proclaimed the autonomy of businesspeople to evade government control and even wreak havoc upon the economy, if they chose to do so in response to unfriendly government policies. Arguments of this latter kind implicitly undercut the former, for if capitalists had such choices in their financial arrangements, then clearly capitalism was a human-made system rather than simply the economic expression of natural laws. But logic did not particularly matter here. The critical issue was one of power—the power that wealthy individuals and corporations wielded over their fellow citizens regardless of populist uprisings or progressive reforms. Plans to fund CAL and CAP were utterly infeasible, for no business would either buy EPIC bonds or even wish to do business in a state committed to their demise: "Scores of big national organizations would immediately close their branch factories in California and suspend all operations. . . . Will any insurance company, any bank, any private individual, who has money, willingly commit financial suicide by buying such bonds?" Another tax provision in EPIC, a steeply graduated state income tax, would of course be evaded by the wealthy, the wordsmiths of Campaigns, Inc., explained; anyone with riches would simply establish their legal residences elsewhere: "Any man with money, that wouldn't do just that, would be crazy, and their lawyers already are telling them just what to do and how to do it. Seriously," the pamphleteers ask conspiratorially, "wouldn't you do the same thing?"[83]

Ultimately, Campaigns, Inc., and other political actors seeking to turn the electorate against Sinclair and EPIC shared this aim: by all necessary means, to encourage Californians of middling class status to identify their aspirations, interests, and views with those of their social and class betters. The Republican appeal certainly did not promise any class leveling between the middle classes and their superiors able to retain tax lawyers, but it nevertheless could succeed by a combination of flattery and threat: flattery that the middling people understood the point of view of the well-heeled; threat that they could just as easily slip into the undifferentiated and ugly mass of the working class and the unemployed. The crowning achievements in this vein were certainly the anti-Sinclair productions of the film industry, whose film shorts (shown between the reels of feature films throughout the fall) could project and validate social fears through a series of images in which the mere association of the Republican administration with respectable, well-groomed citizens, and the Democratic-Socialist contender with shiftless, unkempt migrants, could swing voters toward the former and away from the latter. Beginning in September, California moviegoers were treated to film shorts in which a roving reporter, professing objectivity, conducted a series of brief interviews with actual voters. These *were* bona fide California citizens, but the particular vignettes were carefully selected and edited. Merriam supporters not only formed the clear majority in the films; they also were far better groomed and well spoken, offering various complete-sentence answers about how Merriam was an experienced and reliable officeholder, Sinclair an unpracticed and dangerous huckster. Still more damning were Sinclair's supporters: most were poorly dressed, several spoke in marked nonstandard dialects, and virtually none could offer anything by way of a coherent reason for voting for Sinclair. The most spectacularly damaging of the would-be Sinclair voters—who was seated on the ground and filmed from a high camera angle, as if too lazy or shifty to get up and meet the cameraman eye to eye—explained calmly that Sinclair wished to import the Russian economic model to the United States and commented, "I think that has worked out pretty well for them."[84]

As with the publications of the anti-Sinclair leagues, the most damaging materials were those that took some of Sinclair's more unguarded and utopian pronouncements and treated them as if they amounted to certainties if Sinclair were elected. In *I, Governor,* Sinclair had announced that production for use would transform class divisions and abolish deeply ingrained fears of the revolutionary rabble, so that Californians of all classes would actually welcome the workers who would flock to the state to take part in the new economic system. As Sinclair came to envision the enmeshment of EPIC within the New Deal, prompted by his running mate Downey, he came to believe that the "new system" of production for use must, of necessity, become a federal as well as state program. Consequently, after his apparently successful meetings with Roosevelt at Hyde Park and with members of his administration in Washington, Sinclair announced upon his return to California, "I told Harry Hopkins," head of the Federal Emergency Relief Administration, "that if I am elected half the unemployed of the United States will come to California, and he will have to make plans to take care of them."[85] To the extent the remark was meant seriously at all, it was meant to reflect the virtues of the coming change in political economy, resulting in the greater attractiveness of the state for would-be citizens, and the support of the federal government for that change. But in the newspapers this latest prediction of the future governor took a sinister turn: a Sinclair election would mean a flood of new bums. And the newspapers were only the beginning of Sinclair's trouble. Hiring film extras to pose as hoboes, splicing in scenes from the recently released *Wild Boys of the Road,* MGM produced what the studio purported to be a newsreel showing the arrival of the hordes of ne'er-do-wells whom Sinclair had invited to the state by his offer of openhanded public charity.[86]

It was fantasy fiction, and yet its images provided visual evidence that seemed beyond doubt. Thus did the prospect of Sinclair's election and the certainty of social chaos become melded together, as the most loathed and frightful images of the poor and unemployed became linked, in moving pictures, to EPIC and the Sinclair campaign. Much as Sinclair had argued for the inclusion—even the special place—of the middle classes in EPIC, this was imagery that struck at the heart of bourgeois fears of class insecurity. In the newsreels' representations, the unemployed masses appeared poised to take possession of the state as well as flouting bourgeois restraints of decorum. The poor and the unemployed were already painfully in evidence in California; what if they were actually to be empowered? That was what Sinclair had, in fact, promised; the imaginative work of the newsreels was simply to offer the least generous interpretation of the promise, appealing to the greed and class jealousy of the middle classes where Sinclair had appealed to their more generous impulses.

The EPIC campaign's coup de grâce came from the national leader of the Democratic Party, President Roosevelt himself. Through the summer and fall, Sinclair's claims about the similarity of EPIC to the New Deal had become a principal political strategy for claiming the mainstream, bourgeois credentials of the insurgency. On July 23, a banner appearing above the *EPIC News* masthead had gone so far as to proclaim: "Roosevelt Starts EPIC Plan for U.S."[87] But this assertion, heartily endorsed by Sinclair's running mate Downey, also made EPIC increasingly dependent upon the favor of the president. All seemed well when Sinclair visited Hyde Park and the scheduled half-hour meeting, supposedly a strictly personal and apolitical call, went on for nearly two hours. Sinclair also took a triumphant turn around Washington, DC, including a speaking appearance at the National Press Club and visits with various administration officials including Rex Tugwell at the Department of Agriculture, Harold Ickes at the Department of Interior, Hopkins at the Federal Emergency Relief Administration, and Henry Morgenthau at the Department of Treasury (except for Morgenthau, the arch-liberals of the administration).[88] Afterward, Sinclair made a radio appearance in New York City in which he recapped his friendly conversations with the president and his lieutenants. Sinclair's report about what the government thought and the president knew implied that they, not he, were on the cutting edge of EPIC: "I was egotistical enough to think that I might teach him something, and I started out several times on what I thought were important ideas, but I found that he knew about them and had talked them over with others."[89]

At the meeting at Hyde Park, Sinclair even believed he had received a pledge from Roosevelt that later in the fall, in one of his nationally broadcast speeches, the president would declare in favor of "production for use." Sinclair let it be known among EPIC activists that the president had told him that on or around October 25 Roosevelt would give a fireside chat at which he would discuss unemployment and endorse the concept of production for use.[90] Then, speaking to the San Francisco League of Women Voters on the afternoon of October 23, Sinclair let on before this audience replete with reporters that he expected a Roosevelt endorsement that very evening. By this time the blizzard of pamphlets, the inflammatory quotation boxes in the *Times,* the noxious newsreels, and the almost universally negative newspaper coverage by the state's newspapers had taken their toll upon Sinclair and the campaign. The situation was strikingly similar to that faced by W. E. B. Du Bois roughly half a year earlier, when erstwhile allies as well as powerful foes beleaguered the *Crisis* editor. Sinclair's response invites some of the same metaphors used to describe Du Bois's. Like Du Bois, Sinclair was like a punch-drunk fighter on the ropes, looking to land a wild haymaker for a knockout before collapsing to the canvas. Almost immediately—before the Roosevelt radio address—Sinclair's prediction regarding that night's fireside chat was published in San Francisco newspapers and relayed to the White House for their comment: No, White House officials replied, the president would not be endorsing Sinclair. Back in California, Sinclair and his supporters listened for the president's discussion of persons on relief "producing what they themselves will consume" in vain; what the nation got, instead, was a homily on public charity, in a fireside chat conspicuously shorter than the norm.[91] Sinclair and his supporters were stunned. Lacking Roosevelt's imprimatur of liberal respectability, Sinclair's defeat was from that point practically a foregone conclusion. The fortunes of the California Democratic Party, on the rise in August, were reversed in just ten weeks. Merriam won with 1,138,000 votes, Sinclair was second with 879,000, and Commonwealth Party candidate Raymond Haight, who had run fourth in the Republican primary (with just 84,000 votes), made a respectable third-place showing with 302,000 tallies.

The election over, Sinclair soon returned both to writing as his full-time occupation and to seeing the political world as sharply bifurcated: the enlightened socialist minority versus the clueless capitalist majority. After going into seclusion for a month of writing-therapy and emerging with a new book in hand, *I, Candidate for Governor, and How I Got Licked,* Sinclair redrew the boundary between EPIC and the New Deal, between true social democracy and mere liberalism, the latter being little better than the more straightforwardly procapitalist and inept policies of Hoover: "With no personal bitterness whatever, I tell [Roosevelt] that he cannot go on much longer traveling on two divergent paths. He has to choose between EPIC and Hoover."[92] Sinclair's retreat from collaboration with the liberals took on much the same character as Du Bois's good-riddance of the NAACP. The similarity would grow in the coming years, when first Sinclair sought to transform his campaign to End Poverty in California into a still more grandiose project to End Poverty in Civilization and then, in 1936, when he preferred to dismantle the EPIC organization to prevent its takeover by Communist activists.[93]

Yet at its best, EPIC had succeeded in uniting activists across the liberal-to-radical spectrum even as it had built bridges between working-class and middle-class Californians. Communist fellow-traveler Langston Hughes, just returned in 1933 from his trip to the Soviet Union and residing in northern California, had been too busy to accept W. E. B. Du Bois's invitation to travel east and add his prestige to the social democratic majority at the Amenia conference. In the summer of 1934 he was still in California, collaborating with the Communist writer Ella Winter on a play about the recent agricultural workers' strike there. Hughes did not take an active role in Sinclair's campaign for the governorship, perhaps reflecting the fact that Sinclair's campaign (like Debs's campaigns of the previous generation) did not take any particular notice of the rights of racial minorities. Hughes's sympathies were clear, however, in a September 19 letter to Amy Spingarn updating her on his recent activities: "The Upton Sinclair campaign out here is exciting, too. I hope he wins. His opponents are so terribly reactionary and intollerant [*sic*]. The police and vigilante brutality and intimidation in California these last few months is unbelievable."[94] Unlike Bob Minor, who had led the denunciation of the NAACP and would soon come west to participate in the Communist campaign denouncing Sinclair, Hughes understood from the first how to tell a social fascist from a social democrat. We also might observe, despite Sinclair's postelection pronouncements, that Roosevelt was no Hoover. The changes coming in the national political economy would bring about a historic and social democratic adjustment such as Sinclair and other socialists had long been working for—however reluctant they or New Deal liberals were to admit it.

CHAPTER NINE

READING *THE JUNGLE* AT BREAKFAST: THE NEW DEAL AND OTHER SOCIAL DEMOCRATIC LEGACIES

It is just the kind of story that the politically savvy president might have entirely fabricated, when Roosevelt met with Upton Sinclair a few days after he had won the Democratic gubernatorial nomination of California in a landslide. Yet Franklin Delano Roosevelt's improbable yarn about his mother reading from *The Jungle* at table and spoiling his breakfast may, in fact, be true. Although Roosevelt was twenty-four and in his first year of marriage to Eleanor when *The Jungle* appeared in 1906, Roosevelt's mother lived within a few blocks of the newly wedded couple and was infamously involved in their daily affairs. In an ambitious and publicly spirited household such as theirs, she might well have prescribed Sinclair's sensational exposé as breakfast reading, especially as it touched the fortunes of the Theodore Roosevelt administration with which both Franklin and Eleanor had family ties. At their wedding, "Uncle Ted" had walked Eleanor down the aisle.[1] In any case, in September 1934 Roosevelt needed to encourage Sinclair's belief that he was entirely in accord with the Sinclair candidacy; he did not want trouble with someone who was very possibly going to be the next governor of California. But he also knew how uncertain the election of Sinclair remained—Sinclair had, after all, been a registered Socialist a year earlier and, as we have seen, his plan to End Poverty In California continued to bear the socialist stamp. To be associated too closely with Sinclair—especially if he lost, but even perhaps if he won—would be politically risky. Hence, a story in which Roosevelt connected himself to Sinclair's literary celebrity in 1906 as opposed to his candidacy in 1934 established just the right distance. When Sinclair repeated the story to the press, as he predictably did within a few hours of the meeting with Roosevelt,[2] the press and the public learned only that the president had had just about the same squeamish response to *The Jungle* as practically every other reader in 1906. But such a story recounting the reading of a novel almost three decades earlier could hardly be construed as an endorsement of the present-day Democrat and candidate.

Whether true or invented, though, the story also suggests Roosevelt's conversance with socialism—his awareness of the movement, his acknowledgment of the place of the socialist critique in American culture. In short, it hints at the subterranean persistence and the gradual emergence of socialist ideals and programs in American politics. If Roosevelt could not directly associate with Sinclair's long-standing effort to overturn the profit system, the popularity of Sinclair's candidacy, along with the economic crisis within American capitalism, could help to provide the impetus necessary for Roosevelt's New Deal to challenge and change important elements of that system. Yet Sinclair, together with other American socialists, shaped the New Deal not only as outside political levers. They also helped to identify *which* elements of the system to change, and how. They had helped to define New Deal ideology and rhetoric from the inside and long before it had crystalized as the New Deal. Even as Sinclair was discarded as a person unsuitable for public office, the rhetoric and programs that he and other socialists had long been advocating were adopted and in part implemented by Roosevelt and his political associates. Roosevelt could say little more about his affinity with Sinclair than that *The Jungle* had once spoiled his breakfast. The New Deal's social democratic elements make apparent, however, that Roosevelt and his deputies understood and assimilated the social ends and means advocated by Sinclair and other socialists of the Second Internationale—whether or not Roosevelt could recall the particulars of *The Jungle's* polemical ending as well as the parts about rat feces and human flesh being processed as canned food.

To assess the degree of the cultural assimilation and implementation of social democratic ideals and practices in the era of the New Deal, I will begin with the immediate and demonstrable effects that the EPIC campaign had upon California politics and then proceed to the more equivocal and yet definite influence that socialism exerted upon the New Deal itself. Because, though, that influence was far from complete and the aims of the New Deal itself were but incompletely realized, I will also address some of those legacies of late nineteenth- and early twentieth-century American socialism that had to be pursued outside the transformations taking place in the federal government. Finally, I will turn to legacies of the American socialist tradition that must especially be fought for in our own day, both because they have been neglected and because they may lie within hope of realization.

NEW DEAL FOR CALIFORNIA, EPIC FOR THE NATION

> "The test of our progress is not whether we add more to the abundance of those who have much; it is whether we provide enough for those who have too little."

The influence of EPIC is easy enough to trace within California politics. While soon after the 1934 election the EPIC organization was caught up in internecine battles between social democrats and Communists, the EPIC legislators that *had* been elected went to Sacramento and went to work. Senator Culbert Olson, newly elected from the Los Angeles senatorial district that was the most populous of any in the state, took the lead in systematically introducing legislation corresponding to the planks of the EPIC platform, in versions roughly corresponding to the revised EPIC plan that Sinclair had described in the summer of 1934 in *Immediate EPIC:* reduction of the state sales tax; institution of a graduated state income tax, an estate tax, a state business tax, and a tax on large tracts of undeveloped land; creation of pension programs for the elderly, for the disabled and the blind, and for widows with dependent children; and, finally, state funding for self-help cooperatives. One by one these were reported out of committee, sometimes recommended, sometimes not, and all were either voted down or left to die on the Senate floor—except, that is, for the bill providing funding for the cooperatives, which was approved and signed by Governor Merriam. It was, of course, poignantly ironic that state support for co-ops, meant by Sinclair to be the entering wedge for socialism, was the one piece of EPIC legislation that was signed into law during the annus mirabilis projected in *I, Governor*—and by a formerly reactionary governor. What had meant the coming of Bolshevism if Sinclair had been elected was simply another pragmatic measure for dealing with the Depression in Merriam's administration. This was, however, of a piece with the New Deal conversion of Frank Merriam that the EPIC campaign had helped miraculously to effect. As historian James Gregory points out, Merriam infuriated conservatives in his own party by cooperating extensively on the introduction of New Deal programs in public relief and new taxes.[3]

EPIC also helped open the road for progressives throughout California politics. Former EPIC activists and voter registrants were at the forefront of

Culbert Olson's successful quest to unseat Merriam in 1938—and staged public demonstrations, ultimately also successful, pressuring newly elected governor Olson to stick by his campaign pledge to pardon Tom Mooney, a direct holdover from Sinclair's EPIC campaign promises. Olson's successor, three-term Republican governor Earl Warren, had advised Merriam to reinvent himself in mid-1934 as a pro–New Deal progressive—and Warren, of course, subsequently led the most liberal, activist phase in U.S. Supreme Court history. Another future governor got his start in the 1934 campaign as well: future Democratic governor Edmund "Pat" Brown had been active in the Republican-Progressive campaign of third-place finisher Raymond Haight, whom Sinclair justly described as having split the liberal vote with him and denied Merriam a majority victory. Even losing candidates from the EPIC ranks went on to win public office, support liberal causes, and help in the implementation of the New Deal. Sinclair's running mate, Sheridan Downey, became a two-term U.S. senator from California. Jerry Voorhis, who in 1934 ran and lost as an EPIC candidate in a safe Republican house district, went on to become a U.S. representative from 1937 to 1951 and a lifelong champion of and expert on producer cooperatives.[4]

Gregory observes that both parties were deeply factionalized after 1934: Olson's governorship was in large measure thwarted by the combination of old-fashioned machine Democrats with conservative Republicans, and the party of Earl Warren also gave plenty of latitude for Richard Nixon and Ronald Reagan.[5] The red-baiting tactic used to devastating effect on Sinclair—and exposed relentlessly in *I, Candidate*—would continue to work, some of the time: it backfired in the Merriam campaign against Olson in 1938, but it succeeded when an upstart Republican named Richard Nixon used it to bring down Voorhis, like Sinclair a former socialist, in 1950. But the crucial point, also acknowledged by Gregory, is that Sinclair and EPIC, in combination with FDR and the New Deal, made possible these liberal factions as vigorous caucuses, even if it did not secure the means for them to hold power single-handedly or continuously. Within the Democratic Party, the liberal faction went from being small and ineffectual to being the largest and most powerful bloc, and indeed one of the largest and most powerful forces within the national Democratic Party to this day. This political reality, which today seems self-evident and inevitable, can be traced directly to the EPIC campaign, which, even as it transformed the state Democratic Party into a much more radical and activist organization, had the distinction of recruiting enough new members to bring the party into the majority in the state, a position that it then enjoyed for the first time and it has not yet relinquished.

The influence of EPIC nationally is somewhat more a matter of conjecture and debate. Writing in 1933 in *I, Governor,* Sinclair had announced an ideological kinship between his plans and the president's as well as his intention to exert a further radicalizing influence upon Roosevelt: "I have watched with satisfaction a new birth of the Democratic principle under the leadership of Franklin D. Roosevelt. He has barely got started on his journey, but he is headed in the right direction, towards a government control of business and industry—and I am shoving!"[6] Certainly a prima facie case for Sinclair's success in "shoving" may be built from his subsequent primary victory, his reception at Hyde Park and among the New Dealers, and even the liberalizing pull of the EPIC campaign upon the Merriam administration. And then there is the tantalizing fact that Sinclair's near-miss in the off-year elections came just as several of the more ambitious, socialistic provisions of the first New Deal were being ruled unconstitutional and Roosevelt was preparing a push for the passage of a second round of legislation, the "second New Deal" whose enactments proved to be just as radical and, because more durable, much more revolutionary. Was there some connection between EPIC and the second New Deal that went beyond historical contiguity?

Absolutely so—argues Arthur M. Schlesinger, Jr., in his monumental history of the New Deal. Schlesinger singles out EPIC as foremost among several protest movements that constituted a "Politics of Upheaval" early in the Roosevelt administration: specifically, "The EPIC campaign . . . left behind a ferment of local radicalism not unlike that stirred by Floyd Olson and the La Follettes—a new popular militancy, fairly loyal to Roosevelt and the Democratic party but constituting a leftward pressure on the New Deal. . . . committed to a thesis of American exceptionalism and sharply opposed to the Communists."[7] For Schlesinger, the sharp antinomy on the progressive-socialist spectrum lies not between socialism and liberalism, but between the Communists and everyone else on the left, for the more radical "popular militancy" largely complements New Deal progressivism, to the point of preserving American uniqueness.

Current historian David Kennedy reasserts the divide between the socialists and New Deal progressives—to the detriment of the former and credit of the latter. Kennedy's Pulitzer Prize–winning *Freedom from Fear* groups EPIC with still more unconventional and unstable movements that Americans were wise to reject: the Townsend revolving pension plan, the Share Our Wealth platform of Huey Long, and the anti–Wall Street crusade of Father Charles Coughlin.[8] Kennedy dismisses the insurgent movements as threatening "financial soundness and political prudence" and distances the

New Deal from their political-economic schemes, arguing that Roosevelt was not "stealing their thunder" when he had "stocked his own legislative arsenal with thunder enough."[9] Yet even Kennedy's own account of the relation between the New Deal and more radical insurgent movements implies the dependence of the former upon the latter. In particular, Kennedy's conclusion about the second phase of the New Deal suggests that Roosevelt was taking precisely the classic position of the conservative reformer, and therefore his initiatives were by no means independent of more radical movements. "It was a mark of Roosevelt's reflexive political genius," Kennedy concludes, "that instead of simply bending with the pressure from his left, he capitalized on it. He could now credibly argue to conservative stand-patters that his own program, radical enough by any objective standard, was a prudent bulwark against the irresponsible radicalism of the demagogues."[10] Roosevelt, being the president, could and would ultimately take credit for the landmark New Deal legislation; but in spite of Kennedy's own characterization, his account makes clear the president's political and ideological relation to a threat still further to the left of his agenda, which not only warranted his "reflexive" progressive response but actually made his "radical" remedies look safe and sane in comparison.

Painful as it was to acknowledge after the EPIC campaign that elements of social democracy might be advanced by the New Deal *because* of Roosevelt's repudiation of Sinclair and his movement, Sinclair could gain some satisfaction from having predicted, way back in 1907, this kind of politically constructive rejection. In *The Industrial Republic,* he had imagined the Socialist Party would play a vital role "as a party of the last resort, a club held over Society," creating the conditions for a popular political groundswell bringing the Democratic Party into office and then demanding action.[11] Practically speaking, this is precisely what Roosevelt was doing when he steered a course between Republicanism and "wild radicalism," which in his first inaugural he had presented as having more in common with one another than either had with liberalism.[12] Moreover, Roosevelt's political-economic *via media* was charting the path that Sinclair and other socialists had envisaged for *their* movement. Sinclair's EPIC campaign, with its "one definite, concrete job" and his refusal to be pinned down by radical labels (even *socialist* and *socialism*), had itself been a manifestation of the search for a middle way. American socialism particularly of the Second Internationale had likewise been about finding the middle course between sudden, violent revolution and status quo law and order.

But Sinclair and other socialists provided far more than a political catalyst for progressive reforms implemented by other parties. The ideas and programs for those reforms had been originated by *them* and then, after the fact, adopted by the other parties. This, too, they themselves saw and announced. Sinclair wrote in *I, Governor,* "Nearly thirty years ago I founded an organization, the League of Industrial Democracy, which has had wide influence in American colleges, and helped to train those minds which now constitute the so-called 'brain trust' in Washington. These men [and women], whether they know it or not, are the children of my thought."[13] One close observer of the 1934 election, screenwriter Rob Wagner, noted just this metaphor of intellectual parentage in the general formulation of Socialist Party leader Job Harriman: "Our job is to father socialistic ideas, leave then on the door-steps of the other fellows for adoption." Writing in March 1934, Wagner wove the trope into his own piece asserting that the transmigration of socialist ideas into the Roosevelt administration was well under way before the EPIC campaign gained national notice: "this particular baby, 'I, Governor of California,' was so attractive to the Democratic door-step-takers-in that they began to yip louder and louder for his father. They felt that the baby would make a swell companion for the innumerable pink babies—some of 'em pretty red!—that had been taken into the White House."[14]

The case I am building that socialist ideas were influential within the Roosevelt White House and among New Deal legislation must necessarily be a circumstantial one. After all, neither Roosevelt nor the other principal New Dealers left a bibliography of their sources. Yet—to extend further the investigative metaphor I am here adopting—we may observe that all of the key elements making a case for the socialist provenance of the New Deal are clear: motive, opportunity, means.

The Great Depression itself provided the strongest motive possible for seeking government intervention and hence a widened degree of governmental control in the productive activity of the nation. The impetus for making relatively more overt, socialistic, and socialist interventions into the economy may be found in Roosevelt's political credo of doing something, anything, to deal with the crisis—in counterpoint to his predecessor Hoover's wish to follow economic orthodoxy and let the economy heal itself. Here, Alan Brinkley suggests, was Roosevelt's core philosophy: "Take a method and try it. If it fails, admit it frankly and try another. But above all, try something."[15] Roosevelt himself was quite conscious that his openness to experimentation meant receptivity to any number of heterodox economic and political options, including the EPIC plans being floated in the California gubernatorial campaign. Explaining to Secretary of Labor Frances Perkins why he did not repudiate Sinclair publicly, Roosevelt opined: "Perhaps they'll get EPIC in California. . . . The beauty of our state-federal system is that the people can experiment. If it has fatal consequences in one place, it has little effect upon the rest of the country. If a new, apparently fanatical program works well, it will be copied. If it doesn't, you won't hear of it again."[16]

Still, the *opportunity* for socialist political-economic strategies to become known and preferred in the White House lies only secondarily in the EPIC campaign and other insurgent movements of the 1930s, by which time the ideas and even the specific plans of Roosevelt and his brains trust were already largely formed (and any socialistic influence from outside political sources might be plausibly denied). The greater opportunity for social democracy to become known and embraced by Roosevelt and his administration came earlier, in the mixed socialist and progressive milieu of the pre–World War I era and even stretching back into the nineteenth century. At least four individuals in Roosevelt's inner circle had been schooled in the Social Gospel movement, even according to David Kennedy, a somewhat hostile witness for the socialist case: Roosevelt speechwriter and original Brains Truster Adolf Berle; federal relief administrator Harry Hopkins; Treasury secretary Henry Morgenghau, Jr.; and Labor secretary Perkins.[17] The settlement house work in which Eleanor Roosevelt was involved, and with which she famously acquainted her husband-to-be, was also an unmistakable expression of that milieu. Then there is the testimony of Roosevelt himself that he had had *The Jungle* read to him at breakfast, which regardless of whether the story has any factual basis, points to a historical moment when socialist ideas were widely available and regarded affirmatively in American culture.

We may also note the conspicuous lack of other suspects with the opportunity to effect the kind of intellectual stimulus upon the New Deal that we are describing. Certainly it is evident that the New Deal policies implemented by the Roosevelt administration had their sources outside the conventional wisdom of the Democratic Party. Any number of New Deal enactments ran directly counter to the platform pronouncements of the party, which even in 1932 had proclaimed itself the "advocate [of] an immediate and drastic reduction of governmental expenditures by abolishing useless commissions and offices, consolidating departments and bureaus, and eliminating extravagance to accomplish a saving of not less than twenty-five percent in the cost of the Federal Government."[18] Yet this is the party which under Roosevelt nevertheless wrought the largest expansion of the federal government in U.S. history, which for the first time created a government bureaucracy with sufficient means—if not always political will—to superintend industry and to minister to the basic wants of all citizens.

As for demonstrating that the *means* actually adopted by the Roosevelt administration were socialist, I submit the following partial list of ideas either integral or unique to American socialism, all of which were incorporated into Roosevelt's and the New Deal's philosophy. The first I shall call Exhibit A: the idea that economics was not governed by naturally ordained laws but consisted, rather, of socially constructed relationships that might be studied, challenged, and changed. The view was articulated clearly in Roosevelt's speech accepting the Democratic nomination: "Our Republican leaders tell us economic laws—sacred, inviolable, unchangeable—cause panics which no one could prevent. But while they prate of economic laws, men and women are starving. We must lay hold of the fact that economic laws are not made by nature. They are made by human beings."[19] This was in fact news to orthodox economists of the Democratic as well as the Republican Party, but it had been one of the cornerstones of socialism predating as well as including Karl Marx.

Exhibit B is the idea that the current crisis was a permanent one, from which the nation would not recover without a fundamental change in economic direction. This was likewise articulated in the nomination-acceptance speech, wherein Roosevelt explained that the "enormous corporate surpluses" of the 1920s had not been distributed to consumers, to workers, or even to small stockholders but were, rather, poured into "new and unnecessary plants which now stand stark and idle" and "the call-money market of Wall Street" where it had simply vanished.[20] The notion of permanent crisis, too, was anathema to the prevailing dogma of the business cycle, but it was commonplace among socialists beginning with Marx, imported to the United States by Lawrence Gronlund, and continuing among the whole range of Second and Third Internationale socialists, including Upton Sinclair and W. E. B. Du Bois.[21]

Then there is Exhibit C, a less apocalyptic alternative to the "permanent crisis" postulate, which held merely that the U.S. economy had reached a state of "maturity," historically speaking, with the epoch of building up the nation's wealth led by the capitalist trust-builders being supplanted by an epoch of distributing that wealth more equitably. Prominent among others in the American socialist tradition who held to this view was Edward Bellamy, who from the imagined standpoint of 2000 described the following shift in U.S. political economy as occurring in the years subsequent to the 1888 publication of *Looking Backward:* "The industry and commerce of the country, ceasing to be conducted by a set of irresponsible corporations and syndicates of private persons at their caprice and for their profit, were entrusted to a single syndicate representing the people, to be conducted in the common interest for the common profit. . . . The epoch of trusts had ended in The Great Trust."[22] As for Roosevelt, in a September 1932 campaign speech he announced that "the day of the great promoter or the financial Titan, to whom we granted everything if only he would build, or develop, is over. [Our task] is the soberer, less dramatic business of administering resources and plants already in hand, of seeking to reestablish foreign markets for our surplus production, of meeting the problems of underconsumption, of adjusting production to consumption, of distributing wealth and products more equitably."[23]

Exhibit D suggests that Roosevelt's understanding of political-economic history from rudimentary market economies to modern industrial capitalism—and specifically his understanding of labor within that evolution—stands in tangible relation to a long tradition of socialist analysis. One point of departure in this tradition, indeed, would be the historical analysis of Marx and Engels, as for example their proclamation in the *Communist Manifesto* that "modern industry has converted the little workshop of the patriarchal master into the great factory of the industrial capitalist. Masses of labourers, crowded into the factory, are organised like soldiers. . . . [T]hey are daily and hourly enslaved by the machine, by the over-looker, and, above all, by the individual bourgeois manufacturer himself."[24] Within American socialist culture as in American culture generally, the historical moments of the manufactory workshop and the craft guild are more idealized, so that the essential distillation of the entrance into capitalistic modernity assumes a golden age of relative industrial freedom. Here is the definitive formulation in the Socialist Party platform of 1901, at the party's founding: "Formerly the tools of production were simple and owned by the individual worker. To-day the machine, which is but an improved and more developed tool of production, is owned by the capitalists and not by the workers. This ownership enables the capitalists to control the product and keep the workers dependent upon them."[25] The spirit of this formulation infuses the third of the twelve principles that Upton Sinclair proclaimed as fundamental to the EPIC plan: "Private ownership of tools, a basis of freedom when tools are simple, becomes a basis of enslavement when tools are complex."[26] The socialist formulation, moreover, informs Roosevelt's characterization of modern industry in his pivotal 1936 convention speech. Since the eighteenth century and the successful political revolution beginning in 1776, Roosevelt explains, developments in technology and economies of scale had created "a new problem for those who sought to remain free." Roosevelt's characterization of the present-day situation is careful to enumerate several classes of citizens who suffer from this problem of freedom, and yet the model for that problem is the situation of the exploited proletarian laborer:

> The hours men and women worked, the wages they received, the conditions of their labor—these had passed beyond the control of the people, and were imposed by this new industrial dictatorship. The savings of the average family, the capital of the small-businessman, the investments set aside for old age—other people's money—these were the tools which the new economic royalty used to dig itself in.
>
> Those who tilled the soil no longer reaped the rewards which were their right. The small measure of their gains was decreed by men in distant cities.[27]

If the sympathies of the patrician Roosevelt seem a little too widely cast for a proper inheritor of the socialist tradition, we might consider not only that a moderate pragmatist like Sinclair extolled the virtues of socialism, and EPIC, for almost all classes of Americans, but also that Marx and Engels prophesied the tendency of all workers to gravitate to one class or the other of the two great classes, with the great majority being proletarians.

Habeas corpus is of course one of the earliest and most fundamental principles of law, dating from thirteenth-century England. In the investigative analogy that I am here adopting, it is likewise necessary and vital that we "have the body" of socialism—necessary and vital to show that the New Deal not only proffered the intention of social democratic words but also delivered the actuality of social democratic deeds. That the New Deal produced a substantial body of specifically socialist work might be judged by comparing its enactments with the immediate demands spelled out in the inaugural platform of the Socialist Party, published over three decades earlier. The Socialist Party platform of 1901 consisted of seven planks, which demanded:

1. The collective ownership of all means of transportation and communication and all other public utilities as well as of all industries controlled by monopolies, trusts and combines. No part of the revenue of such industries to be applied to the reduction of taxes on the property of the capitalist class, but to be applied wholly to the increase of wages

and shortening of hours of the employees, to the improvement of the service and diminishing of the rates to the consumers.

2. The progressive reduction of the hours of labor and the increase of wages in order to decrease the share of the capitalist and increase the share of the worker in the product of labor.
3. State or national insurance of working people in case of accidents, lack of employment, sickness and want in old age; the funds for this purpose to be furnished by the government and to be administered under the control of the working classes.
4. The Inauguration of a system of public industries, public credit to be used for that purpose in order that the workers be secured the full product of their labor.
5. Equal civil and political rights for men and women.
6. The education of all children up to the age of eighteen years, and State and municipal aid for books, clothing and food.
7. The initiative and referendum, proportional representation and the right of recall of representatives by constituents.[28]

Understanding that these planks reflect the pragmatic, parliamentary philosophy of the American party and others of the Second Internationale, most of the measures representing ancillary or halfway steps advancing the cause of socialism but falling short of the complete abolition of capitalism, we may nevertheless recognize that the New Deal accomplished much of what Socialists had hoped to accomplish, much on a national scale that Sinclair had sought but failed to do in a single state. In short, the New Deal succeeded in introducing and then institutionalizing elements of social democracy in the United States.

Beginning with the area of *least* achievement, we must confess that plank 7 was not significantly advanced by the New Deal, as Roosevelt was much more inclined to seek wider executive power in the name of the people—in classic populist style—than to seek an extension of direct democracy. In his inaugural address, Roosevelt threatened that he would seek special executive authority akin to war powers, if Congress did not act swiftly against the Depression. Of course, wider democratic participation was a principle with a mixed record among socialists as well. While "proportional representation and the right of recall" was hailed by Karl Marx as the righteous practice of the Paris Commune of 1871[29] and Sinclair sought to use electoral recall, the referendum, and popular initiative as mechanisms to implement EPIC,

Edward Bellamy's *Looking Backward* had hoped largely to insulate the administrators of the nationalized political economy from the popular will, and the authoritarian practices of various really existing socialist states are too well documented either to deny or to need elaboration here. Although, as noted above, Roosevelt welcomed popular initiatives at the state and local levels, he believed—probably rightly—that rapid and sophisticated measures to redirect the economy could only be effected via the initiative of a strong central government, not through popular, grassroots initiatives, as Sinclair proposed.

The other six objectives specified by the Socialist Party in 1901 were, however, substantially advanced or even achieved through the New Deal. Concerning the first plank of the Socialist platform demanding public ownership of utilities and of monopolies, we may note that the New Deal created laws and agencies providing public control of those industries deemed most vital to the common good. Initially, the New Deal of 1933 had sought direct government control of industry through the National Recovery Administration (NRA). Adverse rulings of the Supreme Court based upon the commerce clause of the Bill of Rights forced a shift in strategy, however. Public control over industry then had to be channeled less overtly, through government regulation and oversight bodies. These had been created from the start of the New Deal; they continued to proliferate through the 1930s. The Federal Deposit Insurance Corporation and the Securities Exchange Commission were established in the historic first hundred days of the Roosevelt administration. The Home Owners Loan Corporation, created in 1933, and the Federal Housing Administration, which followed in 1934, established national standards in the businesses of appraising and home-building.[30] The Interstate Commerce Commission (ICC) had been created way back in 1887 to rein in the railroad industry; it was strengthened during the New Deal. So was the Federal Power Commission, which oversaw the oil and gas production industries. The Federal Communications Commission (founded in 1934) supervised telephones and radio; the Motor Carrier Act (1935) extended the authority of the ICC to cover the trucking industry; the Civil Aeronautics Board (1938) anticipated correctly the need for regulation of commercial travel by air.[31] All of these agencies are open to the charge that they helped to save capitalism by protecting the system from its own internal dynamic toward self-immolation; by no means did they represent the full nationalization of the industries they superintended, and therefore they fell short of the prescriptions of the Socialist Party and the Nationalists and even the more modest proposals of the People's Party. But while the profits of business remained in private hands, so did financial risk, and because of these partial steps, industry was held more accountable to the public will than ever before, and more liable than ever before to be circumscribed, redirected, or reformed by democratically responsive public policy.

Concerning the second plank of the Socialist platform that called for "reduction of the hours of labor and the increase of wages" for the working class, we may say that this, one of the more modest immediate demands of the platform, was substantially achieved through the New Deal. The Wagner Act, one of the cornerstones of the second New Deal of 1935, established the right of collective and independent labor bargaining. Largely because of the Wagner Act, American unions grew rapidly, enjoyed unprecedented success in winning increased wages and shorter hours, and finally—after many decades of struggle—came into something approaching parity in the struggle with capital. During the 1930s, the federal government also stepped in to establish national labor norms that had long been sought by Socialists: a nationwide minimum wage, the eight-hour day, and the abolition of child labor.[32] Such measures had until recently been pursued by socialists only, treated as impossibly utopian by mainstream economists affiliated with both major parties. It had been a rally for the eight-hour day, called by the Knights of Labor, that had led to the violence at Haymarket Square and to the arrest and capital convictions of the anarchist leaders there. The cause associated in 1877 with anarchist lawlessness, and judged in 1886 by Laurence Gronlund to be impossible as long as capitalism lasted, was not only championed in the 1930s by one of the major parties but passed into law that has remained to this day.[33]

Almost the same can be said of the New Deal's progress toward those aims specified in the third plank of the Socialist Party's immediate demands: pensions in case of unemployment, debilitating injury, and old age. In his state of the union address for 1935, Roosevelt called for government to provide a social safety net for all citizens, "security of the men, women, and children of the nation against certain hazards and vicissitudes of life."[34] That summer he signed the Social Security Act, which provided unemployment insurance, pensions for the disabled, financial support for widows with dependent children, and monthly stipends for retirees. Although Roosevelt preferred to describe the program in negative terms, as "security" in the event of catastrophe, the "hazards" targeted by Social Security were as predictable as rain, as universal as aging. Social Security might just as reasonably be understood in positive and universal terms, which (as Roosevelt perhaps understood) would help to reveal its socialist provenance: it meant the provision of a certain minimum share of the common wealth for practically all citizens, and a fair, if not equal, opportunity for children to achieve success. To appreciate fully just how revolutionary the changes effected by Social Security were, we should note just how alien its provisions were to the philosophy of Roosevelt's own party coming into the election of 1932, to say nothing of the party of Harding, Coolidge, and Hoover. Whereas the provisions for old-age pensions, unemployment insurance, and support for children had been called for by the Socialist Party for over thirty years, they made their appearance in the platform of the Democratic Party only in 1932, and then only in desultory fashion. Shackled by the states' rights tradition of the party, the 1932 platform called merely for "unemployment and old-age insurance under state laws." In the pre-Depression Democratic platform of 1928, the only items resembling Social Security in the least were accident compensation for employees of the government only—and for work-related injuries only—and a proposed study to develop a limited plan for putting the unemployed to work on "necessary public works," this construction to be phased out when such periods of acute unemployment should abate. But of course Social Security was passed into law as a right of all working Americans, regardless of class; its provisions for the unemployed have been thoroughly institutionalized. Unemployment insurance and old-age pensions have since become part of the fabric of American political and social life.

Concerning the fourth plank of the Socialist platform, demanding "Inauguration of a system of public industries," we may observe that the New Deal established a tremendous network of federally backed employment programs. Though they were deliberately pegged to paying workers *less* than the current labor market (to say nothing of their receiving "the full product of their labor"), these federally instituted programs did something that the marketplace could not do for millions of workers: provide steady, remunerative, and secure employment. A few days after his meeting with Upton Sinclair in September 1934, Franklin Roosevelt indicated his cool response toward Sinclair's hope that the factories and farms of EPIC might be funded by the federal government, telling reporters that the EPIC plan was "impossible, absolutely impossible, on [the] scale" proposed by Sinclair. "If Sinclair has any sense in him," Roosevelt continued, "he will modify at least in practice this perfectly wild-eyed scheme of his and carry it on as a community experiment."[35] But Sinclair might be excused for his wild-eyed scheming given that Roosevelt's New Deal had by this time already initiated a massive federal program of reforestation, public parks construction, and manual labor through the Civilian Conservation Corps, and had initiated a wide-ranging scheme for rural electrification, hydroelectric power, and land conservation throughout the South under the aegis of the Tennessee Valley Authority. Then in 1935 Roosevelt instituted his own scheme for publicly funded industry that altogether dwarfed the scale proposed by Sinclair. The Works Progress Administration (WPA) both expanded federal jobs programs on the model of the CCC and increased funding to state and municipal governments for a whole variety of public works (which Roosevelt stipulated must be "useful—not just for a day, or a year, but useful in the sense that it affords permanent improvement in living conditions or that creates future new wealth for the Nation").[36] The WPA put some three million people back to work in 1935, and approximately eight-and-a-half million before its disbandment in 1943.[37] This was not, decidedly, a permanent program for social and economic equality, but it was demonstrably an instance of government doing what socialists had long been urging, and what antisocialists had always warned against as catastrophic to the future of capitalism: the federal government, through progressive tax policy, was extracting profits from the capitalist economy through corporate and personal taxes and redistributing them among workers who had been deemed expendable in the conventional labor market.

Regarding the aims specified in the fifth and sixth planks of the party's immediate demands—equal rights for women and a share in the commonwealth for children—we may find in the Social Security Act of 1935 and related programs several measures that went some way toward their fulfillment. Roosevelt's 1935 State of the Union Address announced his intention to seek benefits not only for the unemployed and aged but also "for children, for mothers, for the handicapped, for maternity care, and for other aspects of dependency and illness where a beginning can now be made."[38] The resulting legislation was not by any means fully egalitarian, tending to treat both women and children as dependents as opposed to fully fledged citizens with equal rights. To a degree, then, the New Deal reflected the same cultural and political shortcomings that bedeviled the theory and praxis of the socialist movement, as our account of Charlotte Perkins Gilman and her associates has documented. But if the inegalitarian shortcomings of the Social Security Act of 1935 are apparent particularly in the area of gender rights, its provisions continuing to treat men as breadwinners and women as mothers,[39] it did intervene within that traditional matrix to assist women in those situations where social and economic circumstances struck them the hardest: when women's male partners were unwilling or unable to provide for them and their children, and when women were faced with being the primary providers for themselves and their families in a persistently patriarchal society. That portion of the Social Security Act devoted to Aid to Families with Dependent Children, when coupled with New Deal legislation against child labor and compulsory education laws already on the books, brought into being as a matter of federal, nationwide policy virtually all that the Socialists had called for in 1901 in the sixth plank of their immediate demands. Thus it happened, too, that in the final year of her life, Charlotte Perkins Gilman had an opportunity to see the partial fulfillment of her vision of a society that cared for all children as if they were one's own offspring.

A final measure of the ideological and political kinship between Roosevelt's New Deal and the social democratic tradition is the ongoing interplay between ideals of social equality and real-world implementation aiming for, but constantly falling short of, those ideals. The Socialist pattern is evident in Sinclair's quite orthodox formulation of the party's praxis articulated in *The Jungle:* work with non-Socialists where possible to pass measures of immediate assistance to the working classes, but make "no compromise" on the final objective of social equality and the abolishment of the profit system. And that pattern finds its echo in the rhetoric and aims of the New Deal as Roosevelt articulated them at the high-water mark of the New Deal, in his speech to the 1936 Democratic national convention. The New Deal was already substantially in the books, and from a socialist standpoint, many compromises had had to be made. Although Roosevelt himself had been responsible for any number of the compromises, the president turned back instinctively to the rhetoric of no compromise. Having just argued that private ownership of the tools of mass production has led to the enslavement of modern labor, Roosevelt denounced "royalists of the economic order" who have "conceded that political freedom was the business of government, but . . . have maintained that economic slavery was nobody's business," who have "granted that the government could protect the citizen in his right to vote, but . . . denied that the government could do anything to protect the citizen in his right to work and his right to live."[40] He was taking a page practically right out of the American socialist playbook. Bellamy's *Looking Backward,* for instance, had announced "the obvious fact [that] no business is so essentially the public business as the industry and commerce on which the people's livelihood depends, and that to entrust it to private persons to be managed for private profit is a folly similar in kind, though vastly superior in magnitude, to that of surrendering the functions of political government to kings and nobles to be conducted for their personal glorification."[41] Gilman had written,

> We have our religious life.
>
> We have our political life.
>
> We have our industrial life.
>
> In the first two we have made ourselves free, but because we are slaves in the last we are helpless in all.[42]

Roosevelt declared: "Today we stand committed to the proposition that freedom is no half-and-half affair. If the average citizen is guaranteed equal opportunity in the polling place, he must have equal opportunity in the market place."[43]

Much as socialists would and did, Roosevelt saw the measures of the New Deal not as ends in themselves but as stepping-off points in the pursuit of a wider distribution of the national wealth and a deeper commitment to equal opportunity. In his convention speech, Roosevelt spoke of extending as well as sustaining the enactments of the New Deal by defining an "economic bill of rights." The proposal did not call for an equal distribution of the common wealth, but it did envisage the interest of the national community in maintaining a minimum level of economic support for all citizens and in making employment at a living wage available to all American households. It was "the challenge to our democracy," the president said, that "tens of millions of citizens" were being "denied the greater part of what the very lowest standards of today call the necessities of life." Further outlining the crisis through a series of observations melding visionary and muckraking modes, all linked by the memorable anaphora, "I see millions . . . ," Roosevelt propelled his audience toward the conclusion of a common interest of all citizens in each others' economic welfare and, therefore, in the eradication of poverty and unemployment as central tasks of democratic government:

> I see millions denied education, recreation, and the opportunity to better their lot and the lot of their children.
>
> I see millions lacking the means to buy the products of farm and factory and by their poverty denying work and productivity to many other millions.
>
> I see one-third of a nation ill-housed, ill-clad, ill-nourished.
>
> It is not in despair that I paint you that picture. I paint it for you in hope—because the Nation, seeing and understanding the injustice in it, proposes to paint it out. We are determined to make every American citizen the subject of his country's interest and concern; and we will never

> regard any faithful, law-abiding group within our borders as superfluous. The test of our progress is not whether we add more to the abundance of those who have much; it is whether we provide enough for those who have too little.[44]

Roosevelt was not only seeking a more cooperative commonwealth by pushing all Americans regardless of means to take up a struggle against poverty—a cause that he might well have recognized as the rallying cry of the California EPIC campaign, little though he was willing or able to acknowledge it. Unknowingly, no doubt, Roosevelt was also proposing the same "test of the excluded class" that Du Bois had long ago proposed in William English Walling's *New Review*. Without suggesting Roosevelt's means or the ends to greater equality were exactly those sought—or demanded—by his predecessors and contemporaries who were socialists, we might further note the similarity of Roosevelt's ideal to that of yet another socialist, still more venerable than Gilman, Sinclair, or Du Bois. For Roosevelt's demands that Americans should "never regard any faithful, law-abiding group within our borders as superfluous," and that they "provide enough for those who have too little," are but more carefully guarded versions of Marx's famous aphorism: "The free development of each is the condition for the free development of all."

The New Deal was, in fact, the clearest embodiment and most durable legacy of late nineteenth- and early twentieth-century socialism: producing laws, programs, policies, and government apparatuses that changed in fundamental and lasting ways both the means by which citizens might seek by democratic government to direct their nation's economic life and the aims of such a government to promote equal opportunity for every citizen. The New Deal used the national government as an instrument to increase democratic control of industry, to establish workers' rights to a fuller share of the product of their labor, and to extend public support for the sustenance of the most vulnerable members of society. Yet because it increased but did not fully effect that democratic control, because it distributed the common wealth more equally but not equally, and because its assistance to the most vulnerable members was both limited and partial, the social democratic legacy of the New Deal must also be judged to be incomplete. It is to some of these areas where the New Deal itself was flawed as well as the areas where the promise of the New Deal has not yet been realized that I will now, and finally, turn.

"LET US BE DISSATISFIED": THE ONGOING WORK OF SOCIAL DEMOCRACY

> "If you are saving dying babies, whose babies are you going to let die? If you are feeding the hungry, what folk are you (regretfully, perhaps, but none less truly) going to let starve?"

While issues of women's equality were sidestepped by the New Deal, issues of racial equality were trodden upon. African Americans had been hit especially hard by the Great Depression. Black communities had not enjoyed the boom times of the 1920s as fully as had the rest of the nation; the Depression drove black unemployment up to catastrophic levels: 31 percent in Baltimore, 40 percent in Detroit, between 40 and 50 percent in Harlem, and as high as 56 percent in Philadelphia.[45] It would stand to reason that blacks, suffering disproportionately from the effects of the business depression, would benefit disproportionately from federal programs for jobs and agricultural assistance—if such programs were merely race neutral. But they were not. The distribution of agricultural subsidies being left to the states, many in the South prioritized assistance for the largest white-owned farms, leaving relatively little for small-scale white farmers and practically nothing for black ones. When the Works Progress Administration began distributing its largesse, it too worked through the aegis of city political machines, which frequently brought benefits to American ethnics but, again, not proportionately to the U.S. minority group with the least well established political connections, African Americans. When a "Subsistence Homestead Colony" was opened in West Virginia as a New Deal Experiment, Upton Sinclair hailed the development as the transmigration of the EPIC plan to the federal level.[46] The colony was, however, for whites only. After Eleanor Roosevelt stepped in to lobby on behalf of would-be black residents, the government solution was to support a parallel, blacks-only colony—a phenomenon that W. E. B. Du Bois took up as exemplary of the kind of separate, cooperative economic development he had long called for.[47] But the fact that the white colony proved a failure before the black colony could even be built and given a trial testifies not only to the difficulty of making a socialistic economic scheme work within a hostile capitalist environment but also to the New Deal's primary orientation to the needs and predilections of white Americans. It should come as little wonder that black intellectuals were disproportionately attracted to the no-holds-barred philosophy of the Communist

Party, or that the African American populace found enthusiasm for the New Deal mainly on account of the sincere but symbolic antiracism of Eleanor Roosevelt.

Although there were many reasons for the deficiencies of the New Deal on matters of racial justice—chief among them, Roosevelt's political dependency upon the Solid South—one important reason, highlighted by our analysis of the cross-pollination of socialist and New Deal ideas, was the incomplete commitment to racial as well as gender equality across the spectrum of left-wing activism. That failure of commitment did not stem, however, from a failing in socialist ideals. Even critics as attuned to the shortcomings of really existing social democracy as Gilman and Du Bois repeatedly distinguished between an insufficiently developed practice and the egalitarian imperatives of the philosophy. The logic of social democracy and a more consistently implemented socialist program still stood to advance the cause of African Americans, women, and other minorities. Largely because the New Deal established government apparatuses permitting a more democratic direction of industry but implemented that direction unevenly as well as incompletely, preferentially in favor of whites and men, progress toward economic and social equality for nonwhites and women came later and more fitfully, and was driven by activists still further out on the margins than the Second International socialists had been. Although Du Bois lived nearly thirty years longer than Gilman, he was not an active participant in these post–World War II movements for social justice in the United States, either. Yet the social democratic philosophies he and Gilman had articulated were predictive of the directions taken by subsequent activists, and they remain relevant to the possibility of social democracy in our day. These, too, constitute legacies of American socialism.

Beginning with the most immediate and demonstrable of Du Bois's influences, we might note his example of wariness of the Communists. Although in 1938 Du Bois made an appreciative second tour of the Soviet Union, Du Bois rejected Mary White Ovington's despairing suggestion that, after three decades of working for racial equality, "my only hope is in Communism." The methods of the Comintern would not do, Du Bois insisted, in spite of his own inability to transform the NAACP or any other organization into anything like a fit vehicle for black social democracy: As he warned Ovington, "Communism is the hope of us all but not the dogmatic Marxian program with war and murder in the forefront. Economic communism by the path of peace is possible."[48] Soon Du Bois's oft-repeated criticisms of the Comintern agenda and Communist leadership in the United States were affirmed by the disillusion and critique of other black intellectuals who had affiliated themselves with the party, either officially or unofficially, in large numbers during the 1930s. Whether their change of heart came at the time of Stalin's purge of the old-guard Bolsheviks in 1938, his nonaggression pact with Nazi Germany made public in 1939, or—just as likely—a gradual realization that the color line was drawn within the ranks of the Communist Party just as elsewhere in American society, most black Marxists came to renounce their ties with the party or at least distance themselves from it, whether the break was spectacular and public, as with Richard Wright, or more gradual and quiet, as with Ralph Ellison and Langston Hughes.[49]

Du Bois's own odyssey would eventually lead him to embrace several political dangers against which he had warned—and a few with which he had flirted—for practically his entire career. In the 1950s, Du Bois's opposition to the execution of Julius and Ethel Rosenberg was entirely defensible on ethical as well as political grounds. It is of little credit that Upton Sinclair took the patriotic line, supporting the execution vocally as if to make up for those occasions when he stood by his far-left comrades and against the popular will.[50] Less worthy was Du Bois's willingness to throw over his long-standing skepticism about the Comintern. Backed into a corner by Cold War–era surveillance and prosecution as an enemy agent, abandoned by all allies except for Communists who were themselves liable to persecution, Du Bois went so far as to write a defense of Stalin and Stalinism in the unpublished book manuscript, "Russia and America."[51] When Du Bois actually became a member of the Communist Party in 1961, he immediately emigrated to Ghana, where he hailed president Kwame Nkrumah as the incarnation of his black nationalist, socialist vision and Nkrumah, in turn, feted him as the intellectual godfather of Pan-Africanism.

The Ghanese independence movement in fact represented a relatively close fit with Du Bois's projection, via *Dark Princess,* of twenty years of preparation and five years of "intensive struggle," until finally, "In 1952, the Dark World goes free," the question of a violent or peaceable transfer of power being up to "the Pale Masters."[52] The period of "intensive struggle" had begun right on schedule in Ghana, with the creation of various leftist parties in 1947; the victory of Nkrumah's socialist and nationalist Convention People's Party had come in 1951, and official independence had followed almost ineluctably in 1957, in large part owing to the willingness of the British to relinquish their African colonies. But another projection made in *Dark Princess* was also, altogether too fully embodied in Nkrumah—Kautilya and Matthew's concession to realpolitik that there was nothing particularly wrong with "tyrants" so long as they are chosen from the masses and work for the benefit of the masses—"But choose well the Tyrants—there is Eternal Life!"[53] Although it was not until 1964, the year after Du Bois's death, that Nkrumah converted his elected presidency to a dictatorship-for-life, Nkrumah's cult of personality, the persecution of opposition parties, and the centralization of state power were already well under way when Du Bois arrived in Ghana, and these were consistent enough with Du Bois's notion of beneficent, populist tyranny that it is not clear this crowning act would have dampened his enthusiasm for Nkrumah.

If, however, in the last fifteen years of his life Du Bois expended the better part of his energy and hopes chasing dubious materializations of his dreams, there were other portions of his vision that were more positively and durably realized right in the United States. Just as he foresaw the liberation of people of color in colonies throughout Asia and Africa, Du Bois had foreseen that the black church might be the vehicle for welding black communities together behind a common purpose and mobilizing them in a mass movement that went beyond the legal rights fought for—however valuably—by the NAACP as led by Walter White and Roy Wilkins. The black church had, indeed, been one of the final argumentative cudgels he had wielded in his losing struggle against the NAACP board. Replying to Francis Grimke's essay siding with the board, Du Bois had countered that the Reverend Grimke was running down the virtues of his own highly successful and entirely segregated Philadelphia church. In another article penned in the spring of 1934, Du Bois capped a list of successful, self-segregated African American institutions with reference to the spirituals, which as early as *The Souls of Black Folk* he had characterized as not only the highest artistic achievement of black culture but also its principal medium for the message of liberation: "Does [the board] believe in 200 Negro newspapers which spread N.A.A.C.P. news and propaganda? . . . Does it believe in Negro business enterprise of any sort? . . . Does it believe in the Negro spirituals?"[54] The marginality of Du Bois's political position by this point, coupled with his long-standing intellectual and temperamental distance from the African American church, ensured that he would not be an active participant in the social-political work of this most venerable and powerful of black institutions. But the pivotal, social transformative role he had projected for the black church in works ranging from *Souls* to *Quest of the Silver Fleece* and *Dark Princess* (which had correlatives among white socialists in the implicit religiosity of Upton Sinclair and explicit religious theorizing of Charlotte Perkins Gilman) would be substantially realized in the South during the

1950s, even while Du Bois was battling with U.S. authorities over his sympathy with the Soviet state. In fairness to Walter White and the legal strategy he had preferred, the legal decisions won by NAACP lawyers in the 1940s and especially the 1950s were critical, but the grassroots pressure for social and political as well as legal change came from the black churches and associated civil rights organizations, especially the Southern Christian Leadership Conference. Although the civil rights movement did not fully embrace an economic agenda, it used its power as a culturally autonomous force much as Du Bois had envisaged it when he had advocated strategic self-segregation, wielding independent strength as the foundation for interclass and interracial cooperation. Though many whites collaborated with the churches and many civil rights groups were interracial, the movement was also substantially black led—not just nominally, as when the Communists put up black candidates for vice president, but actually.

Eventually, too, social activism rooted in the black church has come to address issues of economics and globalism nearly as forthrightly as Du Bois demanded it should.[55] In a 1968 rally commemorating the centenary of the birth of W. E. B. Du Bois, Martin Luther King, Jr., faced up squarely to the social democratic legacy of Du Bois, framed in terms of his final association with the Communist Party. Just a few months before his own death, King declared to the audience, "It is time to cease muting the fact that Dr. Du Bois was a genius who chose to be a Communist." King then went on to proclaim kinship between socialism and his own ideals:

> Let us be dissatisfied until every man can have food and material necessities for his body, culture and education for his mind, freedom and human dignity for his spirit. . . . Let us be dissatisfied until brotherhood is no longer a meaningless word at the end of a prayer but the first order of business on every legislative agenda. Let us be dissatisfied until our brother of the Third World—Asia, Africa, Latin America—will no longer be the victim of imperialist exploitation, but will be lifted from the long night of poverty, illiteracy, and disease.[56]

This was indeed a vision befitting Du Bois, reprising his test of the excluded class, his social democratic values, and his comprehensive, international conception of equality. Like the vision of Du Bois—and of Gilman and Sinclair, too—by holding the members of the human community to the highest moral and material standards, it constitutes a political program out of reach of any immediately practicable social reality, giving reason again and again for the proclamation and the summons of its central rhetorical figure, "Let us be dissatisfied," and therefore constituting also a vision, a challenge, and a choice for practically any foreseeable future—including our own.

There are two points emerging from the work of the triptych writers, especially when taken together, that in closing I would like to highlight as being of particular relevance to social democracy today. The first is the triptych writers' pragmatic balance between the autonomy of justice struggles and their coordination around a central rubric of economic equality. While Upton Sinclair never fully comprehended the importance of antiracism to a social democratic program, he certainly understood the importance of feminism to such a program—difficult as this was to implement in his own relationships—and his political theory and praxis both gave wide latitude for divergence in socialist philosophies. Charlotte Perkins Gilman, meanwhile, offered a fuller theorization of parallel but semiautonomous struggles for equality. In *Women and Economics,* we might recall, she spoke of "the twin struggle that convulses the world to-day,—in sex and economics,—the 'woman's movement' and the 'labor movement.'" In *With Her in Ourland,* published almost two decades later, Gilman offered much the same account through Ellador's appreciation of the women's and labor movements, whose common interests were best articulated via socialism.[57] Gilman's presentation of the movements as separate from one another is, moreover, a matter of prescription as well as description, given that she also shows that women's and workers' interests are often qualitatively as well as quantitatively different. We have seen the line of reasoning in Gilman's work dating from the 1890s and fully formulated in *Women and Economics:* Because most bourgeois women are not included in the class of individuals paid by wages, and because women of all classes have their labor—sexual, reproductive, and domestic—expropriated by male patriarchs and partners, a revolution within capitalist means of production will not necessarily liberate women whose labor is not organized within capitalism. The inferences to be drawn from this, then, are not only that distinctive interests bind the women's movement together, but also that the uniqueness of those interests demand a certain semiautonomous and self-defensive agenda, lest an insufficiently egalitarian praxis by the labor movement should compromise women's cause.

Although Gilman, with her blindness to racial prejudice at least equaling Sinclair's, hardly anticipated a wider application of her theorization of autonomous and *nonequivalent* emancipation struggles, just such an application was articulated in the social democratic theory of W. E. B. Du Bois. Like Sinclair, Du Bois integrated Gilman's thought into his own: Du Bois's chapter "The Damnation of Women" in *Darkwater* both cites Gilman and draws upon her emphasis on the economic factor as critical in gender relations throughout. Unlike Sinclair—or Gilman, for that matter—Du Bois saw that it would be entirely possible for capitalism to be replaced by socialism in the United States without removing fundamental practices of racially based social and political inequality, just as it would be possible to supplant capitalism without displacing patriarchy. Even while racial identity could be used as an instrument among people of color to establish common ground across class lines (a double-edged ideological sword if ever there was one, either catalyzing the ultimate dissolution of class or concealing class difference within national independence movements), Du Bois saw that racial difference could—and very often did—undermine supposedly natural alliances between working-class groups of differing nations, ethnicities, and colors. This is the analysis we have seen most fully articulated in *Darkwater,* where Du Bois asserted that the "laboring class of all colors," even if theoretically in solidarity with one another, could practically be divided by the color line; especially in Europe and North America, lighter-skinned proletarians might receive economic rewards purchasing their loyalty to the "national middle classes" of their own color. Effectively, then, race can be used as a de facto index of class differentiation, much as Gilman saw gender could be used in this fashion, and just as could the distinction between owning property and owning only one's own labor power. In the 1930s, it was Du Bois's assertion that this class differentiation along color lines was, in fact, occurring in the party that was loudest in declaring its opposition to such differentiation, the Communists. Even when late in life Du Bois became convinced, after all, that Soviet Communism provided the better medium for the development of racial equality than did U.S. liberalism, it is notable that he expatriated himself not to the Soviet state but to black nationalist-socialist Ghana.

Neither Gilman nor Du Bois could claim ownership of the strategy here described, of autonomous and complementary movements for equality within a broad-based social democratic movement. As we have noted, August Bebel's *Woman and Socialism* postulated the complementarity of the women's and labor movement before Gilman did. For that matter, Second International socialism was so insistently polyglot that it might be said to have implied (even if it did not fully act out) the idea of multiple, semiautonomous causes within the one larger socialist movement. But Gilman, Du Bois, and like-minded socialists certainly can claim precedence over late twentieth- and early twenty-first-century critics who articulate the concept of parallel, complementary justice struggles at the confluence of Marxist and

Foucauldian theory. Here is Chantal Mouffe's recent summation of her work with Ernesto Laclau, which I have had some occasion to discuss already at the outset of this study: "For us the radicalization of democracy requires the transformation of the existing power structures and the construction of a new hegemony. In our view, the building of a new hegemony implies the creation of a 'chain of equivalence' among the diversity of democratic struggles, old and new, in order to form a 'collective will,' a 'we' of the radical democratic forces."[58] While the critical vocabulary is new and postmodernist, Gilman's "twin struggle" of the women's movement and the labor movement, wherein each plays a coequal role in social transformation, might readily enough stand in for Laclau and Mouffe's "diversity" and the "chain of equivalence," whereas their "collective will" and "'we' of the radical democratic forces" are unmistakably "the forward-looking system" of socialism. Certainly Laclau and Mouffe's theoretical apparatus is more clearly poised than Gilman's dual movements of women and labor to accommodate the full range of possible liberation movements; as they write in *Hegemony and Socialist Strategy:* "For the defence of the interests of the workers not to be made at the expense of the rights of women, immigrants or consumers, it is necessary to establish an equivalence among these different struggles."[59] Yet the burden of this assertion—the nonidentity and necessary autonomy of the various movements—which marks a clear advantage over the main line of Marxist thought that Laclau and Mouffe interrogate—is a major contention also made by Gilman and Du Bois. Furthermore, while Gilman envisages primarily two movements leading the way toward social democracy, Du Bois's incorporation of the women's movement alongside the black struggle for equality and the labor struggle definitely opens a path for other movements to step forward and show their credentials.

What is more, Gilman and Du Bois make clear just what such credentials would be, in a way that Laclau and Mouffe and other contemporary theorists of social justice often do not. One problem lurking in Laclau and Mouffe's open-ended radical hegemonic coalition is precisely that there is no clear standard by which the justice claims of various groups might be recognized and their justice struggles prioritized. Laclau and Mouffe are active participants in the recent theoretical trend in which the Marxian demand to end exploitation has been balanced—and even in many quarters overwhelmed—by the Foucauldian imperative to subvert social control. The trend is exemplified when they write that "the demand for *equality* is not sufficient but needs to be balanced by the demand for *liberty*."[60] This ostensible refinement opens the door to *any* group becoming equal claimants to participation in Laclau and Mouffe's hegemony, if they are able to attest that their freedom is being infringed upon. The insistence upon "balance" between equality and liberty is reductive of what might reasonably appear to be extraordinarily different "democratic struggles": for example, the challenge of women executives in corporate America to break the glass ceiling as compared with the struggle of many current residents of Sudan or Somalia to stay alive. To call these "equivalent" and thereby to advocate similar degrees of political energy in each case is a prescription for maintaining their inequality (the relative privilege of the former and victimization of the latter). While Gilman's and Du Bois's understanding of social democratic strategy certainly cannot banish factional struggles between various would-be elements of a radical social democratic hegemony, their retention of the key socialist concepts of the economic base and labor exploitation, and the priority they place upon equality over liberty, turn out to be crucial and productive. For thereby they maintain a basis for distinguishing between the relative importance of various social movements and, at the same time, for uniting those who are exploited, dispossessed, or underprivileged.

A fundamental focus upon economic equality, both as the basis for all other forms of equality and as a basic yardstick of social equality, was shared as well by Upton Sinclair. Indeed, consensus between Gilman, Sinclair, and Du Bois upon the importance of the economic base, and a related commitment to tackle the greatest economic injustice foremost, points to what may be the most durable and usable of socialist legacies: the elimination of poverty as the initial step toward genuine social equality. The strategy—and goal—is the second and final point I would offer as pertinent to our thinking about social democracy in our day.

It goes almost without saying that a focused emphasis upon ending poverty is anathema to revolutionary Marxists, for whom any such program would seem a mere palliative, who assert that poverty will be eliminated in any case when the system of private property is abolished, and who insist that this abolishment can only be achieved by concentrating on organization and agitation by the proletariat. Ameliorating the basic material needs of the poorest members of the commonwealth might possibly be accomplished within any number of configurations (or at least, reconfigurations) of capitalism, militant Marxists warn. Alternatively, however, reform-minded American socialists postulated first that social concern for the poor might better mobilize popular support across class lines than would more immediately self-interested alliances between the bourgeois and the militant working classes, and second that the changes necessary to eliminate poverty would presently demand public ownership of the essential industries of the nation—that is, socialism. Upton Sinclair's EPIC campaign operated upon both premises. While believing Californians would find rampant unemployment to be the clearest danger to the social welfare and would, therefore, be willing to back any plausible scheme to put the unemployed to useful work, Sinclair believed that once the virtues of such a program were demonstrated, and when the faults of capitalism were still more fully exposed by its further implosion, then the full development of socialism would be as gradual and inevitable as a force of nature. He predicted in *I, Governor* that the progress of social democracy, through EPIC, "was like a swiftly flowing river eating into a sand bank."[61] Essentially, class competition and division would be undermined by showing the possibility of plenty for all, and this possibility might be realized most directly by a campaign to end poverty.

Other socialists more attuned to the exploitation of minorities, including both Gilman and Du Bois, worried that even the best-case scenario according to doctrinaire Marxists—a socialist regime led by the American working classes and resulting in their dictatorship over the means of production—could leave women or blacks, or both, with little improvement in social and economic status. For these feminist and race-conscious socialists, the best way to ensure a truly egalitarian society was to focus, from the outset, on the needs of those in the greatest material want and social disadvantage. Indeed, among socialists, feminists and race activists were the ones who first formulated the idea of attending to the basic needs of the least privileged members of society as the first rather than the final task of social revolution; it came to the more mainstream writers such as Sinclair only later. As early as his 1913 *New Review* article, Du Bois had suggested that no social democratic system would be worthy of the name until it could face down questions such as these: "If you are saving dying babies, whose babies are you going to let die? If you are feeding the hungry, what folk are you (regretfully, perhaps, but none less truly) going to let starve? If you are making a juster division of wealth, what people are you going to permit at present to remain in poverty?"[62] Only in 1933, under the immediate pressure of the Great Depression, had Sinclair boiled socialism down to the "one definite, concrete job" of ending poverty. But Charlotte Perkins Gilman had insisted upon the elimination of poverty as the social democratic ideal already by 1911. In her novel published that year, *Moving the Mountain,* looking back at an imagined social transformation, she projects that "the real turning point" in social progress was "where the majority of the people recognized the folly and evil of poverty—and saw it to be a thing of our own making."[63] The theme continues in *Herland,* where a general prosperity of all citizens has been the norm for so long that the word for "poor" has passed out of the Herlanders' language, and is asserted again openly in *With Her In Ourland,* in which Ellador urges the eradication of poverty to be both the most immediate, practicable step and the necessary precursor to dealing with other social and physical ills.[64]

The moderation and even conservatism of Gilman's appeal, part of an effort to forge the producing majority sought by the 1890s Populists as well as to exploit conventional conceptions of motherhood, concealed the fact that—so far as Gilman was concerned—an all-out commitment to ending poverty and bringing comfort to all American people would demand the radical transformation of society. The elimination of poverty would be the ultimate opening wedge for social democratic transformation. Perhaps this was not what Roosevelt had in mind when he made the eradication of poverty central to his appeal for an economic bill of rights, when he painted an image of "one-third of a nation ill-housed, ill-clad, ill-nourished" and urged his fellow citizens to "paint it out." No doubt it was not what Lyndon B. Johnson had in mind when a generation later he proclaimed his "War on Poverty," a war superseded by the war in Vietnam much as Roosevelt's campaign for economic justice had been suspended by World War II. Certainly, it remains quite possible that poverty might effectively be dealt with but capitalism left in place. Yet for socialists such as Sinclair, Du Bois, and Gilman, socialism was not an all-or-nothing proposition but a steady process, defined not by the adherence or nonadherence of a particular political-economic system to this or that abstract formula, but rather by whether a real existing society places the good of all its citizens ahead of the interests of its most powerful individuals. And the goal of ending poverty in a global society, a society with clear political boundaries but no real economic boundaries, ends up being not only the most utopian of objectives but the most practical first step toward equality.

Taking a rhetorical cue from another of the legatees of social democracy, Dr. King: Let us be dissatisfied when our society does not prioritize the needs of our least privileged and powerful members above the desires of our most privileged and powerful; dissatisfied when our nation puts its interests ahead of those of other nations, especially when our power and their weakness leads to the exploitation of their labor and natural resources; and dissatisfied, for that matter, when inhabitants living today on earth place their welfare ahead of the welfare of future inhabitants of our planet. Simultaneously, in the pragmatic and idealistic tradition of Gilman, Sinclair, and Du

Bois, we must equally declare our dissatisfaction at any political system or ideological scheme that employs political coercion or in any way compromises the fundamental welfare of the present generation in the name of achieving perfect social equality in some other time and place. Dedicated as they were to socialism as ethical ideal and as political economy, the triptych writers recognized socialism not as an end but as a means to a better community; hence their carelessness at various points in their careers about the labels *socialist* and *socialism.* In our own search for a more perfect national and international union, however, we should recognize how socialism and socialists including Gilman, Sinclair, and Du Bois have already advanced this cause and, as well, how they might yet help us in achieving a national and world community where all members are regarded equally not just in abstract theory but in material fact.

NOTES

Introduction

1. See Walter Rideout, *The Radical Novel in the United States, 1900–1954: Some Interrelations of Literature and Society* (Cambridge: Harvard University Press, 1956); Daniel Aaron, *Writers on the Left: Episodes in American Literary Communism* (1961; repr., New York: Columbia University Press, 1992); and James Gilbert, *Writers and Partisans: A History of Literary Radicalism in America* (New York: Wiley, 1968).

2. The studies include the following: Charlotte Nekola and Paula Rabinowitz, eds., *Writing Red: An Anthology of American Women Writers, 1930–1940* (New York: Feminist Press, 1987); Paula Rabinowitz, *Labor and Desire: Women's Revolutionary Fiction in Depression America* (Chapel Hill: University of North Carolina Press, 1991); James F. Murphy, *The Proletarian Moment: The Controversy over Leftism in Literature* (Urbana: University of Illinois Press, 1991); Barbara Foley, *Radical Representations: Politics and Form in U.S. Proletarian Fiction, 1929–1941* (Durham, NC: Duke University Press, 1993); Bill Mullen and Sherry Lee Linkon, eds., *Radical Revisions: Rereading 1930s Culture* (Urbana: University of Illinois Press, 1996); James Edward Smethurst, *The New Red Negro: The Literary Left and African-American Poetry, 1930–1946* (New York: Oxford University Press, 1999); Robert Shulman, *The Power of Political Art: The 1930s Literary Left Reconsidered* (Chapel Hill: University of North Carolina Press, 2000); and Janet Galligani Casey, ed., *The Novel and the American Left: Critical Essays on Depression-Era Fiction* (Iowa City: University of Iowa Press, 2004).

3. William Maxwell, *New Negro, Old Left: African-American Writing and Communism Between the Wars* (New York: Columbia University Press, 1999); Alan M. Wald, *Exiles from a Future Time: The Forging of the Mid-Twentieth-Century Literary Left* (Chapel Hill: University of North Carolina Press, 2002); and Barbara Foley, *Spectres of 1919: Class and Nation in the Making of the New Negro* (Urbana: University of Illinois Press, 2003). Even the most wide-ranging of these projects, Wald's book, maintains the concentration upon Communist-affiliated writers.

4. Cary Nelson, *Revolutionary Memory: Recovering the Poetry of the American Left* (New York: Routledge, 2001), 2.

5. As I will suggest slightly later in the introduction, there is a strong predilection in contemporary literary criticism and theory toward "radicalism" in several senses—including work interested in various forms of progressive politics. The notable work reflecting this politics and taking up subjects within the period 1890 to 1940 is not, of course, focused entirely on the activities of the Communist Party in the United States, and includes the following: Caren Irr, *The Suburb of Dissent: Cultural Politics in the United States and Canada during the 1930s* (Durham, NC: Duke University Press, 1998); John Whalen-Bridge, *Political Fiction and the American Self* (Urbana:

University of Illinois Press, 1998); Arthur F. Redding, *Raids on Human Consciousness: Writing, Anarchism, and Violence* (Columbia: University of South Carolina Press, 2000); David Kadlec, *Mosaic Modernism: Anarchism, Pragmatism, Culture* (Baltimore: Johns Hopkins University Press, 2000); Laura Hapke, *Labor's Text: The Worker in American Fiction* (New Brunswick, NJ: Rutgers University Press, 2001); John Beck, *Writing the Radical Center: William Carlos Williams, John Dewey, and American Cultural Politics* (Albany: State University of New York Press, 2001); and Michael Szalay, *New Deal Modernism: American Literature and the Invention of the Welfare State* (Durham, NC: Duke University Press, 2000). On many points this work is complementary to mine, and might be read as extending a conversation on progressive politics and American literature back to Herman Melville and other antebellum writers and forward to contemporary authors including Toni Morrison and Kathy Acker; Beck's title, *Writing the Radical Center*, could well have been a subtitle for *American Socialist Triptych*.

It is difficult to generalize about this work, complex and heterogenous as it is, but one common point that emerges is the centrality of "cultural politics" in literature and literary criticism—a formulation that emphasizes the way politics is mediated through the cultural production of literature, and through this process of mediation, literary themes become a substitution for political action. Redding goes so far as to suggest that the specific political affiliations of the Progressive Era were not of particular interest to writers of that period because of (quoting Emma Goldman) "the muddle-headedness of the Left itself," which led to "a failure for political action" but "becomes in fiction a wealth of imagined possibilities" (81). Not only does my study show that Gilman, Sinclair, and Du Bois did show a definite interest in the political groups of their era; it also distinguishes between cultural work and political work in ways that few other studies do (save perhaps some of those examining Communist-affiliated writers!). Certainly, while there were times when all three writers were primarily producing "cultural" work, discussing political themes and ideologies but not otherwise seeking to enact any specific political action, this study emphasizes the ways that this work eventually, in quite definite ways, yielded results in legislative action or institutional change. Hence, even as *American Socialist Triptych* joins these studies in identifying the shortcomings of Progressive Era and New Deal–era politics, it insists the Left was not altogether "muddle-headed" nor a complete "failure" in its political results.

6. For parallel and mutually reinforcing accounts of Ellison's and Wright's breaks with the Communist Party, see Lawrence Jackson, *Ralph Ellison: Emergence of Genius* (New York: John Wiley and Sons, 2002), 286–87; Arnold Rampersad, *Ralph Ellison: A Biography* (New York: Alfred A. Knopf, 2007), 162–63; and Hazel Rowley, *Richard Wright: The Life and Times* (New York: Henry Holt, 2001), 254, 264, 291–93.

7. Kate A. Baldwin, *Beyond the Color Line and the Iron Curtain: Reading Encounters between Black and Red, 1922–1963* (Durham, NC: Duke University Press, 2002), 153.

8. Jacques Derrida, *Of Grammatology*, trans. Gayatri Chakravorty Spivak (Baltimore: Johns Hopkins University Press, 1976), 19.

9. Stephen Greenblatt, *Shakespearean Negotiations: The Circulation of Social Energy in Renaissance England* (Berkeley: University of California Press, 1988), 95, 121.

10. Elaine Showalter, "Introduction: The Feminist Critical Revolution," in *The New Feminist Criticism: Essays on Women, Literature, and Theory*, ed. Elaine Showalter (New York: Pantheon, 1985), 8.

11. Judith Butler, "Performative Acts and Gender Constitution," in *Literary Theory: An Anthology*, 2nd ed., ed. Julie Rivkin and Michael Ryan (Malden, MA: Blackwell, 2004), 904.

12. Fredric Jameson, *A Singular Modernity: Essay on the Ontology of the Present* (New York: Verso, 2002), 134–36.

13. Ibid., 77, 10.

14. Ibid., 137.

15. After the first wave of deconstruction swept through English and other humanities disciplines in the 1980s, Derrida and his exponents worked with notable energy to demonstrate the constructive political and ethical implications of deconstructive interpretation. Among later books by Jacques Derrida in this vein, see *Politics of Friendship*, trans. George Collins (New York: Verso, 1997); and *Ethics, Institutions, and the Right to Philosophy*, trans. Peter Pericles Trifonas (Lanham, MD: Rowman and Littlefield, 2002). Although some critics of the New Historicism have characterized it, too, as mainly concerned with interpretive pyrotechnics, as early as Harold Veeser's groundbreaking 1988 anthology, *The New Historicism* (New York: Routledge, 1988), a number of critics have made a turn toward progressive politics quite explicit. See in this collection, for example, the essays by Louis A. Montrose, Catherine Gallagher, Judith Lowder Newton, Elizabeth Fox-Genovese, and Gayatri Chakrovorty Spivak.

16. Michel Foucault, *Discipline and Punish: The Birth of the Prison*, trans. Alan Sheridan (New York: Vintage, 1979), 26.

17. Charlotte Perkins Gilman, *Human Work* (1904; repr., Lanham, MD: Altamira, 2005), 321.

18. Upton Sinclair, *Mammonart: An Essay in Economic Interpretation* (Pasadena, CA: by the author, 1925), 9.

19. W. E. B. Du Bois, "Criteria for Negro Art," *Crisis* 32, no. 6 (October 1926): 296.

20. Teresa L. Ebert, *Ludic Feminism and After: Postmodernism, Desire, and Labor in Late Capitalism* (Ann Arbor: University of Michigan Press, 1996), 57.

21. Adolph L. Reed, Jr., *W. E. B. Du Bois and American Political Thought: Fabianism and the Color Line* (New York: Oxford University Press, 1997); see especially chap. 8, pp. 127–62; Kenneth W. Warren, "The End(s) of African-American Studies," *American Literary History* 12 (2000): 645.

22. Chantal Mouffe, *On the Political* (New York: Routledge, 2005), 31.

23. Ibid., 88.

24. Eric Lott, *The Disappearing Liberal Intellectual* (New York: Basic Books, 2006), 3.

25. Mouffe, *On the Political*, 33.

26. Ernesto Laclau and Chantal Mouffe, *Hegemony and Socialist Strategy: Towards a Radical Democratic Politics,* trans. Winston Moore and Paul Cammack (London: Verso, 1985), 184.

27. Mouffe, *On the Political,* 53; Lott, *The Disappearing Liberal Intellectual,* 3.

28. For remarkable instances of these three types, see Robert Campin's *Descent from the Cross,* in which the bodies of the criminals executed along with Jesus are represented in the side panels even as Jesus' body is removed lovingly from the cross, and the images of the living in the left-hand panel especially are focused on the action in the central panel rather than upon the lifeless body suspended just over their heads; Rogier van der Weyden's Columba altarpiece, which tells the story of the Virgin Mary's annunciation, the nativity, and the presentation of Jesus at the temple; and Dieric Bouts's *The Last Supper with Four Old Testament Scenes,* in which the side-panel scenes are as various as the healing of Naaman the leper by Elisha and the encounter of Jacob with the angel at Bethel. The first of these two triptychs is reproduced in Barbara G. Lane, *The Altar and the Altarpiece: Sacramental Themes in Early Netherlandish Painting* (New York: Harper and Row, 1984), 90, 61, while the third can be seen in Phillip Lindley, ed., *Making Medieval Art* (Donington, England: Shaun Tyas, 2003), plate 100.

29. See, for example, Rogier van der Weyden's *Last Judgment* altarpiece (Lane, *Altar and Altarpiece,* 141). Because triptychs were intended for the decoration of altarpieces, most of their subjects are treated with extreme reverence, but there are instances that introduce a certain critical distance even on their intensely sacred subjects. The grotesque elements in the *Triptych of Last Judgment* as presented by Hieronymous Bosch (but available today only in a copy) may suggest a later, Renaissance humanist viewpoint, but the virtue of sainthood is not beyond skeptical reflection in Hans Memling, *Altarpiece of St. John the Baptist and St. John the Evangelist,* wherein a remarkably demure Salome averts her eyes from the Baptist's head served upon a platter, while the saint's prostrate, decapitated body lies unceremoniously in the street, center foreground. See, respectively, *Triptych of Last Judgment,* engraving after Hieronymous Bosch, in Lotte Brand Philip, *The Ghent Altarpiece and the Art of Jan van Eyck* (Princeton, NJ: Princeton University Press, 1971), plate 55; and Lindley, *Making Medieval Art,* plate 96.

Chapter 1

1. Daniel Bell, *Marxian Socialism in the United States* (1952; repr., Ithaca, NY: Cornell University Press, 1996), 5.

2. Brian Lloyd, *Left Out: Pragmatism, Exceptionalism, and the Poverty of American Marxism* (Baltimore: Johns Hopkins University Press, 1997), 13. Another key element shared by Lloyd and Bell is their assumption that only Marxist socialism counts as genuine socialism. Indeed, although traditional historiography offers a considerably richer and deeper portrait of American socialism than does American literary history, with its aforementioned predilections for the Communist Party and the 1930s, the long-standing practice among histories of American socialism definitely reflects a bias in favor of Marxism. Whether "Marxism" is featured in their titles or not, the following foundational histories consider the development of Marxian social-

ism as the true socialist lineage: Ira Kipnis, *The American Socialist Movement, 1897–1912* (New York: Columbia University Press, 1952); Oakley C. Johnson, *Marxism in United States History Before the Russian Revolution (1876–1917)* (New York: Humanities, 1974); Robert Hyfler, *Prophets of the Left: American Socialist Thought in the Twentieth Century* (Westport, CT: Greenwood, 1984); Paul Buhle, *Marxism in the United States: Remapping the History of the American Left* (London: Verso, 1987).

3. Karl Marx and Friedrich Engels, "The Manifesto of the Communist Party," in *The Marx-Engels Reader*, 2nd ed., ed. Robert C. Tucker (New York: Norton, 1978), 500.

4. Ibid., 498.

5. Charlotte Perkins Gilman, *The Living of Charlotte Perkins Gilman* (1935; repr., New York: Arno, 1972), 131.

6. Arthur Lipow, *Authoritarian Socialism in America: Edward Bellamy and the Nationalist Movement* (Berkeley: University of California Press, 1982), 17.

7. Edward Bellamy, "Socialism and Nationalism," *New Nation*, January 27, 1894: 38. Bellamy's criticisms of other varieties of socialism are directed largely at their moderation, as he points out that the generic definition allows for socialism on a scale smaller than the nation and for a degree of class readjustment falling short of strict equality.

8. Barbara Taylor, *Eve and the New Jerusalem: Socialism and Feminism in the Nineteenth Century* (New York: Pantheon, 1983), 20–24.

9. Ibid., xi, xii.

10. Brian J. L. Berry, *America's Utopian Experiments: Communal Havens from Long-Wave Crises* (Hanover, NH: University Press of New England, 1992), 27, 29, 119, 124.

11. Ibid., 59–60, 83, 88–89; Carl J. Guaneri, *The Utopian Alternative: Fourierism in Nineteenth-Century America* (Ithaca, NY: Cornell University Press, 1991), 30–34.

12. The substantial Transcendentalist participation at the founding of Brook Farm, as well as the relation between utopian socialist ideology and Transcendentalism, is presented in Richard Francis, *Transcendental Utopias: Individual and Community at Brook Farm, Fruitlands, and Walden* (Ithaca, NY: Cornell University Press, 1997). Hawthorne, it seems, was a participant at Brook Farm less for its philosophical attractions than for what he perceived to be its practical benefits for himself as a writer. He was disappointed to find so little time to write between daily farmwork and chores, and he remained as a full participant in the colony for only about half a year. Annette Kolodny, introduction to *The Blithedale Romance* by Nathaniel Hawthorne (New York: Penguin, 1983), vii–viii.

13. Hawthorne, *The Blithedale Romance*, 246.

14. Ibid. Ironically, given the ungenerous attitude of Hawthorne's narrator toward the Fourierites, Brook Farm might well have come closest to realizing the aspirations of its Transcendentalist founders after it was taken over by them. In 1844, the first full year operating under Fourierite principles, the community for the first time earned a small profit even while, as historian Brian Berry argues, developing a "more democratic system of labor" and seeking more intentionally "to correct the ills of wage la-

bor" than had the original commune in which the Transcendentalists were conspicuous in leadership roles. Berry, *America's Utopian Experiments,* 102, 103.

15. Berry, *America's Utopian Experiments,* 57, 63, 88, 86.

16. On the political side, the following planks of the Knights' platform are of particular interest: government provision of land in the West for settlers only (not privately held railroads and land speculators); establishment of government-owned banks (instead of the present, privately held "national" banks); government printing of paper money (as opposed to paper printed by banks, backed by gold or gold and silver); legislation prescribing equal pay for equal work regardless of gender; government backing for producer and consumer cooperatives; and public ownership of the railroads. Nell Irvin Painter, *Standing at Armageddon: The United States, 1877–1919* (New York: Norton, 1987), 31, 40–41, 44.

17. Laurence Gronlund, *The Cooperative Commonwealth* (1884; repr., Cambridge: Harvard University Press, 1965), 245.

18. Marx and Engels, "Manifesto of Communist Party," 483; Gronlund, *The Cooperative Commonwealth,* 63.

19. Gronlund, *The Cooperative Commonwealth,* 93.

20. Edward Bellamy, *Looking Backward: 2000–1887,* ed. Cecelia Tichi (New York: Penguin, 1982), 64, 65–66.

21. Ibid., 66.

22. Bell, *Marxian Socialism,* 28. George does indeed seem to believe that capital is created by the capitalist rather than by labor. See Henry George, *Progress and Poverty: An Inquiry into the Cause of Industrial Depressions and of Increase of Want with Increase of Wealth; The Remedy* (1879; repr., New York: Doubleday and McClure, 1899), 419.

23. Daniel De Leon, "Reform or Revolution," in *Socialism in America: From the Shakers to the Third International: A Documentary History,* ed. Albert Fried (Garden City, NY: Doubleday, 1970), 246, 244.

24. Ibid., 251, 253.

25. Berry, *America's Utopian Experiments,* 86.

26. Painter, *Standing at Armageddon,* 15–18.

27. Ibid., 30–31, 44–49, 95.

28. Tucker, introduction to *The Marx-Engels Reader,* xxxiv–xxxv. For a sample of Engels's social democratic thinking selected by Tucker, see "The Tactics of Social Democracy," in *The Marx-Engels Reader,* 556–73.

29. The lower two-year figures are first given in John L. Thomas, *Alternative America: Henry George, Edward Bellamy, Henry Demarest Lloyd, and the Adversary Tradition* (Cambridge: Harvard University Press, 1983), 262. The lower overall figure is offered by Cecelia Tichi, introduction to Bellamy, *Looking Backward,* 7. The higher figures, both for the two-year period and overall sales, are given in Jean Pfaelzer, *The Utopian Novel in America, 1886–1896: The Politics of Form* (Pittsburgh: University of Pittsburgh Press, 1984), 48.

30. Mary A. Hill, *Charlotte Perkins Gilman: The Making of a Radical Feminist, 1860–1896* (Philadelphia: Temple University Press, 1980), 170; Gary Scharnhorst,

"Making Her Fame: Charlotte Perkins Gilman in California," *California History* 64 (Summer 1995): 192.

31. Stow Persons, introduction to Gronlund, *The Cooperative Commonwealth,* xxiv.

32. Edward Bellamy, "Shall We Have to Export Socialism?" *New Nation,* September 23, 1893: 434–35. The Social Democratic Workers' Party, founded in 1875 under the leadership of Wilhelm Liebnecht, adopted Marxism as its theoretical basis. But electoral successes and a shift toward reformist principles led Marx to excoriate the party's positions in 1879. See introduction and "Circular Letter to Bebel, Liebnecht, Bracke, and Others," in *The Marx-Engels Reader,* xxv, 549–55.

33. Charlotte Perkins Stetson, "First Class, [First Lesson]," *American Fabian* 3, no. 1 (January 1897): 10. Charlotte Perkins Gilman was later to recall that she had refused, at first, to attend as a socialist delegate because the statement on the membership card was strongly Marxist (Gilman, *Living,* 198). But Gilman's diaries, offering a very detailed daily record in 1896, reveal no particular tumult over her convention credentials, and they regularly name socialists—named as "Socialists," not "Nationalists"—as supporting Gilman when she was short of money.

34. Lawrence Goodwyn, *Democratic Promise: The Populist Moment in America* (New York: Oxford University Press, 1976), xiii.

35. On the historical roots, regional variations, and subsequent regressions of the Populist movement, see Catherine McNicol Stock, *Rural Radicals: Righteous Rage in the American Grain* (Ithaca, NY: Cornell University Press, 1996).

36. Gene Clanton, *Congressional Populism and the Crisis of the 1890s* (Lawrence: University of Kansas Press, 1998), 21.

37. For extensive discussion of the subtreasury proposal, see chapters 6 and 8, and appendices A and B, in Goodwyn, *Democratic Promise.* On the radicalism of the Farmers Alliance and Industrial Union at the heart of Populism, see Goodwyn, *Democratic Promise,* esp. xvii.

38. Goodwyn, *Democratic Promise,* xviii–xix; Painter, *Standing at Armageddon,* 61, 69; Clanton, *Congressional Populism,* 20.

39. Michael Kazin, *The Populist Persuasion: An American History* (New York: Basic Books, 1995), 42.

40. Bell, *Marxian Socialism,* 33.

41. Bellamy, *Looking Backward,* 66.

42. Charlotte Perkins Stetson, "On Human Nature," 3 Lectures on Nationalism, 1890, Charlotte Perkins Gilman Archive, Schlesinger Library on the History of Women in America, microfilm ed. (hereafter cited as CPG Archive), folder 163, pp. 6–7.

43. Gilman, *Living,* 131.

44. Denise D. Knight, ed. *The Diaries of Charlotte Perkins Gilman,* 2 vols. (Charlottesville: University of Virginia Press, 1994), 2: 632–33. Gilman's list of "great names" is in fact notable for its leftist and Marxian tilt: August Bebel and Wilhelm Liebnecht were Marxists and prominent leaders of the German Social Democratic Party; Paul Singer was also a Social Democrat who held the chairmanship in the

1890s; Paul Lafargue was a disciple of Marx active in French leftist politics and married to one of Marx's daughters; Eleanor Marck Aveling was herself one of Marx's daughters, married to Edward Aveling with whom she was active in the English Labour Party.

45. Ibid., 631.

46. Ibid., 632.

47. Mark Pittenger, *American Socialists and Evolutionary Thought, 1870–1920* (Madison: University of Wisconsin Press, 1993), 10.

48. Stetson, "On Human Nature," 25. The passage also appears in the excerpted essay reprinted in *Charlotte Perkins Gilman: A Nonfiction Reader,* ed. Larry Ceplair (New York: Columbia University Press, 1991), 48, which interprets Gilman's manuscript as not having the first paragraph break indicated in my quotation.

49. Kazin, *Populist Persuasion,* 14, 13. According to Nell Irvin Painter, producerism was the guiding ideology not only of the Nationalists and Populists but of the Independent-Greenback Party in the 1870s and the Knights of Labor in the 1880s (*Standing at Armageddon,* 29, 61, 99). This kind of sociopolitical classification—in which "producers" form a single class including all but the idle rich—had been obsolete in England by the middle of the nineteenth century, according to Raymond Williams, *Keywords: A Vocabulary of Culture and Society,* rev. ed. (New York: Oxford University Press, 1985), 63–64. But as Kazin explains, producerism provided not so much a class description as an ethic and a political discourse.

50. Charlotte Perkins Stetson, "Our Human Duties," 12 Talks for Class Series, October 1891–February 1892, CPG Archive, folder 166, pp. 17–18; Charlotte Perkins Stetson, "What the People's Party Means," 5 Lectures, 1890s, n.d., and fragment, CPG Archive, folder 172, p. 15.

51. Stetson, "What People's Party Means"; and fragment, CPG Archive, folder 172, p. 22.

52. Ibid., p. 23.

53. Bellamy, *Looking Backward,* 66.

54. Ibid., 76.

55. Ibid., 77.

56. Charlotte Perkins Stetson, "What We Are Doing," *The Impress,* October 13, 1894: 1–2.

57. The complications of coalition politics are treated productively in Judith Roof and Robyn Wiegman, *Who Can Speak? Authority and Critical Identity* (Urbana: University of Illinois Press, 1995).

58. The influence on Gilman need not be attributed solely to the journal, either. "News from the Clubs," *New Nation,* February 7, 1891: 34, reports both Gilman's regular lecturing at the Los Angeles Club and the club's passage of a resolution supporting "extending the ballot to all above the age of 21, irrespective of sex," while stating that "all such reforms are but preliminary steps toward the final consummation of complete nationalization."

59. Edward Bellamy, "Talks on Nationalism," *New Nation,* April 18, 1891: 192.

60. Ibid.

61. Gilman, *Living,* 187; Charlotte Perkins Stetson to George Houghton Gilman, April 21, 1897, CPG Archive, folder 40, p. 2.

62. Stetson, "First Class, [First Lesson]," 9.

63. Charlotte Perkins Stetson, "The Way Up," 12 Talks for Class Series, October 1891–February 1892, CPG Archive, folder 166, p. 12.

64. Bellamy, *Looking Backward,* 48, 53–54.

65. Charlotte Perkins Gilman, *Charlotte Perkins Gilman's Utopian Novels,* ed. Minna Doskow (Madison, NJ: Fairleigh Dickinson University Press, 1999), 161–62.

66. Charlotte Perkins Gilman, "Preamble to Lecture on 'The Dress and The Body,'" in Andrea Marie Leary, "'To Point to a Solution': A Collection of Charlotte Perkins Gilman's Lectures," Ph.D. diss., University of Delaware, 1998, 201.

67. Gilman, "How Our Work Affects Us," in Leary, "To Point," 427, 428. Leary's dissertation offers a genetic text of selected Gilman speeches, so that she renders accurately the many misspellings that occur in Gilman's originals. When I quote either Leary's dissertation or Gilman's original handwritten texts, I silently alter Gilman's spelling (or handwriting!). I will also, however, give notice of the change in the notes. Here, for example, "character" is spelled as "chenacter" in Gilman's original.

68. Cf. Friedrich Engels, "Origin of the Family, Private Property, and the State," in *The Marx-Engels Reader,* 742; Emma Goldman, "The Traffic in Women," in *Anarchism and Other Essays* (1917; repr., New York: Dover, 1969), 177–94; Voltairine de Cleyre, *Gates of Freedom: Voltairine de Cleyre and the Revolution of the Mind* (Ann Arbor: University of Michigan Press, 2004), esp. section 3, "On Women, Sexuality, and the Body."

69. Charlotte Perkins Gilman, "Socialism as the Cure for The Social Evil," in Leary, "To Point," 508, 522. "Virtuous" is spelled as "vrituous" in Gilman's manuscript.

70. Edward Bellamy, *Equality* (New York: Appleton, 1897), 140–41.

71. Gilman, *Living,* 259.

72. Charlotte Perkins Gilman, *Women and Economics: The Economic Factor Between Men and Women as a Factor in Social Evolution,* ed. Carl Degler (New York: Harper and Row, 1966), 7.

73. Naomi Zauderer, "Consumption, Production, and Reproduction in the Work of Charlotte Perkins Gilman," in *Charlotte Perkins Gilman: Optimist Reformer,* ed. Jill Rudd and Val Gough (Iowa City: University of Iowa Press, 1999), 158–59. Zauderer's article is the best analysis of Gilman's socialism to date, but the distinction she draws between non-Marxist and Marxist socialism must be seen less as a sharp distinction than a difference in emphasis. The imbalance between consumption and production, evident in *Looking Backward,* is addressed directly in Bellamy's subsequent writings including *Equality.* (I would add that even in Marx the production-consumption binary is a misleading one, as for example Marxism's classic adage that all workers should enjoy "the full product of their labor" asserts simultaneously the abolition of capitalist relations of production and an egalitarianism of material consumption among all workers.) As for Gilman, the economic conditions presented in *Women and Economics* as deleterious to women cannot primarily be women's con-

suming power, for this would clearly mark a difference between women married to wealthy husbands and those married to working-class ones, and Gilman stresses that all women are members of an undervalued class roughly to the degree that their labor is either underpaid or not paid at all.

74. Gilman, *Women and Economics*, 3.

75. Ibid., 140.

76. Ibid., 13.

77. Ibid.

78. Ibid., 220, 230.

79. *Equality* was completed no earlier than November and published in time for Christmas 1897 (Thomas, *Alternative America*, 340). *Women and Economics* was drafted in its entirety by October 8, 1897, and taken to the printer on December 16 of the same year (Gilman, *Living*, 237, 239).

80. Bellamy, *Equality*, 132–33.

81. Anne Lopes and Gary Roth, *Men's Feminism: August Bebel and the German Socialist Movement* (Amherst, NY: Humanity Books, 2000), 22; Friedrich Engels, *Origin of the Family, Private Property, and the State in the Light of the Researches of Lewis H. Morgan* (1891; repr., New York: International, 1943).

82. Engels, "Origin of the Family," in *The Marx-Engels Reader*, 744.

83. Quoted in Hill, *Charlotte Perkins Gilman*, 295.

84. August Bebel, *Woman under Socialism*, trans. Daniel De Leon (1904; repr., New York, 1970), 5. I quote De Leon's edition as the one most available today to readers, though Gilman would have read one of the earlier editions described in Lopes and Roth, *Men's Feminism*, 22. But I concur with Lopes and Roth that De Leon's translation of the German title *Frau und Socialismus* is obviously and probably willfully faulty (for *und* in German has a straightforward equivalent in English: *and*).

85. Bebel, *Woman under Socialism*, 5. Lise Vogel, *Marxism and the Oppression of Women: Toward a Unitary Theory* (New Brunswick, NJ: Rutger University Press, 1983), 128–32, objects to Bebel's notion of middle- and upper-class suffragists working toward the same end as proletarians, but the fact that such a debate occurs at all over Bebel reveals the various theoretical permutations possible starting from Marxian premises. Vogel herself acknowledges the influence of Bebel during the Second International (96–103).

86. Bebel, *Woman under Socialism*, 5–6.

87. Ibid.

88. Bellamy, *Equality*, 132–34.

89. Gilman, *Women and Economics*, 340.

90. Ibid., 138.

91. Ibid., 138, 139–40, 139.

92. Ibid., 152–53.

93. Ibid., 63, 152.

94. Ibid., 139.

95. Goodwyn, *Democratic Promise*, 523–25.

96. John Gerring, *Party Ideologies in America, 1828–1996* (New York: Cambridge University Press, 1998), 188, 189.

97. "1896 Democratic Party Platform," from Kenneth Janda, ed., "U.S. Party Platforms since 1840," PoliTxts, http://janda.org/politxts/PartyPlatforms/Democratic/dem.896.html (accessed January15, 2008), par. 14.

98. "1900 Democratic Party Platform," from Kenneth Janda, ed., "U.S. Party Platforms since 1840," PoliTxts, http://janda.org/politxts/PartyPlatforms/Democratic/dem.900.html (accessed January 15, 2008), pars. 14, 15.

99. Ibid., par. 2.

100. "1904 Democratic Party Platform," from Kenneth Janda, ed., "U.S. Party Platforms since 1840," PoliTxts, http://janda.org/politxts/PartyPlatforms/Democratic/dem.904.html (accessed January 15, 2008), par. 14.

101. "1908 Democratic Party Platform," from Kenneth Janda, ed., "U.S. Party Platforms since 1840," PoliTxts, http://janda.org/politxts/PartyPlatforms/Democratic/dem.908.html (accessed January 15, 2008), par. 2.

102. Ibid., pars. 68, 69.

103. W. E. B. Du Bois, *Writings in Periodicals Edited by W.E.B. Du Bois: Selections from "The Horizon,"* ed. Herbert Aptheker (White Plains, NY: Kraus Thomson, 1985), 63, 70.

104. Ibid., 63.

Chapter 2

1. Bell, *Marxian Socialism,* 50.

2. Upton Sinclair, "You Have Lost the Strike! Now What Are You Going to Do About It?" *Appeal to Reason,* September 17, 1904: 1.

3. Upton Sinclair, *The Jungle: An Authoritative Text, Context and Backgrounds, Criticism,* ed. Clare Virginia Eby (New York: Norton, 2003), 319.

4. Ibid., 320–21. The question of industrial efficiency is dealt with at length in chapter 2 of Bellamy, *Looking Backward,* 167–72.

5. Sinclair, *The Jungle,* 322. For discussions of wages and professions that parallel Schliemann's, see Bellamy, *Looking Backward,* 87, 117, 142–43.

6. Granville Hicks, in *Critics on Upton Sinclair: Readings in Literary Criticism,* ed. Abraham Blinderman (Coral Gables, FL: University of Miami Press, 1975), 62.

7. Michael Brewster Folsom, "Upton Sinclair's Escape from *The Jungle:* The Narrative Strategy and Suppressed Conclusion of America's First Proletarian Novel," *Prospects* 4 (1979): 248, 261.

8. Kevin Mattson, *Upton Sinclair and the Other American Century* (Hoboken, NJ: John Wiley and Sons, 2006), 46, 47.

9. Quoted in Hill, *Charlotte Perkins Gilman,* 25; Hill, *Charlotte Perkins Gilman,* 172.

10. Hill, *Charlotte Perkins Gilman,* 171.

11. Pittenger, *American Socialists,* 69.

12. Reed, *Du Bois,* 83; Manning Marable, *W.E.B. Du Bois: Black Radical Democrat* (Boston: Twayne, 1986), 89–90; Wilson Jeremiah Moses, *The Golden Age of Black Nationalism* (New York: Archon, 1978), 139. Only Arnold Rampersad, *The Art and Imagination of W.E.B. Du Bois* (Cambridge: Harvard University Press, 1976), 158, shows any inclination to distinguish between the different kinds of socialism represented among the NAACP directors.

13. Only a minority of the leading American Marxians, whether left, right, or center, could claim a primarily working-class identity or even proletarian background: De Leon was educated in Europe, was at first a lawyer by profession, and taught at the Columbia Law School for six years before becoming active in the Socialist Labor Party; Berger went to university in Vienna prior to emigrating to the United States, taught school in Milwaukee for a time, and edited the German-language *Milwaukee Forwärts* even as he embarked on his career in socialist politics; and Hillquit maintained his law practice in New York City more or less throughout his decades of involvement in socialism (Bell, *Marxian Socialism,* 32–33, 51, 82). Marx, from a family of jurists and rabbis and recipient of the University of Berlin Ph.D., is described by a recent biographer as "belong[ing] to the class of distressed gentlefolk, desperate to keep up appearances and unwilling to give up bourgeois habits." Francis Wheen, *Karl Marx: A Life* (New York: Norton, 1999), 181.

14. For a significant formulation of the interconnection between personal experience and knowledge, see Sandra Harding, "Reinventing Ourselves as Other: More New Agents of History and Knowledge," in *American Feminist Thought at Century's End: A Reader,* ed. Linda S. Kauffman (Cambridge, MA: Blackwell, 1993), 140–41.

15. Folsom, "Sinclair's Escape," 239.

16. Upton Sinclair, *Love's Pilgrimage* (London: Heinemann, 1912), 6.

17. Upton Sinclair, *The Autobiography of Upton Sinclair* (New York: Harcourt, Brace and World, 1962), 34, 49.

18. Though he did not begin his formal education until the age of ten, Sinclair rapidly advanced through grade school to classes at CCNY, which at that time combined high school and the equivalent of the first two years in college—it was the path to higher education for the children of New York City unable to afford preparatory school or a four-year college. He graduated CCNY in 1897, at age nineteen. William A. Bloodworth, Jr., *Upton Sinclair* (Boston: Twayne, 1977), 19.

19. Sinclair, *Autobiography,* 52.

20. Ibid., 112.

21. Ibid., 34, 50.

22. Stetson, "Our Human Duties," 17.

23. Gilman, *Diaries,* 2: 515.

24. Gilman, *Living,* 185, 191.

25. Williams, *Keywords,* 65–66.

26. Cf. Rita Felski, "Nothing to Declare: Identity, Shame, and the Lower Middle Class," *PMLA* 115 (Spring 2000): 33–45.

27. The point is a matter of statistical as well as ideological analysis by Werner Sombart, "The Economic Situation of the Worker," in *Why Is There No Socialism in the United States?* trans. Patricia M. Hocking and C. T. Husbands (1906; White Plains, NY: International Arts and Sciences, 1976), 61–106. The Sombartian thesis carries over as well into Hyfler, *Prophets of the Left,* especially chapter 3, "De Leon and Labor Accommodationism: Two Poles of the American Working-Class Movement," 47–66.

28. David Levering Lewis, *W. E. B. Du Bois: Biography of a Race, 1868–1919* (New York: Holt, 1993), 24–29 (hereafter, *Biography*); quoted in Lewis, 28.

29. Ibid., 144–46.

30. *Correspondence of W.E.B. Du Bois,* 3 vols., ed. Herbert Aptheker ([Amherst]: University of Massachusetts Press, 1973), 1: 169–71.

31. Lewis, *Biography,* 387, 404–5.

32. Ibid., 408–9.

33. Ibid., 313.

34. Ibid., 327.

35. Ibid., 328.

36. Bell, *Marxian Socialism,* 71. For an account of Socialists in office, see Donald T. Critchlow, *Socialism in the Heartland: The Midwestern Experience, 1900–1925* (South Bend, IN: University of Notre Dame Press, 1986), 8–9.

37. The summary is of socialist historian James Weinstein by Isabel González Díaz, "Whose Chicago, Anyway? 'Aesthetics' vs. 'Propaganda' in Upton Sinclair's Ending for *The Jungle,*" *Revista Canaria de Estudios Ingleses* 32–33 (1996): 102.

38. John Graham, ed., *"Yours for the Revolution": The "Appeal to Reason," 1895–1922* (Lincoln: University of Nebraska Press, 1990), 7.

39. Sinclair, *Love's Pilgrimage,* 415, 420; Sinclair, *The Jungle,* 309n; Anthony Arthur, *Radical Innocent: Upton Sinclair* (New York: Random House, 2006), 21.

40. Quoted in Folsom, "Sinclair's Escape," 250.

41. Sinclair, *The Jungle,* 310.

42. Ibid. 309–10. Compare Sinclair's description of the "Little Giant," for whom "The Lord had used up so much material in the making of his head that there had not been enough to complete his legs," with the brief account given by Daniel Bell: "Slight-bodied and of small stature, [De Leon] had a large head which, with his piercing black eyes, fine-etched features, and carefully modeled beard, gave him a commanding presence" (*Marxian Socialism,* 33).

43. Sinclair, *The Jungle,* 323–24.

44. For the critics who find favoritism toward Lucas, see Folsom, "Sinclair's Escape," 253, and Díaz, "Whose Chicago, Anyway?" 102. For the critics who assert Sinclair's preference for Schliemann, see Scott Derrick, "What a Beating Feels Like: Authorship, Dissolution, and Masculinity in Sinclair's *The Jungle,*" *Studies in American Fiction* 23, no.1 (Spring 1995): 90, and June Jacobs, introduction, *The Jungle,* by Upton Sinclair (New York: Modern Library, 2002), xiv.

45. Sinclair, *The Jungle,* 315, 316, 318, 317–18.

46. Ibid., 314, 313.

47. Ibid., 318–19.

48. Quoted in Folsom, "Sinclair's Escape," 246.

49. Sinclair, *The Jungle,* 318.

50. Eugene V. Debs, "Arouse, Ye Slaves!" in Graham, *Yours for the Revolution,* 110.

51. George Allan England, *Story of the Appeal* (n.p.: n.p., [1914]), 68.

52. All of the following letters from 1910 may be found in Haldemann MSS II, Manuscripts Department, Lilly Library, Indiana University, Bloomington, Correspondence 1909–1917, with Sinclair's correspondents and the dates of their letters as follows: Gilman (November 12), Steffens (December 1), Untermyer (December 1), Markham (December 2), and Darrow (December 9).

53. Frederick Upham Adams to Upton Sinclair, February 4, 1911, Sinclair MSS, Manuscripts Department, Lilly Library, Indiana University, Bloomington (hereafter Sinclair MSS), box 1, January–February 1911.

54. Sinclair, *The Jungle*, 324; Upton Sinclair, *The Industrial Republic: A Study of the America of Ten Years Hence* (New York: Doubleday, Page, 1907), 88.

55. Upton Sinclair, *My Lifetime in Letters* (Columbia: University of Missouri Press, 1960), 109.

56. Howard H. Quint, "*The Challenge* and *Wilshire's Magazine*," in *The American Radical Press, 1880–1960*, 2 vols., ed. Joseph R. Conlin (Westport, CT: Greenwood, 1974), 1: 80.

57. Upton Sinclair and Gaylord Wilshire, "A Butterfly Net for a Rhinoceros Hunt: A Continuation of the Upton Sinclair-Wilshire Debate," *Wilshire's*, October 1913, 1–2.

58. "Paterson Pageant—Important," Sinclair MSS, box 1, n.d. file in November–December 1914. Document erroneously dated as [1914?] by Lilly Library—a rare mistake in their filing of materials lacking date information.

59. Rose Pastor Stokes to Upton Sinclair, May 26, 1913, Sinclair MSS, box 1, January–July 1913, pp. 3–4.

60. Anne Huber Tripp, *The I.W.W. and the Paterson Silk Strike of 1913* (Urbana: University of Illinois Press, 1987), 179–80.

61. Sinclair and Wilshire, "Butterfly Net," 4.

62. Sinclair, *Industrial Republic*, 207.

63. Ibid., 209.

64. Ibid., 206. I would not wish to overstate the originality of Sinclair's analysis here. Cf. especially Gronlund, *The Cooperative Commonwealth*, 244.

65. Sinclair, *Autobiography*, 126.

66. Robert M. Crunden, *Ministers of Reform: The Progressives' Achievement in American Civilization, 1889–1920* (New York: Basic Books, 1982), 172, 183–88.

67. Crunden is the most thorough of the depreciators of Progressive Era reforms, though the critical trend has been widespread. It is aptly described and well documented by David Sarasohn, *The Party of Reform: Democrats in the Progressive Era* (Jackson: University of Mississippi Press, 1989), vii–xii. See also William M. Morgan, *Questionable Charity: Gender, Humanitarianism, and Complicity in U.S. Literary Realism* (Durham, NH: University of New Hampshire Press, 2004).

68. David Traxel, *Crusader Nation: The United States in Peace and the Great War, 1898–1920* (New York: Knopf, 2006), 15–16; Sarasohn, *Party of Reform*, 4; Robert Harrison, *Congress, Progressive Reform, and the New American State* (Cambridge: Cambridge University Press, 2004), 265; Crunden, *Ministers of Reform*, 195–96.

69. Quoted in Sarasohn, *Party of Reform*, xv.

70. Sarasohn, *Party of Reform*, 166–69, 183–88.

71. Traxel, *Crusader Nation*, 21.

72. John Graham, introduction to *The Coal War: A Sequel to "King Coal,"* by Upton Sinclair (Boulder: Colorado Associated University Press, 1976), xxiii, xxv–xxvii. Graham's account of conditions in the Colorado coal mines is confirmed by a source otherwise more sympathetic with the Rockefellers and corporate capitalism, H. M.

Gitelman, *Legacy of the Ludlow Massacre: A Chapter in American Industrial Relations* (Philadelphia: University of Pennsylvania Press, 1988), 3.

73. Graham, introduction to *The Coal War,* xvi, xxx–xxxi.

74. Gitelman, *Legacy of Ludlow Massacre,* 18.

75. Graham, introduction to *The Coal War,* xlvii; Gitelman, *Legacy of Ludlow Massacre,* 18–20, 117.

76. Quoted in Graham, introduction to *The Coal War,* xlvii.

77. See "Rockefeller Balks Sinclair Mourners," *New York Times* April 30, 1914: 5; "Night Picketing at Rockefeller's," *New York Times* May 1, 1914: 4. For a sampling of out-of-town coverage at a conservative newspaper, see the following items in the *Chicago Tribune:* "Mourn in Street for Dead Miners," April 30, 1914: 5; "Sinclair Freed; Parade Resumed," May 2, 1914: 4; "Sinclair Calls John D. Jr. A 'Tool,'" May 4, 1914: 5; "'Silence Leaguers' at New York Funeral Service for Colorado Strike Victims, in Front of Standard Oil Office," illus., May 6, 1914: 15; "Brands Sinclair Falsifier," May 19, 1914: 7; "Upton Sinclair Insists 'John D.' Is at Lake Forest," May 23, 1914; "Sinclair Warns Rockefeller Jr. of Death Charge," June 1, 1914: 1. Even the story in which Colorado governor Ammons "Brands Sinclair Falsifier" reports essentially Sinclair's version of events.

78. Graham, introduction to *The Coal War,* lix–lx.

79. Leon Harris, *Upton Sinclair: American Rebel* (New York: Crowell, 1975), 144; Sinclair, *Autobiography,* 200–201.

80. Graham, introduction to *The Coal War,* lxvi.

81. Sinclair, *Autobiography,* 201; Graham, *Yours for the Revolution,* 61.

82. Upton Sinclair, "John D.'s Governor of Colorado Lied to President Wilson, and Associated Press Suppressed the Facts," *Appeal to Reason,* May 30, 1914: 1.

83. Ibid.

84. Ibid. Sinclair's telegram to the president (which he sent to other AP newspapers both to get the word out and to demonstrate its newsworthiness) may be found in "Swears Guardsmen Looted Tent Colony," *New York Times* May 19, 1914: 3.

85. Creel's article is referenced in a letter from Ben Lindsey: "To say that we all appreciated your wonderful article in Everybody's is to feebly express it. I think it is just about the greatest thing you ever did." Ben Lindsey to George Creel, June 13, 1914, Sinclair MSS, June 1914, box 1, p. 2. Reed's article is recommended by Sinclair: letter to Annie Gould, June 25, [1914], Sinclair MSS, box 1, June 1914.

86. Upton Sinclair, letter to John D. Rockefeller, Jr., May 26, 1914, Sinclair MSS, box 1, May 1914, 6–7.

87. Quoted in Graham, introduction to *The Coal War,* lxi.

88. Julius Gerber to Upton Sinclair, May 7, 1914, Sinclair MSS, box 1, May 1914.

89. Morris Hillquit to Upton Sinclair, June 5, 1914, Sinclair MSS, box 1, June 1914.

90. Graham, introduction to *The Coal War,* lx, lxvi–lxix.

91. Upton Sinclair, "To my Friends in Tarrytown," July [1914], Sinclair MSS, box 1, July–August 1914, p. 5; Graham, introduction to *The Coal War,* lix–lxx.

92. Quoted in Annie Gould to Upton Sinclair, June 23, 1914, Sinclair MSS, box 1, June 1914, p. 1.

93. Ibid., 1–3.

94. Graham, introduction to *The Coal War,* lxxv.

95. Upton Sinclair, *The Brass Check: A Study of American Journalism* (Pasadena, CA: by the author, 1920), 193.

96. Arthur, *Radical Innocent,* 154.

97. Annie W. Gould to Upton Sinclair, July 10, [1914?], Sinclair MSS, box 1, July–October 1915, p. 3. My narrative assumes that in the Sinclair MSS the letter is misfiled in being placed among the July 1915 letters.

98. Sinclair, "To my Friends," 6–7.

99. Sinclair, *Autobiography,* 203. By the beginning of August 1914 Sinclair was already hearing from colleagues whom he had solicited for suggestions as to selections; Leonard Abbott to Sinclair, August 6, 1914, Sinclair MSS, box 1, discusses suggestions for the anthology at length.

100. Sinclair, *Autobiography,* 203.

101. Ibid., 207; Graham, introduction to *The Coal War,* lxxvii–lxxviii.

102. Quoted in Graham, introduction to *The Coal War,* l.

103. Quoted in Graham, introduction to *The Coal War,* lii.

Chapter 3

1. See Sally Alexander, ed., *Women's Fabian Tracts* (London: Routledge, 1988).

2. Quoted in Mary Jo Buhle, *Women and American Socialism, 1870–1920* (Urbana: University of Illinois Press, 1981), 105. Buhle's chapters 3 and 4 trace the rise of women's activity in the Socialist Party from a marginal role at its founding to the national visibility achieved by declaration of the Women's National Committee in 1908, as well as noting how turn-of-the-century women's socialist activism had its roots in the Nationalist and Populist movements.

3. Matthew Hild, *Greenbackers, Knights of Labor, and Populists: Farmer-Labor Insurgency in the Late-Nineteenth-Century South* (Athens: University of Georgia Press, 2007), 146–47.

4. Engels, "Origin of the Family," in *The Marx-Engels Reader,* 744.

5. Gilman, *Women and Economics,* 106–7.

6. Ibid.

7. Ibid., 118–19.

8. Ibid., 151.

9. Charlotte Perkins Gilman, "Our Excessive Femininity," in Leary, "To Point," 250. There are several silent corrections in this passage: "ornamentation" is "orneementation" in Gilman's original MS, "required" is "requied," and "develop" is "develope."

10. Gilman, "The Real Woman," in Leary, "To Point," 216. Silent correction in noun number: "helpmate" is "helpmates" in the original.

11. Gilman, "A Married Child," in Leary, "To Point," 480.

12. Joseph B. McCullough, *Hamlin Garland* (Boston: Twayne, 1978), 53–54. The critics are divided on whether he drew back from Populism because the movement became too conservative for him, or he for the movement. McCullough joins Donald Pizer in taking the former stance; the latter position is adopted by Walter F. Taylor,

"Hamlin Garland and Economic Reform," in *The Critical Reception of Hamlin Garland, 1891–1978,* ed. Charles L. P. Silet, Robert E. Welch, and Richard Boudreau (Troy, NY: Whitson, 1985), 148.

13. Gilman, *Diaries,* 2: 506, 752.
14. Ibid., 328–29.
15. Ibid., 402.
16. Ibid., 380.
17. Ibid.
18. Sinclair, *The Jungle,* 323–24.
19. Sinclair, *Industrial Republic,* 234.
20. Arthur, *Radical Innocent,* 88–89.
21. Ibid., 30–31.
22. Sinclair, *Love's Pilgrimage,* v.
23. Ibid., 282–83.
24. Hamlin Garland to Upton Sinclair, March 14, [1911], Sinclair MSS, box 1, March–April 1911, pp. 1, 3; Charlotte Perkins Gilman to Upton Sinclair, August 31, 1910, Sinclair MSS, box 1, July–August 1910.
25. Sinclair, *Love's Pilgrimage,* 286.
26. Ibid., 562–63.
27. Ibid., 498.
28. Ibid., 474.
29. Ibid., 142–43.
30. Ibid., 650–51.
31. Ibid., 656.
32. Ibid., 662–63.
33. Arthur, *Radical Innocent,* 130.
34. Upton Sinclair to Harry Kemp, July 21, 1910, Sinclair MSS, box 1, July 1910–April 1911, p. 4.
35. Ibid., p. 3.
36. Arthur, *Radical Innocent,* 134.
37. Ibid., 135–36.
38. William Brevda, "Love's Coming-of-Age: The Upton Sinclair-Harry Kemp Divorce Scandal," *North Dakota Quarterly* 51, no. 2 (Summer 1983): 69.
39. Quoted in ibid., 71.
40. Brevda, "Love's Coming-of-Age," 75; Arthur, *Radical Innocent,* 137.
41. Arthur, *Radical Innocent,* 119–20.
42. Ibid., 134, 136.
43. Arthur suggests that Craig went to England not only to meet Sinclair but also to terminate in relative secrecy a pregnancy begun by a previous liaison with Upton (*Radical Innocent,* 143–44).
44. Ibid., 145.
45. Craig gave up her literary ambitions by the time of their marriage, at the latest. Arthur, *Radical Innocent,*146.
46. Ibid., 202–3, 229, 241.
47. Ibid., 146.

48. Arthur, *Radical Innocent,* 146; Mattson, *Upton Sinclair,* 85.

49. Jean Holloway, *Hamlin Garland: A Biography* (Austin: University of Texas Press, 1960), 151, 150, 192.

50. Quoted in Holloway, *Hamlin Garland,* 157.

51. Holloway, *Hamlin Garland,* 192.

52. Ibid., 281.

53. W. E. B. Du Bois, *Darkwater: Voices from Within the Veil* (1920; repr., New York: Schocken, 1969), 146.

54. Ibid., 181.

55. Ibid., 164.

56. Lewis, *Biography,* 177–78.

57. Du Bois, *Darkwater,* 19.

58. Ibid., 186.

59. Lewis, *Biography,* 432, 463–64.

60. David Levering Lewis, *W.E.B. Du Bois: The Fight for Equality and the American Century, 1919–1963* (New York: Holt, 2000), 185 (hereafter *Fight*).

61. Ibid., 186–87.

62. "Had Ideas of Her Own," *Boston Globe,* December 17, 1892: n.p.; CPG Archive, Newsclippings, Divorce 1892–97, n.d., reel 282.

63. See CPG Archive, Newsclippings, Divorce 1892–97, n.d., reel 282.

64. "His Tale of Woe," *Los Angeles Times,* December 22, 1892: n.p.; CPG Archive, Newsclippings, Divorce 1892–97, n.d., reel 282.

65. "Women of Brains as Wives," *San Francisco Examiner,* December 25, 1892: n.p.; CPG Archive, Newsclippings, Divorce 1892–97, n.d., reel 282.

66. "Nationalists on Marriage," *Boston Herald,* December 20, 1892: n.p.; CPG Archive, Newsclippings, Divorce 1892–97, n.d., reel 282.

67. "A Cook-Stove Throne," *San Francisco Examiner,* March 2, [1894]: n.p.; CPG Archive, Newsclippings, Divorce 1892–97, n.d., reel 282.

68. Quoted in Hill, *Charlotte Perkins Gilman,* 188.

69. Quoted in Hill, *Charlotte Perkins Gilman,* 189–90.

70. Hill, *Charlotte Perkins Gilman,* 143.

71. Ibid., 180.

72. Ibid., 220.

73. Ibid., 221.

74. Gilman, *Diaries,* 2: 804.

75. Initially no more than half the cost of the magazine was paid for by subscriptions, and the publication never reached the circulation of 3,000 subscribers that would have covered its costs. Madeleine Stern, introduction to *The Forerunner,* vol. 1: 1909–1910 (Westport, CT: 1968), v–xii. Stern assumes that Gilman was able to make up the difference by lectures and other publications. But a check of Gary Scharnhorst, *Charlotte Perkins Gilman: Bibliography* (Metuchen, NJ: 1985), shows that during *The Forerunner's* run from 1909 to 1916 Gilman seldom published anywhere else, and surely she was too busy writing the entire monthly magazine to take on many lecture engagements.

76. Carol Farley Kessler writes, for example, that "[Gilman's] subsequent produc-

tivity suggests . . . this marriage created the safe place for her to do her work that [Walter] Stetson had earlier wanted from her for his work." *Charlotte Perkins Gilman: Her Progress Toward Utopia and Selected Writings* (Syracuse, NY: Syracuse University Press, 1995), 33.

77. Du Bois, *Darkwater,* 165.

Chapter 4

1. Sinclair, *The Jungle,* 261.

2. Hill, *Charlotte Perkins Gilman,* 172.

3. Charlotte Perkins Gilman, "A Suggestion on the Negro Problem," *American Journal of Sociology* 14, no. 1 (July 1908): 75.

4. Quoted in Philip S. Foner, *American Socialism and Black Americans: From the Age of Jackson to World War II* (Westport, CT: Greenwood, 1977), 114. Foner argues, however, that the Second Internationale Socialist Party was far more progressive on the question of race than is usually supposed, as race issues were constantly discussed and a progressive stance fought for by most party leaders (xiii).

5. W. E. B. Du Bois, Editorial, "Politics," *Crisis* 4, no. 4 (August 1912): 181.

6. Reed, *Du Bois,* 83.

7. Ibid., 84.

8. In 1904 Ovington was beginning her second settlement-house position but her first in a predominantly black neighborhood of New York City. She wrote to Du Bois for advice, though she was never timid about espousing her own views. Du Bois, *Correspondence,* 1: 78.

9. Mary W. Ovington to W. E. B. Du Bois, August 29, 1908, Papers of W. E. B. Du Bois, microfilm edition, University of Massachusetts, Amherst (hereafter Du Bois Papers), reel 2, frame 1116.

10. Quoted in Lewis, *Biography,* 313.

11. Isaac Rubinow to W. E. B. Du Bois, November 12, 1904, Du Bois Papers, reel 2, frame 1296, pp. 1, 2.

12. W. E. B. Du Bois to Isaac Rubinow, November 17, 1904, Du Bois Papers, reel 2, frame 1300.

13. W. E. B. Du Bois to C. C. Owens, April 17, 1908, Du Bois Papers, reel 2, frame 1119.

14. Du Bois, *Writings in Periodicals,* 6.

15. Ibid.

16. W. E. B. Du Bois, *The Quest of the Silver Fleece* (1911; repr., Miami, FL.: Mnemosyme, 1969), 79.

17. Neither in Zora's speech nor in Du Bois's writing of this period are the concepts considered with a high degree of sophistication. But the key point here is Du Bois's conversance with socialist ideas. Rampersad is virtually alone in noting Du Bois's socialist mind-set at this relatively early moment in his career, quoting Zora's quip, "You don't own what you don't need and can't use" as a "rephrasing" of "a key Marxist slogan" (*Art and Imagination* 122). Zora's speech also reflects Du Bois's awareness of the socialist analysis offered by Bellamy and other American socialists, who saw need as the only humane principle of distribution. See Bellamy, *Looking Backward,* 66, 87, 110–12.

18. Du Bois, *Quest*, 73.

19. Ibid., 362.

20. Ibid., 430.

21. Ibid., 398.

22. In the 1920s and 1930s, biographies of John Brown would proliferate among American socialists, precisely because he provided a favorable opportunity to discuss political violence in a U.S. context. See Michael Gold, *Life of John Brown* (n.d.; repr., New York: Roving Eye, 1960), and David Karsner, *John Brown: Terrible "Saint"* (New York: Dodd, Mead, 1934), besides W. E. B. Du Bois, "John Brown: An Estimate of the Great Emancipator on His One Hundred and Twenty-sixth Birthday," *Crisis* 32, no. 1 (May 1926): 13.

23. Upton Sinclair, *Manassas: A Novel of the War* (1904; Tuscaloosa: University of Alabama Press, 2000), 214.

24. W. E. B. Du Bois, *John Brown*, ed. John David Smith (1909; Armonk, NY: M. E. Sharp, 1997), 174. It is also instructive to compare and contrast Du Bois's representation of John Brown with that of another activist soon to be a member of the NAACP board alongside him—Oswald Garrison Villard, editor-in-chief of the *Nation* and the *New York Evening Post*, and grandson of the great abolitionist William Lloyd Garrison. Oswald Garrison Villard, *John Brown, 1800–1859: A Biography Fifty Years After* (1909; New York: Knopf, 1943). Villard's account holds that Brown resorted to violence only as a last resort, and amounts to a reshaping of the historical John Brown to align his philosophy more closely with that of Villard's grandfather. Du Bois, with considerably stronger historical foundation, asserts bloody retribution as the key to Brown's antislavery campaign.

25. Du Bois, *John Brown*, 200. Lewis, *Biography*, attempts to use *John Brown* to demonstrate Du Bois's "Edwardian aversion to the justification of means by ends" and contrasts his stance in the 1909 biography with his later views as a Marxist (359). But Lewis quotes only the first instance of Du Bois's statement about "the price of liberty is less than the price of repression," omitting the later instance of it in the very same 1909 edition that adds "even though that cost be blood." As observed by the editor of the most recent reissue of the biography, the addition of that clause complicates any simple dividing line between Du Bois's early and later socialism. John David Smith, introduction to Du Bois, *John Brown*, xix.

26. Du Bois, *John Brown*, 200–201.

27. Lewis, *Biography*, 444.

28. Along the Color Line, "Economics," *Crisis* 4, no. 4 (August 1912): 163.

29. Along the Color Line, "The colored voters of St. Louis . . . ," *Crisis* 6, no. 1 (May 1913): 11.

30. W. E. B. Du Bois, Editorial, "Forward Backward," *Crisis* 2, no. 6 (October 1911): 244. Du Bois indicates that the title's allusion to the Bellamy movement is quite self-conscious, when he additionally refers to "the traveler from Altruria" in this editorial.

31. The *New Review* was published by Walling beginning in January 1913, with financial support from Mabel Dodge. Marable, *W.E.B. Du Bois*, 84.

32. W. E. B. Du Bois, "Socialism and the Negro Problem," *New Review* 1 (1913): 39.

33. "The Annual Children's Number," *Crisis* 8, no. 5 (September 1914): 251.

34. W. E. B. Du Bois to C. C. Owens, April 17, 1908, Du Bois Papers, reel 2, frame 1119.

35. W. E. B. Du Bois, Editorial, "The Last Word in Politics," *Crisis* 5, no. 1 (November 1912): 29.

36. W. E. B. Du Bois, Editorial, "Tillman," *Crisis* 16, no. 4 (August 1918): 165.

37. Du Bois, "Last Word in Politics."

38. W. E. B. Du Bois, Editorial, "The Oath of the Negro Voter," *Crisis* 15, no. 1 (November 1917): 1.

39. W. E. B. Du Bois, "The Strength of Segregation," *Crisis* 7, no. 2 (December 1913): 84.

40. [W. E. B. Du Bois,] Opinion, "Segregation," *Crisis* 7, no. 4 (February 1914): 174.

41. W. E. B. Du Bois, Editorial, "Occupations" and "Co-Operation," *Crisis* 14, no. 4 (August 1917): 166.

42. W. E. B. Du Bois, Editorial, "Consecration," *Crisis* 14, no. 6 (October 1917): 284.

43. W. E. B. Du Bois, "The Migration of Negroes," *Crisis* 14, no. 2 (June 1917): 63.

44. W. E. B. Du Bois, Editorial, "East St. Louis," *Crisis* 14, no. 5 (September 1917): 216.

45. Du Bois, *Darkwater*, 255–56.

46. Lewis, *Biography*, 555–57.

47. W. E. B. Du Bois, "The Races Congress," *Crisis* 2, no. 5 (September 1911): 208.

48. W. E. B. Du Bois, "Peace," *Crisis* 6, no. 1 (May 1913): 26.

49. W. E. B. Du Bois, Editorial, "World War and the Color Line," *Crisis* 9, no. 1 (November 1914): 28, 29.

50. "Out of Africa Have I Called My Son!" illustration, *Crisis* 9, no.1 (November 1914): 26–27.

51. W. E. B. Du Bois, *The Negro* (1915; repr., Philadelphia: University of Pennsylvania Press, 2001), 233, 235.

52. Ibid., 241–42.

53. Ibid., 242.

54. Murray B. Levin, *Political Hysteria in America: The Democratic Capacity for Repression* (New York: Basic Books, 1971), 31.

55. Ibid.; Robert K. Murray, *Red Scare: A Study of National Hysteria, 1919–1920* (1955; New York: McGraw-Hill, 1964), 59, 61, 63; Neil A. Wynn, *From Progressivism to Prosperity: World War I and American Society* (New York: Holmes and Meier, 1986), 189.

56. William M. Tuttle, Jr., *Race Riot: Chicago in the Red Summer of 1919* (New York: Atheneum, 1970), 5–10, 64.

57. Wynn, *From Progressivism to Prosperity*, 189.

58. Ibid.

59. W. E. B. Du Bois, Editorial, "To the Rescue," *Crisis* 10, no. 6 (May 1916): 31.

60. [W. E. B. Du Bois], "Direct Action," *Crisis* 13, no. 5 (March 1917): 246.

61. Lewis, *Biography*, 541.

62. A poem selected by Du Bois for *The Crisis* hailed the soldiers as martyrs and heroes: Lucian Watkins, "These," *Crisis* 15, no. 4 (February 1918): 185. Their calm dignity in the face of death was hailed by a newsclipping that prefaced the poem as well, which read in part: "Without a tremor they stepped out with soldierly tread and singing a hymn they walked to their places. . . . Resuming their song they stood erect and displayed the greatest fortitude while the ropes were adjusted." The poem's defiant imagery is also reflected in the illustration that surrounds it on the page of *The Crisis*: black soldiers marching in ranks of four, flags unfurled; an echo deliberate or not of St. Gaudens' relief of Colonel Shaw's black regiment, but this time without the figure of Shaw hovering over them on horseback.

63. Lewis, *Biography*, 578.

64. Quoted in Foley, *Spectres of 1919*, 33.

65. See, for example, Du Bois's analysis linking racism and class exploitation, capitalism and imperialism, in "The Hands of Ethiopia" and "Of Work and Wealth." Du Bois, *Darkwater*, 56–74, 81–104.

66. Ibid., 95.

67. Lewis, *Biography*, 540.

68. Claude McKay, "If We Must Die," *Liberator* 2, no. 7 (July 1919): 21; Lewis, *Fight*, 11.

69. John H. Owens, quoted in Opinion, "Socialism and the Negro," *Crisis* 22, no. 6 (October 1921): 245.

70. Du Bois, *Darkwater*, 158.

71. Ibid., 101.

72. Ibid., 155–57.

Chapter 5

1. Susan M. Matarese, *American Foreign Policy and the Utopian Imagination* (Amherst: University of Massachusetts Press, 2001), 9. Matarese provides the fullest bibliography of works between 1888 and 1900: 212 texts, all but 25 of which were full-length fictional or speculative nonfiction works (137–45). Pfaelzer, *Utopian Novel in America*, locates an additional 20 book-length texts published between the years 1880 and 1887 (181–88).

2. Thomas Peyser, *Utopia and Cosmopolis: Globalization in the Era of American Literary Realism* (Durham, NC: Duke University Press, 1998), 10.

3. Quoted in David Shi, *Facing Facts: Realism in American Thought and Culture, 1850–1920* (New York: Oxford, 1995), 196.

4. The most comprehensive examination of the connections among white Protestants between American religion and working-class social activism is Jama Lazerow, *Religion and the Working Class in Antebellum America* (Washington, DC: Smithsonian Institution, 1995). Lazerow's work is notable especially because it emphasizes the

relative theological conservatism of working-class activists before the Civil War (a distinction from the later activists of the Social Gospel movement) and because it shows the diversity of attitudes taken by these activists toward the material means they considered justifiable, for whereas many believed that religion demanded a brotherly and sisterly attitude of nonviolence toward all members of society, regardless of class, others saw in the religion of the Old Testament a warrant for bloody vengeance against oppressors. For similar accounts of white Catholic workers later, during the New Deal, see Neil Betten, *Catholic Activism and the Industrial Worker* (Gainesville: University Presses of Florida, 1976) and Kenneth J. Heineman, *A Catholic New Deal: Religion and Reform in Depression Pittsburgh* (University Park: Pennsylvania State University Press, 1999).

5. W. E. B. Du Bois, *The Souls of Black Folk* (1903; New York: Bantam, 1989), 134–35.

6. Ibid., 137, 139, 143, 145.

7. Sinclair, *The Jungle,* 284.

8. Du Bois, *Souls of Black Folk,* 138.

9. Ibid.

10. Sinclair, *The Jungle,* 285.

11. Ibid., 287, 289–90, 288, 291.

12. Ibid., 285.

13. Ibid., 287, 289, 290, 291.

14. Frederick Douglass, *Frederick Douglass Papers,* Series 2: Autobiographical Writings, vol. 1: *Narrative,* ed. John W. Blassingame et al. (New Haven: Yale University Press, 1999), 49.

15. Ibid., 54.

16. Sinclair, *The Jungle,* 291–92, 292.

17. Douglass, *Narrative,* 50.

18. Sinclair, *Love's Pilgrimage,* 248.

19. Sinclair, *Autobiography,* 101.

20. Sinclair, *The Jungle,* 301, 298, 312.

21. Folsom, "Sinclair's Escape," 257–58; Sinclair, *The Jungle,* 312.

22. Sinclair, *The Jungle,* 306, 313.

23. Michael Folsom's complaint is representative as well as particularly lucid, as he opines that the ending "demeans and hobbles Jurgis" to a "remarkable" degree, leads Sinclair "away from engagement with (even sympathy for) working class life," and "reduces to naught [Jurgis's] role—the worker's role—in the political climax of the fiction." Folsom, "Sinclair's Escape," 258, 262.

24. Sinclair, *The Jungle,* 289, 290.

25. Moses, *Golden Age,* 162; Rampersad, *Art and Imagination,* 121.

26. Du Bois, *Quest,* 78.

27. Ibid., 99, 75.

28. Ibid., 188.

29. Ibid., 215.

30. Ibid.

31. Ibid., 293.

32. Ibid., 294, 295.
33. Ibid., 296.
34. Ibid., 373, 374, 375.
35. Ibid., 400.
36. Ibid., 430.
37. Ibid., 395.
38. Ibid., 396.
39. W. E. B. Du Bois, Editorials: "Co-operation," "Cooperation," and "Co-operation," *Crisis* 15, no. 1; 16, no. 5; and 17, no. 1 (November 1917, September and November 1918): 9–10, 215, and 268.
40. Gilman, *Utopian Novels,* 39.
41. Ibid., 50, 51, 88.
42. Mark 11:23; Matthew 17:20 (New International Version).
43. Gilman, *Utopian Novels,* 86.
44. Ibid., 101.
45. Ibid., 38.
46. Ibid., 57, 55, 57.
47. Ibid., 77, 86, 136.
48. Daniel Borus, "Introduction: Edward Bellamy's Utopia in His Time and Ours," in *Looking Backward: 2000–1887,* ed. Daniel Borus (Boston: Bedford / St. Martin's, 1995), 1–28, skillfully describes the social and historical grounding of Bellamy's novel.
49. Gilman, *Utopian Novels,* 98.
50. Ibid., 37.
51. Ibid., 56.
52. Ibid., 64.
53. Ibid., 103, 92–93.
54. Ibid., 59.
55. Ibid., 58.
56. Ibid., 102, 91, 104.
57. Ibid, 105.
58. Peyser, *Utopia and Cosmopolis,* 88.
59. Gilman, *Utopian Novels,* 91.
60. Ibid., 64, 91. Hallie's account of the raising and slaughtering of food animals makes clear that the human-centered world imagined by Gilman demands, as well, the humane treatment of animals: "A proper proportion of edible animals are raised under good conditions, nice healthy happy beasts; killed so that they don't know it!—and never kept beyond a certain time limit" (64).
61. Ibid., 87.

Chapter 6

1. Du Bois, "Peace," 26.
2. Charlotte Perkins Gilman, *The Man-Made World: Or Our Androcentric Culture* (1911; repr., New York: Johnson Reprint, 1971), 225.
3. Sinclair, *Industrial Republic,* 70.
4. Ibid., 186, 98.

5. For instance, none of the essays in Denise D. Knight and Cynthia J. Davis, eds., *Approaches to Teaching Gilman's "The Yellow Wall-Paper and* Herland (New York: MLA, 2003), highlight the possibility that the nonviolent, all-female society of Herland provides any commentary whatsoever on the war in Europe, circa 1915–16. Significantly, the one essay that mentions Gilman's fiction as offering a commentary on the war, Lisa Ganobcsik-Williams, "Confronting Issues of Race, Class, and Ethnicity in *Herland*," is the rare essay that includes discussion of *With Her in Ourland*—although even there the mention is only brief.

6. Ganobcsik-Williams, "Confronting Issues," 112.

7. Gilman, *Utopian Novels*, 364.

8. Candice Millard, *River of Doubt: Theodore Roosevelt's Darkest Journey* (New York: Doubleday, 2005).

9. Gilman, *Utopian Novels*, 184.

10. Ibid., 193–94.

11. Ibid., 230.

12. Ibid., 206.

13. Ibid., 142.

14. Ibid., 246.

15. See Margit Stange, *Personal Property: Wives, White Slaves, and the Market in Women* (Baltimore: Johns Hopkins University Press, 1998), 26; Robert L. Griswold, "Law, Sex, Cruelty, and Divorce in Victorian America, 1840–1900," in *Family and Society in American History*, ed. Joseph M. Hawes and Elizabeth I. Nybakken (Urbana: University of Illinois Press, 2001), 145–72.

16. Gilman, *Utopian Novels*, 265.

17. Ibid., 194.

18. Ibid., 257.

19. Ibid., 342.

20. Ibid., 347.

21. Ibid.

22. Traxel, *Crusader Nation*, 183, 250–51.

23. See, for instance, "One Effect of the War," *Forerunner* 6, no. 3 (March 1915): 74; "Pacifists, Militarists, and Money," *Forerunner* 7, no. 9 (September 1916): 244; "War," *Forerunner* 7, no. 10 (October 1916): 303–8.

24. Gilman, *Utopian Novels*, 281, 282, 278.

25. Ibid., 264.

26. Ibid., 283.

27. Ibid., 296, 298.

28. Ibid., 304.

29. Henry Louis Gates, Jr., introduction to Du Bois, *Souls of Black Folk*, xxvi–xxviii; Du Bois, *Souls of Black Folk*, 143–44.

30. Gilman, *Utopian Novels*, 268, 269.

31. Ibid., 303.

32. Ibid., 307.

33. Ibid., 307–8.

34. Ibid., 296.

35. Ibid., 322.
36. Ibid., 355–56, 339, 335–36.
37. Ibid., 386.
38. Karl Kautsky to Upton Sinclair, September 25, 1909, Sinclair MSS, box 1, September–December 1909, p. 3.
39. Scharnhorst, *Bibliography,* 156–74.
40. Upton Sinclair to the Committee of the Anti-Enlistment League, September 27, 1915, Sinclair MSS, box 1, July–October 1915, p. 2.
41. Upton Sinclair, *Jimmie Higgins* (1919; repr., London: Hutchinson, [n.d.]), 16.
42. Ibid., 18.
43. Ibid., 16.
44. Ibid., 93.
45. Ibid., 159–60.
46. A. M. Simons to Upton Sinclair, May 23, 1917, Sinclair MSS, box 1, June–August 1917.
47. Charles Edward Russell to Upton Sinclair, May 4, 1917, Sinclair MSS, box 1, April–May 1917.
48. Upton Sinclair, "Jimmie Higgins: An Announcement," *Upton Sinclair's,* September 1918: 2.
49. Upton Sinclair to William English Walling, May 16, 1917, Sinclair MSS, box 1, April–May 1917, 1.
50. Upton Sinclair to Woodrow Wilson, October 22, 1917, Sinclair MSS, box 1, September–October 1917, pp. 4–5.
51. A letter from Eugene Debs thanked Sinclair for his tribute to "The Candidate." Eugene V. Debs to Upton Sinclair, September 19, 1918, Sinclair MSS, box 1, pp. 2–3.
52. Sinclair, *Jimmie Higgins,* 255.
53. Sinclair's depiction of the "water cure" probably was informed by public hearings and press coverage of court-martial proceedings against U.S. servicemen who used this method of torture against Filipino freedom fighters in the first decade of the century, a story told by Paul Kramer, "The Water Cure: Debating Torture and Counterinsurgency—A Century Ago," *New Yorker,* February 25, 2008, http://www.newyorker.com/reporting/2008/02/25//080225fa_fact_kramer (accessed December 21, 2010). Although Sinclair, as usual, stood by the factual accuracy of his novel, there is no definite record of U.S. soldiers torturing one of their own during the World War I Archangel expedition.
54. Sinclair, *Jimmie Higgins,* 275.
55. Ibid., 276.
56. Ibid., 277.
57. Ibid.
58. Ronald Gottesman, *Upton Sinclair: An Annotated Checklist* (Kent, OH: Kent State University Press, 1973), 62, 69. The various forms of intervention undertaken by the United States and Great Britain did not conclude until 1920. For a detailed account of the intervention, see David S. Foglesong, *America's Secret War Against Bolshevism* (Chapel Hill: University of North Carolina Press, 1995).

59. Upton Sinclair, "A Letter to the Socialist Party," *Appeal to Reason*, July 17, 1920, 3.

60. Sinclair, *Jimmie Higgins*, 287–88.

61. Floyd Dell, *Upton Sinclair: A Study in Social Protest* (New York: Doran, 1927), 147–48.

62. Sinclair, "Letter to Socialist Party," 3.

63. Du Bois, *Darkwater*, 256–57.

64. Ibid., 258, 259.

65. Ibid., 268.

66. Ibid., 269, 270.

67. Ibid., 269.

68. Bellamy, *Looking Backward*, 43.

69. Du Bois, *Darkwater*, 270.

70. Ibid., 271–72.

71. Ibid., 272.

72. Ibid., 273.

Chapter 7

1. Entering 1919 with over 108,000 members, that section of the Socialist Party of America which retained this name and its parliamentary principles had a membership of little more than 15,000 at the end of the year. Though at its founding in 1919 the Communist Labor Party could count some 70,000 members—as it drew off over half the SPA's membership—its primary successor, the Workers Party (Communist), had a membership under 16,000 by the midtwenties. Richard W. Judd, *Socialist Cities: Municipal Politics and the Grass Roots of American Socialism* (Albany: State University of New York Press, 1989), 174; Murray, *Red Scare*, 276.

2. Bell, *Marxian Socialism*, 120.

3. Mike Gold to Upton Sinclair, Sinclair MSS, January 7, [1925].

4. Quoted in James Woodress, *Willa Cather: A Literary Life* (Lincoln: University of Nebraska Press, 1987), 333.

5. The comparisons I am offering here offer a clear basis for Perry Anderson's "triangulation" between artistic modernism, cultural modernity, and radical politics, wherein Fredric Jameson insists on a correspondence between the artistic avant-garde and the "immense new social forces, political suffrage and the growth of the labour unions and the various socialist and anarchist movements" even though so many "artists of the modern [do not] occupy the same space as these new social forces, nor even manifest any ideological sympathy for or existential knowledge for them." Jameson, *A Singular Modernity*, 134. They lend weight as well, to the by-now commonplace reference to literary modernism as being "revolutionary" as well as "radical," for the political and literary transformations appear to have happened simultaneously and therefore, it seems, in sympathetic harmony with one another. Thus the mixing of political and literary terminology seems not at all incongruous in Jerome Rothenberg, ed., *Revolution of the Word: A New Gathering of American Avant-Garde Poetry, 1914–1945* (New York: Seabury, 1974), and is a matter practically of received knowledge in Alan Filreis's recent book about later poetry, *Counter-*

Revolution of the Word: The Conservative Attack on Modern Poetry, 1945–1960 (Chapel Hill: University of North Carolina Press, 2008). To these accounts, I would merely add that the revolutions in art and politics were not, after all, so revolutionary when one considers the preceding realist and socialist traditions in something other than stereotyped versions.

6. Gilman, *Living,* 284–85.

7. Scharnhorst, *Bibliography,* 157–78.

8. Charlotte Perkins Gilman, "Anarchists and Jokes," *Louisville Herald,* December 19, 1919: 7; "Exiling Dissenters," *Louisville Herald,* February 17, 1920: 6.

9. Charlotte Perkins Gilman, "The Peoples of America," *Louisville Herald,* February 12, 1920: 12; "Real America," *Louisville Herald* March 29, 1920: 6.

10. Gilman, *Living,* 317, 316, 324.

11. Ibid., 320.

12. For an account of Wyndham Lewis's politics as typical of modernism, see Fredric Jameson, *Fables of Aggression: Wyndham Lewis, the Modernist as Fascist* (Berkeley: University of California Press, 1979). Recently, Keith Gandal, *The Gun and the Pen* (New York: Oxford University Press, 2009), has shown that Hemingway, Fitzgerald, and Faulkner responded bitterly to modern, meritocratic tests used by the military during World War I, which facilitated the advancement of minority ethnics to officer status, whereas they were rejected for service.

13. For a remarkably similar later argument, see Gayle Rubin, "The Traffic in Women: Notes on the 'Political Economy' of Sex," in *Toward an Anthropology of Women,* ed. Rayna R. Reiter (New York: Monthly Review, 1975), 157–210.

14. Charlotte Perkins Gilman, *His Religion and Hers: A Study of the Faith of Our Fathers and the Work of Our Mothers* (1923; repr., Walnut Creek, CA: AltaMira Press, 2003), 263–64.

15. Ibid., 262–63, 266–67. See Michael Haynes and Rumy Husan, *A Century of State Murder? Death and Policy in Twentieth-Century Russia* (London: Pluto, 2003). Among their calculations, Haynes and Husan estimate one million prison camp deaths during the Stalinist period, one million executions of political enemies just between 1928 and 1940, and execution of over 30,000 kulaks in 1930–31 during the forced collectivization of Soviet agriculture (69–71).

16. Emma Goldman to Upton Sinclair, Sinclair MSS, December 14, 1931; Upton Sinclair to Emma Goldman, Sinclair MSS, December 28, 1931.

17. Gilman, *His Religion and Hers,* 275, 238, 42.

18. Quoted in Joshua Muravchik, *Heaven on Earth: The Rise and Fall of Socialism* (San Francisco: Encounter Books, 2002), v. Muravchik's exposition of religious analogues within the socialist movement is complementary to certain points of my own arguments. His conclusion that socialism is a religion with no morality, however, is a monstrous overgeneralization, challenged on many points by the examples of Gilman, Sinclair, and Du Bois.

19. Gilman, *His Religion and Hers,* 7.

20. Ibid., 276.

21. On the pervasive theological liberalism of the Social Gospel, see Paul T. Phillips, *A Kingdom on Earth: Anglo-American Social Christianity, 1880–1940* (Uni-

versity Park: Pennsylvania State University Press, 1996). For a sample of the writings of Social Gospel advocates, see Elden J. Eisenach, ed., *The Social and Political Thought of American Progressivism* (Indianapolis: Hackett, 2006), chap. 7: "The Social Gospel and Social Christianity."

22. Gilman, *His Religion and Hers,* 292.

23. W. E. B. Du Bois, Opinion, "Negro Writers," *Crisis* 19, no. 6 (April 1920): 299. This was five years prior to the date when the coinage appeared in the *New York Herald Tribune,* the source credited as its origin in Lewis, *Fight,* 160.

24. W. E. B. Du Bois, Opinion, "The Negro and Radical Thought," *Crisis* 22, no. 3 (July 1921): 103. In the early 1920s Du Bois published two feature articles by McKay about his experiences in the U.S.S.R., where he was honored as an important American poet and political comrade: Claude McKay, "Soviet Russia and the Negro," *Crisis* 27, no. 2 (December 1923): 61–63; and "Soviet Russia and the Negro (Concluded)," *Crisis* 27, no. 3 (January 1924): 114–18.

25. W. E. B. Du Bois, "Russia, 1926," *Crisis* 32, no. 1 (November 1926): 8.

26. W. E. B. Du Bois, "Judging Russia," *Crisis* 33, no. 4 (February 1927): 189.

27. Ibid.

28. Du Bois, "Criteria for Negro Art," 296.

29. Ibid., 292.

30. Lewis, *Fight,* 203.

31. W. E. B. Du Bois, *Dark Princess: A Romance* (1928; Millwood, NY: Kraus-Thomson, 1974), 22.

32. Eric J. Sundquist, *To Wake the Nations: Race in the Making of American Literature* (Cambridge: Harvard University Press, 1993), 620.

33. David Levering Lewis suggests Marcus Garvey as the model for Du Bois's Perigua, but the particulars of that character's militant schemes actually seem to fit better the account he gives of the Hamitic League and the African Blood Brotherhood. Lewis, *Fight,* 216.

34. Du Bois, *Dark Princess,* 60–61.

35. According to Left historian Philip S. Foner, the ABB subscribed to a platform of "immediate protection and ultimate liberation" for blacks, including a call for "armed resistance to lynching"—specifics that describe Perigua's group with some precision. *American Socialism,* 309.

36. As with the ineffectiveness of militant nationalist groups in *Dark Princess,* the futility of organization among the Pullman Porters has its counterpart in the world outside the novel—as in the mid-1920s the porters were largely content to stand by the company unions set up by Pullman. Eric Arneson, *Brotherhoods of Color: Black Railroad Workers and the Struggle for Equality* (Cambridge: Harvard University Press, 2001), 87–88.

37. Du Bois, *Dark Princess,* 92, 90, 86.

38. Lewis, *Fight,* 218.

39. Du Bois, *Dark Princess,* 283, 284.

40. Ibid., 266, 279, 285, 287, 286.

41. Ibid., 310.

42. Sundquist, *To Wake the Nations,* 623.

43. Du Bois, *Dark Princess,* 256–57.

44. Ibid., 297, 296–97.

45. "Foes of Freedom," *New Republic* June 13, 1923: 61. See also Editorial, *Nation,* July 4, 1923: 2; "Upton Sinclair Braves Prison in Fight to Uphold People's Constitutional Rights," *Haldeman-Julius Weekly,* May 26, 1923: 1.

46. Johan Smertenko, "Upton Sinclair at His Best," *Nation* June 8, 1927: 643.

47. James Fuchs, "Reviewers Reviewed," *New Masses,* August 1927: 27.

48. Foley, *Spectres of 1919,* 76.

49. Michael M. Topp, *The Sacco and Vanzetti Case: A Brief History with Documents* (New York: Palgrave Macmillan, 2005), 29–36.

50. Upton Sinclair to editor, *Road to Freedom,* April 22, 1929, Sinclair MSS, box 11, April 19–24, 1929, p. 2. Sinclair refers to an article "published in the Sunday supplements of all the Hearst newspapers" and "reprinted again and again by the Sacco-Vanzetti Committee," although it is not entirely clear in this instance if he means the 1922 Vanzetti appeal or the review of Vanzetti's *Story of a Proletarian Life,* published the next year: "Now as in the Days of Henry D. Thoreau, Massachusetts Has Its Greatest Soul in Jail," *New York American,* September 16, 1923: 3.

51. [W. E. B. Du Bois], "Evil," *Crisis* 24, no. 2 [January 1922?]: 107; "Sacco and Vanzetti: A Play," W. E. B. Du Bois Papers, Beinecke Rare Book and Special Collections Library, Yale University.

52. Aaron, *Writers on the Left,* 170–72, 452 n. 21.

53. Upton Sinclair, *Boston* (Pasadena, CA: by the author, 1928), v.

54. Aaron, *Writers on the Left,* 171.

55. Ibid., vii; Sinclair, *Autobiography,* 240–41. A number of these women are named in the dedication of the most extensive brief of the case to be published after the execution, by associate defense attorney Herbert Ehrmann. Herbert B. Ehrmann, *The Case That Will Not Die* (Boston: Little, Brown, 1969).

56. Sinclair, *Boston,* 53.

57. R. N. Mookerjee, *Art for Social Justice: The Major Novels of Upton Sinclair* (Metuchen, NJ.: Scarecrow, 1988), 98.

58. Sinclair, *Boston,* 532.

59. Ibid., 231, 233.

60. Mike Gold to Upton Sinclair, n.d. 25, Sinclair MSS, box 64, Mike Gold n.d., p. 2.

61. Gardner Jackson to Upton Sinclair, Sinclair MSS, February 1, 1928.

62. Bob Minor, telegram to Upton Sinclair, February 14, 1928; Upton Sinclair to Robert Minor, February 17, 1928; Upton Sinclair to Lydia Gibson Minor, February 18, 1928; Fred Moore, telegram to Upton Sinclair, February 21, 1928; Upton Sinclair to Robert Minor, February 21, 1928; all in Sinclair MSS.

63. Upton Sinclair to Michael Gold, April 4, 1928, Sinclair MSS, April 1–6, 1928.

64. Upton Sinclair to Robert Minor, February 18, 1928, Sinclair MSS, February 18–23, 1928, pp. 1, 2.

65. Sinclair to Robert Minor, Sinclair MSS, February 16, 1928, p. 5.

66. Sinclair, *Boston,* 329, 344–45.

67. Ibid., 283.

68. Ibid., 735.

69. Sinclair to editor, *Road to Freedom,* 3.

70. Carlo Tresca to Upton Sinclair, May 17, 1929; Upton Sinclair to Carlo Tresca, May 25, 1929; both in Sinclair MSS, May 10–17 and 25–31, 1929.

71. Joseph North, "The Electric Chair," *New Masses,* October 1929: 25.

72. Sinclair, *Boston,* 754.

Chapter 8

1. Ann J. Lane, *To Herland and Beyond: The Life and Work of Charlotte Perkins Gilman* (New York: Penguin, 1990), 346–47, 353, 359–61.

2. Countee Cullen, "Scottsboro, Too, Is Worth Its Song (A Poem to American Poets)," in *On These I Stand: An Anthology of the Best Poems of Countee Cullen Selected by Himself and Including Six New Poems Never Before Published* (New York: Harper and Brothers, 1947), 160.

3. Dan T. Carter, *Scottsboro: A Tragedy of the American South* (Baton Rouge: Louisiana State University Press, 1969), 146.

4. Ibid., 53.

5. James E. Goodman, *Stories of Scottsboro* (New York: Pantheon, 1994), 24–25.

6. Ibid., 83.

7. Quoted in Kenneth Robert Janken, *White: The Biography of Walter White, Mr. NAACP* (New York: New Press, 2003), 398; quoted in Goodman, *Stories of Scottsboro,* 84.

8. Carter, *Scottsboro,* 56–58, 90–91; quoted in Carter, *Scottsboro,* 91.

9. Robert Minor, "The Negro and His Judases," *Communist* 10 (1931): 639.

10. Eugene Gordon, "The Negro's New Leadership," *New Masses* July 1931: 14–15.

11. See, for instance, Walter White, "The Negro and the Communists," *Harper's,* December 1931: 62–74.

12. W. E. B. Du Bois, Postscript, "The Negro and Communism," *Crisis* 38, no. 9 (September 1931): 313.

13. Ibid., 313–14.

14. Ibid., 313.

15. Ibid., 315.

16. Ibid., 318–19.

17. Carter, *Scottsboro,* 123–24, 125–27.

18. Earl Browder, "For National Liberation of the Negroes! War Against White Chauvinism!" *Communist* 11 (April 1932): 299.

19. W. E. B. Du Bois, Postscript, "The Strategy of the Negro Vote," *Crisis* 42, no. 2 (June 1933): 141.

20. Ibid., 142.

21. Lewis, *Fight,* 275, 293; Janken, *White,* 138, 172–73.

22. Quoted in Janken, *White,* 172.

23. Abram Harris to W. E. B. Du Bois, July 6, 1929, NAACP Papers, microfilm edition, Correspondence Records-H, reel 28, frame 595; W. E. B. Du Bois to Abram Harris, July 17, 1929, NAACP Papers, microfilm edition, Correspondence Records-

H, reel 28, frame 597. Sterling Spero and Abram Harris, Jr., *The Black Worker: The Negro and the Labor Movement* (1931; Port Washington, NY: Kennikat, 1966), 469.

24. Lewis, *Fight,* 320–21.

25. "Negro Editors on Communism: A Symposium of the American Negro Press," *Crisis* 39, no. 6 (April 1932): 117–18.

26. W. E. B. Du Bois, "Postscript: Toward a New Racial Philosophy," *Crisis* 41, no. 4 (February 1933): 45.

27. Ibid., 21.

28. Lewis, *Biography,* 517–22.

29. Lewis, *Fight,* makes clear Du Bois's nearly complete control over the list of invitees (315–16, 319).

30. [W. E. B. Du Bois], "Youth and Age at Amenia," *Crisis* 44, no. 6 (October 1933): 226–27.

31. W. E. B. Du Bois, "On Being Ashamed of Oneself: An Essay on Race Pride," *Crisis* 44, no. 5 (September 1933): 199.

32. Ibid., 199–200.

33. Foley, *Radical Representations,* 174.

34. Jos. Prokopec, "Negroes As an Oppressed National Minority," *The Communist* 9 (March 1930): 239–40.

35. Du Bois, "On Being Ashamed," 200.

36. Ibid.; Prokopec, "Negroes," 242.

37. Lewis, *Fight,* 335–36.

38. W. E. B. Du Bois, Postscript, "Segregation," *Crisis* 45, no. 3 (January 1934): 20.

39. W. E. B. Du Bois to Abram Harris, January 22, 1934, NAACP Papers, microfilm edition, Correspondence Records, reel 42, frame 429.

40. W. E. B. Du Bois, Postscript, "Segregation in the North," *Crisis* 45, no. 6 (April 1934): 115.

41. Janken, *White,* 29–33.

42. Both quoted in Lewis, *Fight,* 341.

43. W. E. B. Du Bois to Abram Harris, January 16, 1934, NAACP Papers, microfilm edition, Correspondence Records, reel 42, frame 428.

44. Lewis, *Fight,* 343; quoted in Lewis, *Fight,* 344.

45. Lewis, *Fight,* 344, 346–47.

46. "Preliminary Report of the Committee on Future Plan and Program of the N.A.A.C.P.," James Weldon Johnson Manuscript Collection, Correspondence, Beinecke Rare Book and Manuscript Library, Yale University Library, box 24, folder 544, p. 7.

47. Janken, *White,* 194–95.

48. "Preliminary Report of the Committee," p. 7.

49. W. E. B. Du Bois, Postscript, "Violence," *Crisis* 46, no. 1 (May 1934): 147–48.

50. Upton Sinclair, *The Lie Factory Starts* (Los Angeles: End Poverty League, 1934), 44.

51. Upton Sinclair to Bronson Cutting, January 22, 1934, Sinclair Archive, Correspondence, box 25.

52. Upton Sinclair, *I, Governor of California, and How I Ended Poverty: A True Story of the Future* (Pasadena, CA: by the author, 1933), 9.

53. "Sinclair New Clubs Reach 300 Total," *Upton Sinclair's Paper: End Poverty,* February 1934: 10. In his January 22, 1934, letter to Bronson Cutting, Sinclair reported that 289 clubs had been formed.

54. "Organization Manual: Upton Sinclair Club, Plan, Constitution and Pledge Card System" (End Poverty League, n.d.), Sinclair Archive, box 6, no. 7.

55. Sinclair, *I, Governor,* 10.

56. Ibid., 14.

57. Ibid., 15.

58. Ibid.

59. Upton Sinclair to David Sinclair, May 16, 1934, Sinclair Archive, Correspondence, box 26.

60. Greg Mitchell, *Campaign of the Century: Upton Sinclair's Race for Governor of California and the Birth of Media Politics* (New York: Random House, 1992), 192. What being "middle-aged" has to do with being either middle class or politically moderate, I am uncertain, but in any case, the middle-class status of Sinclair and a number of other EPIC leaders is a common enough phenomenon in radical political movements, and the status of the leaders cannot be taken as a measure of the popular base of the Sinclair campaign.

61. Morton Newman, interviewed by Fay Blake, May 28, 1984, Upton Sinclair's "EPIC" Campaign for Governor of California, 1934, donated phonotape collection, Regional Oral History Organization, Bancroft Library, University of California at Berkeley, collection 1651, tape 19.

62. Archie Brown, interviewed by Claudia Williams, June 20, 1984, Upton Sinclair's "EPIC" Campaign for Governor of California, 1934, donated phonotape collection, Regional Oral History Organization, Bancroft Library, University of California at Berkeley, collection 1651, tape 1.

63. Louise Lambert, interviewed by Claudia Williams, June 29, 1984, Upton Sinclair's "EPIC" Campaign for Governor of California, 1934, donated phonotape collection, Regional Oral History Organization, Bancroft Library, University of California at Berkeley, collection 1651, tape 13.

64. Sinclair, *I, Governor,* 24.

65. Ibid., 53.

66. Ibid., 60.

67. Upton Sinclair, *EPIC Answers* (Los Angeles: End Poverty League, 1934), 14.

68. See "Real Issues Fogged by Rivals," *Upton Sinclair's EPIC News,* July 16, 1934: 3.

69. "Meet Sheridan Downey . . . Sinclair Running Mate"; "Noted Democrat Swings Power Behind Sinclair"; both in *Upton Sinclair's EPIC News,* May 28, 1934: 1.

70. Downey to Sinclair, March 14, 1934, pp. 1–2.

71. Upton Sinclair, *Immediate EPIC* (Los Angeles: End Poverty League, 1934), 24.

72. Upton Sinclair, "National Hookup Address," KHJ, August 29, 1934, Sinclair Archive, Series III, box 34, p. 4. See also in the same box "Address of Upton Sinclair, KNX, Shrine Auditorium, August 27, 1934," pp. 3–4.

73. Clarence Frederick McIntosh, "Upton Sinclair and the EPIC Movement, 1933–1936," Ph.D. diss., Stanford University, 1955, 158, 161.

74. Mitchell, *Campaign of the Century*, 31.

75. Ibid., 86, 128, 154, 201–2, 217.

76. Ibid., 291.

77. Ibid., 144.

78. See the following pamphlets, all in Sinclair Archive, Box VI A, item numbers as indicated: "Upton Sinclair on the Catholic Church," no. 2; "Upton Sinclair's Opinion of Christian Science," no. 4; "Upton Sinclair Publishes His Opinion of the Seventh-Day Adventists," no. 5; "Upton Sinclair Attacks All Churches," no. 9.

79. All in Sinclair Archive, Box VI A, item numbers as indicated: "Upton Sinclair on the Legion," no. 10; "Upton Sinclair Reviews the University of California," no. 12; "Sinclair: Dynamiter of All Churches," no. 7; "The Proof That Upton Sinclair *Preaches* Revolution," no. 17; "Upton Sinclair *Discusses* the Home," no. 13; "Sinclairism Means," no. 18.

80. Mitchell, *Campaign of the Century*, 335.

81. "What Sinclair's Epic Means to You," pamphlet (San Francisco: Young Liberal League, [1934]), Sinclair Archive, Box VI A, no. 30, p. 6.

82. Ibid., p. 4.

83. Ibid., p. 5.

84. Mitchell, *Campaign of the Century*, 369–71, 415–16; quotation transcribed from "We Have A Plan," vol. 4 of *The Great Depression*, videotape, PBS Video, 1993.

85. Quoted in Mitchell, *Campaign of the Century*, 246.

86. Mitchell, *Campaign of the Century*, 499–501.

87. "Capital Jobless to Operate Idle Land, Factories," "Huge Tennessee Valley Rehabilitation Project Parallel to EPIC Plan," and "Two States Operate Idle Factories"; all in *Upton Sinclair's EPIC News*, July 23, 1934: 1–2.

88. Mitchell, *Campaign of the Century*, 108–9, 112–13.

89. "Upton Sinclair Address, WEAF, New York City, Saturday, September 8, 1934, 'My Meeting with the President,'" Sinclair Archive, Series III, box 34, pp. 2–3.

90. The news was widely enough disseminated among campaign workers to be known by Mort Newman, a teenage campaign volunteer whose main work was selling campaign literature. "We Have A Plan."

91. Sinclair, *I, Candidate for Governor: And How I Got Licked*, ed. James N. Gregory (1934; Berkeley: University of California Press, 1994), 202–3.

92. Ibid., 204.

93. James N. Gregory, introduction to Sinclair, *I, Candidate*, xi.

94. Langston Hughes to Amy Spingarn, September 19, 1934, Joel Spingarn Papers, James Weldon Johnson Manuscript Collection 11, Beinecke Rare Book and Manuscript Library, Yale University Library, box 1, folder 15, p. 3.

Chapter 9

1. Kenneth S. Davis, *FDR: The Beckoning of Destiny, 1882–1928: A History* (New York: G. P. Putnam's Sons, 1971), 197–98, 192–93.

2. Sinclair, *I, Candidate*, 87.

3. Gregory, introduction to *I, Candidate,* xii.

4. Mitchell, *Campaign of the Century,* 438–39, 236–37, 562–63, 546, 572.

5. Gregory, introduction to *I, Candidate,* xii–xiv.

6. Sinclair, *I, Governor,* 2.

7. Arthur M. Schlesinger, Jr., *The Politics of Upheaval,* vol 2. of *The Age of Roosevelt* (Boston: Houghton Mifflin, 1960), 123.

8. David M. Kennedy, *Freedom from Fear: The American People in Depression and War, 1929–1945* (New York: Oxford University Press, 1999), 215, 241–42.

9. Ibid., 244.

10. Ibid.

11. Sinclair, *Industrial Republic,* 207.

12. Franklin D. Roosevelt, *Public Papers and Addresses of Franklin D. Roosevelt,* ed. Samuel I. Rosenman (1938–50; New York: Russell and Russell, 1966), 1: 649.

13. Sinclair, *I, Governor,* 2.

14. Ibid., 26.

15. Quoted in Alan Brinkley, "The New Deal Experiments," in *The Achievement of American Liberalism: The New Deal and Its Legacies,* ed. William H. Chafe (New York: Columbia University Press, 2003), 2.

16. Quoted in Mitchell, *Campaign of the Century,* 259.

17. Kennedy, *Freedom from Fear,* 146.

18. "1932 Democratic Party Platform," pars. 12 and 6, and "1928 Democratic Party Platform," pars. 8, 71, and 73; both from Kenneth Janda, ed., "U.S. Party Platforms since 1840," PoliTxts http://janda.org/politxts/PartyPlatforms/Democratic (accessed July 31, 2008).

19. Roosevelt, *Public Papers,* 1: 657. Cf. Stetson, "On Human Nature," 25.

20. Roosevelt, *Public Papers,* 1: 651.

21. In *The Industrial Republic,* for example, Sinclair explained in a vivid reductio ad absurdum that the final outcome of the profit system (and a fairly accurate projection of the Great Depression) was that able-bodied workers—say a shoemaker, fish peddler, and baker—had made all the shoes, caught all the fish, and baked all the bread necessary—for those able to *buy* it, not themselves—and therefore could be judged expendable by their capitalist society. These workers would be told: "Everything is complete, and of course there is no more room for you. Therefore, you had best be off to another planet!" (18).

22. Bellamy, *Looking Backward,* 66.

23. Quoted in Kennedy, *Freedom from Fear,* 123. Kennedy notes that the speech, given to the San Francisco Commonwealth Club, was written by one of the original members of Roosevelt's so-called Brains Trust, Adolf Berle (*Freedom from Fear,* 123).

24. Marx and Engels, "Manifesto of Communist Party," 479.

25. National Committee of the Socialist Party of America, "The Socialist Platform Adopted by the Socialist Party in National Convention at Indianapolis, Ind., July 31, 1901," 1.

26. Sinclair, *I, Governor,* 10.

27. Roosevelt, *Public Papers,* 5: 232, 233.

28. National Committee of the Socialist Party, "Socialist Platform," 2–3.

29. Karl Marx, "The Civil War in France," in *The Marx-Engels Reader,* 632. See also Friedrich Engels's commentaries in the reprinting of Marx's tract upon the occasion of the twentieth anniversary of the Commune (627–28).

30. Kennedy, *Freedom from Fear,* 366–67, 369; Brinkley, "The New Deal Experiments," 14.

31. Kennedy, *Freedom from Fear,* 367n, 371–72.

32. Brinkley, "The New Deal Experiments," 8.

33. Gronlund had declared: "Therefore we say it is Utopian to hope to have a legal normal working day of eight hours . . . as long as the Established Order lasts" (*The Co-operative Commonwealth,* 81).

34. Franklin Delano Roosevelt, "Social Security," in *Speeches of the American Presidents,* ed. Janet Podell and Steven Anzovin (New York: H. W. Wilson, 1988), 491.

35. Mitchell, *Campaign of the Century,* 121.

36. Franklin Delano Roosevelt, "Second Annual Message to Congress, January 4, 1935," in *The State of the Union Messages of the Presidents, 1790–1966,* ed. Fred L. Israel (New York: Chelsea House, 1967), 3: 2816.

37. The WPA's limited life, its redundancy in the wartime economic boom, was not Roosevelt's original plan, Kennedy asserts (*Freedom from Fear,* 252–53, 374–75).

38. Roosevelt, "Second Annual Message," 2813–14.

39. Alan Brinkley, for one, notes that the New Deal "continued mostly to reflect traditional assumptions about women's roles and made few gestures toward the aspirations of those women who sought economic independence and professional opportunities" ("The New Deal Experiments," 17).

40. Roosevelt, *Public Papers,* 5: 232.

41. Bellamy, *Looking Backward,* 66.

42. Gilman, *Nonfiction Reader,* 76.

43. Roosevelt, *Public Papers,* 5: 233, 234.

44. Ibid., 6: 4–5.

45. Lewis, *Fight,* 284; Kennedy, *Freedom from Fear,* 87.

46. One article in *EPIC News* reports that the Federal Subsistence Homestead Corporation had authorized the Interior Department to "build and operate factories," "buy, construct and operate mines . . . industries, power plants farms, commercial establishments, parks and forests." "Stop! Look! Read! Here Epic Plan, Roosevelt Plan," *Upton Sinclair's EPIC News,* June 25, 1934: 6.

47. "Segregation—A Symposium," *The Crisis* 45, no. 5 (March 1934): 82.

48. Mary White Ovington to W. E. B. Du Bois, March 11, 1938, Du Bois Papers, reel 49, frame 386; W. E. B. Du Bois to Mary White Ovington, March 21, 1938, Du Bois Papers, reel 49, frame 385.

49. On Ellison's and Wright's falling out with the party, see Jackson, *Ralph Ellison,* 286–87; Rampersad, *Ralph Ellison,* 162–63; and Rowley, *Richard Wright,* 254, 264, 291–93. Arnold Rampersad suggests that Langston Hughes worked with the Communist Party as much for professional as for political motives, insists that he never actually joined the party, and asserts that Hughes's drift away from fellow-traveler sta-

tus commenced at least as early as the public announcement of the Hitler-Stalin nonaggression pact. Arnold Rampersad, *The Life of Langston Hughes,* 2nd ed., vol. 1 (New York: Oxford University Press, 2002), 215, 374–75.

50. On Du Bois's public statements in defense of the Rosenbergs, see Lewis, *Fight,* 555. For a specimen of Sinclair's thinking on the Rosenbergs' execution, see "Upton Sinclair Replies to *Daily Worker* Open Letter," *New Leader,* February 16, 1953: 27.

51. W. E. B. Du Bois, "Russia and America: An Interpretation," typescript, Du Bois Papers, reel 85, frames 395–561.

52. Du Bois, *Dark Princess,* 297.

53. Ibid., 285–86.

54. Lewis, *Fight,* 343–44, 346.

55. For just a slice of the voluminous literature of black church leaders who were active in the civil rights movement, see Davis W. Houck and David E. Dixon, eds., *Rhetoric, Religion, and the Civil Rights Movement, 1954–1965* (Waco, TX: Baylor University Press, 2006).

56. Martin Luther King, Jr., "Honoring Dr. Du Bois," in *Darkwater,* by W. E. B. Du Bois, new ed. (New York: Schocken, 1968), xv, xvii.

57. Gilman, *Utopian Novels,* 364.

58. Mouffe, *On the Political,* 53.

59. Laclau and Mouffe, *Hegemony and Socialist Strategy,* 184.

60. Ibid.

61. Sinclair, *I, Governor,* 59.

62. Du Bois, "Socialism and Negro Problem," 39.

63. Gilman, *Utopian Novels,* 61, 84.

64. Ibid., 340.

INDEX